INTERRELIGIOUS LEARNING

Taking the theme of learning as central to the responsible practice of interreligious dialogue, Michael Barnes S.J. discusses a Christian spirituality that builds on virtues of hospitality and welcome to the other, while maintaining the importance of difference and particularity in the search for meaning. Each chapter explores how faith grows as a person crosses a threshold into another religious world and learns sensitivity to echoes of the known in the unknown. Encounters with the religious other, refracted through texts, conversations, artefacts and places, are used to illustrate the ancient Patristic theme of 'seeds of the Word'. Cumulatively they show that a faith that learns how to engage imaginatively with another religious world constantly returns to the 'home' tradition, reinvigorated in its appreciation of the other.

Michael Barnes S.J. is Reader and Senior Lecturer in Interreligious Relations at Heythrop College, University of London. He has written a number of articles and books on interreligious relations, including *Walking the City* (1999), *Traces of the Other* (2000) and *Theology and the Dialogue of Religions* (Cambridge, 2002).

INTERRELIGIOUS LEARNING

Dialogue, Spirituality and the Christian Imagination

MICHAEL BARNES S.J.

CAMBRIDGE
UNIVERSITY PRESS

CAMBRIDGE UNIVERSITY PRESS
Cambridge, New York, Melbourne, Madrid, Cape Town,
Singapore, São Paulo, Delhi, Tokyo, Mexico City

Cambridge University Press
The Edinburgh Building, Cambridge CB2 8RU, UK

Published in the United States of America by Cambridge University Press, New York

www.cambridge.org
Information on this title: www.cambridge.org/9781107012844

First published 2012

Printed in the United Kingdom at the University Press, Cambridge

A catalogue record for this publication is available from the British Library

Library of Congress Cataloguing in Publication data
Barnes, Michael, 1947–
Interreligious learning : dialogue, spirituality, and the Christian imagination / by Michael
Anthony Barnes.
p.   cm.
Includes bibliographical references (p.   ) and index.
ISBN 978-1-107-01284-4
1. Christianity and other religions.   2. Dialogue – Religious aspects – Christianity.   I. Title.
BR127.B335   2012
261.2–dc23
2011043210

ISBN 978-1-107-01284-4 Hardback

for Richie
1966–2009
'a life beyond words'

Contents

vii

Contents

Preface

DIALOGUE AND LEARNING

Few words are as susceptible to misunderstanding as 'dialogue'. In the popular imagination it conjures up pictures of formal meetings in which speakers work towards agreement on some clearly defined topic. In this sense, dialogue may not be the enemy of truth, but the relationship can become problematic; if the object of the exercise is the negotiated settlement of some knotty problem, a degree of compromise and accommodation enters the picture. Thus the term gets associated with the activities of politicians and public officials – and inevitably gives off a whiff of vested interest and undisclosed motives. Small wonder that when the word is applied to the encounter of religions it often attracts a degree of suspicion, as if to enter into dialogue with people of another tradition is to collude with a relativising disregard for religious integrity.

There is, however, another side to the experience of dialogue. When people meet each other as people of faith, the term dialogue comes to connote less the type of reasoning found in Socrates' insistent questioning of his students than the more mystical encounter of 'I and Thou', which is associated with the thought of personalist philosophers like Martin Buber. A Buberian model of dialogue subordinates the issues discussed to the significance of the encounter itself. It is concerned not with the negotiation of outcomes but with a meeting of persons that is almost an end in itself.

In practice, of course, the distinction between the two meanings is never that clear – and no doubt people engage in interreligious dialogue for a variety of reasons. For the intellectually curious, it introduces them to the challenge of different ways of speaking about reality. For the more traditionally religious, it makes for an acceptable form of mission, one that fits the cultural mood of the age. For the politically conscientious, it is one way of answering the demands of justice, getting to know one's neighbours and developing resources for social cohesion. Sometimes the emphasis is on clarifying ideas and concepts; sometimes it is about building confidence and understanding. Nevertheless, whether we are talking about what is sometimes called the dialogue of theological exchange or the more practical dialogue of common life, the one thing all forms of dialogue share is the experience of learning. When common projects are worked on, when important concerns are shared, when different accounts of ultimate reality are discussed, not only is mutual understanding built up and barriers broken down but a new light is often cast on whole areas of life that have largely been taken for granted. It is not just that one learns more about 'the other'; one also learns more about the self.

This book takes its rise from that experience. For many people in a pluralist multicultural world, faith is deepened, not diluted, by the encounter with another religion or way of life. Learning about another religious tradition goes hand in hand with learning about one's own. But how precisely is faith deepened – and what is learned? How can the beliefs and symbolic structures of one tradition become the source of reflection for another? In addressing these questions, people of faith face something of a dilemma. Either they move towards some sort of universalism, identifying supposedly common elements that are shared by all religions, or they incorporate the most attractive and useful elements of other traditions into one all-inclusive pattern – their own. The former flattens out difference, the latter just absorbs it. That there are ethical as much as theological considerations here is obvious. Some would argue, however, that the risk has to be taken – indeed, that the risk is taken every time people engage with one another and seek to go beyond the politeness and pleasantries of everyday exchange. In today's world of volatile religious and anti-religious commitments, in which fundamentalist and liberal secular sensitivities rub up against each other, dialogue and learning are imperatives not luxuries.

I write as a Christian theologian. Inevitably I 'read' the world of religious difference from within that tradition and seek to give as much attention to the internal philosophical coherence of other traditions as I do to the theological integrity of my own. The tension between virtues of faithfulness and openness runs through this book, and, in what I coyly call a 'Postface', intended to mirror this Preface, I return briefly to the dilemma. There I shall attempt some summary remarks about how interreligious learning is more than a valuable resource for promoting social cohesion in a pluralist society but essential to the proper articulation of Christian faith. My hope is that by that time the key elements of the thesis will have emerged through what is primarily a reflection on the actual experience of interreligious encounter, of living in an ever-developing relationship with other people of faith.

In style and method, the approach in what follows has similarities to what has come to be called 'comparative theology', the close reading of the texts of another religious tradition from a consciously Christian theological perspective. That this is an important development within theology of religions there is no doubt, even if, as a new development, its theoretical foundations are still contested. In our globalised world, translations of sacred texts that even a few years ago would have stayed safely locked away are freely available. Anyone can read them. But mere availability is not everything – indeed, it can be problematic. The question is how to read intelligently, prayerfully, theologically, so that what is being assimilated becomes a source of wisdom and learning beyond the community of faith to which it originally belonged. In what follows I shall be commenting on some important texts, but it is not the expertise of the technical exegete that I bring to this book.

Basing interreligious dialogue on textual tradition has obvious advantages and in practice can be extraordinarily fruitful. Christianity is nothing if not a religion of the Word, and, while different religions value their sacred scriptures in different ways, there are clearly links and analogies between religions as textually based ways of thinking about the world. The risk, however, is that too strong an emphasis on textuality risks projecting onto other religious traditions Christian, and more generally Western, philosophical notions of literacy and literature. There is much more to any religious tradition than its written, or even oral, teachings. My contention, very simply, is that the 'life of texts' is the 'life of a community'. If interreligious learning begins with the meeting of persons, then attention needs to be given not just to the textual tradition itself but to the context of everyday living that it both forms and expresses. I therefore use 'texts' in a loose sense to refer not just to canonical scripture and authoritative commentary but to the forms of practice that inhabit the narratives of faith and give them flesh and blood reality. My subject is the interpersonal engagement and the ideas, events, meetings and particularly places that sound echoes and resonances of the known in the unknown and provoke an imaginative re-engagement with the Christian tradition.

This book builds on and complements the approach to dialogue worked out in my earlier *Theology and the Dialogue of Religions*. In the final chapter of that book, I described a practice of Christian faith nourished by the Eucharist that built up a Christian habitus, an instinct of hospitality and welcome to the other. I spoke of the Christ celebrated by the Church not as the 'Christ of conquest' but as the 'homeless Christ' who through the continuing yet hidden action of the Spirit goes on drawing all people to himself. I ended by picking up the ancient Patristic theme of the 'seeds of the Word'. God is to be known through the single mystery of creation and redemption, through everything that enhances that sense of participation in the very life of God to which all people are called. My aim was to commend the resources of Christian faith for generous engagement with the other. This book continues that project, but does so through the prism of lived examples.

Each chapter can be read as a discrete reflection on a particular experience of crossing a threshold into another religious world. From this sense of being in 'the middle of things' I seek to discern and follow a trace of the other that stimulates the imagination, opening up half-formed connections, sparking the odd insight, pointing to something that has been missed or not properly understood about the ways of God. What sense can I make of this particular experience, what is seen and heard and touched – indeed, been touched by? What does it take to learn from the unfamiliar and other?

However, what I present in this book is more than a record of one person's interreligious encounters. Vatican II's unequivocal statement in *Nostra Aetate*, the 'Declaration on the Relationship of the Church to non-Christian Religions', that the Church 'rejects nothing of what is true and holy', and the call to Christians to 'acknowledge, preserve and encourage the spiritual and moral truths found among non-Christians, also their social life and culture', makes theological reflection on the experience of dialogue an essential feature of responsible Christian living in a multi-faith society. If that is correct, then the dilemma noted above is not to be solved in advance of the engagement with the other. Certainly the Church, as, indeed, other communities of faith, must work out the principles on which dialogue and encounter are to be based. But it will be through the actual experience of being in relationship that will lead to those principles being tested and deeply rooted in the tradition. By setting these reflections in particular places – in a Hindu temple or in a Buddhist meditation centre or with a discussion about Shi'a theology in the back of a bus – my aim is not just to paint an evocative picture of the messy reality of life in a thoroughly pluralist world: the chapters are intended to build on one another, developing a cumulative argument for an interreligious learning that grows out of a range of meetings, encounters and conversations.

The first chapter begins with a place that is more metaphorical than real: the 'marketplace' of human interaction that comes at the end of the Buddhist ox-herding pictures. Even (perhaps, especially) here, the object is to anchor dialogue in the reality of the everyday. That familiar set of images takes the form of a journey, in which certain key moments open up the possibility of enlightenment. My aim, however, is not to extract a universal paradigm from the Buddha story, nor to impose some Christian template on someone else's religious experience. I work a stage further back, as it were, with the terms of what Charles Taylor calls a 'social imaginary'. The practices of faith, from the prayerful cultivation of interiority to the more exterior works of witness, build up a certain learned ability to move between religious worlds.

In teasing out the logic of interreligious learning, the book describes three moments that speak of shifts in understanding of the relationship with whatever is other. The first section, under the general title of 'Meetings', is an attempt to situate interreligious encounter within a broad theological and historical context and thus to question certain modern assumptions about the nature of 'religion' and its familiar instantiations, 'the religions'. To build an interreligious social imaginary that attends to both the creative and destructive sides of human religiosity means paying attention to the ways in which religion can, on the one hand, be turned into an oppressive ideology and, on the other, be reduced to 'mere culture'. Self-critical attention to the possibility of corruption is always necessary in any human institution – let alone those that seek to speak of divine things. The point I argue here is that by developing a model of a religious tradition as a 'school of faith', where teachers and learners can meet, a forum is created within which theological questions about the meaning of beliefs, actions, prayers and rituals can be addressed with proper integrity.

The second section, entitled 'Crossings', takes 'translation' as the primary metaphor for a process of growing engagement with the other. While it is obviously the case that concepts and ideas have to be translated into other languages if a communication across cultures is to take place, translation is an art rather than an exact science. Thus I seek to argue, largely through examples taken in the first place from the Christian dialogue with Judaism, that persons need to be translated, crossing over a cultural border, if they are to learn the skills and sensitivities that dialogue demands. Two further chapters in this section continue this theme, with a specific focus on the spirituality of dialogue. I argue, through an engagement with Buddhist and Hindu meditative traditions, that the 'dialogue of spiritual experience' provokes an interiority in which desire is channelled by the virtue of a humble and hopeful waiting upon ultimate mystery, however that is conceived.

The third section, 'Imaginings', takes up some of the more ethical and political implications of dialogue that have been touched on throughout the book, particularly the theme of religiously inspired violence. Here the focus is on the return, back across the threshold of engagement, to consider how Christian faith has been enhanced by the meetings, crossings and, crucially, the imaginings that it provokes. Although any number of examples could have been chosen (any significant encounter with the religious other stimulates the imagination to think otherwise), I have restricted myself here to Islam and the Indian religions. The engagement with Islam, I argue, raises questions not just about revelation but also about the nature of the human person as called to witness to the creative power of God. Devotional Hinduism and Sikhism begin from different theological premises but, as I seek to argue, mirror the Christian focus on the God revealed in the very depth of everything that makes us most human – in tragedy and loss, in joy and delight, in passion and suffering. It is important, therefore, in a work of Christian theology, to take back into the 'marketplace' some response to Jesus's own question: 'who do you say that I am?'

The last thing I want to do, however, is press these examples into some pan-religious Procrustean bed. They are the fruit of textual and contextual reading, one person's reflection on learning something of the traces of the ever-surprising God. I shall return briefly to the logic that I seek to develop in a final concluding section that offers some further elucidation of a Christian spirituality of dialogue. More important than any such logic is the conviction that guides me throughout that, while Christian faith and the beliefs and practices of Jews, Muslims, Hindus and Buddhists may be saying different things, the very attempt to grapple with difference in a spirit of generous respect can be mutually supportive and illuminating. By beginning in the middle of things, with particular people in particular situations, what emerges is a considered and thoughtful response to the Spirit who leads all people into the mystery of God's providence. Deliberately to avoid the imposition of some sort of magisterial overview is not to collude with the worst excesses of postmodern relativism, it simply acknowledges that any account of the form of God's presence in the world raises complex issues about how to discern that form and how to live with, as well as learn from, that sometimes irreducible difference.

Acknowledgements

This book is, first and foremost, a record of experience. I am indebted to my neighbours, the good people of Southall in all their splendid diversity, and particularly the parishioners of St Anselm's Catholic Church, thanks to whom I have been happily immersed in the multicultural mix of West London for some years. I am also grateful to many students at Heythrop College who have, with unfailing sharpness, asked awkward questions and kept my theology of religions honest. In particular I thank the two groups who formed the *Faiths Together* project, an experiment at Heythrop in interreligious learning that tested old ideas and generated new ones. Thanks also to friends and students at the Muslim College, where the task of teaching Christianity has enabled me to appreciate the richness of the living tradition of Islam. Many friends and colleagues have contributed in great ways and small, making the right noises at the right time. A special debt is owed to Ahmad Achtar, Jim Bernauer, Frank Clooney, Swami Dayatmananda, Manfred Deselaers, Gwen Griffith Dickson, Martin Ganeri, Gokal Singh Gill, Anil Goonewardene, Jonathan Gorsky, Chris Hewer, Damian Howard, Gerry Hughes, Robert Kennedy, David Lonsdale, Tony McCaffry, Joachim Russek, Philip Sheldrake, Mohammad Shomali, Frank Sullivan, Bill Tomkiss, Sister Theoktisti, who all in their different ways have given time, advice and support. I am grateful to them all. Thanks also to my Jesuit brethren in Southall for putting up with my distractedness, and to the community at Boston College, Massachusetts, whose hospitality enabled me to get the final drafts finished. Nor should I forget Brother Daniel Faivre, my late and much missed mentor, whose firm but gentle criticisms of my earlier work got this one going.

Finally, a brief word about the dedication. Richard was my first nephew. He was born with a severe mental and physical handicap, and died, a day short of his forty-third birthday, as the first draft of this book was being finished. He never spoke, yet somehow became the centre of a web of human relations. His was very much a life beyond words, one that in giving and receiving love witnessed eloquently to the Word of God. Like a good theologian, he reminds me that not everything can or should be said about the ways of God. To his memory this book is respectfully dedicated.

I

Meetings

CHAPTER I

The middle of things

In his collection of essays, *Zen and the Taming of the Bull*, the learned Buddhist teacher Walpola Rahula introduces the well-known series of Zen pictures that illustrate the way to enlightenment. In the version that Rahula discusses, the bull – a metaphor for the unruly mind – is depicted as changing gradually from black to shining white. 'The underlying idea', he says, 'is that the mind, which is naturally pure, is polluted by extraneous impurities and that it could and should be cleansed through discipline and meditation'.[1] The *yogi* or seeker after truth begins by confronting the wild beast, catches it and then tethers it. He ties it to a tree and trains it to follow after him. In the next picture, the bull lies passively by the river while the *yogi* plays his flute. Then we find the bull drinking from the water while the *yogi* sleeps in the background. In the next, bull and seeker stand observing each other. In the penultimate picture, the seeker is alone; the bull has been transcended altogether. The final picture in Rahula's series is nothing more than a round circle; now both bull and self have been transcended and all traces of ego eradicated.

That is as far as Rahula's account takes us. His aim is to link the contemporary practice of Zen, where the emphasis is usually on 'sudden' enlightenment, with the most ancient traditions, particularly his own Theravada, with its disciplines and meditative practices that build up a mindful attention to the present moment. But in the more familiar Japanese versions, which go back to the fifteenth century, a further stage is indicated: what is often called the 'return to the marketplace'.[2] Here we find the *yogi*

---

[1] Walpola Rahula, *Zen and the Taming of the Bull: Towards the Definition of Buddhist Thought* (London: Gordon Fraser, 1978), pp. 15–23.

[2] In Rahula's book, the origin of the pictures is ascribed to the twelfth-century Zen master Kaku-an Shi-en. The version he refers to was painted by Shubun, a fifteenth-century Zen priest. They may represent a Zen Buddhist interpretation of the ten stages of enlightenment traced by the *Bodhisattva*, as outlined most notably in the *Avatamsaka Sutra*. They have become widely known in the West owing to their inclusion in Paul Reps, *Zen Flesh, Zen Bones* (Harmondsworth: Penguin, 1972), a collection of Zen and pre-Zen writings, published originally in 1957.

encountering others and talking with them. One commentary, by the Zen scholar Yanagida Seizan says:

The relationship between bull and herdsman is indeed an allegory of the process of meditation, where we succeed in capturing and quieting this present arrogant heart of ours, which runs wild. . . . Zen training only begins when we become aware, in the midst of our dreaming, that the bull has run away from us. . . . [The ox-herding pictures] are an expression of that element in Zen thought which finds the profoundest miracle in the dialogue between plain ordinary people, where any religious coloration of charity, salvation or satori has completely disappeared.[3]

Depicted here is something of the spirit of the Mahayana, with its paradoxical assertion that *samsara* is *nirvana* and *nirvana samsara*. Ultimately, the round of rebirth, life in the world as we experience it, is no different from the truth discovered in that moment of enlightenment. To be enlightened does not entail some escape to a transcendent realm but the attaining of freedom from all forms of attachment – whether from control by the inner passions or, more paradoxically, from the very desire for some 'spiritual realm'. What Buddhists refer to as *upaya*, 'skilful means', is as much a quality of detachment that values the potential for enlightenment in the world of ordinary everyday experience as it is a practical exercise of compassion that leads and teaches other suffering sentient beings.[4]

I begin this book in the 'marketplace of religions' not because I want to short-circuit the complex and arduous process of the journey of faith but in order to draw attention to the intrinsic value of being in the middle of things. The very metaphor of the 'spiritual journey' begs a serious question. The end of the quest is, of course, described in the great religious traditions in different ways – as enlightenment or *Nirvana*, as the beatific vision of God, as eternal life and indescribable bliss. But how is what is, strictly speaking, unknown and beyond experience related to what is known and familiar? Whatever the language that is used, if the end of the journey is indescribable then we have no way of knowing *in advance* whether we are on the right path – let alone whether we have reached the end. Metaphors, of course, always limp and should never be pressed too far. Religious language is not intended to afford an exact representation of reality but to support the life of holiness by providing the necessary

---

[3] Quoted by Stephen Addiss in his introductory article, 'The History of Ox-Herding Poems and Paintings', in the book accompanying the exhibition *John Cage: Zen Ox-Herding Pictures* (Richmond, Va.: University of Richmond Museums, 2009).

[4] See the account of the training of the *bodhisattva* as taught by the *Avatamsaka Sutra* in the essay by Luis O. Gomez, in Takeuchi Yoshinori (ed.), *Buddhist Spirituality*, vol. i, *Indian, Southeast Asian, Tibetan, Early Chinese* (London: SCM, 1994), pp. 160–70.

signposts. *Nirvana* in this sense is a regulative concept, what Steven Collins calls the 'limit condition' that gives the early Buddhist tradition its coherence.[5] It only makes sense within the framework of the terminology established in the Buddha's first sermon, the 'setting in motion of the wheel of truth', the Middle Way, the Four Noble Truths and the Noble Eightfold Path. Such language is given its own peculiarly transformative power by both the link that these words forge with the originating witness of the Buddha and the time-honoured tradition of practice that has preserved them. The Buddhist meditator comes to learn that the disciplines that lead to the conquest of self have to be set within a broader contemplative context of mindfulness of the whole of reality. Rahula's pictures make it seem like a straightforward linear progress. That would be to forget the key word 'return'. In returning to the world of the everyday, prepared to share the fruits of the *Buddhadharma* with others, the mindful meditator has become deeply conscious of the paradox that that world was never left in the first place.

Not that this is a peculiarly Buddhist insight. Speaking out of a very different religious world, Martin Buber recounts stories of the Hasidim that stress, he says, not any esoteric teaching but the 'mode of life' that shapes a community. God is not the utterly transcendent mystery but a familiar companion, to be discerned as much in the ordinary activities of life as in moments of other-worldly bliss. The conviction that there is no essential distinction between sacred and profane generates a certain sacramental quality in Hasidic mysticism. 'Everything', says Buber, 'wants to be hallowed, to be brought into the holy, everything worldly in its worldliness . . . everything wants to become sacrament'.[6] These are words that might have come from a St Teresa of Avila, words that speak of a profound awareness of the sacred at home in the everyday, of the Word of God alive and active among the 'pots and pans' of daily distraction. If this is mystical experience, then it challenges our idea of what makes for the holiness of things. In fact,

[5] Steven Collins, *Nirvana and other Buddhist Felicities* (Cambridge University Press, 1998). Collins begins Part 1 with a comment on Wittgenstein's celebrated observation at the end of the *Tractatus* that 'whereof one cannot speak, thereof one must be silent'. What it *is* possible to speak about, insists Collins, are the patterns of imagery that make up the 'collective memory' behind a religious tradition like Pali Buddhism.

[6] Martin Buber, *The Origin and Meaning of Hasidism*, ed. and trans. Maurice Friedman (Horizon Press: New York; 1960), p. 181. For Buber's collections, see *Tales of the Hasidim: The Early Masters* (New York: Schocken Books, 1947) and *The Later Masters* (New York: Schocken Books, 1948). The first volume of Buber's interpretation of Hasidim is to be found in *Hasidism and Modern Man*, ed. and trans. Maurice Friedman, 2nd edn. (Atlantic Highlands, NJ: Humanities Press, 1988). See also Maurice Friedman, *Martin Buber's Life and Work: The Later Years, 1945–1965* (New York: E. P. Dutton, 1983), especially pp. 177 ff.

of course, it witnesses to something more elusive, and more profound –
what in Christian terms might be called an incarnational sensibility. When
Christians gather to celebrate the Eucharist they are not taken out of the
everyday but plunged more deeply into it.[7] Christianity, says Karl Rahner,
in an essay on 'The Foundation of Belief Today',

calls for a whole-hearted and straightforward profession of hope, amidst all the
mysterious twists and turns of our life, and assures us that in this mystery there lies
what we call God, eternal life, ultimate value and the salvation of our being.[8]

Within the ordinary lies the extraordinary. To be more precise, within the
embrace of all manner of limitation, from the weakness of the will to the
more intractable traumas of particular histories, lies the possibility of
true human freedom. The challenge, as Rahula tries to show, is how to
practise the traditions and disciplines in such a way that one is for ever
coming back to the world of everyday experience with a fresh vision and
renewed energy.

THEOLOGY OF THE ORDINARY

This book carries the title 'interreligious learning' – and already I hope I
have given a taste of the sort of cross-religious reflection that is to come. In
what follows I seek to map out something of an impalpable process of
learning, as much about the self as about the other, from the initial
curiosity excited by the challenge raised by the strangeness of another
religious world to the leaps of the imagination that generous engagement
always demands. Throughout I am guided by the conviction that it is the
very *ordinariness* of life in the marketplace that builds interreligious
understanding and turns out to be theologically significant. By contrast,
Western culture, fixated on much-hyped extraordinary 'events' and
heightened states of consciousness, sees the religions as alternative versions
of some 'spiritual commodity': less the cultural axis around which the
marketplace revolves than competing brands in the curiously anodyne
'retail outlets' of town-centre shopping malls. For every Zen practitioner
prepared to delve into the traditions created by Bodhidharma, Hakuin
and Dogen, many more remain content with the 'beat' version:

[7] In the words of Timothy Radcliffe, the Eucharist is a 'transformative event' that brings the Word alive.
See 'The Sacramentality of the Word', in Keith Pecklers (ed.), *Liturgy in a Postmodern World* (London:
Continuum, 2003), pp. 133–47.
[8] Karl Rahner, *Experience of the Spirit: Source of Theology, Theological Investigations*, vol. xvi (London:
Darton, Longman and Todd, 1979), p. 22.

Zen-generated forms of meditation as a lifestyle choice. Sales of books on Islam may have rocketed in the months after 9/11, but how much was this generated by a genuine concern to understand the deepest inspirations of Islamic civilisation, and how much by a morbid fascination with a tradition that could stir up suicide bombers with visions of virgins in paradise? Religion is trivialised when reduced to a cultural straitjacket for the psychologically immature or an alternative therapy for the spiritually jaded.

The various forms of interreligious dialogue that have grown up in recent years, not just the formal debates between the theologically expert but those rooted in neighbourly concern and commitment to common action, challenge this type of neo-orientalist fantasy. Before religions like Buddhism and Islam can be categorised as systems of belief, they are communities of faith, groups of struggling human beings who, like their Christian dialogue partners, seek to bring certain sources of wisdom – rituals, texts, devotions, legal and commentarial traditions – into a correlation with the exigencies of everyday life. However different their practices of faith may be, and however different the questions they ask, they do share a desire to make intellectual and affective sense of *this* world and *this* moment. Exactly how that commitment to an informed and responsible everyday life is informed by visions of a future state varies from tradition to tradition. The mistake, however, is to think of the great or 'world religions' as different configurations of certain purely 'religious' or 'spiritual' phenomena. While religions are often rightly understood as conservative forces within society, it does not follow that they are unchanging and monolithic; indeed, forms of revivalism are always growing side by side with new developments that in some ways mirror the spiritual eclecticism of postmodernity. At stake here is not just the definition of religion or how the history and relationship of the great religions is to be narrated, but theological questions that arise from the interpersonal relationship, questions about *human meaning*.

I will return to these themes – essentially the clash between two different conceptions of 'religion' as it faces modernity – in more detail as we proceed. In this first chapter, I am concerned with the task of theology – what Rowan Williams refers to as the work of the religious intellect.[9] I write from a Christian perspective but with the conviction that the sort of

---

[9] Notably in a lecture given at Birmingham University, 11 June 2003, 'Christian Theology and Other Faiths': 'Theology, the work of religious intellect, tries to work out what the implications are of seeing everything in relation to a holy reality that is never absent.'

questions with which this book is concerned cross religious boundaries – if only because, whether we like it or not, Christians and others live as neighbours in the middle of things. We do not share common beliefs, we do not even share a common religious language with which to speak of ultimate reality. Even to talk of 'we' is problematic – for what makes for 'us'? Yet the demands for mutual learning and understanding are real. All communities of faith have to learn how to respond generously yet with integrity to the questions that others put. All face similar issues that the life of faith and the pursuit of holiness raise – questions about truth and language, reason and revelation, grace and freedom. These and other themes are implicit in what follows, but comparative questions as such are not my main concern. If theology is the work of religious intellect, then it is important to reflect on the experience of being in dialogue and the activity of learning that any interreligious engagement provokes. To that extent I am concerned less with the common ground between religions or points of particularity and difference than with putting together the terms of what Charles Taylor calls a 'social imaginary'.

Our commentator on the ox-herding pictures noted that Zen thought finds its 'profoundest miracle in the dialogue between plain ordinary people'. The world of everyday 'ordinary' experience may seem prosaic and uninteresting but it betrays its own inner harmonies without which enlightenment and learning would be impossible. A 'social imaginary', Taylor tells us, is something much deeper than the 'intellectual schemes' that people think about when in 'disengaged mode'. It is about what is implicit in the ways people behave and react, what gives their actions a certain cognitive and affective coherence. To be more specific, he is thinking of

the ways in which [people] imagine their social existence, how they fit together with others, how things go on between them and their fellows, the expectations that are normally met, and the deeper normative notions and images which underlie these expectations.[10]

Religiously inspired practices, from 'internal' rituals and prayer to forms of dialogue with those external to the community, develop over time. And not the least important aspect of any theology of religions must be a reflection on what makes life coherent – what gives it a sense of 'moral order', to use Taylor's term. However, this is precisely *not* to say that

---

[10] Charles Taylor, *A Secular Age* (Cambridge, Mass.: Harvard University Press, 2007), p. 171. See also Charles Taylor, *Modern Social Imaginaries* (Durham, NC and London: Duke University Press, 2004), p. 23.

practices drive theory, any more than the other way round. Rather, the relationship is reciprocal. Ordinary life or life in the marketplace is driven by certain implicit understandings of what makes for harmony and order. To bring these to light means giving attention to two dimensions of any 'social imaginary': on the one hand, assumptions about the meaning of existence and what makes for human flourishing, and, on the other, the context of practice that shapes, and is in turn shaped by, such assumptions. Through a process of questioning and engagement, comparison and dialogue, the 'religious intellect' is brought to bear on the complex dialectic of theory and practice that gives meaning to people's lives.

At the end of this chapter I return to Taylor's provocative thesis about religion and modernity, so carefully developed in *A Secular Age*, in order to give some theological shape to a question that has long fascinated me – a question as much about human growth and transformation as about theology and the philosophy of religion. What happens to faith when it becomes 'interfaith'? This is not just a practical question about how one language of faith can speak to and learn from another, or a philosophical question about how different languages can speak truthfully. It is more specifically concerned with what the effort of communication, to speak across cultural and religious gaps, does to the way I regard my own tradition. Set alongside that question is another, an ethical question that is perhaps more intractable: what the effort of communication does to the other. Does interreligious learning simply instrumentalise the other? Such questions lie behind the themes discussed in the chapters that follow and will, I hope, become more explicit as we proceed. What will emerge will be less a theology than a spirituality of dialogue – an account of the transformative practices of learning in community that are undergirded by ritual, worship and prayer.

Here, however, I want to stay with the developing tradition of Christian discourse about the other that is seeking its own proper integrity. In this chapter, I offer no more than a sketch of the theology of religions that has emerged in Christian circles in the last few decades. This will give something of the background to a certain trajectory that I will characterise at this stage as moving from a liberal normative pluralism to a much more tradition-centred form of post-liberal theology, and particularly what in recent years has come to be called 'comparative theology'.

THEOLOGY AND THE DIALOGUE OF RELIGIONS

Christian engagement with other religious traditions is as old as Christianity itself and has generated a variety of theological responses. The popular

'threefold paradigm' typology, usually ascribed to Alan Race, has the great
merit of gathering various different ideas and approaches into a single
coherent pattern.[11] The first two positions, 'exclusivism' and 'inclusivism',
take their rise from a question that derives from Christian soteriology: can the
non-Christian be saved? 'They' are deliberately placed outside the boundaries
of a Christian world or they are given a secondary place within. The first
option is to draw very strict lines of demarcation; the second option is more
benign: to extend the boundary, recognising 'aspects' of Christian identity in
the other. The third pattern, named simply 'pluralism', begins from different
premises – and is consciously *not* centred on Christianity as the normative
tradition of faith.[12] Following the thesis of John Hick, the pluralist hypothesis
states that there is no fundamental difference between religions; all are simply
descriptions of a more or less common core or experience. Three theological
positions are thus run together as stages of development. A hard-edged
evangelical tradition gives way to a more generous Catholicism, but this is
shown to rest ultimately on a claim to Christianity's unique finality; the
saving truth of Christianity is present to people from other faith traditions in
an implicit or 'anonymous' way. In due course, given the increasingly
manifest similarities between Christianity and other faiths to be discerned
in our contemporary world, it seems only reasonable to shift away from such
an insistence on the ultimate superiority of one tradition and cross a 'theological Rubicon' into a much simpler world where Christianity is acknowledged as but one of many religions.[13]

---

[11] The threefold paradigm typology has proved remarkably resilient. It was first proposed by Alan Race in his
Christians and Religious Pluralism: Patterns in the Christian Theology of Religions (London: SCM, 1983) and
later developed in his *Interfaith Encounter: The Twin Tracks of Theology and Dialogue* (London: SCM.
2001). Without using the typology form, much the same approach is to be found in Paul Knitter, *No Other
Name?* (London: SCM, 1985). A similar approach, but with a very different reading, is taken by Gavin
D'Costa in *Theology and Religious Pluralism* (Oxford: Blackwell, 1985). D'Costa provides a brief critique in
'Theology of Religions', in David Ford (ed.), *The Modern Theologians*, 3rd edn. (Oxford: Blackwell, 2005),
pp. 626–44. The most thoroughgoing critique from a Roman Catholic perspective, and setting the debate
within the broad perspective of theology of religions, is that of Jacques Dupuis, *Toward a Christian
Theology of Religious Pluralism* (New York: Orbis, 1997), especially pp. 180–201. Attempts to move beyond
the paradigm approach include Michael Barnes, *Religions in Conversation* (London: SPCK, 1989) and
James L. Fredericks, *Faith among Faiths: Christian Theology and Non-Christian Religions* (Mahwah, NJ:
Paulist, 1999). The most thoroughgoing reprise, bringing the story up to date, comes from D'Costa,
Christianity and World Religions: Disputed Questions in the Theology of Religions (Oxford: Wiley-Blackwell,
2009), especially pp. 1–45.

[12] 'Pluralism' is, however, not understood in any univocal sense. There are variations within the pattern –
and, indeed, within the different religions themselves. See, e.g., Paul Knitter (ed.), *The Myth of
Religious Superiority* (New York: Orbis, 2005).

[13] The image of the 'theological Rubicon', an irrevocable step into a new way of conceiving interreligious relations, occurs first in John Hick's essay 'The Non-Absoluteness of Christianity', in John
Hick and Paul Knitter (eds.), *The Myth of Christian Uniqueness* (London: SCM, 1987), pp. 16–36.

This all sounds plausible. While Hick's initial proposals have been nuanced over the years, the basic thesis remains much the same: modernity demands a paradigm shift in thinking about the relationship of religions from a Christianity-centred theology that seeks to 'place' the other to a more open-ended or 'global' theology. He defends it from a number of angles, developing historical, sociological and ethical considerations, which are backed by a philosophical account of religious experience. This is based, ultimately, on a Kantian distinction between the particular phenomena of the religions and the single noumenon or the 'Real-as-such' to which they all in some way point. As a philosophical project these proposals have received an enormous amount of attention, not all of it entirely favourable.[14] My interest lies with the implications for theology. Apart from reducing the rich and complex traditions of mainstream Protestant and Catholic theology to rather dull schemes for placing a troublesome other, they also beg a number of questions – about the nature of religion, about the scope of theology, about modernity itself, about human relations and the human capacity for understanding what is other. The not so hidden assumption is that religions share certain things in common and that with enough effort and good will clarity of meaning and purpose will be achieved. Sooner or later people of different faiths will all end up understanding the 'truth' that lurks undetected in the interreligious undergrowth.

Everyone would agree that in a multi-faith world Christian theologians can no longer be content to regard 'other religions' with indifference; the perceived relativity and historicality of all religions makes claims to some overarching superiority of one tradition over all others much more difficult to make. The suspicion remains, however, that a normative pluralism squeezes complex traditions into a carefully prepared stereotype as if they are versions of the same thing instead of richly diverse patterns of living and learning. Indeed, there seems to be something faintly contradictory about a 'pluralist'

---

[14] See, e.g., Gerard Loughlin, 'Prefacing Pluralism: John Hick and the Mastery of Religion', *Modern Theology*, 7.1 (1990), pp. 29–55; Gavin D'Costa, 'The Impossibility of a Pluralist View of Religions', *Religious Studies*, 32 (1996), pp. 223–32; Charles T. Mathewes, 'Pluralism, Otherness and the Augustinian Tradition', *Modern Theology*, 14.1 (1998), pp. 83–112; Keith Ward, 'Truth and the Diversity of Religions', *Religious Studies*, 26 (1990), pp. 1–18; essays collected in Harold Hewitt (ed.), *Problems in the Philosophy of Religion: Critical Studies of the Work of John Hick* (Basingstoke: Macmillan, 1991). Within the perspective of religious studies, see also Michael Barnes, 'Religious Pluralism', in John Hinnells (ed.), *The Routledge Companion to the Study of Religion*, 2nd edn. (London and New York: Routledge, 2010), pp. 426–41. Placing Hick's approach to pluralism within the context of his philosophical work as a whole, see David Cheetham, *John Hick: A Critical Introduction and Reflection* (Aldershot: Ashgate, 2003).

theology of pluralism. It is one thing to recognise a plurality of possible answers to a question; another to turn such a plurality into a theory that somehow accounts for the facts. Pluralist thinkers like Hick are surely right to insist that in a world of many faiths any reflection on religious identity must take account of a plurality of other views. But they are wrong to abstract their own position from that plurality. Otherwise what we have is a 'view from nowhere', a theory that, precisely because it seeks to stand apart from and above the living reality of religious traditions, has nothing to say to that reality.

This failure to take 'the religions' seriously spills over into a very limited critique of Christian theologies of religion. The ranking of complex theologies as 'isms', systemic variations on a soteriological theme, ignores the key insights of the mainstream Evangelical and Catholic traditions – and thus fails to appreciate the nature of theology itself. Neither Barth nor Rahner – the 'usual suspects' set up by the pluralist hypothesis – fits the 'exclusivist'/ 'inclusivist' label. Barth's theology is *kerygmatic*. His is a religious rhetoric that is intended to move the heart with its power of persuasion. While he does make a notorious distinction between religion and revelation, this is not a matter of setting 'the religions' over against Christianity.[15] A similar note of caution about theological genre needs to be sounded with regard to Karl Rahner. When Rahner uses the term 'Anonymous Christianity' for the first time, he is reflecting on the possibility of belief in today's world. Here, using the sort of language appropriate to a pastoral rather than systematic theologian, Rahner confesses that he is not troubled by what he sees. 'Why not? Because I see everywhere a nameless Christianity and because I do not see my own explicit Christianity as one opinion among others which contradict it.'[16] When Rahner turns to the specific question of salvation outside the Church, the dominating context is again ecclesial and pastoral.[17] He is concerned with the integrity of the Church in an apparently faithless, or, at any rate, increasingly post-Christian world. In some ways, Rahner's intention is similar to that of Schleiermacher, with his theme of the religious *a priori* that would bring home to the 'cultured despisers' of religion some

---

[15] At issue, of course, is 'unbelief – human superstition and self-righteousness – which exists in dialectic with God's self-revelation in Christ, a position developed in Book I of the *Church Dogmatics*. By Book IV, the emphasis has changed from the sovereignty of God to the humanity of Christ.

[16] Karl Rahner, 'Thoughts on the Possibility of Faith Today', *Theological Investigations*, vol. v (London: Darton, Longman and Todd, 1966), pp. 3–22.

[17] See Rahner's development of the 'four theses' in 'Christianity and the Non-Christian Religions', *ibid.*, 115–34, especially the fourth thesis with its return to the theme of the Church as the 'vanguard' of God's saving work, the beginning of that 'unification of the whole human race', which is properly *God*'s work of salvation.

awareness that the truth of Christianity is a truth for all people. The 'Anonymous Christian' is best understood, therefore, as a theological intuition arising out of Rahner's theological anthropology. His basic presupposition is that the relationship between God and humanity contains an immanent dimension; that is to say that within human experience are contained the seeds of human understanding of God.

For Rahner in particular soteriology needs to be set within the context of themes of grace and human freedom that are proper to Christian anthropology. It is worth noting that, while the seven great ecumenical Councils of the universal Church came to binding conclusions about Christology and the Trinitarian mystery of God, nothing was ever said about soteriology *as such*.[18] Strictly speaking, the notorious statement that 'outside the Church there is no salvation', seized upon with such glee by pluralist theologians, is in its origins a statement abut the nature of the Church not salvation.[19] The ultimate state of the righteous individual is known only to God and may not be second-guessed by others, not even by the Church. For both Barth and Rahner the issue is not how to avoid the 'exclusivist' edges of Christian rhetoric but how to speak of the merciful purposes of the God revealed in Jesus Christ without colluding in a naive universalism. They see the function of theology in different but complementary ways.[20] In Anselm's sense they both produce not monologues but dialogues, 'allocutions' – faithful responses to God's

---

[18] The focus is, of course, on Christology. That salvation comes through Christ was not a subject of controversy, hence the Christological principle that 'what has not been assumed has not been saved'.

[19] A point which comes out strongly in the survey of the subject in Francis A. Sullivan, *Salvation Outside the Church: Tracing the History of the Catholic Response* (London: Chapman, 1992). See especially Sullivan's discussion of the origins of the '*Extra Ecclesiam Nulla Salus*' adage in Cyprian's *De Unitate Ecclesiae*, pp. 20–4. On the same point, see Gavin D'Costa, '"Extra ecclesiam nulla salus" Revisited', in Ian Hamnett (ed.), *Religious Pluralism and Unbelief: Studies Critical and Comparative* (London: Routledge, 1990), pp. 130–47. Sullivan concludes that the theological value of the saying lies in its being 'one way, and a very imperfect way at that, in which Christians have expressed their belief that God has given to his church a necessary part to play in his plan to save the world' (p. 204).

[20] I am conscious that this book does not make adequate reference to developments in theology of religions from a Protestant evangelical perspective. The most significant shift, from which many Catholic theologians have drawn inspiration, lies with the neo-Barthian 'Yale school' and specifically with George Lindbeck's highly influential *The Nature of Doctrine: Religion and Theology in a Postliberal Age* (Philadelphia, Pa.: Westminster, 1984). Although Lindbeck's thesis about the 'cultural-linguistic' model of religion and his 'regulative' understanding of doctrine stem from his ecumenical concerns, both have important implications for theology of religions, opening up the possibility of a more tradition-centred dialogue. For a detailed survey of this development and its roots in the dialogue of Jewish and Christian theologians in the USA, see Peter Ochs, 'An Introduction to Postcritical Scriptural Interpretation', in Peter Ochs (ed.), *The Return to Scripture in Judaism and Christianity* (Mahwah, NJ: Paulist, 1993). For an excellent commentary on new developments (especially Scriptural Reasoning) since Lindbeck's original publication, I am indebted to C. C. Pecknold, *Transforming Postliberal Theology: George Lindbeck, Pragmatism and Scripture* (London: T & T Clark, 2005).

Word.[21] Central to that response are the classical theses that have defined
Christian theology over the centuries – including Christology, ecclesiology,
the doctrine of creation, as well as soteriology. In this regard perhaps the most
perceptive comment of Vatican II, which has so much influenced the thinking of all Christian theologians about other faiths, does not come from the
formal declaration on the relationship of the Church to non-Christian
religions, *Nostra Aetate*, but from *Lumen Gentium*, the Dogmatic
Constitution on the Church, which speaks about persons of other faiths
being 'orientated to' or 'related to' the Church (*Lumen Gentium*, 16). This
vision of the single life-giving mystery of God's love in which Christians and
other people of faith participate together sets the 'old question' of the
salvation of the non Christian in a new light. In particular it questions the
dichotomy implicit in much pluralist thought, between the tradition of
Church teaching and the actual experience of dialogue. The question is not
how to adjust the former in order to accommodate the latter, but how to
speak of the *social and relational nature of human existence* while maintaining
the proper integrity of faith.[22]

Since the Council, official or magisterial teaching from the Catholic
Church about other religions has been concerned with the implications of
this question. One constant theme of Pope John Paul II's encyclicals has
been respect for human dignity;[23] another is the universal action of the Holy
Spirit, which is at work 'in every individual, according to the eternal plan of
salvation'.[24] In focusing specifically on the topic of Christian mission and its
relationship with the practice of dialogue, he goes so far as to extend the
activity of the Spirit from individuals to culture and religions. 'It is the Spirit
who sows the "seeds of the Word" present in various customs and cultures,
preparing them for full maturity in Christ.'[25] This is classic Catholic fulfilment (or, in Race and Hick's terms, 'inclusivist') theology; the grace that
makes salvation possible is given in virtue of Christ, through the Paschal
Mystery of Christ's death and resurrection. But John Paul also adds a new
dimension, raising the much more complex issue of the mediation of grace
through other faiths and cultures. It would, of course, be easier for theologians to stick with individual salvation and avoid getting into the awkward
business of discerning the 'truths and values' present in other religions. The
pope does not do this. Thus in the address he gave to the plenary of the then

---

[21] See Nicholas Lash, *The Beginning and the End of 'Religion'* (Cambridge University Press, 1996),
pp. 5–6.
[22] The theme developed in my earlier work, *Theology and the Dialogue of Religions* (Cambridge
University Press, 2002).
[23] *Redemptor Hominis*, 6.   [24] *Dominum et Vivificantem*, 53.   [25] *Redemptoris Missio*, 28.

Secretariat for Non Christians in 1987, he raises what could be considered merely speculative questions. 'How does God work in the lives of people of different religions? How does the saving activity of Jesus Christ effectively extend to those who have not professed faith in him?'[26] They are, however, intensely pastoral and theological. A few years later, the Pontifical Council for Interreligious Dialogue went so far as to speak of people from other religions being saved 'through their own religious traditions and by following the dictates of their conscience'.[27]

The direction of such authoritative statements is clear: grace is present in other religious traditions. Even the suspicious *Dominus Iesus* tempers its concerns about relativism in the theology of religions by acknowledging the need for theologians to engage in a positive dialogue with other religions in order 'to explore if and in what ways the historical and positive elements of these religions may fall within the divine plan of salvation'.[28] The subtitle of *Dominus Iesus*, 'On the Unicity and Salvific Universality of Christ and the Church', witnesses to a very Catholic principle: Christology and ecclesiology are all of a piece. However the relationship of Christianity and other religions is configured, we are talking about *one* mystery, a *single* mystery of God's salvific action in the world. What can be known of God through the doctrine of creation and what can be known through God's own act of self-revelation in Christ are not two distinct things; there is a continuity between them. This does not rule out but positively demands attention to the task of discerning the action of the Holy Spirit who brings to a fullness that mystery of human participation in God's love to which all people of faith are 'orientated' (*Lumen Gentium*, 16).

At issue, in other words, is not *whether* people from other faith traditions can be saved – they always remain within the gracious providence of God and do not lack for the means of salvation – but what substantive part in that dynamic of salvation can be granted to the religions themselves. Are they saved *despite* their traditional beliefs and practice or more exactly *through* them? Rahner steers us quite clearly in the direction of the latter position. In his later work it is worth noting that when he addresses the issue of 'non-Christian religions' he does not use the term 'Anonymous Christian'. The question is the 'presence' of Jesus Christ in the history of salvation and how

---

[26] *Acta Apostolicae Sedis*, 79 (1987), 1319–20. The Secretariat's name was changed to the Pontifical Council for Interreligious Dialogue (PCID) in 1988.

[27] A joint statement of the PCID and the Congregation for Evangelisation: 'Dialogue and Proclamation: Reflections and Orientations on Inter-religious Dialogue and the Proclamation of the Gospel of Jesus Christ', *Bulletin* [of the PCID], 26/2 (1991), pp. 210–50. Quotation from section 31.

[28] *Dominus Iesus*, 14.

that question shapes Christian life and practice *and* the Christian understanding of the very nature of the self-communicating God. Rahner postulates two principles: first, the 'universal and supernatural salvific will of God which is really operative in the world', and, secondly, the historical and social nature of the 'event' of salvation. It is the Christian experience of grace mediated through a historical and social form that enables Christians to speak of the form God's salvific action takes in the world.[29] The Incarnation reveals God through that which makes people most human – their rootedness in temporally bound forms. In other words, if for Christians God is made manifest in and through the world of our everyday experience, then something analogous is true for others as well. *For Christian and non Christian alike*, then, divine grace is made present not apart from but precisely through concrete forms of human religious belief and practice. Paradoxically, by stressing the ecclesial form in which grace is mediated, Rahner manages to build a bridge between different communities of faith. God does not deal with human beings independent of those historically bound sociocultural institutions – 'the religions' – which constitute and inform human existence in the world. This shift, away from a focus on soteriology alone and towards the theological significance of the beliefs and practices of people of faith, is to be noted in *Nostra Aetate* with its extraordinary exhortation to Christians to 'recognize, preserve and promote the good things, spiritual and moral, as well as the socio-cultural values found among these people' (*Nostra Aetate*, 2). Dialogue begins in the wake of the Council as a matter of learning *about* what motivates people of faith, even to the extent of working and learning *with* them.[30] In the post-conciliar period, however, it also opens up another possibility, one that is implied by the direction of Rahner's thought: learning *from* them about what God may be saying. This raises a challenge with which the Catholic Church is still seeking to come to terms.[31]

[29] Karl Rahner, *Foundations of Christian Faith* (London: Darton, Longman and Todd, 1978), pp. 313 ff.

[30] Christians are exhorted to enter into 'conversations and collaboration' ('colloquia et collaborationem'), *Nostra Aetate*, 2.

[31] At issue are the limits of the typically Catholic fulfilment theology. Jacques Dupuis, with his Rahnerian 'Mystery of Christ' model of interreligious relations, makes a distinction between the religions as a *de iure* and *de facto* reality; religions need to be seen in a fully graced perspective as a willed aspect of God's constitution of the world, not a merely contingent factor. See *Toward* and the development of 'asymmetrical complementarity' in Dupuis's later *Christianity and the Religions: From Confrontation to Dialogue* (New York and London: Orbis/Darton, Longman and Todd, 2002). The distinction was one of the problematic topics raised by the Congregation for the Doctrine of the Faith in *Dominus Iesus* in September 2000. For a summary of the 'Dupuis affair', see Gerald O'Collins, 'Jacques Dupuis: His Person and Work', in Daniel Kendall and Gerald O'Collins (eds.), *In Many and Diverse Ways* (New York: Orbis, 2003), pp. 18–29. A more theological commentary in found in Gerald

THE CHRISTIAN IMAGINATION

It is not surprising that this should be so. The 'question of the other' – the resistant voice that contests the move to mastery on the part of the same – cannot be domesticated by a theoretical system. Ironically, this point is never properly addressed by a normative pluralism, which prides itself on openness to the other. Being based on a type of philosophical universalism that, however benignly, would seek out common values and essences rather than allow for the highly complex ways in which people of faith seek to identify themselves, pluralism fails to take seriously the variety of religions and the differences between them. At issue is not just the truth about the relationship between God, the world and humanity on which Christian faith takes its stand but the integrity of other religious traditions as well.[32] While there is always a risk that theology may trespass beyond the boundaries of what can legitimately be said, the questions that people of faith put to each other deserve an honest response and serious engagement – as the framers of *Nostra Aetate* realised. This changes the context for doing theology – not just theology of religions. Thus, David Tracy goes so far as to say: 'On strictly theological grounds, the fact of religious pluralism should enter all theological assessment and self-analysis in any tradition at the very beginning of its task.'[33] For Tracy, the enterprise of theology in a multi-faith context demands that Christian faith be articulated as it emerges through a critical dialogue with other traditions. To invoke the language noted above, the aim is to learn how to become a learner, how to listen attentively for the Word of God wherever that Word may be spoken. In this sense, all theology, the work of religious intellect, is dialogical; it depends on an engagement with the other.

From the call to engage directly with the 'good things, spiritual and moral' of other religions has emerged the practice of comparative

O'Collins, 'Jacques Dupuis's Contributions to Interreligious Dialogue', *Theological Studies*, 64 (2003), pp. 388–97. For a detailed discussion of the implications of the *de iure/de facto* distinction and the position adopted by *Dominus Iesus*, see the debate between Terrence Tilley, Gavin D'Costa and Perry Schmidt-Leukel, *Modern Theology*, 22.1 (2006), pp. 51–63; *ibid.*, 23.3 (2007), pp. 435–68; *ibid.*, 24.2 (2008), pp. 271–97.

[32] For a Muslim perspective on religious pluralism, see Muhammad Legenhausen, *Islam and Religious Pluralism* (London: Al-Hoda; 1999). For a Buddhist account, see Kristin Beise Kiblinger, *Buddhist Inclusivism: Attitudes towards Religious Others* (Aldershot: Ashgate, 2005). For a brief summary, see Barnes, 'Religious Pluralism', *Routledge Companion to the Study of Religion*, pp. 433–8. For a sustained non-reductive discussion of common themes and ideas in Islam and Christianity, see Paul L. Heck, *Common Ground: Islam, Christianity and Religious Pluralism* (Washington, DC: Georgetown University Press, 2009).

[33] David Tracy, 'Theology: Comparative Theology', in *The Encyclopaedia of Religion*, vol. xiv (New York: Macmillan; 1986), pp. 446–55. Quotation from p. 446.

theology.[34] In its contemporary form, this is an example of what Paul Griffiths calls 'religious reading', a process of submission to and interrogation of canonical and key commentarial texts from which emerges a religious account of things.[35] As a form of theology of religions, comparative theology represents a theological hospitality in which the texts of another tradition are allowed to sound familiar echoes and resonances in one's own. Texts are read together, or in close relation to each other. That is to say that proper attention is given to the defining doctrines of the tradition while at the same time is cultivated an awareness of how analogous themes and ideas are conceived and ordered by another religious tradition. For Francis Clooney, its most noted exponent, 'Comparative theology is a manner of learning that takes seriously diversity and tradition, openness and truth, allowing neither to decide the meaning of our religious situation without recourse to the other.'[36] In a series of books that have brought Christian and Hindu spiritual and theological classics into conversation, Clooney shows that what is at stake is a particular type of scriptural or textual rationality.[37] He is not just making the obvious point that all religious traditions depend on certain canonical texts for their internal coherence. Against the pluralist tendency to set up points of comparison that are intended to show that ultimately religions are alternative versions of the same religious essence, Clooney stresses the intrinsically *theological* value of practices of reading and study. It is not that Rumi or the Quran or a commentary on the *Mimamsa Sutras* act as some sort of reminder of God's cross-religious presence; more profoundly the *act of reading* is itself religious experience. In words reminiscent of an important distinction made by Griffiths, Clooney insists that

---

[34] The project of comparative theology has come to be associated in recent years with the name of the American indologist Francis X. Clooney. His most important apologia is to be found in *Comparative Theology: Deep Learning across Religious Borders* (Chichester: Wiley-Blackwell, 2010). See also his chapter in John Webster, Kathryn Tanner and Iain Torrance (eds.), *The Oxford Handbook of Systematic Theology* (Oxford University Press, 2007), pp. 653–68 and a review article, 'Comparative Theology: A Review of Recent Books, 1989–1995, *Theological Studies*, 56 (1995), pp. 521–50. For lucid theological discussion, see James L. Fredericks, 'A Universal Religious Experience? Comparative Theology as an Alternative to a Theology of Religions', *Horizons*, 22 (1995), pp. 67–87. Clooney has edited an important collection of essays, many with special attention to methodology and theoretical foundations: *The New Comparative Theology: Interreligious Insights from the Next Generation* (London: T & T Clark, 2010). D'Costa offers some critical appraisal of the project in *Christianity and World Religions*, pp. 37–45.

[35] Paul J. Griffiths, *Religious Reading: The Place of Reading in the Practice of Religion* (Oxford University Press, 1999).

[36] Clooney, *Comparative Theology*, p. 8.

[37] Among Clooney's most important exercises in comparative theology are *Theology after Vedanta* (Albany, NY: SUNY Press, 1993), *Seeing Through Texts: Doing Theology among the Srivaisnavas of South India* (Albany, NY: SUNY Press, 1996) and *Divine Mother, Blessed Mother: Hindu Goddesses and the Virgin Mary* (Oxford University Press, 2005).

'Comparative theology requires readers, not consumers, and our reading comes to fruition in teaching or in writing that enables our listeners to take up the work themselves with spiritual sensitivity.'[38] What he speaks of as 'deep learning across religious borders' is in this sense a 'double learning'. A largely unstructured process of moving back and forth across religious borders leads not just to my learning something new about another tradition but to a deeper and perhaps different way of perceiving my own.

In sketching out a genealogy of comparative theology, Clooney notes a variety of forms, including the historian of religion Max Müller and such influential figures in contemporary theology of religions as Keith Ward, Robert Neville and Raimon (Raimundo) Panikkar. What distinguishes Clooney's approach is his disavowal of theory in favour of unlocking the theological potential of particular instances of religious reading. The word 'intuition' runs through the book, a witness to a Catholic faith that knows no bounds and seeks to be drawn into the graced world defined by Hindu texts. In the spirit of Anselm's 'faith seeking understanding', his practice continues the dialogue that the likes of fellow-Jesuits, Roberto de Nobili and Matteo Ricci, held with Indian and Chinese cultures respectively. Clooney thus sees his work as in harmony with the Catholic inclusivist theology inspired by Rahner and Dupuis. Like them, he seeks to balance claims to Christian uniqueness with a necessary openness to the truths claimed by other traditions. But he goes further in commending a practice of the imagination that deliberately seeks the leading of the Spirit – a practice based on a prayerful *lectio divina*. To the objection that his deliberate avoidance of any 'grand theory' ignores presuppositions and undeclared influences, he responds that what is important is 'to bring specific learning about specific other traditions into the conversation'.[39] The aim is to get the conversation going, to enter into another world, with all its strangeness, in faith that here too can be experienced something of the power of a 'transformative vision'. The emphasis is not on unearthing the 'message' behind the text (for that may remain strictly impenetrable) but on the very act of praying and pondering the message – or, to invoke the title of another of Clooney's studies, 'seeing through texts'. Rather than decide in advance where any act of reading will lead, he insists that

[h]onest study has its own dynamics, and we cannot predetermine the conclusions to which our encounter with other religions will lead. We are better off if we remain

---

[38] Clooney, *Comparative Theology*, p. 60.

[39] See Kristen Beise Kiblinger, 'Relating Theology of Religions and Comparative Theology', *The New Comparative Theology*, pp. 21–42, with Clooney's response, pp. 195–6.

patiently and persistently committed to actual instances of learning, specific experiments, deriving our insights from the actual comparisons and not from a theory about religions or about the methodology of comparison.[40]

The hard work of engagement, says Clooney, can easily be deferred by talking about it rather than doing it. This distinctively pragmatic approach, which should characterise a theology of religions done in the middle of things, reflects a shift in the nature of the dialogical context itself. Where de Nobili worked out of a typically Catholic instinct that expected to find 'seeds of the Word' in the Sanskrit and Tamil texts that he explored so thoroughly, his modern-day counterparts are only too well aware that Hinduism, which is itself so much given to the assimilation of other traditions, presents a more profound challenge to Christian faith. Today's Hindus are less happy with some vague universalism and much more ready to argue for the specificity of an incredibly rich and diverse tradition. Clooney's model of comparative theology is derived very much from his engagement with Hinduism, which, as he shows, boasts a commentarial tradition richly deserving of the title theology – the act of 'the religious intellect'.[41] It is the extraordinary vitality and genial chaos of the various spiritualities that have gown up on the Indian subcontinent that make Hinduism such an attractive and life-giving ground for comparative engagement.

It is not just Hindu religious texts, whether devotional or more overtly theological, which form the focus of reading. In a telling example, Clooney prefaces a brief discussion of one particular evocation of the goddess Laksmi by telling us about a visit to a small and unpretentious temple in south Chennai. 'To visit this temple ... opened for me new possibilities of vision beyond what I had seen or thought before.'[42] The building sets the scene for reading, for setting the story of Laksmi within the wider perspective of the relationship between the goddess and her consort, the god Vishnu. The world of Hindu gods and goddesses is far removed from Christian theism, and there is no easy way to uncover some elusive inner meaning. To attempt to do so, however, is to make the mistake of reading in Griffiths's 'consumerist mode', utilising the texts to satisfy curiosity or to build up a command of the language and literature of

---

[40] *Ibid.*, p. 41.
[41] This theme is present in all Clooney's work, but comes out most powerfully in *Hindu God, Christian God* (Oxford University Press, 2001). Subtitled *How Reason Helps Break Down the Boundaries between Religions*, the book opens up common themes such as God's existence and divine embodiment in a dialogue between major theologians from the two traditions.
[42] Clooney, *Comparative Theology*, p. 88.

the Indian world.[43] Comparative theology approaches sacred texts differently, seeking to develop a sensitivity not just to the meaning of the text but to the context of faithful practice that texts both embody and form. Although Clooney does not make this point explicitly, I suspect that what drives much of his thought is the act of *darśana* – literally, 'seeing', or having sight of the beloved. To see the image is also to be seen – for the image is more than a static representation and has what Catholics might call a sacramental quality. In other words, in looking at the figure of the goddess and reciting the words of the prayer, I am brought into the presence of a God who, manifested as a divine couple, draws me to Godself through participating in that relationship. I find it significant that the same word *darśana* is used as the title for the six orthodox philosophical systems of classical Hinduism. Study and the reasoned analysis of experience have an analogous function to the more obviously religious activity of going to the temple for *darśana* of God. In seeing I am seen; I am brought up against myself and enter more deeply into a world suffused by the divine presence.

This plunge into the middle of Hindu *bhakti*, with its wild mood-swings and conflicting emotions, seems a far cry from the abstract formalism of normative pluralism. Yet, almost by definition, the 'question of the other' is not to be answered by a self-referential scheme. Difference cannot be side-lined without doing serious violence to the fragile fabric of human religiosity – a point to which I will return at the end of this chapter. At this stage, however, I want only to argue that no practice of comparative reading is ever done in a cultural and religious vacuum. Texts need to be read as part of the wider and more complex framework that makes up religious life – and that must include the buildings and artefacts and practices of faith and even the people who make up communities of faith. In a certain sense, they too present themselves to be read. They possess their own textuality. The version of comparative theology that is developed in this book differs from that espoused by Clooney in that the examples, the starting points for reflection, are embodied in the lives of persons of faith and inscribed in the places of worship and artefacts that give voice to their faith – sometimes more eloquently than their words and conversation. These are, in other words, embodied comparisons – requiring particular responses to particular people in particular situations. Yet they

---

[43] *Religious Reading*, pp. 40 ff. For Griffiths, religious learning does not just involve reading. While it is 'largely constituted by reading', this is a practice which is 'in many ways deeply different from the kinds of reading taught in the schools of contemporary nation-states' (p. 40). That is to say, that what makes religious reading formative of a particular sense of religious identity is its *reverential* rather than purely *consumerist* mode.

also speak of the principles necessary for any theology of religions, principles of integrity and faithfulness as much as those of openness and respect for the other. To read a religious text, still more to respond sympathetically to the religious context in which they are inscribed, is to enter into a sacred landscape that cannot be reduced to a few more or less spiritual generalisations. Whether at the academic and theological levels, where the underlying issue is very often to do with the place of reason itself within the practice of faith, or in considering such analogical practices as people of faith living and talking together about personal and public concerns, the activity of comparison, explicit or implicit, is a work of the religious imagination. In these terms, comparative theology – whether engaging with texts or with persons or with both – is born from an abiding curiosity about the different ways human beings speak about themselves and whatever they take to have ultimate value.

A SPIRITUALITY OF DIALOGUE

Life in the middle of things raises any number of questions, some theological, about the ways of God with human beings, some more precisely philosophical, about the limits of knowledge, or ethical, about the relationship with the other. What are the resources and practical skills that communities of faith have developed for addressing issues about what is other, strictly beyond the ambit of what is known? What are the limits of adaptation and accommodation? How can the dual responsibilities of faithfulness and openness be exercised with integrity? How are practical considerations about social cohesion or the common good affected by different religious motivations? And what do our all too human responses and reactions to strangers and 'difference' say about the nature of divine reality and human perfection? To these may be added my earlier question – about what happens to faith when it becomes 'inter-faith' – a question less about theology of religions than the spirituality of dialogue, about how faith may be transformed by the engagement with the other. Such questions, which imply not just a 'double learning' but a *double responsibility* of being a Christian, run through these chapters. To that extent, my reflections develop their own narrative – or, to be more precise, follow that set by the self-revealing Word of God. In one sense, the particular examples and the stories they tell speak for themselves – and readers will bring their own 'seeds of the Word' to set in dialogue with my experience. But, in another, they trace an ever-deepening path through the words spun by both self and other, from considerations about the nature of religion and the religions through a range of interreligious encounters to that sense of the unity of all things promised by life in the Spirit of Christ. What holds them all together is the experience of life in the middle of things, engaged in the never-ending task of interreligious learning.

More so than in Clooney's admirably intuitive interrogation of Christian and Hindu scriptures, I am concerned to highlight the hermeneutical principles that underpin the reverential reading of our increasingly multi-faith pluralist world. As noted at the beginning of this chapter, I am proposing a restructuring of a 'Christian imaginary' through a conscientious and discerning dialogue with the other. In the first place, that means recognising the significance of the power of any social imaginary to order and direct human experience. Various themes suggest themselves and in the chapter that follows I want to open up the narrative by addressing the problematic concept of religion itself. Let me conclude this opening chapter, with its sketch of contemporary theology of religions, by returning briefly to the theme that has guided us thus far – life in the middle of things – and to what Charles Taylor, in his account of religion in a secular age, refers to as 'the great disembedding'.[44]

This centuries-long shift from a society in which everyone believes in an enchanted world to one in which belief is the exception and requires explicit justification sets the hierarchical ordering of pre-Reformation Europe against the rampant individualism of post-Enlightenment modernity. Taylor's analysis is detailed and complex and is designed to question the coherence of the familiar secularisation thesis about the destructive impact of modernity on religion. His more nuanced view, noted earlier, is that religion is always changing, producing new forms and practices that continue to negotiate the familiar exigencies of human living. More is at stake, however, than retrieving some long lost model for religion. For Taylor, one of the most significant aspects of the 'great disembedding' is not just the emergence of the 'buffered self', which has marginalised itself from an enchanted world, but the creation of what is – literally – 'secular' time: time which belongs to *this* age.[45] Without a sense of a God-given *telos* at work in human society, the conviction that people are guided by the goal of salvation that governs all aspects of their lives, society finds itself going nowhere. Time is flattened out and turns itself into a sort of procession of events, one thing following after another with very little shape or direction.

For Taylor, the challenge is to find a new way of reading this history of 'homogenised, empty time' that is neither naive nor nostalgic but remains

---

[44] *Modern Social Imaginaries*, pp. 49–67; *A Secular Age*, pp. 146–58.   [45] *A Secular Age*, pp. 54–5.

alive to new forms of spiritual sensibility.[46] Here an alternative model of time suggests itself. 'Time for us', says Taylor,

continues to be marked by cycles, through which we orient ourselves. Even those who are most thoroughly immersed in the packed, measured schedules of a demanding career – perhaps especially they – can be totally at a loss if their routine is interrupted. The frame gives a sense to their lives, distinguishing different moments from each other, giving each its sense, creating mini-kairoi to mark the passage of time. It's as though we humans have a need for gathered time, in one form or another.[47]

Whatever else religions may or may not do for their communities, they gather and shape the flow of time. To give but one example of a practice that has formed Catholic Christianity: the rhythms of the monastic chant – regular, formal, measured – give a certain pattern to the day, structuring the lives of the monks and anchoring them solidly in ancient formative memories. In its origins, of course, this is a form of timekeeping, marking the key moments of the day – sunrise, midday, sunset – with a time of remembrance and praise of God. The structure is almost as old as Christianity itself. It is also reminiscent of the practice of prayer in Islam. Muslims too order the day with prayer at five specific moments. In the mosque a clock keeps the times that are to be observed not just by those present but by all Muslims, the complete community or *umma*. And, to return to the example of traditional Buddhist practice with which I began, the time of meditation is part of a much broader and more structured *marking of time* that gives a certain rhythm to life as a whole. The particular fruit of meditation, the building up of 'mindfulness' or attention to the present moment, emerges from and flows back into the daily pattern of life as it is lived. Islam, Christianity and Judaism have always maintained highly developed liturgical cycles that pattern the year. Analogous points can be made about the religions of India and the Far East. Checking on the appearance of the new moon, calculating the date of Easter, consulting complex stellar horoscopes, may seem like a mind-dulling legalism, but it represents something so obvious, yet so subtle, that it is easily missed. The practice of regular prayer or meditation, through the day, through the year, gives hope and meaning to people's lives. Communal rituals and formal practices give clarity and authority to the community of faith. Durkheim speaks of the object of religion being 'to raise man above himself and to make him lead a life superior to that which he would lead'.[48] Putting it very simply, rituals

[46] *Ibid.*, p. 594.   [47] *Ibid.*, p. 714.
[48] Émile Durkheim, *Elementary Forms of Religious Life* (London: Allen and Unwin, 1915), p. 414.

socialise individuals, giving them not just a sense of belonging but a conviction of moral worth and power.

In practice, of course, nothing is ever that simple; the desire for a ritualised ordering of reality exists in tension with life in the messy middle of things. Convictions, especially those that would seek to preserve the self against the inexorable flow of time, not to mention the incursions of the other into a familiar space, can be ambivalent – not to say dangerous. So let me finish this chapter with a couple of summary remarks that may act as a sort of *leitmotif* that will colour the rest of this book.

Against the popular tendency, with which I began, to associate 'religion' with versions of some discrete area of 'spiritual' experience, I want to argue for religion in terms of a 'social imaginary' that structures people's lives and gives rise to a whole way of life. When people do *puja* in the temple or walk in pilgrimage or sit in silent meditation or celebrate particular rituals or read canonical texts, they are not concerned with a purely personal or private spiritual activity that can be set apart from their other concerns. Rather, religion is about the sanctification of *the whole of life*. A religious account of things, says Griffiths, is comprehensive and unsurpassable; it is learned in particular ways, through particular linguistic and institutional contexts.[49] There is more to religion than some sort of glorified timekeeping mechanism, a quaint relic of an age before timetables ruled our lives. Rather, as Augustine realised, the mystery of time, and the uncanny human capacity to mark time and to negotiate its passing, is one of the profoundest aspects of the religious instinct.[50] It goes on informing the human condition because it touches one of our most basic needs – the desire for meaning and purpose.

The second point is a corollary of the first – and touches upon one of the most problematic areas in what follows, namely the pathology of religion. If a religious faith sets up a total view of the world, then the other, whether other religious communities or deviant members of one's own community, or just whatever threatens internal harmony, can become problematic – and a provocation to violence. How does one cope with difference and diversity, with the awkward things that simply do not fit the pattern? Is there not a limit to what any total view of things can comprehend? Indeed, is not such a 'totality', as Levinas warns us, deeply corrupting? I shall seek to argue that too strong an emphasis on 'content', an uncritical account of religion as no more than a 'security structure' or guiding set of rules for the pathway through life, turns faith into a closed system that inevitably ends up total-ising the other. An account of any religious tradition without a pedagogy,

---

[49] *Religious Reading*, pp. 3–21.   [50] St Augustine, *Confessions*, Bk. XI.

teaching not just the skills of discernment but a lifelong *process* of learning, is likely to be seriously flawed and oppressive. Traditional stories and rituals give people a rooting in time and a way of structuring the ordinary and everyday, but how people respond to everyday exigencies and pressures depends on a whole range of factors – not all of which are easily accommodated within the traditional timetable of regular ritual and prayerful practice. In other words, the security established by a community's tradition *raises* the question of the other, it does not take it away.

Taylor speaks not of social theory but social *imaginary*, because, among other things, it accounts for beliefs and practices shared by a wide variety of 'ordinary' people.[51] This is where we began: the ordinariness of life that is yet the source of the most profound of truths. The logic implicit in the ways of acting and responding that bind people together is as important, if not more so, than the theoretical overviews that such logic develops. Interreligious learning is one practice that, I wish to argue, characterises a pluralist age. Undoubtedly it needs in due course to be theorised and given a proper integrity. Taylor warns us, however, that shifts in any social imaginary take time to emerge. The crucial task, therefore, is not to impose some overarching theory in the anxiety to comprehend a rapidly changing world. It is, first and foremost, to tease out the complex process by which 'we' find ourselves interrogating – and being interrogated by – the other, and that allows us to go on being recognisably 'us' while maintaining a positive harmony of relationships. To live in the middle of things without making premature assumptions about the extent of our understanding of, let alone mastery over, the other is the heart of interreligious learning.

---

[51] *A Secular Age*, pp. 171 ff.

CHAPTER 2

Schools of faith

Dindigul is a typical Indian provincial town nestling on the fringes of the Kodai hills in the southern state of Tamil Nadu. I spent several months there during the final stage of my training as a Jesuit. It was a time of prayer and study, time marked by a wonderful freedom to get to know a world that, up to that moment, had been transmitted to me mainly through novels, travelogues and the standard textbooks on Indian religions. What I remember from those days was no great insight into Vedantic philosophy as it impacted on Christian theology, but, rather more prosaically, a sense of the religious routine somehow built into the land itself. Early in the morning I used to stand and watch the sun as it rose over the lip of the distant horizon. Day after day I found myself totally captivated by this symbol of new life. The whole world seemed to respond with a symphony of noise – birds and insects, traffic on the road, and the strains of devotional music from the temple by the railway. 'They are waking up the god', one helpful old man told me. During the day the sun crossed the sky and I took refuge in the shade. In the evening a deep stillness attended the setting of the sun – often in a brilliant array of reds and purples. Those wonderful moments of twilight were always so short, as if the sun was in a hurry to put the world to bed. Small wonder that Vedic mythology is so powerfully endowed with references to the mysteries of nature and the power of the seasons.

Since then I have been back many times and seen a lot more of this vast subcontinent with its array of spiritualities and religions. There is, of course, more to Hinduism than romantic images of wizened *sannyasis* at their *puja* and sacred cows wandering languidly into the setting sun. But if I begin with this particular memory it is not because I wish to obscure the complex ways in which the aesthetic, mystical and social dimensions of religion are interweaved or to ignore its dark and destructive side. It is, rather, that I have always been struck by the deep harmony between the practices of faith, the cycles of nature and the human mapping of history. Sometimes that harmony is palpable – as in a religion like Hinduism, which is so much bound up with the land. Sometimes one struggles to discern its life-giving rhythms – as in the prophetic religions of the Middle East that seem more concerned to dominate the world rather than live at peace with it. But in both – and in all the vast array of religious phenomena that it would be possible to quote – religious practice and 'ordinary life' are intimately related, part of a single, complex and mysterious tapestry.

That connection is less obvious in 'the West'. Yet even here are plenty of reminders of what I alluded to briefly at the end of the previous chapter – religious faith as the patterning of time's relentless movement. It may not be possible to observe the sun with such contemplative fascination, but the instinct to mark everyday existence with the order of ancient rituals remains, and goes on building both traditional and novel forms. Within a one mile radius of the house in London where I live there are more than sixty different places of worship.[1] Apart from the various Christian churches, chapels and meeting places that have been there for generations, there are four mosques, three Hindu temples, a dozen Sikh *gurdwaras* and a small Buddhist *vihara*. Some are eked out of terraced houses and reordered halls and garages. Some are purpose-built, with no expense spared. The main *gurdwara* is a mix of traditional Panjabi and modern British architecture. Bare concrete and polished marble, with stained-glass windows and an array of white and golden domes, it stands on a road named after General Sir Henry Havelock who was prominent in the first Indian war of independence in 1857. When this magnificent building was formally opened a few years ago, I remember hearing the sound of music and went to investigate. There coming down the road resplendent in the red uniforms of the Grenadier Guards was a military band. The irony was not missed on many of the folk who turned up to enjoy the event.

TRADITION AND MODERNITY

Let that juxtaposition stand for all the complex anomalies and paradoxes that confront 'traditional religion' in a multicultural city like London. While some communities shift across social and cultural borders with relative ease, others find the process of putting down new roots in a very

[1] Reference to Southall is made in my *Theology and the Dialogue of Religions*, especially the final chapter. A 'pilgrim's guide' to places of worship in Southall is set out, with brief historical details, in Daniel Faivre, *Glimpses of a Holy City* (privately published, 2001). For a much more detailed ethnographic study of practices of integration across community boundaries in Southall, see Gerd Baumann, *Contesting Culture: Discourses of Identity in Multi-Ethnic London* (Cambridge University Press, 1994).

untraditional diaspora extremely painful.[2] Some become more isolated and fixed into self-defining enclaves; others show a remarkable creativity, using architecture, decoration, dress, forms of internal organisation and smart hi-tech means of self-presentation in order to adapt to changed conditions. But the business of re-rooting and adjusting to changed circumstances cuts both ways. According to Taylor, the modern post-Enlightenment West has long lost any instinctive sympathy for the 'enchanted' world and constructed instead a secularity with a 'self-sufficient humanism'.[3] Inevitably this causes tensions and misunderstanding between home and immigrant communities. At times, 'other religions' can seem very other indeed: strange relics of an age long past with customs and culture that refuse integration and threaten social cohesion. Hence the use of popular descriptors like 'moderate' and 'mainstream' to define beliefs and behaviour that are deemed acceptable in modern society. Such language is, however, thoroughly question-begging, for where is the mainstream and who has the right to define it? Demands that supposedly pre-modern religions like Islam need their own Reformation if they are to catch up with the rest of the world often seem arrogant and short-sighted. The world historian Marshall Hodgson neatly turns this sort of Western ethnocentrism on its head. The exception is not 'the vast, vague "Orient"', he says, but Europe. 'The appropriate question is not "Why did the Muslims lag behind?" but "Why did the Occident suddenly become so different?"'[4] If that is correct, if it is not anti-modern non-Christian religion but post-Christian Western culture that is other, then the burden of proof changes dramatically. The project of interreligious learning assumes ethical and political as well as 'purely' theological dimensions.

I do not intend to pursue that political issue here. I note only certain underlying assumptions about the relationship of religion, modernity and the secular democratic state. They go something like this. To be properly cohesive society depends on some sort of agreement about shared common values and matters of mutual concern. But since religions disagree about what is true and holy and good, *ipso facto* they cannot provide the necessary 'social glue'. Indeed, left to themselves, communities of faith seek only to

[2] 'Diaspora religion' as a theme in Religious Studies has gained considerable prominence in the last two decades. For an excellent guide and bibliography of recent material, see Sean McLoughlin, 'Religion and Diaspora', in John Hinnells (ed.), *The Routledge Companion to the Study of Religion*, 2nd edn. (London and New York: Routledge, 2010), pp 558–80.
[3] Charles Taylor, *A Secular Age* (Cambridge, Mass.: Harvard University Press, 2007), pp. 1–22.
[4] Marshall Hodgson, *Rethinking World History: Essays on Europe, Islam, and World History* (Cambridge University Press, 1999), p. 217.

safeguard their particular vision of things; sooner or later the pursuit of narrow self-interest is bound to breed resentment and even to break out in violence. Underlying this narrative, it would be fair to say, is an account of 'the religions' as versions of some generic 'religion'. Islam, Hinduism, Buddhism, Sikhism etc. are really versions of the same thing. There can be little doubt that for politicians and policymakers religion presents a major challenge; they are, after all, charged with managing a pluralist society founded on ideals of democratic consensus.[5] It is important, however, not to mistake a *diverse* society for a *divided* society. Just because religions believe different things it does not follow that they cannot and do not talk to each other.[6] Indeed, as I seek to argue, the exploration of difference can provide an impetus to open up conversations across boundaries. But, if that is to happen and religious communities are to be regarded as a force for social cohesion and not a problem that prevents it, then a different 'social imaginary' needs to be constructed, an alternative to the tendency to lump all communities of faith together as versions of the same sort of social structure, with similar basic patterns of belief and similar structures of organisation and authority.

How are 'the religions', including Christianity, to be released from the modern tendency to homogenise and reduce to some easily assimilable generic formula? In response to that question I find myself in substantial agreement with the argument advanced by Gavin D'Costa, that an alternative narrative to 'the new religion of secularism' is needed if theology is not simply to collude with the pretensions of modern culture.[7] That may be accounted a starting point for what follows.

[5] Such assumptions (in many ways influenced by the principled liberal secularist thought associated with John Rawls) about the place of religion in the public sphere are being subjected to an increasingly sophisticated critique. See especially Kristin Deede Johnson, *Theology, Political Theory and Pluralism: Beyond Tolerance and Difference* (Cambridge University Press, 2007); Charles T. Mathewes, *A Theology of Public Life* (Cambridge University Press, 2007); Thomas Banchoff (ed.), *Religious Pluralism, Globalization and World Politics* (Oxford University Press, 2008); Nigel Biggar and Linda Hogan (eds.), *Religious Voices in Public Places* (Oxford University Press, 2009). The formation of liberal modern ideas about the place of religion in the public sphere (essentially, of course, a privatisation of religion) is recounted in William Cavanaugh, *The Theopolitical Imagination* (Edinburgh: T & T Clark, 2002). For a different reading of 'modernity's story' about religion, with due acknowledgement of William Cavanaugh, see Gavin D'Costa, 'The Secular Construction of the Sacred', in *Christianity and World Religions: Disputed Questions in the Theology of Religions* (Chichester: Wiley-Blackwell, 2009), pp. 74–102.

[6] See remarks made by Rowan Williams in his keynote address to a seminar at Lambeth Palace on Bilateral Inter Faith Dialogue in the United Kingdom, 30 March 2009. Report published by the Inter Faith Network for the UK, 2009.

[7] Drawing on a variety of historical studies, D'Costa distinguishes what he calls 'ideological secular readings' of religion (e.g., Freud, Durkheim) that exclude theology a priori from 'principled secular

My first aim in this chapter is to distinguish the modern concept of religion (with its connotations of some sort of purely spiritual activity) from the more complex version to be found in those great communities of faith that are usually referred to in the literature as the 'world religions'. The discourse of normative pluralism makes no such distinction; the role of theology is to negotiate between more or less similar versions of the same thing. I have already noted that this impoverishes the aims of theology. However, it also imposes an uncritical stereotype on traditions that, whether in their traditional world of origin or scattered through a diaspora, make up richly diverse patterns of holiness that shape people's lives. Vast amounts have, of course, been written about religion as a cultural and social phenomenon, from detailed ethnographic studies to magnificent theoretical explorations. My concern, however, is not with the nature and origins of human religiosity as such (which, as Keith Ward lucidly demonstrates, easily gets explained away in terms of 'something else'[8]) but with religion as a practice of faith that is bound up with the search for understanding and wisdom. According to Jonathan Z. Smith, 'religion' is not a first-order characterisation but a designation imposed from outside on 'some aspect of native culture'.[9] In the religions that take their rise in India – Hinduism, Buddhism, Jainism, Sikhism – there is no word for religion; the nearest is the Sanskrit *dharma*, with its root meaning of what is solid or dependable, an elusive term that is often translated as truth, justice, right or teaching. In Islam, the nearest equivalent is *din*, a word with connotations of that complex of obligations that God's revelation imposes. In none of these traditions do we find the deracinated essence of 'religion' as a set of purely

readings', which allow some form of intra-religious interpretative framework. Both, however, turn out to be value-laden positions – thus opening the way for a renewed theological form of religious study. See *Christianity and World Religions*, pp. 91 ff.

[8] See Keith Ward, *The Case for Religion* (Oxford: Oneworld, 2004). Although I am here concerned less with the nature and definition of religion as such and more with shifts in the way the word itself is used and the effect these have on interreligious relations, the place of theology within the wider discipline of Religious Studies does have some significance. To omit theology is to lose the most important dimension of the practitioner's self-description. Thus, according to Clayton Crockett, 'the study of religion necessarily possesses a theological component or moment, even if only in a formal sense'. 'On the Disorientation of the Study of Religion', in Thomas A. Idinopulos and Brian C. Wilson (eds.), *What is Religion? Origins, Definitions and Explanations* (Leiden: Brill, 1998), p. 5. The inclusion of a major article on theology (by David Ford) in *The Routledge Companion to the Study of Religion* is one indication that the rigid distinction of theology from Religious Studies is breaking down. For more detailed discussion of these issues, see Gavin Flood, *Beyond Phenomenology: Rethinking the Study of Religion* (London: Cassells, 1999).

[9] See Jonathan Z. Smith, 'Religion, Religions, Religious', in Mark Taylor (ed.), *Critical Terms in Religious Studies* (University of Chicago Press, 1998), p. 269. According to Wilfred Cantwell Smith, 'religions' tend to be named by outsiders who, 'in their conception of other men's religions, have tended to drain these of any but mundane content'. *The Meaning and End of Religion* (London: SPCK; 1978), p. 141.

spiritual beliefs and practices that is typical of the post-Enlightenment West. Rather, each one proposes variations on the theme of what makes for human flourishing and learning about the nature of transcendent mystery. Once the shift is made away from Orientalist impositions to what practitioners of the traditions in question *say of themselves*, a more interesting and theologically challenging perspective begins to open up.

Secondly, therefore, I want to identify a different sort of 'social imaginary'. I argue that religions should be understood in dynamic terms as 'schools of faith' where the traditions that sustain people of faith and the skills that communicate wisdom are learned. This image I take from a persuasive suggestion of Nicholas Lash with echoes not just of Wilfred Cantwell Smith but also of the patterns of Christian living and learning that are represented in the Creeds.[10] With his discerning enthusiasm for uncovering the uncounted ways in which religious traditions have interacted with each other over the course of time, Cantwell Smith is concerned with bringing the history of religion into theology. Whatever they may or may not have in common, each of the religions needs to be approached as a community of faith – or, more exactly, an aggregation of communities – which finds their coherence through a complex process of historical engagement between a particular theological vision of the nature of things and the challenges and questions that the wider world puts to the tradition. In short, he reminds us that religious communities are made up of learners, and that religion is about learning in the broadest sense. This will take us back to my main thesis. Interreligious learning, to repeat the earlier point, begins not with the assimilation of data *about* the other but in the middle of a 'school of schools' when one learns *from* and *with* the other.

'RELIGION' AND 'THE RELIGIONS'

At the end of the previous chapter, I ventured a description of religion in terms of a 'social imaginary' that gives rise to a whole way of life. Here I want to set this idea against the more popular account noted above by tracing just one strand through a complex history of development. That strand is implied in Cantwell Smith's observation that the Latin adjective

---

[10] See especially Wilfred Cantwell Smith, *The Meaning and End* and *Towards a World Theology: Faith and the Comparative History of Religion* (London: Macmillan, 1981). Nicholas Lash outlines his own account of 'the religions' as 'schools of faith' in *The Beginning and the End of 'Religion'* (Cambridge University Press, 1996), especially pp. 19–21. For the Creed as 'The Pattern of Christian Pedagogy', see Lash, *Easter in Ordinary* (Notre Dame, Ind.: University of Notre Dame Press, 1988), pp. 254–85. On the Apostles' Creed, see Lash, *Believing Three Ways in One God* (London: SCM: 1992).

'*religiosus*' 'had a considerably more stable history than the substantive'.[1] His 'person-orientated' approach to religion seeks to reinstate the position of the participant and to correct what he sees as too strong an emphasis on the position of the outsider or observer. Where observers identify things, participants are caught up in processes. He therefore draws attention to the 'notion that human history might prove more intelligible if we learned to think of religion and the religions as adjectives rather than as nouns – that is, as secondary to persons or things rather than as things in themselves'.[12] I will return to the implications of this idea towards the end of this chapter. Meanwhile, I want to stay with this shift from the 'adjectival' to the 'substantival' quality of 'religion'. What precisely is it about 'religion as process' that can be retrieved from this history?

The tendency to reify what are really qualities of persons or what is intrinsic to the actions that persons perform is the mechanism that creates abstract nouns, or even personifications. When the substantive *religio* begins to emerge, notably in Lucretius and Cicero, it has already gathered connotations of obligation or vow or duty. But it still keeps its connection with cult and ritual, the formal commitment or 'binding' that people make, whether to the gods or some other object worthy of respect. Lucretius, in *De Rerum Natura*, uses the impersonal term rarely but he does refer to *Religio* at one point as a shadowy goddess figure who embodies qualities of piety, reverence or due diligence, which are typical of one who is *religiosus*.[13] The Latin Fathers of the Church inherited the idea, applying it to their own practices that expressed a 'binding' to the God of Israel. In some instances, as with Tertullian, it tended to assume a polemical force, setting Christian faith over against pagan practices. St Augustine, however, with his intensely felt vision of the God of love struggling to reveal himself to sinful human beings, retained the older meaning of committed engagement. When he wrote his great treatise *De Vera Religione*, his target is Manichaean dualism and all manner of 'false opinions'; but more exactly the object of the treatise is to commend that worship of the one God that by 'binding ourselves tightly to him alone' overcomes all superstition.[14] *Religio* is used along with *cultus* (cult, or worship – what 'cultivates' the relationship with God or makes it flourish). While Augustine writes clearly from a Christian Trinitarian perspective, the 'true religion' he commends is not the right

---

[11] Cantwell Smith, *The Meaning and End*, p. 20.   [12] *Ibid.*
[13] Lucretius, *De Rerum Natura*, 1.62–5. See Cantwell Smith, *The Meaning and End*, p. 22.
[14] St Augustine, *De Vera Religione*, 1.1: 55.III. Translation from *The Works of St Augustine: A Translation for the Twenty-first Century*, Pt. 1, vol. viii (New York: New City Press, 2005).

system or set of beliefs to be contrasted with the wrong one; he is more concerned with describing the personal confrontation with the splendour and love of God that his Christian faith has taught him. Similarly, for the greatest of the medieval scholastics, St Thomas Aquinas, 'true religion professes faith in one God'. '*Religio*' is one of the virtues; in the *Summa* it comes under the general heading of justice. That is to say, 'religion' is that service or observance that is due to God alone and is to be contrasted with vices of idolatry and superstition.[15] Religion is an activity of the soul, the inner motivation that prompts someone to express the worship proper to God. In other words, for these two theologians, 'religion' is not coterminous with any particular version or form of human religiosity. Rather it refers to what constitutes the highest aspiration of the human spirit, the 'bond' that in and through prayer unites the creature with the Almighty Creator.

A shift in meaning begins to take place with the European Renaissance and the period of the great voyages of discovery.[16] In 1453, in the wake of the sack of Constantinople by Muslim armies, Nicholas of Cusa wrote *De Pace Fidei*, an extraordinary theological tract that takes the form of a heavenly dialogue between the *Logos* with Saints Peter and Paul and seventeen individuals, including a Greek, an Indian, a Jew, a Persian, a Turk, a German, an Armenian and even an Englishman. The participants are made to represent typical religious beliefs or attitudes. There is a nice moment towards the end when '*Anglicus*' raises a question about 'fastings, ecclesiastical duties, abstinences from food and drink'.[17] The response he gets is that different people do things differently and there is always a legitimate pluralism of religious practice that has to be respected. This is a theme that runs throughout the text. The key phrase, which Cusa repeats, is '*one religion in the variety of rites*'. 'Religion' exists in tension with 'rites'. At work in Cusa's imagination is the spirit of Renaissance humanism: a delight in the sheer variety and richness of human endeavour. Here we find ourselves on the edge of the modern era, marked by the opening up of new knowledge about different peoples and cultures. Travellers to Asia observe people praying in ways that are similar to Christian practices; the worship and devotion of the natives of the Americas seem to reflect

---

[15] *Summa Theologiae* 2a2ae, 81, 2a2ae, 92, 94. 'To act justly', says Lash commenting on Aquinas, 'is to render people or things their due. To act religiously is to give God *God's* due.' See *Theology for Pilgrims* (London: Darton, Longman and Todd, 2008), p. 28.

[16] Cantwell Smith, *The Meaning and End*, pp. 32 ff.; Smith, 'Religion, Religions, Religious', pp. 270–2.

[17] James E. Blechler and H. Lawrence Bond, *Nicholas of Cusa – Interreligious Harmony: Text, Concordance and Translation of* De Pace Fidei (Lampeter: Edwin Mellen, 1991).

something of what is familiar in Europe. This focus on ritual, suggests Jonathan Z. Smith, had an unintended consequence; for similarities to what is known require some sort of explanation.[18] Patristic theories of accommodation, such as had inspired Irenaeus and Justin, now come into their own, inspiring the Jesuit missionaries of the late sixteenth and early seventeenth centuries to build new syntheses of the 'seeds of the Word'.

This side of Cusa's account of 'religion' has been overlaid by another, one that is indebted less to a fascination with other people's rituals and religious practices than to the spirit of understanding and discovery itself, which in many ways anticipates the Enlightenment. If the Age of Discovery was entranced by the strange and exotic, releasing a new spirit of missionary endeavour that developed within the Catholic Church in the wake of the colonial empires, the Age of Reason grappled with the more philosophical problems about truth and authority that were raised by the massive expansion of human knowledge in the seventeenth century. The Enlightenment was, of course, founded on disillusion with the theological claims of Christianity to be based on a special revelation of the divine. This is not to say that the quest for the foundations of true knowledge was intrinsically anti-religious; Descartes, for instance, was a devout Christian who was educated by Jesuits. But it does raise the question to which I drew attention at the end of the previous chapter – how the other is to be accommodated. The medieval strategy was to demonise the other as 'anti-Christian'; if the Word of God had been proclaimed openly then non Christians, Jews and Muslims were guilty of refusing a manifest truth. With the so-called discovery of the Americas, and therefore of people who had never known anything of Christ, the 'problem of the other' has to be configured differently. The other lacks proper understanding – not anti-Christian but simply non-Christian, and therefore in need of true knowledge.[19]

The challenge is how to order this vast array of new data, new material and new ideas. But the fascination with worlds to the east and west of Europe was compounded by a problem nearer home: the wars of religion of the early seventeenth century, which showed, all too starkly, how divisive

---

[18] 'Religion, Religions, Religious', p. 270. In a collection of essays in *Imagining Religion: From Babylon to Jonestown* (University of Chicago Press, 1982), Smith draws attention to how the discovery of connections and coincidences builds theoretical reflection. See especially pp. 53 ff. and the observation, with regard to ritual and sacred place, that '[t]here is nothing that is sacred in itself, *only things sacred in relation*' (emphasis added).

[19] A point made with great cogency by Bernard McGrane in his *Beyond Anthropology: Society and the Other* (New York: Columbia University Press, 1989).

religious commitments could be. How to make sure that religious commitment did not provoke discord and even violence? The political solution in Europe, codified with the Treaty of Westphalia, which ended the Thirty Years War in 1648, began the process by which religion becomes politicised (more exactly, privatised), that is to say, removed from the public or political sphere.[20] The philosophical (and therefore theological) solution is for all partisan commitments, all particularities, all differences, to be brought under one unifying foundation. The huge variety of 'religion' is reduced to a single essence or 'thing'. Religion is less about what human beings actually *do* in terms of worship and prayer, and much more concerned with what they take to be true.

To flesh out this philosophical shift, let me turn briefly to Lord Herbert of Cherbury (1582–1648), much quoted and still influential, and one of the first rationalist philosophers to speak of 'natural religion', an essence that underlies particular traditions. Herbert distils five basic principles or 'common notions concerning religion' out of the variety of religious beliefs: the existence of one supreme God, the duties of worship, the demands of an ethical life, repentance for sin, and 'that God avenges crimes which are committed with impunity in this life'.[21] At work here is a version of religion that can be traced back to the distinction common to the three Semitic religions, as well as to Platonism, between the world of the Infinite or Transcendent and the world of the senses; such an essence of all religion appears to have more to do with a desiccated Christianity than some deep structure of all human religiosity.[22] More important, however, than the content of this rationalist approach to religion is the presupposition behind it: the truth of a religion is to be found in its doctrines. Religion is about knowledge; the standard is set by what is intelligible and open to reason. No longer are we talking about rituals and a rule of life, or even about that personal commitment and respect that is owed to the Divine, but the external standard of behaviour and its systematised mode of justification that are open to scrutiny. Religion has become an object

[20] See D'Costa, *Christianity and World Religions*, pp. 60 ff., 74 ff. and William T. Cavanaugh, '"A Fire Strong Enough to Consume the House"', *Modern Theology*, 11.4 (Oct. 1995), pp. 397–420. Cavanaugh's point is that to speak of the 'wars of religion' is anachronistic; what was at stake was the creation of 'religion' as a universal category, separate from an activity called 'politics'.

[21] 'Common Notions Concerning Religion', from Ivan Strenski (ed.), *Thinking about Religion: A Reader* (Oxford: Blackwell, 2006), pp. 2–8.

[22] The beginnings of one form of contemporary atheism, namely the rejection of a deistic God rather than the biblical God of Israel, and therefore of the 'secular religion' of modernity, are charted in Michael Buckley, *At the Origins of Modern Atheism* (New Haven, Conn.: Yale University Press, 1987). For a theological commentary on what continue to be influential ideas, see Lash, 'The Impossibility of Atheism', *Theology for Pilgrims*, pp. 19–35.

of observation, of study – no longer the means to stimulate learning, but its primary focus.[23]

To sum up this rapid overview: in the seventeenth century, the clash of religious interests at home, and growing information about other worlds and cultures, created a category of religion as an intellectual system. But this is precisely *not* to say that 'the religions' were treated objectively as discrete social and cultural phenomena in their own right. On the contrary, they are identified by approximation to the 'essence' of Christianity (more exactly, a rationalist theism) that gives privileged place to a transcendent Absolute reality, the ultimate object of human understanding. This perception of 'religion' was to have an important influence on how the colonialist administrators of a later age were to construct an identity of the peoples they came to govern.[24] It is not, perhaps, going too far to suggest that the European desire to overcome all rivalry between religions is projected on to the wider world of colonialist expansion. The disparate and diffuse cultures, philosophies and value systems that were encountered, from the 'New World' of the Americas to the distant and fabled lands of China and Japan, were easily regarded as players in some great interreligious competition. Cantwell Smith tells us that the first book on 'the religions of the world' appeared in 1508.[25] It is, admittedly, rather more polemical than Cusa's eirenic vision of the peoples of the world gathered around the Logos. Nevertheless, it is an interesting example – perhaps the first – of how the word 'religion' is used in the plural. According to Peter Harrison, from the beginning of the eighteenth century, the plural becomes a commonplace – usually with four variants: Judaism, Islam or 'Mahometanism', Christianity and 'paganism'.[26] Each is a version of generic 'religion'. What they have in common is their relative approximation to the Enlightenment philosophers' concern to find and order the proper foundation for what can be known. The rationalism of this period constructed a normative template that fitted all forms of religion. But it did so by promoting an all-pervading dualism of sacred and profane. As God (the ultimate object of knowledge) was set apart from the world, so the practices of religion came to be divorced from everyday living – with the inevitable result

---

[23] See D'Costa, *Christianity and World Religions*, pp. 65–8, 91–102. For an excellent overview of such theories of religion, ranging from the search for 'natural religion' to the phenomenology of Mircea Eliade, see Ivan Strenski (ed.), *Thinking about Religion: A Reader* (Oxford: Blackwell, 2006).

[24] See, e.g., Tony Ballantyne, *Between Colonialism and Diaspora: Cultural Formations in an Imperial World* (Durham, NC and London: Duke University Press, 2006), p. 42.

[25] *Dyalogus Johannis Stamler Augustn. de diversarum gencium* [sic] *sectis et mundi religionibus*. Reference from Cantwell Smith, *The Meaning and End*, p. 236 n.

[26] Peter Harrison, *'Religion' and the Religions in the English Enlightenment* (Cambridge University Press, 1994), p. 39.

that religion became privatised. It is this dichotomy that has formed our thinking about 'the religions' ever since.[27]

THE 'OTHERNESS' OF THE RELIGIONS

Let me now return to my opening remarks with the observation that religion is not just about what people believe about transcendent verities. It is concerned with what people *do* and, more specifically, with the many and varied ways people try to bring some sort of harmony and inner understanding to existence. What goes on in a tiny Vaishnava temple by a railway line in rural India – 'waking up the god' – sounds quaint and medieval to the sophisticated Westerner but it speaks of a world shot through with traces of holy being. Of course, to use that sort of language to describe the pilgrimage to one of the major shrines of Shi'a Islam during the festival of Ashura or to account for the Vipassana practices of Theravadin monks in a Thai monastery would be totally inappropriate. The demanding process of understanding 'religion' can easily be subverted by unexamined assumptions – especially about what is supposed to hold religious practices together. It seems plausible to say that there is a common pattern in the contact that ritual or prayer or meditation establishes between this visible world of human relations and some other, non-visible world of 'transcendent' reality. And no doubt all religions do, as Lord Herbert surmised, raise questions about the nature of transcendence, about the purpose of human life, about how ultimate reality and this world are related. The problem, of course, is that the attempt to isolate 'common notions' or patterns can become so vague and general as to be meaningless. Raised here are questions about meaning, theological questions – by which I do not mean questions about the inner coherence of a faith system but more intractable questions about how faith and hope, understanding and judgement, experience and imagination, wonder and love, all work together. They arise from different experiences of the world of human and divine interaction and, therefore, different motivations for approaching that world.

Without that context, the risk is that religion is reduced to an object of study. What then happens is that the rich complexity of 'social imaginaries' gives way to a dualism of public and private, material and spiritual, what we can agree upon because we can observe it and what we cannot agree upon

[27] The sharpest theological commentary on this development comes from Lash, *The Beginning and the End*, pp. 3–25.

because it is, by definition, beyond observation. The modern fixation on the measurable can be fatal not just to the truth of religion but also to any practical purchase that that truth might have on the political and practical reality of life in a multi-faith world.

Religion can, of course, be described. Social imaginaries are never incommensurable; links and patterns and continuities can always be found. But, where human behaviour is involved, and especially where that behaviour must be set against the horizon of what people believe has ultimate value and significance, care needs to be taken not to short-circuit the process of description, to turn complex phenomena like Hindu *bhakti* or Shi'a Islam or Buddhist *Abhidharma* study into versions of the 'same thing'. Once that happens, and the richness of religious phenomena gets reduced to some overarching essence, the religious universe that results becomes bland and uninteresting. The reality is very different – if infuriatingly diffuse. To go into a Hindu temple is to be confronted by a number of statues and pictures ranged around the walls. Even the central sanctuary will have more than one figure; usually it is a pair, the god with his consort. (Or should that be the goddess with *her* consort?) Although Hindus will speak of these figures as all representing different aspects of the one God, it is not immediately obvious what this means, how the diversity relates to the one.[28] If this is monotheism, it is significantly different from the insistent uncompromising proclamation of the one supreme God of the three Semitic or Abrahamic religions. Again, to spend some time in a Theravada Buddhist *vihara* is to become aware of the presence of the Buddha at the centre of the ritual and the meditation practices. Buddhist practice always begins with the taking of the three refuges – to the Buddha, the *Dharma* or teaching and the *Sangha*, the community of disciples. Buddhists will insist, however, that the Buddha is not another version of the Hindu god figures. In Buddhism, the gods are all relativised, no more than superhuman spirits – and often further from true enlightenment than sentient beings, human or animal. Buddhism appears to deny the existence of God; it is certainly sceptical about the possibility, let alone the value, of basing one's life on worship of or devotion to 'God'. In short, there is a lot more to Hinduism and Buddhism than systems of belief, variants on some universal cross-religious model. Both are very different, sometimes very strange and certainly very other.

---

[28] An interesting example of creative explanation of the Hindu concept of God appeared in a mimeographed handout available in the Vaishnava Ram Mandir in Southall. The three letters G O D are interpreted as referring to qualities or attributes of God as Giver, Ordainer and Destroyer, and ascribed to the figures of Brahma, Vishnu and Śiva.

Something analogous can be said for the more familiar traditions from the Middle East 'Semitic' traditions. There is a complexity about the different schools of Islam, the various Christian denominations, even the multiple forms into which Judaism divides, which does not fit the Enlightenment account of 'religion' as variations on a single pattern. This is not to say that all attempts to describe, let alone order, the variety of 'traditional religion' are fruitless and should be abandoned; only that more attention needs to be paid to the historical dynamics of change and interaction that have produced such proliferating forms. There is never a single finished reading to history – and certainly not to the history of religion and interreligious engagement.

This is why Cantwell Smith's refusal to homogenise religions is so intriguing – the scholarly expertise of the historian of religion combined with the instinct of the theologian. What fascinates him is the *meaning* of the plurality of religions – that is to say, the whole history of dialogue and encounter that has formed the great religious traditions, and most notably Christianity, in a particular way. He once remarked: 'we explain the fact that the Milky Way is there by the doctrine of creation, but how do we explain that the *Bhagavad Gita* is there?'[29] A similar question might be raised about the Quran, about Gotama the Buddha, about the Sikh tradition, about Zoroastrianism and the Jains. What are they all *for*? Cantwell Smith's nagging conviction that the reason for studying the history of religions is not just in order to account for various discrete amalgams of religious phenomena – from prayer and ritual to cultural artefacts and social organisations – but to show how these traditions are always interacting and responding to each other makes him an inspiration for interreligious learning. His overriding thesis is that humankind is today called to 'participate in God's creative process of bringing into actual reality what has until now been an ideal reality only, that of the world-wide community'.[30] He may not manifest the theological nuance of a Rahner or a Dupuis, but he does raise the possibility of a different sort of theological judgement – one based not on a priori speculative theory but on the reality of interreligious engagement itself. While some aspects of his work are problematic, he does force us to think more carefully about what we mean by 'religion'.

The original edition of Cantwell Smith's classic study *The Meaning and End of Religion* came out in 1962. In it he proposed to replace 'religion' as a misunderstood and now thoroughly misleading concept with

---

[29] From Wilfred Cantwell Smith, *Religious Diversity*, ed. W. G. Oxtoby (New York: Harper and Row; 1976), p. 16.
[30] *Ibid.*, p. 137.

two terms: 'faith' and the somewhat ponderous 'cumulative traditions'. The former he sees as some sort of human invariant that can be discerned in those historical institutions that we call 'religions' but which cannot be separated from them. Faith is to be distinguished from belief; belief is one among many of the overt expressions of faith, along with ritual and social action, which reflect the inner attitude or conviction that is faith.[31] His point is that while religious beliefs vary considerably from tradition to tradition, faith for the most part maintains a certain constancy across the traditions. What the cumulative traditions – 'the religions' – do is maintain and channel faith. This idea – what I shall try to explore in the next chapter as the 'conviction of meaning' – raises a number of questions.[32] At that point we will need to open up a theological critique that will take forward the issue raised at the end of the previous chapter, the 'question of the other'. Here, however, I want to stay with the external 'institutions' of religion as 'cumulative traditions' – the diffuse reality alluded to at the beginning of this chapter. Even tiny shrines next to a railway line have a history that needs to be related not just to the history of texts and traditions but to the people and the land that they inhabit. If religions are not to be reduced to versions of generic 'religion' or emasculated into a series of 'isms', we need to find an alternative model that accounts for the growing and changing nature of religious traditions without occluding the particular insight or vision that they seek to preserve.

CONSTRUCTING RELIGIONS

For examples of how the Western obsession with essences has constructed a whole series of 'religions', let me stay in India. Strictly speaking, there is no such thing as 'Hinduism' before the beginning of the nineteenth century. The colonial administrators and missionaries who travelled through India identified what is really a series of 'families' or collections of more or less related religious practices and beliefs as a 'religion', a dim reflection of the Christian religion they knew. In this they were preceded by Muslim invaders in the second millennium CE. 'Hindu' was a title

---

[31] See the conclusion to Cantwell Smith, *The Meaning and End*, pp. 193–202. The ideas are worked out in a further study on the nature of faith as personal 'engagement': *Faith and Belief: The Difference between Them*, new edn. (Oxford: Oneworld, 1998).

[32] His characterisation of faith as an 'inner piety' sometimes has resonances of a liberal protestant 'common essence' of all religious experience. See D'Costa, *Christianity and World Religions*, p. 73.

given by outsiders, a term of exclusion and demarcation.[33] For the Muslims it designated the aliens whom they had conquered and whose non-Muslim status in a newly Islamic world had now become religiously significant. For a long time, the designation meant little more than Indian or native, and included all indigenous communities, including Buddhists and Jains. Only in the nineteenth century did the term begin to be used by Indians themselves. This was triggered by an organised reaction to Christian missionaries and the British Raj with which they were identified. Reform and revival movements proliferated, seeking to rediscover the pure origins of the tradition in the classical *Vedas* and *Upanishads* that date back to the second millennium BCE. To speak of this early tradition as 'Hinduism' is an anachronism. It is, more properly, the religion associated with the Brahmin priests – the 'brahmanical' or Sanskritic tradition. But even that designation is strictly inaccurate; what we are dealing with is a fluid and ever-changing amalgam of hymns and ritual prayers, spells and philosophical reflection, devotion and ascetical instructions. What is now called Hinduism is essentially an *assimilative or integrative tradition*, which gathers up heterogeneous material, always drawing in new material so that it is quite impossible to say which is 'original' or 'pure'. Even to raise the question risks colluding with Orientalist preconceptions. Although there are any number of excellent introductions and surveys of 'Hinduism', most of them are uneasy with the way the term gives the impression of system and order, which is simply not there. Instead, they stress the role of the Brahmins, whose mastery of the classical language Sanskrit provided them with a tool for holding together a number of seemingly disparate strands of religious practice.[34] Which is not to say that all Hindu texts are in Sanskrit, or that all 'Hindu' traditions are brahmanical in the broad sense. Rather, the language is acknowledged as the ideal medium, to which all other, local vernaculars approximate. 'Hinduism' is more correctly a whole series of philosophies, devotions, practices and ways of life associated with the subcontinent.

---

[33] The construction of Hinduism and the other great religious traditions of India has to be seen against the background of the growing European fascination with 'the Orient' that began with the voyages of discovery and reached a height with the Romantic movement. The classic study that gave its name to the movement is Raymond Schwab, *The Oriental Renaissance* (New York: Columbia University Press, 1984). The most detailed study of the contacts between India and Europe is Wilhelm Halbfass, *India and Europe: An Essay in Understanding* (Albany, NY: SUNY Press, 1988). Covering the field from the perspective of the History of Ideas is J. J. Clarke, *Oriental Enlightenment* (London and New York: Routledge, 1997).

[34] See, e.g., Julius Lipner, *Hindus* (London: Routledge; 1994) and Gavin Flood, *An Introduction to Hinduism* (Cambridge University Press, 1996).

Much the same process of construction applies to Buddhism, which originated out of the great brahmanical complex of religion in the mid-first millennium BCE, at about the time of the later *Upanishads*. Cantwell Smith tells us that the first recorded use of 'Boudhism' is 1801 and the earliest study 1828.[35] First judgements by Westerners on this enigmatic tradition were unequivocally negative. The way of the 'Bauddhas' was safely sidelined as a heretical sect of 'Hinduism', associated with the sage Gautama. By the middle of the nineteenth century, with access to scholarly texts, the originality of Buddha's teaching was recognised. In 1844, the first of the great scholarly buddhologists, Eugene Burnouf, wrote of this 'brilliant light' as a 'page from the origins of the world'.[36] But if the figure of the Buddha quickly emerged as a noble moralist to rival Jesus, his doctrines seemed disturbingly nihilistic. Perhaps the most difficult, and counter-intuitive, thesis in Buddhism is *Anatmavada* – the 'theory of no-self'. The human person is a collection of fleeting, passing, insubstantial entities; nothing lasts for more than a moment. I shall have occasion to examine this idea in greater detail later, for it sets up an important challenge to the limits of interreligious learning. Here I note only that there is a philosophical coherence to Buddhism that, for all its complexity, makes it easier to grasp than the many divergent philosophies that make up the ever-proliferating tradition that is Hinduism. Care needs to be taken, however, not to make Buddhism a philosophically aware practice of yogic meditation techniques. The focus on interiority is no doubt one important reason why nineteenth-century Western philosophers and artists, notably Schopenhauer and Wagner, were able to plunder Buddhist ideas to back their own thoughts and interests.[37] For Buddhists themselves, however, Buddhism is not a concept or system but the *Buddhadharma*, the teaching of the Buddha. To be a Buddhist is not to believe in a set of doctrines, it is to 'take refuge', to seek *Moksha* or *Mukti* by going to the Buddha, the *Dharma* and the *Sangha*. The Buddha taught in the vernacular; he sought to communicate a message of enlightenment for all suffering sentient beings. He taught not a system but a practice, both an ethical and a meditative way. The teaching is to be adapted for different individuals and different needs. Thus, the Buddhism of ancient India is different from what was later established in Tibet or China. Much of the Buddhism practised in

---

[35] In German by Isaac Jakob Schmidt. Closely followed by E. Upham, *The History and Doctrine of Buddhism* (London: R. Ackermann, 1829). See Cantwell Smith, *The Meaning and End*, p. 61 n. 36, p. 253.
[36] Quoted in Stephen Batchelor, *The Awakening of the West* (London: Thorsons, 1994), pp. 239–40.
[37] *Ibid.*, pp. 250 ff.

Europe and the USA today – a sort of postmodern Buddhism[38] – has its own particular quality, as we shall see later. The attraction of Buddhism is that it is practical and adaptable, concerned with the 'welfare of all sentient beings', not with the maintenance of some given revelation or a priori dogmatic position.

Cantwell Smith would remind us that neither of these traditions can be separated from the other. Historically they are interdependent – part of a single developing process of challenge and exchange. Perhaps the best example of his thesis is another of the great Indian religious traditions, Sikhism. Again, I will focus on the theme of interreligious learning with Sikhs in a later chapter. Here my concern is to question the standard wisdom that sums up Sikhism as a mixture or even a syncretism of Hinduism and Islam. It is true that the faith was formed under cultural and political pressure, and that the contemporary stereotype owes much to the British attempt to 'militarise' the Sikhs in the nineteenth century. However, its origins lie within a particular tendency and development in Indian religion that is often referred to as the '*sant* tradition' – the following of a holy man whose life and teaching incite deep devotion to God. The inspiration came from Guru Nanak (1469–1539), a devotee or *bhakta* who preached sincerity in personal relations and worship of the overwhelming majesty of God. He was not so much the founder of a 'new religion' as a reformer of the formalised rituals and heartless asceticism that he saw around him in his homeland of Panjab. The tradition that took after him led through the authority of his successors – together they make up the ten *gurus* – to the establishment of the *Khalsa*, the 'community of the pure', in 1699. Cantwell Smith comments on this historical emergence of a new tradition, noting it as an example of the gradual process of reification: 'the preaching of a vision, the emergence of followers, the organisation of a community, the positing of an intellectual ideal of that community, the definition of the actual pattern of its institutions.'[39] Certainly a number of stages can be distinguished. Nanak's vision is of the one God who brings creation into being with a single word, who yet wills to make himself known by placing his name in human hearts. The fifth *guru*, Arjun, was responsible for gathering the verses of his predecessors into the *Guru* Granth Sahib, and the tenth *guru*, Gobind, left instructions that the Granth should henceforth be the source of authority, the 'visible body of the *Gurus*'. With the

---

[38] See Stephen Batchelor, 'The Other Enlightenment Project', in Ursula King (ed.), *Faith and Practice in a Post-Modern Age* (London: Cassells, 1998), pp. 13–27.
[39] Cantwell Smith, *The Meaning and End*, p. 67.

establishment of the *Khalsa*, Gobind succeeded in giving a very precise shape to the heroic spirit of Sikh identity. The story that is told of that event is part of the formative folklore of the Sikh tradition and I shall return to it in more detail later. It is sufficient to note here that a history of resistance, both to assimilation by the broad 'Sanskritic' tradition and to domination by Mughal Islam, has given Sikhism a unique identity.[40] That history continues into the contemporary diaspora and is symbolised by the great *gurdwara* described at the beginning of the chapter, a place that for all its modern style keeps alive a venerable tradition by providing for the needs of a large and vibrant community of faith.

SCHOOLS OF FAITH

The major Indian religious traditions are part of a complex developing structure; they do not exist in a hermetically sealed historical vacuum. Cantwell Smith's account of 'cumulative traditions' is a welcome corrective to what might be called the 'spiritual commodity' version of religion. Indian religions need to be set within the same historical continuum but they also need to be distinguished. If there is a prevailing image that runs through what I have just described, it is not that of religion as a set of ideas and concepts, or even as a set of practices. Both are there, of course, but they are subject to a deeper structure – that which is vested in the relationship between pupil and teacher, the devotee participating in God's love, the searcher for truth attracted by the enlightened one, or the householder living in close proximity to the *sant*. In the next chapter I will develop this point under the concept of faith and will offer my own critique of Cantwell Smith. Here let me stay a little longer with the other side of his proposal, the concept of the 'cumulative tradition' and to link it with my theme of interreligious learning. My point is that the concept of 'religion' needs to be understood not as some deracinated essence but as embodied in the activities of teaching and learning that make up 'the religions'.

As historically developing communities, the great religions maintain forms of human conversation in which truth is taught and the integrity of ancient wisdom maintained. Lash's version of Cantwell Smith's reading of religious interaction argues that religions act like schools. 'Christianity and *Vedantic* Hinduism, Judaism and Buddhism and Islam are schools ... whose pedagogy has the twofold purpose – however differently conceived

---

[40] For the historical evolution of the Sikh Panth, see especially Pashaura Singh, 'Sikh Identity in the Light of History' in Pashaura Singh and N. Gerald Barrier (eds.), *Sikhism and History* (Delhi: Oxford University Press, 2004), pp. 75–110.

and executed in the different traditions – of weaning us from our idolatry and purifying our desire.'[41] The qualification *Vedantic* might seem to limit the scope of Hinduism as a school to the classical philosophical *darśanas*. But that title, with its connotations of 'sight' and 'vision', extends the meaning and scope of philosophy beyond the analytic and critical activity familiar in the West. It is not that the *Vedanta* (or, indeed, *Nyaya* and *Samkhya*) schools work within the broader religious tradition to give it a proper intellectual coherence. They are themselves concerned intimately with the pursuit of *moksha* or liberation. It would also be a mistake, as Clooney's scholarly engagements teach us, to presume that *bhakti-marga* does not have its own commentarial tradition. It is for that reason that the sketch I gave above, of the 'cumulative tradition' which is Hinduism, emphasised devotional *bhakti*, the form in which the vast majority of Hindus express their faith. In the context of a tradition like Hinduism that recognises a number of different paths and practices, distinctions between 'process' and 'content' are misleading and artificial. Something similar can be said for other schools; my point is that the cumulative traditions that are 'the religions' are first and foremost communities of persons whose religious account of things includes not just a comprehensive vision but also the learned skills that go with assimilating and interpreting that vision. As Paul Griffiths puts it, 'any religious account must contain a pedagogy'.[42] What people of faith learn and how they learn, the object of study and the skills of teaching that together give them identity, are all of a piece.

This chapter began in a place brought to life by time given to prayer and contemplation. In the chapters that follow I will take up further examples of such a hermeneutical 'reading' of places. As exercises in comparative theology, they are intuitive and imprecise, seeking more for echoes and resonances than hard and fast points of similarity and likeness. To that extent these are pragmatic explorations,[43] avoiding premature closure and the temptation to subordinate the open-ended mystery of life in the middle of things to a set of final meanings. Much as that may sound like an invitation to enter the confusion of the postmodern condition, the reality is rather more creative and imaginative and, as I shall hope to show, more central to the project of Christian, as much as interreligious, learning than at

---

[41] *The Beginning and the End*, p. 21.　　[42] Griffiths, *Religious Reading*, p. 20.
[43] Taking 'pragmatic' from the sense given by Peter Ochs in his study of the pragmatism of Charles Sanders Pierce. Pierce, says Ochs, offers 'pragmatic definitions of indefinite things. My thesis is that pragmatic definition is not a discrete act of judgment of classification but a *performance of correcting other, inadequate definitions of imprecise things.*' Peter Ochs, *Pierce, Pragmatism and the Logic of Scripture* (Cambridge University Press, 1998), pp. 4–5.

first appears. In anticipation of what I shall develop in my final two chapters, let me quote Nicholas Lash, who, in describing Christianity as a school of 'discipleship of the crucified', says that 'there is *nothing* that we do and suffer, think, or feel, or undergo, which may not contribute to such schooling.'[44] To those who have learned how to reflect on their learning, the middle of things can be the site of a strange revelation.

This is what a school of faith teaches. Like any good school it will seek to bring the processes of teaching and learning into a proper correlation. It will ensure an appropriately critical attention to the search for understanding and wisdom. It will cherish the symbolic worlds of discourse that have formed a tradition of learning. It will introduce pupils to the world that exists beyond the borders of their experience and expand the horizons of the imagination. And, perhaps most importantly, it will teach not just knowledge and information about the world but the skills necessary for engagement with that world. The further question, touched on earlier, is whether it is possible to envisage a situation in which 'the religions' meet within the same space as a 'school of schools', passing on purpose and value to successive generations – and to one another. Can such a commitment to meeting and encounter, conversation and learning, address the problem of the other that I noted at the end of the previous chapter? Interreligious learning in itself will not create such a community. But it remains a necessary if not sufficient condition. Without a process of learning across borders that seeks to discern truth in the resonances and echoes that dialogue always throws up we risk either further fragmentation into 'parallel lives' or a postmodern eclecticism – or both. It is clearly important not to allow the secular culture so to weaken the internal sources of energy that characterise religious traditions as comprehensive accounts of the world that they end up being marginalised, emasculated into essentially private spiritual practices. On the other hand, if the energy that religion motivates is not controlled or directed, we may end up not with schools but with sects, each competing for its own rapidly diminishing slice of the secular space. To open up these issues – about how religious communities are to find space both for themselves and for others in a pluralist world, about the broader political responsibilities of faith, about what can be acknowledged in the other's world and what cannot, what is of God and what is not, what is faith and what is superstition or unquestioning ideology – we must now turn to the concept of faith itself and what I have referred to above as the 'conviction of meaning'.

---

[44] Lash, *Easter in Ordinary*, pp. 258–9.

CHAPTER 3

Communities of conversation

No name more chillingly sums up the bloody twentieth century than Auschwitz. The original concentration camp, housed in the red-brick barracks built for the Polish army in the 1920s, lies hidden behind forbidding grey walls on the outskirts of the sleepy provincial town of Oświęcim, an hour's bus journey from Cracow. Nowadays, the mocking sign over the entrance, *Arbeit Macht Frei*, welcomes gaggles of tourists and students. The museum's excellent guides explain everything with a calm objectivity that allows the full horror of what happened there to speak for itself. Nothing, however, prepares the casual visitor for Auschwitz-Birkenau, the massive death camp where more than a million Jews were systematically annihilated as part of the 'Final Solution' between 1943 and 1945. Situated a kilometre away, across the railway line, the infamous gateway stands incongruously close to some very ordinary modern houses. Such comforting signs of domesticity do little to overcome the sheer desolation of the place.

I was just such a casual visitor on my first trip there – a dull weekday afternoon with enough time to see the sights but not enough to absorb more than a few details. For my second visit, a couple of years later, I was fortunate to have my own guide, a German Catholic priest who has dedicated his life to prayer and interreligious dialogue at a centre in the old town. We did a sort of pilgrimage, silent and meditative, across the flat landscape, past the remains of the huts and the gaunt rust-daubed concrete posts that seem to run endlessly into the distance, and down as far as the trees that border the distant boundary, away from the buses and the tourist memorabilia. We inspected the ruins of the crematoria and paused before the abstract stone sculpture and the great bronze plaques that memorialise the victims who had been transported there from all over Europe. We saw the ponds where the ashes of the dead had been dumped, then looked at a set of photographs and read about what had happened on that precise spot more than sixty years earlier. It was there that the priest told me how he had learned to listen – as he put it – to the 'voice of the earth'. Bending down he parted the rich tufts of grass and picked

48

tiny traces of bone from the soil. 'Terra sancta', he said quietly to himself. It was as if the remains of the murdered millions were continuing to nourish our battered world. For him, Auschwitz was a deeply religious place because it preserved the most harrowing yet precious of memories.

That image of a suffering land that never forgets its own people stayed with me as I read Martin Gilbert's monumental study of the Shoah.[1] Gilbert gives us a detailed chronicle of what happened. Day after day, week after week, month after month, it reads like a relentless record of survivors' memories. This labour of love, keeping the memory of his people alive, does not seek for explanations. Indeed, it is almost as if Gilbert restrains himself from comment, allowing the facts to speak for themselves. One story stood out – perhaps because it happened near the Galician town of Tarnow, which I knew from an earlier visit to Poland.

Quoting an eyewitness account, Gilbert recounts how children were separated from their parents, taken to a shed on the side of the town square and shot. 'One could go mad', said the witness. Then he went on to recall how an old man was kneeling in the corner of the square with his daughter at his side. Casually a Gestapo officer drew his revolver and killed the old man. The witness continues:

'His daughter then leaped to her feet and cried to the Gestapo man in German: "You scoundrel! What did my father do to you that you shot him?" The Gestapo man flew at her, hit her and threatened to kill her too. The girl looked at him with a penetrating gaze. When he turned away, avoiding her eyes, she insulted him again, called him a mean coward who shot defenceless people, and shouted that he dared not look into her eyes. "Look straight into my eyes, you coward", she cried, "and shoot! These eyes will pursue you and haunt you all your life!" The Gestapo man winced, turned away from the girl, as if to muster his courage, and after a moment aimed his revolver at her and shot her'.[2]

Did those eyes haunt him for the rest of his life? We do not know, of course. But the story certainly inspired the eyewitness – and the historian. In that sense, the young woman's act lives on. The story reminds me of one of Levinas's most important themes. Levinas, with his own personal experience of the Shoah, is one of those thinkers whose complex, even tortuous, writing plays endless variations on a simple theme – the disturbance of the self-referential order by the other. Human living is shot through with experiences of something strange, something different, something that awkwardly refuses to be controlled – and may not be dominated by self-centred need. In a section of *Totality and Infinity* entitled 'Ethics and the

[1] Martin Gilbert, *The Holocaust: The Jewish Tragedy* (London: Fontana 1987).   [2] *Ibid.*, p. 404.

Face', Levinas speaks of murder as 'this most banal incident of human history'.[3] Banal does not mean trivial; he is not seeking to deny the enormous moral import of such an act. Murder – the attempt to *efface* another – is, rather, an extreme example of how human beings seek to impose their will on others. Levinas's point is that such an act of obliteration of the other is, strictly speaking, impossible. I may desire to kill my enemy; I may indeed succeed in doing so – as the Gestapo officer did. But something remains. Something of that encounter refuses ever to go away. The memory of the glare of those eyes goes on haunting me. The desire to murder is countered by a resistance, the fierce refusal willingly to submit. Gilbert's story is exceptionally powerful. Of course, not all those murdered at Auschwitz went to their deaths with such courageous defiance. But the efforts of others who came after, historians and museum curators, philosophers and contemplative priests, speak volumes for their determination that the deaths of those with no one to defend them should not be in vain.

In so many tales of depravity and unspeakable cruelty there are glimmers of light, records of moral courage and extraordinary heroism. For those prepared to look hard enough there will always be signs of hope in the darkness. However, Levinas is very definitely not making some facile point about the incurable optimism of human beings. For him, what is revealed in the ordinariness of human relations, in the murderous intent of a psychopath as much as in the loving caress of husband and wife, is the revelation of the other, a force or presence or reality that can be sensed but never comprehended, touched but never controlled. This is not to say that we do not try to do just that – to remain in control. But comprehension, in the literal sense of totally grasping, is beyond us. Traces of Infinity – the God beyond all knowing, as a Christian might want to say – cannot be commanded, still less obliterated, but remain stubbornly challenging our desire to exercise mastery and control. Or, as my guide to Auschwitz-Birkenau so simply demonstrated, the earth goes on bearing the traces of its people.

I will return to the Shoah in a later chapter when I consider the significance of Judaism and the chequered history of Jewish–Christian relations for Christian faith. There I will seek to argue that the retrieval of Christianity's roots in its relationship with the people of the Covenant forms the matrix or creative heart of a new way of relating to people from other faith traditions. At that point we can begin to talk about interreligious learning in terms of 'crossings', the movement across the threshold of another religious world. This chapter is still concerned with 'meetings', the exploration of the encounter

---

[3] Emmanuel Levinas, *Totality and Infinity* (Pittsburgh, Pa.: Duquesne University Press, 1969), p. 198.

between people of faiths and the conversations that it provokes. It begins in the shadow of Auschwitz to make the point that so many interreligious meetings today are already shot through with an ambivalence that may not be ignored. This is not the place to consider the nature of religiously inspired violence; again, that theme will be taken up later in a different context. Here I take it for granted that *homo religiosus* can be corrupted, that the respect and reverence that I understand as the root meaning of *religio* can mistake its object. In short, 'religion' can be reified into ideology. The first part of this chapter explores the concept of faith; the second part returns to the scene with which I opened, and the dark side of religion.

FAITH, BELIEF AND THE RELIGIONS

This ambivalence of human religiosity has already been hinted at. Levinas begins his masterwork with a question: 'what sense can we make of morality after the failure of morality?'[4] It is, of course, a not so veiled reference to the Shoah, but also a guarded statement of faith in the capacity of human beings to overcome their murderous instincts when faced by, and prepared to enter into relationship with, the other. Naive optimism about natural human goodness may have died in the gas chambers, but hope did not. In the first chapters of this book I have argued that before the religions settle into systems and institutions and formalised sets of beliefs they are to be understood as the social imaginaries that bring groups of individuals gathered together into a moral community. Outward forms – prayers and rituals, icons and architecture, stories, poems and myths – build into the great cultural institutions that get named as Christianity, Hinduism, Islam etc. But those forms are for ever changing, as people interact with one another, and new questions get asked. However the complex motivations that gather the phenomena of religion together are to be understood – that is to say, however they are to be explained in psychological or sociological terms – religious communities are dominated by the desire to make sense of life by keeping faith with the past, bringing present experience into line with what has gone before. This is what makes religions akin to schools where practices of teaching and learning are preserved and promoted. Guiding these practices, I now want to argue, is faith – what I call the 'conviction of meaning', a certain capacity to correlate and make sense of the sheer variety of human experience, from its special moments of consolation through to times of intense darkness.

[4] *Ibid.*, p. 21.

I have already drawn attention to Wilfred Cantwell Smith's proposal to deconstruct the term 'religion' by substituting two correlative terms, 'cumulative traditions' to refer to the fluid historical reality taken by the religions and faith as that 'human quality' that animates them. According to Cantwell Smith, faith is a 'personal quality of which we see many sorts of expression'.[5] He begins with the reality of religious plurality and argues against the tendency identified earlier to reduce 'religion' to sets of beliefs or doctrines. This is not to say that the latter do not exist – that they are not of major significance for practitioners. Rather, his point is that before people identify themselves as Christian or Buddhist, or whatever, we are 'all persons, clustered in mundane communities no doubt, and labelled with mundane labels but, so far as transcendence is concerned, encountering it each directly, personally, if at all. In the eyes of God each of us is a person, not a type'.[6] This is very much not to say that faith is some disembodied Platonic idea. Faith can only be discerned in its instantiation in the communities of faith – that is to say, within the meaning-giving activities that grant people security and a sense of identity.

At its best it has taken the form of serenity and courage and loyalty and service; a quiet confidence and joy which enables one to feel at home in the universe, and to find meaning in the world and in one's own life, a meaning that is profound and ultimate, and is stable no matter what may happen to oneself at the level of the immediate event.[7]

Faith in this sense is what characterises *homo religiosus* – a certain capacity of commitment or (to go back to the original connotations of *religio*) 'binding' in human beings that enables them to create meaning by exploring the ideals and the visions that 'cumulative traditions' present to them.

Cantwell Smith's careful dissection of the modern discourse of 'religion' and the shift away from an intellectualist towards a more personalist reading of the dynamic processes at work in the lives of people of faith is a vast improvement on the 'spiritual commodity' version of religion. Yet the emphasis that he puts on faith does at times make it seem like another post-Enlightenment form of generic religion, albeit one in which outer forms and practices are animated by inner conviction. To that extent, his argument tends to play into a version of normative pluralism that earlier I found seriously lacking; people of faith share the same 'personal quality' of

---

[5] Wilfred Cantwell Smith, *The Meaning and End of Religion* (London: SPCK; 1978), p. 185.
[6] *Ibid.*, p. 91.
[7] Wilfred Cantwell Smith, *Faith and Belief: The Difference between Them*, new edn. (Oxford: Oneworld, 1998), p. 12.

faithfulness but differ in the beliefs expressed in the various cumulative traditions.[8] Clearly there is an issue here. People of faith are motivated not just by a personal quest for God but by a serious commitment to the truth taught within their own faith tradition. Even (perhaps, especially) the desire for learning with and from the other has cognitive as well as affective dimensions. Nevertheless there is, I suggest, more to Cantwell Smith's argument than an appeal to some generalised inner essence or cross-religious invariant rooted in feeling. In a later study, when he writes about the possibility of a Christian theology of comparative religion, he describes faith as 'an orientation of the personality, to oneself, to one's neighbour, to the universe; a total response; a way of seeing the world and handling it; a capacity to live at a more than mundane level; to see, to feel, to act in terms of, a transcendent dimension'.[9] Even allowing for the rhetorical flourishes with which his writing is peppered, he is commending faith not just as a quality that typifies the person but as something with an intrinsically *interpersonal* dimension. Truth and falsity, he argues elsewhere, are not just functions of statements and propositions; they are also – '*and primarily*' – properties and functions of persons.[10] As a historian of religion, his aim is not to analyse the conflicting claims of different religions but to comment on developments within the ever-changing relationships of communities of faith. In particular, he is exercised by the observer–participant or insider–outsider dichotomy noted in the previous chapter and draws attention to what he regards as an important development. Dialogue between persons of faith, he feels, is where the future of interreligious relations is leading: the emergence of a 'third type'. He tells us that

One reason why it has been necessary, and indeed one reason why it has been possible, to construct a single theory adequate to serve simultaneously both observer and participant, is that in our day these two roles are beginning to coalesce, as men of faith become aware of themselves as incipiently or potentially members of

---

[8] For critique of Cantwell Smith on this point, see Gavin D'Costa, *Christianity and World Religions: Disputed Questions in the Theology of Religions* (Chichester: Wiley-Blackwell, 2009), pp. 69 ff. D'Costa draws our attention to the foreword by John Hick to the 1978 edition of *Meaning and End*.

[9] *Towards a World Theology: Faith and the Comparative History of Religion* (London: Macmillan, 1981), pp. 113–14 – the first and only time, says Cantwell Smith, that he dared write a book of theology. As the title of the book and the title of this chapter – 'A "Christian" theology of comparative religion?' – indicate, Cantwell Smith shifts uneasily from a traditional Christocentric to a more overtly pluralist theocentric perspective.

[10] My emphasis added. Quotation is from a paper entitled 'A Human View of Truth', in John Hick (ed.), *Truth and Dialogue: The Relationship between World Religions* (London: Sheldon, 1974), pp. 20–44. Cantwell Smith concludes caustically that '[A] conception of truth that is impersonal handles the natural world well, but comprehends the world of man ineptly' (p. 39).

the total corporate religious complex of mankind, composed of different but no longer separated communities.[11]

This is the common experience of observers who have become participants, the experience of interreligious learning. But how to become such a person of faith, one guided by a 'conviction of meaning', which is rooted in one's own 'cumulative tradition', yet open to and respectful of others' similar convictions? If the terms of my 'Christian imaginary' are drawn in the first place from a Catholic sacramental sensibility, this is not to deny that there may be analogous ways in which such 'third types' can emerge, dependent on the skills and virtues taught by the particular 'schools of faith'. It is the interpersonal and, therefore, interreligious quality of faith with which I am primarily concerned.

IMAGINATIVE EXPRESSIONS

In the opening chapter, I quoted the important statement of Vatican II's *Lumen Gentium*, that other religions 'are related to' the Church.[12] A continuum can be traced across different communities. The problem is how to speak of this continuum without either totalising the particularity of the other or reducing all areas of difference to some sort of religious 'essence'. In more recent documents from the Catholic Church, most obviously *Dominus Iesus*, a distinction between 'faith' and 'belief' is drawn.[13] Faith is theological in the sense that it describes only that revelation and personal response to God that the writers of the document consider to be proper to Christians, whereas belief describes a much more human quality of aspiration.[14] It is clear that some version of this distinction needs to be made if the specificity of the truth revealed in Christ is to be maintained and 'faith' is not to be collapsed into some well-meaning desire for ultimate truth. The document does, however, make it clear that God never fails to make himself present, not just to

---

[11] *The Meaning and End*, p. 200. [12] *Lumen Gentium*, 16. The Latin word is 'ordinantur'.

[13] *Dominus Iesus*, written under the auspices of the Congregation for the Doctrine of the Faith, appeared in September 2000. It was not unconnected from a process enacted against some ideas in the work of Jacques Dupuis, especially *Toward a Christian Theology of Religious Pluralism* (New York: Orbis, 1997). For a reliable guide to the 'Dupuis affair', see introductory articles by Franz Cardinal Koenig and Gerald O'Collins in a Festschrift for Dupuis: Daniel Kendall and Gerald O'Collins (eds.), *In Many and Diverse Ways* (New York: Orbis, 2003).

[14] 'If faith is the acceptance in grace of revealed truth which "makes it possible to penetrate the mystery in a way that allows us to understand it coherently" [*Fides et Ratio*, 13], then belief, in the other religions, is that sum of experience and thought that constitutes the human treasury of wisdom and aspiration which man in his search for truth has conceived and acted upon in his relationship to God and the Absolute.' *Dominus Iesus*, 7.

individuals but to 'entire peoples', through the 'spiritual riches' of their traditions. This gets us closer to the wisdom of the Council. In articulating correctly the mystery of God's invitation to human beings to participate in God's own life, distinctions must be made, but they need to be kept within the broader unity of God's providential purposes. If the distinction is not to become a dichotomy, faith has to be given a broader connotation – one that does not appear to speak of altogether different religious attitudes.[15] In retaining something of that typically generous Catholic sensibility, we can do no better than go back to Augustine, for whom 'true religion' as proper reverence and worship is to be expressed through the virtues of faith, hope and love. Thus, at the beginning of the *Enchiridion*, building on Galatians 5:6, he says: 'When a mind is filled with the beginning of that faith which works through love, it progresses by a good life even toward vision, in which holy and perfect hearts know that unspeakable beauty, the full vision of which is the highest happiness.'[16] Faith works through love, indeed, is inseparable from love. When I speak of faith as the 'conviction of meaning', therefore, my intention is not to turn it into some systemic gnosis but to recognise, quite simply, that what draws meaning out of darkness is a trust in the power of persons to mediate that meaning. Such was the message of that extraordinary walk around the death camp of Birkenau: to have a wise and thoughtful companion makes all the difference. The faith of another, shared in companionship, ensures that meaning emerges even from the darkest of places, that a vision of completeness is always kept open. This is a model of Cantwell Smith's 'third type' – neither impartial external observer nor uncritical absorbed participant but a mediator capable of moving across boundaries and enacting the patterns of hospitality that make religious communities not closed enclaves but welcoming schools of faith. To explore this personal quality of faith further we need to consider some of its particular imaginative expressions, the cultural forms that give the 'conviction of meaning' its specific flavour, as it were.

The religions of India, as I have already noted, are full of examples of searchers seeking out the *guru*, the *jñani*, the 'one who knows' or learned teacher. The very word *Upanishad*, the name of the philosophical texts that are held to sum up and bring to a fulfilment the Vedic revelation, has the

---

[15] The Barthian overtones in the document are clear and somewhat problematic. See the discussions on *Dominus Iesus* in Stephen J. Pope and Charles Hefling (eds.), *Sic et Non: Encountering Dominus Iesus* (New York: Orbis, 2002), especially the chapter by Francis X. Clooney, 'Implications for the Practice of Inter-religious Learning' (pp. 157–68).

[16] *The Enchiridion on Faith, Hope and Charity*, 1.5. Translation from *The Works of St Augustine: A Translation for the Twenty-first Century*, Pt. 1, vol. viii (New York: New City Press, 2005).

basic meaning of 'sitting down near'. It reminds us that the texts express a relationship in which the teacher initiates the pupil into the secrets behind the text. Sikhism, with the dominating figures of the ten founding *gurus*, and the two great ascetic traditions of India, Buddhism and Jainism, follow the same general pattern. When, for example, the Buddha preaches the *Dharma*, it is said that those who hear him put their *śraddha* in him, express their *confidence* in him, a personal devotion that gives a particular focus and direction to their desire for *Nirvana*.[17] It therefore makes sense to say that around the person of the Buddha *śraddha* coalesces and is given shape; it is the necessary basis on which the practice of the Noble Eightfold Path becomes possible. Of course, the Buddha goes on to teach self-reliance. In the Theravada tradition the last words of the Buddha are given as 'Decay is inherent in all component things! Work out your salvation with diligence!'[18] His followers are not to take what they have received merely on trust. They are to make it their own, to become themselves *Buddha*, 'awakened' to the true nature of reality. Nevertheless, the Path begins with the act of placing one's confidence in another human being. A famous early text that structures the ever-developing progress on the way to enlightenment makes clear that the personal relationship with the one 'who knows' gives rise to a vision of new possibility, albeit only dimly glanced at this early stage. 'Full of hindrances is household life, a path for the dust of passion. Free as the air is the life of him who has renounced all worldly things. How difficult is it for the man who dwells at home to live the higher life in all its fullness, in all its purity, in all its bright perfection!'[19]

This metaphor of the way or path is so deeply rooted in religious consciousness that it is easy to take it for granted. Early in Chapter 1, I drew attention to the question that it raises: how do I know I am on the right path? That, of course, is the point. I do not. But to call setting out on a journey an act of faith (the example of Abraham, of course, springs immediately to mind) does not turn faith into gnosis or make it any less profoundly human. In our technological age, it is easy to forget that paths are not motorways that politicians and planners have decreed and massive tractors have gouged through the countryside. As Stephen Batchelor reminds us, a path is a path for at least three very human reasons. It gives a sense of direction, it allows

---

[17] The Sanskrit root is *śrad*, meaning 'to have faith or faithfulness, have belief or confidence, believe, be true or trustful'. Monier Williams Sanskrit–English dictionary, p. 1095. See Cantwell Smith, *The Meaning and End*, pp. 59 ff.

[18] See *Mahaparinibbana Sutta*, 'The Book of the Great Decease'. *Digha Nikaya*, ii. 156 (Pali Text Society edition, p. 173).

[19] From the *Samaññaphala Sutta*, 'On the Fruits of Being a Recluse'; *Digha Nikaya*, i. 62 (pp. 56–95).

unhindered passage and – maybe most importantly – it is made up of the traces of those who have gone before.[20] Paths are not planned. But they do not just happen either. They have a history. Indeed, they *are* history in the sense that they describe certain practices (of walking, following and remembering) that themselves give rise to and embody ideas. They invite a simple act of trust: they are there for a reason, a reason that someone else has discovered. They witness to a hidden yet very human wisdom that those who follow, if they are not put off by the meanderings and deviations, will eventually discover for themselves.

Indian religions are often called 'mystical', to distinguish them from the 'prophetic' religions of the Middle East. There is something significant in the distinction – even though it can be overstated and become misleading.[21] There are plenty of examples of Indian religiosity – its *bhakti* or devotional forms, for instance – which, strictly speaking, do not fit the pattern. Here the person of the god or goddess draws the devotee. Nevertheless, one element of the path image continues to hold: truth, enlightenment, revelation, *moksha* or freedom, begins with faith, a conviction that truth is to be found at the end of the path. *Bhakti*, with its many forms of the God who draws devotees to him or herself, is much closer in spirit to Christianity and the other two Semitic religions than it is to the strict mystical path of Vedantic Hinduism or the scholastic traditions of Buddhism. Here the initiative lies with the teacher, the prophet who actively searches for pupils, for disciples. Each is dominated by imperatives. After Jesus's baptism he begins his ministry by calling Peter and James and John – fishermen who will themselves become 'fishers of men'. Christianity begins with a command: 'follow me'. The Word is spoken by Jesus; more exactly, God's Word *is spoken* in and through the person of Jesus and becomes embodied in that person. Hence the way to respond to God's Word is to enter into a relationship with the person of Jesus. The Word is made flesh. The truth is to be found not so much at the end of the way but *on the way*, in the company of the one who identifies himself as 'Way, Truth and Life'. Later I shall return to this Christian imperative and juxtapose it with others that are to be found in Judaism and Islam. Here I just note that the tendency to regard the three monotheistic religions of the Middle East as

---

[20] Stephen Batchelor, 'The Other Enlightenment Project', in Ursula King (ed.), *Faith and Practice in a Post-Modern Age* (London: Cassells, 1998), pp. 113–27.

[21] Not the least valuable feature of Friedhelm Hardy's *The Religious Culture of India* (Cambridge University Press, 1994) (based on the Wilde lectures given at the University of Oxford between 1985 and 1987) is that he manages to bring the three major strands of Indian spirituality (very often summarised as the *trimarga* of *karma, bhakti* and *jñana*) into a rather more complex focus which shows how themes of power, love and wisdom are forever interacting with each other.

variations of a single 'Abrahamic' tradition needs to be treated with care. If Indian religions turn out on closer examination to be more complex than the 'mystical' stereotype might allow, something similar applies to the 'prophetic'. There are many ways of responding to the God who calls.

What such responses have in common is that personal quality of trust in the ultimate order of things. It does not follow, however, that 'order' fits some neat predictable pattern. That is precisely the danger of which Levinas speaks when he inveighs against the controlling character of Western philosophy and culture. Faith is the 'conviction of meaning', but convictions can be destructive. Hence the corollary of the 'school of faith' model of religion – that faith is not the imposition of order but the *sine qua non* for exercising the skills of relationality, the willingness to work within the limits of human imagining. In this sense, faith teaches us how to cope with the lack of order, to work (or, more likely, to wait patiently) for order to assert itself. Maybe this is one reason why people of faith cherish traces of the past and mark them with memorials of some kind – names inscribed in stone, family genealogies traced, stories of the past recounted. Such acts represent very tangible signs of the value human beings give to relics and memories of ancestors. They remind us of their story. The memory, whether of the victims of genocide, of soldiers killed in war, of much-loved parents and children, is to be preserved because there is something intrinsically significant about human life – even, perhaps, especially – when the pieces cannot be fitted together again. Again I will pick up on this theme later.

Here I want to focus on what faith *does*. In the first place, it is, of course, the pain of loss, and maybe a sense of guilt for the past, which such memorialising seeks to assuage. Even if the guilty may never be punished, and the unknown soldier remains unknown, the innocent and the forgotten can get some sort of vindication if a collective, if not individual, memory is kept constantly in view. There is, however, much more at stake here. In Chapter 1 I referred to Charles Taylor's concept of 'gathered time'. In a culture dominated by the homogeneous and horizontal, people still go on looking for a different way of marking what is significant and meaningful, even if through laments for what has been lost.[22] Faith looks forward as well as keeps the past alive, and the quality of our remembering and our capacity to re-imagine what has gone before forms that hope that looks to the future with realism and confidence. The past cannot be changed, but it is important to set the record straight. The ideal is clear. To keep faith with the past somehow gives a moral quality to the present and a sense of purpose as we seek to anticipate the

---

[22] Charles Taylor, *A Secular Age* (Cambridge, Mass.: Harvard University Press, 2007), pp. 714 ff.

future. The reality, of course, is often much more difficult. Faith also involves a struggle with the lack of resolution that most clearly mirrors our inability to make sense of life's often stultifying confusions.

This approach to faith is very different from what is to be discerned in the polemics of the 'new atheism'.[23] In the writings of Richard Dawkins, Christopher Hitchens and their ilk, faith is regarded as an irrational determination to believe certain odd things despite the fact that science and careful experiment have proved otherwise. In his best-seller, *The God Delusion*, Dawkins argues forcefully against the 'God hypothesis', which has kept religious folk in blissful ignorance of the demonstrably scientific truth about human existence. Dawkins buys into the Enlightenment essentialising of religion noted in the previous chapter. Religion is a cognitive system, a set of theories about the way things are, which locks people into an immoveable mindset. Religious folk are like gullible children. Once infected with the 'virus' of religion, they will grow up with a fatal tendency for wishful thinking and make-believe. What is most puzzling about Dawkins's curiously uncritical ramble through the byways of religious and scientific speculation is precisely that it is so unscientific. Very little evidence is offered. Assertion often takes the place of real argument. Religion is thus sidelined as an 'accidental by-product – the misfiring of something useful'.[24] A little gentle probing beyond the heavy rhetoric soon reveals the reason for this type of aggressive reductionism: a suspicion of the more intangible and elusive edges of human experience. Human nature, like every other aspect of the world of experience, is assumed to be open to investigation. In principle, that may be true, but it does not follow that the world and everything in it is just one great complex machine, the rules of which will eventually lay themselves open to scrutiny – and control.

It is almost as if for the new atheists religion presents an awkward challenge to the coherence of the scientific account of things, instead of answering different questions in different ways. Not everything in human experience is patent of explanation, not least the fickleness and fragility of human nature itself. Religious language may find it difficult to make sense of the intangible –

---

[23] The term comes from an important critique in Tina Beattie, *The New Atheists: The Twilight of Reason and the War on Religion* (London: Darton, Longman and Todd, 2007). Beattie argues for a broader conception of reason that addresses questions about justice and power and which the narrow focus of the 'new atheism' ignores.

[24] Richard Dawkins, *The God Delusion* (London: Bantam, 2006), p. 188.

the fear of death, the joy of discovery, the peace of freedom – but it does not seek to explain it away, to reduce it to biological impulses and mechanical links in the brain. Set within the broad context of a way of life that gives meaning to experience, the language of faith opens up a horizon of understanding, a way of looking at the world and coping with the most elusive and threatening aspects of our experience. Which is not to say that religion comes up with a set of answers, a normative 'explanation' of the way things are. The polarising of contemporary debate about religion between diehard fundamentalists and enlightened rationalists closes off more-important and interesting options. Thus, Richard Kearney begins his thoughtful response to aggressive atheism by asking 'What comes after God? What comes in the wake of our letting go of God?'[25] His response is to chart the terms of a type of hermeneutical pondering that recognises the continuing possibility of 'God after God', God discerned at the heart of the everyday, in the secular and the stranger. Kearney calls it a wager 'that it is only if one concedes that one knows virtually nothing about God that one can begin to recover the presence of holiness in the flesh of ordinary existence'.[26] In the wake of Auschwitz, philosophers like Levinas and Paul Ricoeur go on asking the 'faith question'. Faith is not a dogmatic determination to hold on to some given set of meanings come what may, still less an indulgence in childish fantasies and romances with a 'happy ending'. Even when so much counts against faith, human beings still make the wager, looking for the traces of God who still approaches – often in the guise of the 'stranger in your midst'. Religious faith, as Augustine knew, comes from that sense of being taught and being led, which itself builds the confidence that *ultimately it all makes sense*. The important word, of course, is 'ultimately'.

HOPE AND THE MYSTERY OF SELF

Faith enacts memory and sustains hope. What is past is never lost but provides the impetus for fresh enquiry into how experience can best be configured. It is always possible to see things differently; fresh experience may well force us to re-imagine the way things appear to be. Put like that, faith as trust in the deep patterning of human living is not at variance with

---

[25] Richard Kearney, *Anatheism (Returning to God after God)* (New York: Columbia University Press, 2010), p. 3. The word may be new, but Kearney insists that there is nothing particularly new about anatheism as a 'movement – not a state – that refuses all absolute talk about the absolute' (p. 16). While having features in common with a pragmatic or agnostic atheism, anatheism differs by keeping open the possibility of the divine discerned in practices of hospitality and meetings with the stranger.

[26] *Ibid.*, p. 5.

that spirit of open and honest enquiry that characterises the constant scientific dialectic of hypothesis and experiment. Indeed, it very much supports it. I regularly give lectures on Christian faith to students at the Muslim College in Ealing, West London. On one occasion I was accused of pushing fideism by stressing so much the Christian narrative of death and resurrection. In response, I invoked St Anselm's adage, '*fides quaerens intellectum*', faith seeking understanding. I pointed out that Anselm did not mean that one must accept a given intellectual superstructure in order to make sense of the world. If one took anything on trust, I said, it was the rationality set deep into creation itself, and the God-given capacity of human beings to make sense of that world and thus give glory to its Maker. That rather Islamic way of looking at the issue touched off a great conversation. Later it caused me to reflect and to go back to the beginning of Anselm's famous *Proslogion* – which he calls an 'allocution' – to contrast it with the earlier *Monologion*, or 'soliloquy'. There he rouses himself to the contemplation of God.

I acknowledge, Lord, and I give thanks that You have created Your image in me, so that I may remember You, think of You, love You. But this image is so effaced and worn away by vice, so darkened by the smoke of sin, that it cannot do what it was made to do unless You renew it and reform it. I do not try, Lord, to attain Your lofty heights, because my understanding is in no way equal to it. But I do desire to understand Your truth a little, that truth that my heart believes and loves. For I do not seek to understand so that I may believe; but I believe so that I may understand. For I believe this also that unless I believe, I shall not understand.[27]

The passage ends with a quotation from Isaiah (7:9), which reminds us of how the prophet at the very beginning of his calling finds himself purified by the coals of fire taken by the seraphim from the altar of the Temple. Like Isaiah, Anselm is drawn into the mystery of a loving God who enables him to overcome the darkness of sin and to become more conformed to the power that draws him to his natural end, to enjoy the glory of God's face. Faith for Anselm is not a capacity to believe some esoteric doctrine about God; it is an act of trust in God himself who leads and teaches and brings to perfection human skills of enquiry and understanding. It is this leading conviction – that God is the supreme teacher and that true understanding begins with the prayerful contemplation of the mystery of God – that dominates all Anselm's writings. He does not lay down Christian truth in dogmatic form (though no doubt he could have done) so much as invite his pupils into a journey of

[27] St Anselm, *Anselm of Canterbury: The Major Works*, ed. Brian Davies and G. R. Evans (Oxford University Press, 1998), p. 87.

self-discovery that will issue in fully understanding the purpose for which they were created. To invoke the Cantwell Smith distinction, he teaches not belief but faith. For Anselm, as for Augustine, faith is inseparable from love; only by learning how to love all that has been given by God does one come to understand and rejoice in its meaning. This is the life of the Spirit. The *Proslogion* ends with words of hope and praise.

I ask, Lord, as you counsel through our admirable counsellor. May I receive what You promise through Your truth so that 'my joy may be complete' [John 16:24]. . . . Until then let my mind meditate on it, let my tongue speak of it, let my heart love it, let my mouth preach it. Let my soul hunger for it, let my flesh thirst for it, my whole being desire it, until I enter into the 'joy of the Lord' [Matt. 25:21], who is God, Three in One, 'blessed forever. Amen'. [Rom. 1:25][28]

These are, of course, the words of a Christian theist. Even the more philosophical of Anselm's works are written out of the conviction that understanding only comes about through the co-operation of divine and human. But – as the Muslim students recognised – that does not make him a fideist, subordinating understanding to faith, making knowledge of God dependent on the particularity of certain truths given only to privileged initiates. Anselm took delight in the powers of human reason, which, like Augustine before him, he saw as opening up an inner journey into the mystery of a self that is made in the image of the Trinitarian God. Faith and understanding can be distinguished but not separated – two dimensions of Cantwell Smith's 'human quality' of courage, loyalty, humility and hope. If that is correct, then what the different religious traditions of the world give us are versions of the desire to learn, to discern the rich patternings of human experience that orientate human beings towards their final end – however that is to be conceived. What we are talking about is a certain way of structuring experience, of bringing together into an initial harmony the sometimes clashing and discordant voices of the past and orientating them towards an uncertain future. I say 'initial' because the faith that seeks understanding cannot, and should not, presume to synthesise the full data of human experience. It opens up the spirit of enquiry by providing a purchase on reality, a place from which the questions can be asked, if not answered. Religious questions about the meaning and the final purpose of things are not the same as scientific questions about how the objects of direct experience of the world hang together. But, as St Anselm would have reminded us, they do overlap at various points.

[28] *Ibid.*, p. 104.

FAITH BECOMING IDEOLOGY

So far, what I have described is a faith that 'gathers time', which seeks to remember (literally, put back together) the past, and uses the imagination to reconstruct a future that answers the 'conviction of meaning'. The new atheists do, however, have a point. Christopher Hitchens is not concerned to deconstruct religion as a pseudo-science. He is more interested in religion as 'an enormous multiplier of tribal suspicion and hatred'.[29] Since 9/11, we have become only too well aware of how apparently ordinary men and women can unleash acts of the most appalling cruelty, in the sincere belief that what they are doing is sanctioned by God, that suicide is some sort of ticket to paradise. However, to dismiss this as an Islamic phenomenon, the worst result of 'fundamentalism', is to reduce a complex phenomenon to a Feuerbachian 'something else', some human need that can be explained in purely sociological or psycho-analytic terms. A much more discerning critic of modern religiosity than Dawkins and Hitchens is the philosopher John Gray. His eloquent plea for realism about human nature and the destructive capacity of religious impulses is a welcome warning to religious romantics and anti-religious dogmatists alike about the limits of post-Enlightenment accounts of human rationality. 'Theories of progress', says Gray, 'are not scientific hypotheses. They are myths, which answer the human need for meaning.'[30] Gray's point is that religious faith can become ideology; utopian ideals can overwhelm not just an imagined future but the comforts of a gathered present as well.

It is for that reason that I talk about using the imagination to *re*-construct a future. This is a task that demands careful discernment and constant repetition in the face of failure. When the meaning to which convictions point becomes over-defined, when the commitment to the path loses that humility which knows it is still on the path and has not yet reached an end, the present moment can become destructive – both of the other and, more subtly, of the self. Acts of faith, as I have described them, look back to the past, seeking always to link people with a sense of their origins and to project them forward into a much more risky encounter with the future. As Richard Fenn reminds us in his study of apocalyptic texts, faith can become over-determined. When communities find themselves under pressure the temptation to play up old animosities becomes almost overwhelming. When they face persecution or

---

[29] Christopher Hitchens, *God is not Great* (London: Atlantic, 2007), p. 36.
[30] John Gray, *Black Mass: Apocalyptic Religion and the Death of Utopia* (New York: Farrar, Strauss and Giroux, 2007), p. 2.

find themselves faced with the collapse of their dreams, otherness is demonised, and hopes for future fulfilment get replaced by an at times almost paranoid vision of immediate judgement. 'We' are set apart from 'them'. By developing 'dreams of glory', usually understood in terms of a catastrophic reversal of fortunes, the apocalyptic vision 'not only embodies the end of time but promises compensation to the faithful for lost futures'.[31]

It is not always fear that demonises the other; a naive confidence in the myths of the past can be equally corrupting. In a later chapter I will draw attention to some examples of the pathology of the religious instinct. For the moment, however, I want to complete this chapter by returning to my opening illustrations from Auschwitz and the Shoah. If religion can give people a creative and self-sustaining power, it can also be dangerously destructive.

The factors that led to the rise of Nazi totalitarianism are many and complex. And the extent to which it was dependent on a skewed version of Christianity is still hotly contested. It remains a moot point whether the Shoah would ever have been possible without the fertile ground prepared by centuries of European anti-Semitism. Be that as it may, the point I want to make is that we are dealing with a normative ideology, not just an idea, but, in Gray's terms, a utopian ideal of progress, an account not of the way things are but of the way things should be. Tzvetan Todorov distinguishes wisely between the 'grammar of humanism' and the 'grammar of totalitarianism'. The former is based on three persons – *I*, *thou* and the collective *they*; the latter, by contrast, has only two persons: '*us*, among whom the distinctions between individual *I*s have been suppressed; and *them*, the enemies who must be fought, not to say slaughtered'.[32] The totalitarian world is conceived in Manichaean terms and founded on a radical opposition, the good and the bad, the right and the wrong. There is no room here for manoeuvre or nuance, still less for a neutral view of things. Difference is opposition; the other an enemy to be annihilated. In the case of the Nazis such an ideal had overt racist overtones. To repeat the terms that I noted at the end of my first chapter, Nazism, like all other totalitarian ideologies, was based on a comprehensive pattern with no place for the other.

---

[31] Richard Fenn, *Dreams of Glory: The Sources of Apocalyptic Terror* (Aldershot: Ashgate, 2006), p. 22.

[32] Tzvetan Todorov, *Hope and Memory: Reflections on the Twentieth Century* (London: Atlantic, 2003), p. 39. Todorov concludes: 'In a distant future, when utopia will have been made real on earth, *they* will be nothing more than slaves (in Nazi ideology) or they will have ceased to exist (in the Communist vision, which will then have a grammar with only one person).'

However, to speak of faith becoming ideology may itself play into the idealist fallacy, what Taylor calls 'the attribution to ideas of an independent force in history'.[33] Following Cantwell Smith, I have tried to argue that religion, and specifically *the* religions and the stories they seek to tell, must be conceived and understood through the lens of history. Motivations for action differ, and may not be run together into single all-encompassing explanations. That said, the past always has its lessons for the present; that is why human beings go on remembering. While the Shoah certainly teaches us how the consequences of action can be justified in the name of some high-minded ideology, something more particular and paradoxical is also going on, the casual obliteration of the human imagination. This is what Hannah Arendt, in her absorbing account of the Eichmann trial, referred to as the 'banality of evil'.[34] That evocative phrase was developed not to excuse or dismiss what happened but to contest the prevalent depictions of the Shoah as motivated by some malevolent will to do evil, a delight in murder. I have already noted that Levinas saw it differently. So far from resembling some gothic monster, Eichmann appeared as ordinary and innocuous. He operated unthinkingly, following orders, efficiently carrying them out, with no consideration of their effects upon those he targeted. The extermination of the Jews was just a task to be done, indistinguishable in principle from any other bureaucratic responsibility. In a final reflection on this theme, published posthumously, Arendt notes how struck she was by

a manifest shallowness in the doer that made it impossible to trace the incontestable evil of his deeds to any deeper level of roots or motives. The deeds were monstrous, but the doer – at least the very effective one now on trial – was quite ordinary, commonplace and neither demonic nor monstrous ... it was not stupidity but *thoughtlessness*. ... Clichés, stock phrases, adherence to conventional codes of expression and conduct have the socially recognized function of protecting us against reality, that is, against the claim on our thinking attention that all events and facts make by virtue of their existence. ... It was this absence of thinking – which is so ordinary an experience in our everyday life where we have hardly the time, let lone the inclination, to stop and think – that awakened my interest.[35]

[33] Charles Taylor, *Modern Social Imaginaries* (Durham, NC and London: Duke University Press, 2004), p. 31.

[34] See Hannah Arendt, *Eichmann in Jerusalem: A Report on the Banality of Evil*, rev. edn. (New York: Viking Press, 1965).

[35] From Hannah Arendt, *The Life of the Mind* (New York: Harcourt Brace Jovanovich, 1978), p. 4. Quoted in Jean Bethke Elshtain, *Augustine and the Limits of Politics* (Notre Dame, Ind.: University of Notre Dame Press, 1998), pp. 86–7.

It is the lack of thought or critical awareness that is so corrupting. In other words, tempting though it is to explain the Shoah, or any other act of human wickedness, as the stage on which some titanic Manichaean struggle of the forces of good and evil is played out, the reality is probably rather more prosaic – and therefore so much more easily ignored or patronised. Arendt's reflections call to mind Levinas's point about the impossibility of the murderer achieving his object; the other continues to haunt even the most evil of minds. Be that as it may, Arendt does spell out one implication of Levinas's argument. Evil is not some countervailing force to the power of good. It is, in the language of classical Christian theology, the *privatio boni*, the falling away from the good. Devils in Christian tradition are fallen angels. When we lose sight of the other we become literally irresponsible, unable to respond and blandly content with the convictions that have brought us to this point. The present becomes everything; even memories fail to create – let alone disturb. Arendt's point reminds us that, although Nazism was an extreme form of a totalitarian ideology, its seeds are there in any system that is fixated on the preservation of the self – for the self can easily be subordinated to the coercive system, whether that is proclaimed in some set of overarching principles or embodied in the will of the great leader. To become part of such a collective 'us' defined over against an opposing 'them' means privileging conformity over creativity, compliance over the imagination. The destructive side of the religious instinct is just that – a failure to imagine how things could be different and a refusal to summon up the courage to make them so.

None of this suggests that somehow Auschwitz can be 'explained'. In so many ways Auschwitz is beyond comprehension. Nevertheless, as I discovered that warm summer afternoon, some sort of meaning can emerge when we are in the company of those who have invested time and emotional energy in coming to terms with even the most ghastly of events. All that remains of the death camp are the wrecked crematoria and the decaying concrete posts of the boundary fence. Empty relics, lacking any real substance, with no reality of their own, they fill the present with a totalising vision that admits not of an other. That that place is also *terra sancta* because it inspires memory and motivates new resolution is testimony to those who refuse to have their imaginations totalised by the banal grammar of us and them. Truth emerges in relationship, in the community that conversation forms. The challenge is how to be sustained by that conversation, to keep faith with the memories that it calls to mind, while recognising and not seeking to obliterate the painful elements of otherness that it may uncover. If a 'school of faith' describes a centre of learning where otherness is engaged without being totalised, what are the processes by which faith becomes embedded in the world of everyday experience? In the next chapter I will pursue further this aspect of the contemporary interreligious social imaginary, by broadening the context in which the learning that flows from conversation takes place. To build a 'school of schools' that is proof against the temptation to turn faith into ideology means paying some attention to another temptation, to reduce the properly religious to the 'merely' cultural.

CHAPTER 4

Thresholds of meaning

The Orthodox monastery of St John the Baptist – *prodromos* or forerunner – is perched half-way up an enormous mountain, with glorious views over the plain of Thessaly in central Greece. A small international community of nuns came here from Athens at the turn of the millennium to inherit a concrete shell, a building begun but soon abandoned by monks from Mt. Athos in the mid-1980s. Relying largely on their own labour and not inconsiderable energy, these indomitable women have managed to finish the main monastery building as well as constructing from scratch a little church next door. They run a dairy farm, grow vegetables, restore icons, produce mosaics and play host to a growing number of guests and pilgrims. At the end of a long winding road, as well-tilled fields give way to rock and scrubby wilderness, it comes as a total surprise to discover this tranquil spot almost hanging over the edge of the valley. The cluster of buildings is a triumph of architectural ingenuity and artistic harmony. Brilliant white stuccoed walls contrast with the red tiles of the roof – a perfect setting for the richly gilded icons that decorate the walls of the church. Despite its remote location, the monastery acts as a magnet for local people who, when they are not inspecting the cheese and pickles in the monastic shop, attend long and beautiful liturgies that keep them in touch with the formative rhythms of faith.

The monastery is beautiful in its very simplicity. This is no magnificent showpiece, a cathedral dominating the landscape, but a functional piece of architecture with a specific purpose, to provide shelter and sanctuary for community and worshippers. Its beauty comes from the truthfulness with which this purpose is met. The very lack of pretence in the building betrays an aesthetic honesty that builds up a sense of the harmony and wholeness of the monastic life. The nuns do not spend their day immersed in the theology of the Greek Fathers and then, reluctantly, get on with the more prosaic business of making ends meet and keeping body and soul together. More exactly, they are involved in a regular round of activities – from singing in choir to milking the cows. It is that combination of the prayerful and the practical, the work that goes on in church and farm, which gives shape to their lives and links them to the deeper rhythms of the world around them. The place seems to grow out of the land, not overcome or suppress it. It witnesses to the process by which human beings engage with the world of their experience and shape it imaginatively to meet their deepest needs and desires.

I have called this chapter 'thresholds of meaning' because the inner harmony created by such places introduces the possibility of learning. The nuns of St John the Forerunner show us one way in which, precisely by becoming securely rooted in the everyday world, it is possible to encounter something new. They are heirs to the monastic tradition of Christianity that contemplates the reality of God's presence in everyday forms. The monastery is neither 'high culture', in the elitist sense, nor popular (or, more exactly, populist) culture that deliberately panders to mass stereotypes and ease of reproduction. The building and adorning of a place of worship enables this community to establish itself and find a new way of living an ancient tradition. The same applies to other buildings; they may not possess the same measure of aesthetic decoration but they do take their place as cultural artefacts, the tangible result of the meaning-making activities that define human beings as people of faith, in Cantwell Smith's sense. What is illustrated in the monastery of St John, therefore, is not just the practical difficulty of engaging with the messiness of conflicting desires and demands. Something more human (or, more exactly, *humane*) is at stake, for, in Clifford Geertz's well-known phrase, human beings are creatures 'suspended in webs of significance'.[1] The point is that those desires have value; a sense of the divine other is somehow made present in and through the world of everyday experience. Certain normative ideals, in other words, are refracted through particular tangible forms – from buildings and clothing to rituals and customs – to which collectively is given that singularly obscure term 'culture'.

The previous chapter ended with Todorov's 'grammar of humanism' – the formation of social groupings from the 'I–Thou' relationship. This, I suggested, offers an important counter to the 'grammar of totalitarianism', which builds a comprehensive system with no place for the other. Implicit in Todorov's distinction, with its two radically different notions of what makes for cohesive community, is the contested relationship between 'religion' and 'culture'. How are the two distinguished – and held together?

[1] Clifford Geertz, *The Interpretation of Cultures* (London: HarperCollins, 1973), p. 5.

How, to repeat the point on which I ended, are we to avoid the temptation of reducing religion to some aspect of human culture? I shall address those questions as we proceed, in the context of the contemporary missionary paradigm of 'inculturation', and return to it at the end. More immediately, let us turn to a discussion of the term that Kathryn Tanner, quoting Raymond Williams, refers to as one of the 'most complicated in the English language'.[2]

TENDING NATURAL GROWTH

Tanner's interest is in theology as a cultural activity. If theologians are to engage with the conflicting forms of discourse that make up a pluralist world, they have to attend to the work of ethnographers and cultural anthropologists for whom culture refers to the ways people make sense of their lives and the civilisations that result. Culture is the whole amalgam of customs and traditions, many unspoken and implicit but nonetheless real, which make up a way of life. Terry Eagleton begins his critique of postmodern 'culturalism' with the same observation as Tanner but goes in a very different direction. Culture may be complicated but the term often considered its opposite, namely nature, 'is commonly awarded the accolade of being the most complex of all'.[3] Eagleton focuses on the nature–culture dialectic, that is to say the transformation of 'nature' by 'culture' through forms of artistic or aesthetic expression. Culture here means literature and the arts. The two sets of connotations of culture – Tanner's anthropological and Eagleton's aesthetic – fade into each other at various points. If the former is more concerned with how communities of interest give value to their existence, the latter looks at the things that people *do* and what they actually *make* in order for life to become meaningful. If the former looks to the broad forms of life that emerge from meaning-giving activities, the latter tends to focus on the objects that can be said to 'carry' culture. Whatever we mean by the word culture – and it clearly has many levels of complexity – it is in the first place about 'making'. However the relationship between nature and culture is conceived it involves *work*, an effort of the creative imagination.

All cultural critics, theological or otherwise, recognise that before culture becomes objectified in ways of life or artefacts it is a process (a verb rather

---

[2] Kathryn Tanner, *Theories of Culture: A New Agenda for Theology* (Minneapolis, Minn.: Fortress Press, 1997), p. 3 (quoting Raymond Williams, *Keywords: A Vocabulary of Culture and Society* (Oxford University Press, 1976), p. 76).

[3] Terry Eagleton, *The Idea of Culture* (Oxford: Blackwell, 2000), p. 1.

than an abstract noun). To that extent culture comes close to 'religion' as I tried to describe it in the opening chapters of this book. Just as 'religion' needs to be dissected into two elements – 'faith' (as the inner dynamic search for meaning) and the 'cumulative tradition' (as the historically instantiated community of persons that practises that faith) – something similar needs to be done for culture. With culture, however, the shifts in meaning are impalpable and description is more difficult. The word originally came from the world of husbandry, 'the tending of a natural growth', as Eagleton puts it, and gradually took on much more moral and intellectual connotations to refer to the object of the mental and spiritual quest.[4] The 'cultivated' person was the one with taste, someone who exhibited a proper sensitivity to the harmony of form and a feeling for the correctness of expression. That may be accounted the inner dynamic of culture – what the Victorian poet Matthew Arnold famously defined as 'a pursuit of our total perfection by means of getting to know ... the best which has been said and thought in the world'.[5] Here are the origins of the aesthetic meaning of culture. Interestingly, at almost exactly the same point in history, with the rapid growth of social and human sciences, the other meaning emerges. Just two years after Arnold, the great British anthropologist Edward Tylor speaks of culture as 'that complex whole which includes knowledge, belief, art, morals, law, custom, and any other capabilities and habits acquired by man as a member of society'.[6] Culture has now become associated with particular ways of life, shifting in meaning from cultured activity to the cultured communities and people themselves, the civilisations that have resulted. Thus, today we find that the word is often used either as a sort of catch-all for creative achievement – the arts, music, literature and the fine things of life – or in a more sociological sense to refer to the way of life associated with particular interest groups – celebrity culture, youth culture, football culture etc.

What such abstractions tend to miss is the dynamism of a complex process of coming to terms with the world of experience. Raymond Williams, that most perceptive and influential of cultural historians, speaks of culture as a 'structure of feeling'.[7] It is almost an oxymoron. How can feelings take on a *structure*? Yet that is precisely what the work of cultivation, shaping the world around us, does: it gives shape and form to our innermost

[4] *Ibid.*, p. 2.
[5] Matthew Arnold, *Culture and Anarchy*, ed. R. H. Super (Ann Arbor, Mich.: University of Michigan Press, 1965).
[6] Edward Tylor, *Primitive Culture* (London: John Murray, 1871).
[7] Raymond Williams, *The Long Revolution* (Harmondsworth: Penguin; 1965), p. 48.

hopes and desires. Human beings aspire to all sorts of things, some fairly confused, and therefore in need of proper direction. But we are never *tabula rasa*. We have a history. We never begin at the beginning; our feelings are already formed in the middle of things. We inherit a whole series of traditions and rituals and customs and ways of doing things. But what is known and tested is always being brought up against what is new and challenging, what demands creativity and a certain learned ability to see the world differently in order to meet new demands. For Williams, therefore, the word culture is always used in two senses that have to be held together.

A culture has two aspects: the known meanings and directions, which its members are trained to; the new observations and meanings, which are offered and tested. These are the ordinary processes of human societies and human minds, and we see through them the nature of a culture: that it is always both traditional and creative; that it is both the most ordinary common meanings and the finest individual meanings. We use the word culture in these two senses: to mean a whole way of life – the common meanings; to mean the arts and learning – the special processes of discovery and creative effort. Some writers reserve the word for one or other of these senses; I insist on both, *and on the significance of their conjunction.*[8]

The question that Williams raises is how the 'aesthetic' and the 'anthropological' – feeling and structure – are related. The monastery of St John the Forerunner, as I have described it, gives us one example. Culture means 'cultivating' history and tradition. A new community has established itself in a new place by tapping into the wisdom of the past. *These* beginnings depend on other ones, not just the founding monastery outside Athens where the nuns originated, but the gathered experience of the Orthodox Church and its traditional ways of engaging with the world. It also means establishing a sense of belonging, of being at home in *this* place. Thus, as I noted earlier, the nuns have built their own place with their own way of doing things, particular artefacts, forms of decoration and liturgical style. In this way it is possible to speak of feeling becoming structured or channelled in certain directions, in tune with the demands both of time, what has gone before and what is still to come, and place, the particular site they have chosen and the wider religious environment to which it is related. Scattered across that mountain are any number of small hermitages, many no more than caves set deep into the rock. The monastery continues that way of life – living in harmony with the local environment. Clinging precariously to its corner of a wild landscape this little complex of buildings speaks eloquently

[8] Raymond Williams, *Culture is Ordinary*, repr. in John Higgins (ed.), *The Raymond Williams Reader* (Oxford: Blackwell, 2002), p. 11 (emphasis added).

of how the religious instinct combines with the artistic impulse not just to *manage* the land but to endow it with meaning, to make it attractive not just to the intellect but to all the senses. It illustrates better than any theoretical construct how the two meanings of 'culture' hang together. Artefacts, from icons to architecture, mediate meaning. A 'culture of humanism', therefore, speaks in the first place of how human beings make things *in order to make sense of things.*[9]

FAITH BECOMING CULTURE

In a pluralist world, for faith to take on an interpersonal dimension it has to become 'cultivated' or embedded, living in harmony with the local environment and responding to the particular questions raised by particular peoples. In the previous chapter I noted the cognitive and affective connotations of the life of faith; faith is inseparable from virtues of hope and love. In the terms developed by Charles Taylor, they represent his distinction between 'moral order' and 'social imaginary': the articulated theory of what makes for the good life in society and that more impalpable array of implicit meanings, background practices and forms of social cultivation that give a people a sense of shared purpose and meaning.[10] The tension between the two is not easily resolved.

At some stage in any interreligious exchange the question of why a particular group behaves in a certain way comes up – usually something to do with dress or food or ritual or social structures. Very often no coherent response is forthcoming: maybe because the origins of the issue are lost in the backstreets of history, maybe because a degree of embarrassment surrounds it – especially if it has something to do with the treatment of women. If there is an answer, such and such a practice is defended as 'only culture'. But this insistence that religion and culture can be separated rests on a fallacy, that we are talking about discrete and essentially different 'things'. Rather, they have a reciprocal relation. We are dealing with dynamic processes, what people *do* in order to make sense of the world, which cannot be reduced to a neat formula. By the same token, however, whatever their similarities, they cannot be collapsed or elided together, as if

---

[9] This formulation is a gloss on an observation of Rowan Williams in a lecture given at Toynbee Hall, London on 16 May 2007 entitled 'Multiculturalism: Friend or Foe'. 'If culture is a word for making things and making sense of things, it is never something that can be abstracted from history. . . . People learn to make different things and say different things.'

[10] Charles Taylor, *Modern Social Imaginaries* (Durham, NC and London: Duke University Press, 2004), chaps. 1 and 2; Taylor, *A Secular Age* (Cambridge, Mass.: Harvard University Press, 2007), chap. 4.

the one is merely a form of the other. Similar processes do not mean *same* processes. It is the relationship between the two, the way in which the 'religious instinct' tends 'natural growth' that needs further elucidation.

As a general principle it makes sense to say that while both religion and culture provide visible, tangible structures or frameworks for human living the identity established by religion is much stronger and less malleable than that provided by culture. This ought to make the discerning of some sort of unchanging essence of any religion straightforward. In practice, of course, nothing is ever that easy; as I have tried to argue earlier, 'the religions' as they exist are complex sedimentations of historical processes. The 'schools of faith' are charged not just with preserving age-old wisdom (which would imply a reified – or deracinated – version of 'culture') but with finding that appropriate form of language that makes the task of communication possible. This is where theology as the exercise of the religious intellect comes into its own. The 'work' of cultivation is never a purely human activity. At stake is the conviction that God or the source of transcendent value is already active in the world of ordinary everyday human activity. The human work, so to speak, is to recognise what is already happening – and work with it. As Nicholas Lash says, in an essay on the 'impossibility of atheism', 'Learning to use the word "God" well, learning to speak appropriately of God, is a matter of learning that we are creatures, and that all things are created, and created out of nothing. And learning this takes time.'[11] The determination to remain faithful to a vision of a universal truth while yet recognising that it is only ever manifested through changing cultural forms takes time because it raises real dilemmas. In domesticating the world around us does faith risk becoming domesticated itself? Just how does one preserve that vision of God at work in particular privileged ways – such as Torah, the Incarnation of Jesus, or the Holy Quran – while allowing God the freedom to be God? How to keep a sense of the transcendent, the Other, who is forever challenging our tendency to replace hope and idealism with the comfort of the present moment?[12]

That this is more than a practical issue of adapting the language of faith to different cultural contexts becomes clear when we look at the experience of those who have struggled to live out this universal vision with feet, as it were, in two cultural camps. Let one example suffice for the moment. The extraordinary French monk, Henri le Saux, who styled himself Swami Abhishiktananda and lived as a wandering *sannyasi* in India until his

[11] Lash, *Theology for Pilgrims* (London: Darton, Longman and Todd, 2008), p. 25.
[12] See T. J. Gorringe, *Furthering Humanity: A Theology of Culture* (Aldershot: Ashgate, 2004) for some sharp comments on the danger of the Church being assimilated to culture.

death in 1973, was determined to practise his Christian faith in a philosophical world formed by the *Upanishads*. Like so many missionaries before him he was convinced that Christianity spoke a universal message, a truth for all people. It therefore had to be translated if it was to be understood. But how to translate that message without losing the particular nuance of the Hebrew and Greek-speaking worlds from which it originated? If Christian faith was expressed in Sanskrit or Tamil, in the formulae of the *Vedanta* or Hindu devotional *bhakti*, would translation just turn it into yet another of the proliferating cults that have flourished on Indian soil? On the other hand, as he mused in his diary, 'if Christianity cannot be expressed in the religious-cultural terms of India without dissolving away, then it is not catholic. I do not see how one can escape from this dilemma.'[13] The attempt to resolve it almost broke him. Like the early Jesuit pioneers of a new and radical approach to Christian mission, Matteo Ricci and Roberto de Nobili, he tried to live a style of life attuned to local customs and ways of behaviour. But at some point the more flexible fabric of culture fades into the hard-edged structures of religion. Abhishiktananda found that negotiating that particular space was anything but easy.

Before taking his dilemma further, it may help to summarise the argument thus far and to link it with what has gone before. My initial point is that if it is to enable people to make sense of their world religion must become rooted in local cultural forms. The 'conviction of meaning' needs a structure, a 'handle' on things, as it were, a way of unifying experience. Particular artefacts, such as a statue to a local worthy set up in the town square, or cultural activities, like the parish bazaar or cricket on the village green, form a community. Secondly, to pick up the questions noted above: if a religious tradition becomes too much caught up in or dominated by particular cultural expressions it risks becoming no more than a variation on that culture, subject to the forces and values that have formed it. I spoke of one version in the previous chapter; external threats can very easily harden the harmonising force of tradition into an uncritical ideology. Here I note another. One does not have to agree with the 'new atheists' when they dismiss religion as an inadequate science-substitute or the particular lifestyle choice of the psychologically immature to see that religion can become an uncritical personalised myth that infantilises people. At that point faith does

---

[13] For the most revealing insights into Abhishiktananda's struggles to express his Christian faith in a different theological and cultural idiom, see *Ascent to the Depth of the Heart. The Spiritual Diary (1948–1973) of Swami Abhishiktananda: A Selection*, ed. and trans. David Fleming and James Stuart (Delhi: ISPCK, 1998).

not become at home in a culture, challenging it and responding to it, so much as gets turned into a 'subculture', an aspect of the culture rather than an active partner in dialogue. I therefore find myself in agreement with Tim Gorringe when he insists that culture and religion can be distinguished but not separated. Gorringe is concerned to develop a Christian theology that is proof against the temptation to assimilate faith to culture.[14] But similar concerns apply to the equally delicate work of interreligious learning. For both it is important to ensure that the dynamic process of making sense or giving meaning to life is not subverted by some comfortable formula or system.

This is the point where we must return to culture as what I called above a work of the creative imagination. In the second half of this chapter, I want to focus on what missionary theologians refer to as inculturation, bringing faith into an engagement with culture. This will enable us finally to return to the concept of culture as a dynamic process in which place and memory are brought into a creative correlation.

CORE-TO-CORE DIALOGUE

Inculturation, a somewhat ponderous neologism, dates from the period of the Second Vatican Council and expresses the retrieval, through the influence of kerygmatic theology, of 'mission' as an intrinsically theological concept.[15] Mission is what *God does*. The Church, in the language of the Council, is 'missionary of its very nature' because it has its origin in the *Missio Dei*, God's work of sending the Son and the Spirit into the world.[16] Again a sacramental vision of a world that bears the signs of the transforming power of God makes itself felt, and again the 'question of the other' is raised. As Robert Schreiter expresses the dilemma, 'How much emphasis should be placed on the dynamic of faith entering into the process, and how much emphasis should be given to the dynamics of culture already in place?'[17] Schreiter's conclusion, that the poles of the dilemma are not 'an either-or proposition' but 'two moments' that require greater or less

---

[14] *Furthering Humanity*, pp. 42 ff.
[15] According to David Bosch, *Transforming Mission* (New York: Orbis, 1992), the term was first coined by Joseph Masson in 1962 after which it 'soon gained currency among Jesuits' (p. 442). Peter Schineller, in *A Handbook of Inculturation* (New York: Paulist, 1990), pp. 21–2 tells us that Cardinal Sin used it at the Synod on Catechesis in Rome in 1977, after which it was given 'papal approval' by Pope John Paul II and was used in apostolic exhortations.
[16] *Ad Gentes*, 2.
[17] Robert Schreiter, 'Inculturation of Faith or Identification with Culture', *Concilium*, 2 (1994), pp. 15–24.

emphasis depending on circumstances does not make the dilemma any easier to resolve. But it does focus attention away from the maintenance of some sort of balance between conflicting demands, 'theirs' and 'ours', and raises the question of how religious practice of various kinds, from prayer to preaching, roots communities in the world. Other universalist traditions such as Islam and Buddhism face similar challenges; if a message is for all people then it needs to find expression in forms appropriate to the needs of particular people. Clearly more is at stake here than finding 'word equivalents'. It is not just that faith has to 'become culture' if it is to communicate truth and not act as an alien imposition; faith only becomes alive when it is communicated. As I shall argue in the next chapter, the art of translation is not just a practical skill; it is also theological, an act of the 'religious intelligence' that learns how to speak of what it discerns God to be doing in the world. The point I want to make here is that the sacramental sensibility that informs all interreligious learning is not infused from on high, as it were; it is itself formed by the various processes and practices through which we 'make things in order to make sense of things'.

If the monastery with which I began is a good example of how a community manages to make sense of life in a particular place by becoming part of that place, attuned to local mores and ways of doing things, something similar can be said for all sacred places.[18] In order to inject a more interreligious element into the discussion, I turn now to two examples of the dialogue between Buddhism and Christianity, which illustrate how, before conversations ever emerge between partners, faith becomes rooted in particular places – the Seimeizan inter-faith centre near the village of Kikusui in Japan and the Tulana centre outside Colombo in Śri Lanka.

Strictly speaking, Seimeizan is a branch of a Buddhist temple named after the great Christian theologian and missionary, Albert Schweitzer. The founder of Seimeizan, Franco Sottocornola, came to Japan in 1978 as superior of the Xaverian missionaries. An expert in the history and theory of liturgy, he got to know the head of the temple, Roshi Furukawa, and together they set up Seimeizan as a centre for interreligious exchange in 1987.[19] Writing about the centre's first five years, Sottocornola describes it as

---

[18] For a survey of the mutual influence of places and religions, see Kim Knott, 'Geography, Space and the Sacred', in John Hinnells (ed.), *The Routledge Companion to the Study of Religion*, 2nd edn. (London and New York: Routledge, 2010), pp. 476–91. For a more theological commentary, see Philip Sheldrake, *Spaces for the Sacred: Place, Memory and Identity* (Baltimore, Md.: Johns Hopkins University Press, 2001).

[19] The story of the foundation and early period is told (in Italian) by Maria de Giorgi in *Seimeizan* (Bologna: EMI, della cooperativa Servizio Missionario, 1989) (subtitled 'Fragments of a Dialogue between Christians and Buddhists' and with a 'theological-pastoral reflection' by Carlo Molari).

a 'place of prayer or spiritual experience' where people from different faith traditions can come to explore the richness of each other's texts, rituals and religious symbols.[20] Dialogue is centred on mutual friendship, shared study and a commitment to social involvement 'for the total liberation and salvation of humankind'.[21] Like a number of Jesuits, such as Hugo Enomiya Lassalle and William Johnston, who follow the Ricci–de Nobili tradition and have entered deeply into the practice of Zen as an expression of the 'dialogue of religious experience', Sottocornola has found striking similarities between the teachings of Zen masters and Christian mystics. For him, however, the experience has led not to theological reflection on commonalities and difference, but to consideration of ways in which the Eucharist can be celebrated in respectful dialogue with Japanese culture.

Mass is celebrated at Seimeizan in a style inspired by Japanese customs and aesthetics, many elements of which Sottocornola finds reflected in the 'tea ceremony' – originally a Chinese practice adopted by Zen monks as a suitable preliminary to meditation. Sottocornola's point is not that Mass celebrated sitting on *tatami* mats and using slow graceful movements makes Christians somehow more at home in a strange world or that it demonstrates the underlying shared affinity between different faiths; in fact, for him it is important to stress that this is only one, and not always the most appropriate, way in which Mass can be celebrated in 'Japanese style'. Rather, the encounter with Japan develops in the participants an attentiveness to the other that allows Japanese spirituality, its customary actions and symbolic forms to sink into the heart and change it. Again, this is not to argue for the adoption of some acculturated hybrid. In fact, the most surprising resonance that Sottocornola discerns in *zazen*, the 'silent sitting' that anchors the meditator in the present moment and leads to an emptying of the 'ego', is adoration of the sacrament of the Eucharist. Whatever the differences in their account of Ultimate Reality and the nature of the 'true self', both rely on the fixing of the attention on one thing. The very physicality of Zen, its focus on the body and all the senses contemplated in utter stillness, brings the Christian to a deep awareness of the Eternal Word which is spoken out of God's silence and of the Body of Christ in which the Word becomes incarnate.[22]

To interject the central thesis of this book: as so often happens, dialogue with the other enables interreligious learning, a rediscovery, sometimes

---

[20] Franco Sottocornola, 'Seimeizan 1987–1992: Five Years of Interreligious Experience', *Japan Mission Journal*, 47.2 (1993), pp. 119–29.

[21] *Ibid.*, p 127.

[22] Franco Sottocornola, 'Zazen and Adoration of the Eucharist', *Japanese Mission Bulletin*, 49.1 (1995), pp. 44–56; 'The Tea Ceremony and the Mass', *Japan Mission Journal*, 44.1 (1990), pp. 11–27.

inarticulate yet deeply felt, of the meaning of one's own tradition. Place creates a context within which resonances and echoes of the other can be sensed. The aesthetic dimension, embodied most obviously in architecture and artefacts, what is made, is important not just in creating a harmonious atmosphere but in affirming the spirit of the place itself. Nowhere is this more obvious than at Tulana, the dialogue and study centre developed by the Jesuit theologian Aloysius Pieris. In many ways, Tulana is an unremarkable set of buildings, hovering on the edge of small villages and sharing their simplicity. What makes it unusual is that it is decorated by works of art on Christian subjects, many done by Buddhist artists. One of these – two figures depicting the story of Jesus and the woman at the well – dominates the main area. Another is a more grating image – a depiction of the victims of Śri Lanka's civil war, which is almost beyond description. It stands as a reminder that for all its atmosphere of tranquillity Tulana sits in the middle of a nation torn apart by inter-communal strife. With his commitment to liberation and justice issues, Pieris widens the sphere of 'culture', bringing social and political issues into his practice of interreligious learning.

This context gives the inculturation dilemma a much sharper edge. As a Buddhist scholar committed to a theology of liberation, Pieris's first concern is to make the 'Church *in* Asia' become the 'Church *of* Asia'. The primary metaphor that Pieris develops for this form of inculturation is 'baptism': as Jesus was baptised in the waters of the Jordan and then on the cross, so must the Church be 'humble enough to be baptized by its precursors in the Jordan of Asian religion and bold enough to be baptized on the cross of Asian *poverty*'.[23] The Church has throughout its largely Western history of domination always sought to judge the other, to impose its own cultural baggage along with the message of the Gospel. Pieris, like so many Asian Christians who are enormously sympathetic to the religions with which they have grown up and through which they have come to appreciate the depth of meaning in their own tradition of faith, sets them firmly apart. The question that they are asking is this: in Asia, where it remains a minority, can Christianity accept a different sort of singularity or uniqueness, willing to be judged by the other while holding up the example of the self-denying Christ who alone judges all human pretensions? Put like this, Pieris's rhetoric of liberation seems like a powerful restatement of the best of the Jewish and Christian prophetic tradition. He repeats the same themes, the same juxtaposition of images and word plays, over and over again. For Pieris, prophetic judgement has a

---

[23] Aloysius Pieris, *Love Meets Wisdom* (New York: Orbis, 1988), p. 41.

part to play in any dialogue. Nevertheless, the context of place and its Buddhist ethos give a very particular quality to Pieris's deeply felt theology of liberation. The prophet does not always have to take the active or lead role in the relationship. Silence can also be prophetic, just as the passive or suffering Christ continues to speak God's Word.

Thus Pieris reminds us that without a harmony of speech and silence words cannot be heard; without the prior spirit of stillness and self-denial there can be no effective engagement. This leads him to recognise a similar, though quite profoundly 'singular', process of integration within Christian faith. For the Buddhist, the dominant religious 'idiom' or 'language of the Spirit' is gnostic. In other words, wisdom or *prajña* is intrinsically salvific; compassion or *karuna* is the indispensable prelude. For the Christian, the correlative idiom is agapeic or affective because Christian faith is essentially a response to the revelation that God is love; love brings knowledge of God or, more properly, a God-given wisdom. Pieris knows that 'gnosis' has always had a poor press in Christianity and is at pains to retrieve a properly Christian 'agapeic gnosis'. He also seeks to commend the value for Buddhists of a 'gnostic agape' that would make the Buddhist path less a relentless search for forms of discriminative knowledge and more a harmony of wisdom and compassion.

It is not far-fetched to conclude that the core experience of Christianity is not agape pure and simple but agape in dialogue with gnosis; conversely, the core experience of Buddhism is not mere gnosis, but a gnosis intrinsically in dialogue with agape. Hence, a true Buddhist–Christian encounter is possible only at the depths of our being where the core-to-core dialogue has already taken place![24]

How can such a programme be accomplished? Not through a speculative theology of accommodation but, according to Pieris, through the ascesis or life of faith of the community that brings together the Buddhist *gnostic detachment* of voluntary poverty and the Christian *agapeic involvement* in the struggle against poverty. In the silence generated by the Buddhist practice of mindful meditation is heard the voice of the other.

CROSS-CULTURAL TRADITIONS

I shall return to this point about learning from the encounter with Buddhist meditation in a later chapter. Here I want to reflect further on this particular meeting point, the growing engagement between Buddhism and

[24] *Ibid.*, p. 119.

Christianity, as an example of the problems and pitfalls – and promise – of inculturation. Most Christian accounts of the meeting of Buddhism and Christianity give a very one-sided impression; travellers, missionaries, philosophers and colonialist administrators have long been fascinated with Europe's 'silent other'. All too often Buddhism was misunderstood either as an obscure variation on the overarching Hindu tradition or as a projection of the fears, hopes and prejudices of 'the West'. Stephen Batchelor's survey rather redresses the balance, contributing a Buddhist commentary to a very Eurocentric story.

There are as many kinds of Buddhism as there are ways the fragmented and ever-changing European mind has to apprehend it. In each case 'Buddhism' denotes something else. For rationalists it means a philological object, something to be dissected and known. For romantics it is a fantasy object, where all is pure and good, a justification for one's disdain of the corrupt West. Yet while rationalists *think* they understand Buddhism and romantics *feel* they know – what is it really?[25]

The answer, he feels, is 'nothing you can put your finger on'. Buddhism includes a number of things – ethics, psychology, philosophy, mysticism, devotion – but as the Middle Way between extremes it transcends them all. The forms it has taken are all contingent on particular historical circumstances. And will continue to be so. A new diffusion of Buddhist teaching, aided by the process of immigration and a number of Buddhist 'exiles' to the West – Tibetans, Vietnamese etc., has put paid to the Orientalist constrictions noted earlier. Scholarly interest in Buddhism now seeks to combine anthropological with historical-critical and philological readings of Buddhism, seeking to link the immense variety of contemporary practice with a renewed awareness of the significance of the ancient Indian background. Meanwhile, some academic Buddhologists have developed forms of 'Buddhist theology' – shifting the emphasis from a purely descriptive to a normative account of Buddhism – and now make their own contributions to comparative theology.[26] In many ways this sort of creative reflection represents a recovery of the ancient commentarial tradition of monastic training, but by taking intellectual engagement out of the monasteries and into the academy it also returns to an important dimension of the Buddhist

---

[25] Stephen Batchelor, *The Awakening of the West* (London: Thorsons, 1994), p. 274.
[26] For an interesting collection, see Roger Jackson and John Makransky (eds.), *Buddhist Theology* (London: Curzon, 2000). In his introduction, Jackson brings 'Buddhist theology' close to Rowan Williams' 'work of religious intelligence'. 'We may use the term "theology" to describe conceptual activity within and about a particular religious tradition, without thereby implying that such activity is itself an avenue to the ultimate; it is just as true, after all, that the God of Christian theology is ineffable as it is that *nirvana* or buddhahood transcends the range of thought' (p. 3).

tradition, its strict avoidance of 'unskilful' forms of purely metaphysical speculation. No longer is it so easy to set up oppositions between Christianity and Buddhism, between a personal God and an impersonal 'world-process', between a providential created order and the beginningless cycles of existence, between grace and the lonely realisation that all is *śunyata*, 'emptiness'. Even the Buddhist teaching of *anatmavada* or 'no self' seems less alien and more patent of Christian understanding.

That is not to erase profound differences, but to set them in a different perspective. The *Buddhadharma* can never be defined as a single religious tradition that exists as a number of different sects. Buddhism is, in Christian parlance, a 'missionary' tradition not because it actively proselytises (which would imply that its teachings are always to be opposed to others) but because, of its very nature, it exists always in relationship with others. Buddhism is naturally 'cross-cultural'; it constantly adapts and changes. There is no 'essence' that can be extracted, systematised and set over against a 'religion' called Christianity. Both traditions are bound up with and inseparable from particular symbolic forms. Buddhism needs to be understood against its brahmanical background and Christianity through its Jewish roots. To that extent both are inseparable from very particular religious origins. But, as Pieris reminds us, both traditions are also critiques of and, to some extent, reactions against these origins.[27] In different ways such a conscious distancing was provoked by the conviction of their *universal significance*; the Gospel is Good News for all peoples while the *Dharma* is to be preached for the welfare of all sentient beings. Both are committed to the communication of a message and therefore needing consciously to find appropriate translation and inculturation. Like Christianity, Buddhism tells a story that has formed not a philosophy or ideology but a civilisation, a whole complex way of life. As 'world religions' Buddhism and Christianity are defined by particular engagements and by the dialogues with others that the engagements provoke. In this sense the two traditions are considerably more fluid and diffuse than the textbook versions might allow. Like the story of Jesus's Death and Resurrection, the story of the Buddha's Enlightenment gives birth to a practice, a 'path' or *pratipada*, from which arise key principles and dominating symbolic forms that infuse Buddhism with a richly mystical and ethical flavour. They are, however, just as rooted in ritual acts – chanting in a particular way, offering flowers to the Buddha-image, adopting a certain posture – as the more obviously liturgical tradition of Christianity. In both

[27] For example, 'Western Christianity and Asian Buddhism: A Theological Reading of Historical Encounters', in *Love Meets Wisdom*, pp. 17–42.

traditions, through cultivating the sense of place and marking the passing of time, a whole variety of practices are rooted in the everyday.

All this suggests, remembering what was said by Sottocornola about the Seimeizan experience, that the way to any intellectual or theological dialogue is to be conducted through the medium of the experiential. For Christians seeking to forge links with or 'inculturate' into Buddhism, it is only through shared religious practice that the all too enigmatic quality of the *Buddhadharma* can be grasped. In which case perhaps the key distinction between Buddhism and Christianity lies not so much in any set of 'oppositions' as in the valuation put upon language itself. Invoking a version of the prophetic-mystical distinction, David Tracy reminds us that the Buddhist speaks a word *realised for oneself* while the Christian speaks a word that *belongs to another*, to God.[28] Each represents a different, but perhaps complementary, configuration of the relationship between word and silence. For Buddhists, the linguistic forms in which the 'way' is expressed and explained are 'crutches' to keep the sick and suffering going, or the boat with which one crosses to the 'farther side' but which, once used, should be left behind. Buddhism is conscious of how language can divide and separate. In this sense the Buddhist challenge to the ease with which Christians speak about God can be understood as, in an important sense, 'prophetic'. *Nirvana* is not the 'final word' and certainly not a 'new word', but rather relativises all words, every positive statement about ultimate reality, reminding us that the language of faith always risks idolatry. Having said that, it is important not to reduce Buddhism to an arid intellectualism. The Dalai Lama is supposed to have remarked that 'there is no Absolute in Buddhism but, if there were, it would be compassion'.[29] There is a hint here that whatever else *Nirvana* may mean it is more than a matter of realising the ultimate truth, the radical emptiness of things, *alone*. If the quality of Wisdom cognises so-called 'ultimate reality', emptiness, then Compassion acts as a corrective to it, realising a different sort of ultimate – perhaps that value of Compassion that makes a practical reality of *pratityasamutpada*, the radical relatedness of all. For Christians this distinction between ultimate truth and ultimate value does not hold (at least not with the same force) because the source of both, indeed of all things, lies in God.

---

[28] David Tracy, *Dialogue with the Other: The Interreligious Dialogue* (Louvain and Grand Rapids, Mich.: Peeters/Eerdmans, 1990), especially pp. 12–26.

[29] Quoted, for example, by Roger Corless in 'Buddhism and Violence'. www.purifymind.com/BuddViolence.htm.

COSMIC AND METACOSMIC RELIGION

What the two traditions hold in common is – again – more a process than an essence, a capacity (albeit worked out in very different ways) to shape or bring into focus the faith of particular communities and to make them, more exactly, 'schools'. Buddhism and Christianity are complex amalgams of what Pieris refers to as cosmic and metacosmic religiosity – terms that roughly translate the Pali *lokiya* and *lokuttara* ('this-worldly' and 'other-worldly').[30] The former represents what he calls 'an ecological spirituality', a basic human religious response to the numinous disclosed in various 'cosmic forces', while the latter describes what lies at the heart of all the major world religions: 'an immanently transcendental horizon … salvifically encountered by human beings'.[31] The two can be distinguished but not neatly separated; they coexist as a sort of 'intra-religious dialogue' that produces different configurations of a never-ending dialectic between what Panikkar calls '*mythos*' and '*logos*', the 'outer' spiritual language and the 'inner' intellectual grammar of faith.[32] If this is correct, then it would explain why for many theologians it is at the meeting point between cosmic and metacosmic that mutual understanding and mutual transformation are to take place. Franco Sottocornola's reflections, for example, are in many ways *pre*-theological. The life of the Seimeizan community is largely concerned with the dialogues of common life, common action and religious experience. Unlike Pieris, Sottocornola does not seek to reflect on their theological implications. On the other hand, a theology is implied in the unspoken conviction that the community draws its life not from some a priori ideology or speculative scheme but from a life of prayerful engagement with another community of faith. God, to put it in Christian terms, goes on making God present wherever the 'other-worldly' becomes incarnate in the responsible practice of a people.

In the Buddhist–Christian encounter, therefore, theologians are not trying to accommodate two more or less comparable stories or 'language games', one drawing its inspiration from the Buddha, the other from Jesus, or even seeking to adapt the language of one to the other. For Pieris, the dialogue is about bringing two different but complementary religious 'idioms' into a creative correlation. Christianity is more 'prophetic' or 'agapeic' while Buddhism is more 'mystical' or, in Pieris's term, 'gnostic',

---

[30] See Aloysius Pieris, *An Asian Theology of Liberation* (Edinburgh: T & T Clark, 1988), pp. 71–4.
[31] Aloysius Pieris, 'Does Christ Have a Place in Asia? A Panoramic View', *Concilium*, 2 (1993), pp. 33–47.
[32] Raimundo Panikkar *The Intra-Religious Dialogue* (New York: Paulist, 1978), p. 102.

in ethos, style and practice. As with Sottocornola's understated dialogue of life and religious experience, Pieris grounds his own engagement with the Buddhist culture of his native Śri Lanka in a *communicatio in sacris*, by which he means not just shared meditation but a participation in the broader religious culture that shapes the lives of the rural poor – metacosmic *and* cosmic religiosity.

While the project of inculturation began in the years after the Second Vatican Council as an approach to mission that would lead to a more effective engagement between the Gospel and non-Christian cultures, in more recent years it has become a metaphor for interreligious dialogue itself. As noted earlier, religion and culture are distinguishable but never entirely separable; faith must always, to repeat, 'become culture' if it is to be properly embedded in the ordinary life world of ordinary folk. The twin dangers, Schreiter's dilemma, through which such influential interreligious theologians as Pieris seek to navigate the Church, are either to impose a faith that destroys rather than enhances what is already there or to produce so accommodating a version of Christianity that it loses all specificity and power to challenge and change. To acquiesce in the first is to turn Christianity into an imperialist force, the like of which has been experienced all too often in the history of Christian mission. To move in the other direction is to make of Christian faith what I called above a subculture, a settled set of responses to life, identified in terms of clothing, routines and familiar customs, a 'thing' rather than a dynamic process of engagement with the world of experience. To avoid the stridency of the former and the anonymity of the latter means paying careful attention to Pieris's ascesis of faith and the skills and virtues of communication within and across boundaries that it seeks to develop.

In the next chapter I shall examine further the dynamic or verbal account of culture as inculturation, with particular reference to these personal qualities, which I describe under the heading of *translation*. Here let me conclude with a final thought about the themes that have run through the first section of this book and which sets the scene for what follows.

CROSSING THRESHOLDS

I began this series of 'meetings' with that guiding image of the return to the marketplace where the 'unruly mind' lives and works in a world transformed. The other places – real rather than metaphorical – all share certain characteristics. Most obviously, they are all bounded configurations of space. Some, like the monastery of St John the Forerunner, are remarkable for the sheer quality of the boundary-making. Others work on a far less grand scale. Simple wayside shrines, crudely constructed out of a few slabs of stone daubed with paint, make up for their lack of artifice with the simple clarity of the act of boundary-making. Others, of course, like Auschwitz-Birkenau, are much more alien impositions on nature – not because they witness to the triumph of technology over art – although they are, of course, graphic illustrations of the 'banality of evil' – but because they eradicate the need for a 'grammar of humanism'. When the conviction of meaning is over-determined, the boundary separating 'us' from 'them' becomes a barrier. The need for security trumps the desire to explore and learn.

It is obvious that places are built with a variety of motives, from welcome and hospitality to the aggressive assertion of power. What I have sought to describe in this chapter is something of the conditions that make a 'school of faith' (and more importantly a 'school of schools') possible. My argument is that culture interacts with nature to construct not just an aesthetically pleasing place but a centre of human engagement. What I began by calling the middle of things is also a network of interpersonal relations. Thus the care with which space is cultivated often testifies as much to the harmony between human artifice and the indefinable power intrinsic to magnificent scenery as to the capacity of people to make themselves 'at home' both within their environment and with each other. For Levinas, 'home' is the first major theme in his phenomenology of otherness: 'I am at home with myself in the world because it offers itself to or resists possession.'[33] The act of domesticating the world, making it conform to one's needs, provokes a degree of resistance – the first inklings of an otherness at the heart of the project of self-making that puts the self in question. This is what gives certain places a life of their own; they do not just embody the 'comprehensive scheme' which is a religious tradition, they also leave space for what, following Levinas, might be called the 'resistant other'. Churches, temples, mosques, gurdwaras, holy sites of all kinds, are tangible records of the myriad ways human beings negotiate this mysterious world. Architecture and artefacts, the rituals and the life of prayer that they support, the processes of social interaction that they inspire, are all of a piece. What gives them life, however, is not some intrinsic quality of 'the sacred', but that elusive quality of 'otherness' in all its forms with which they seek to engage. In brief, they map out crossing-places for the imagination. In the gnomic but provocative utterance of Michel de Certeau, 'Space is a

[33] Emmanuel Levinas, *Totality and Infinity* (Pittsburgh, Pa.: Duquesne University Press, 1969), p. 38.

practiced place.'[34] What he means is that we do not begin with space as some sort of natural or pristine void by which we are somehow surrounded, and then proceed to control it with constructions and cultural objects of all kinds. More exactly it is the other way round. The space in which we find ourselves is already marked irrevocably by the traces of human interaction. It consists not of some 'arena' that I can dominate through self-assertive action, but of a much more ill-defined network of human interactions that are strictly limitless and therefore can never be mastered.

How to seek out and identify the rhythms and harmonies that natural geography *and* the history of human cultivation have built into the world? Like all records and inscribed memories, places can be read as texts. Their many layers of meaning, reflected in the oral and written material they embody and the art and custom they preserve, reveal the 'webs of significance' in which human community is held together. Significant places, the aesthetically pleasing and the more starkly hideous, are all records of the struggle to order the raw material of life in the middle of things. In that sense they have about them a certain moral ambivalence; beauty of form is no guarantee of the probity of purpose. The challenge – as much ethical as it is theological – is to engage with the rich experience of our cultured environment in such a way that traces of Divine Reality are not suppressed in favour of some all-dominating ideology but discerned with the wisdom and understanding that only a properly formed 'grammar of humanism' can guarantee.

In these four chapters, held together with the word 'meetings', what I have done is reflect on my initial question about what happens to faith when it becomes 'inter-faith' – faithful to the terms of one's own tradition yet responsible before the face of the other. Moving from religions as versions of some spiritual commodity to the model of 'schools of faith', and drawing attention to the twin dangers that any such school has to face – rigid ideology, on the one hand, and cultural accommodation, on the other – I have mapped out the terms of a comparative theology that takes values of openness and faithfulness seriously and leads to a learning that has two dimensions and two responsibilities – a clearer understanding of the other and deeper wisdom about my own. For the schools of faith to become communities of conversation, where humane values of reverence and

---

[34] Michel de Certeau, *The Practice of Everyday Life* (Berkeley: University of California Press, 1984), p. 117. De Certeau speaks of place as 'an instantaneous configuration of positions' whereas space 'is composed of intersections of mobile elements'. He notes that the distinction is rather like that between the unspoken and spoken word (*ibid.*).

respect can flourish, a certain threshold has to be crossed. When the project of interreligious learning is generously embraced boundaries perceived as barriers give way to boundaries as centres of intersection, places where people of faith can gather and where meeting points can become crossing points. To make such a manifesto more than a neat juxtaposition of spatial metaphors, however, we now need to consider in more detail the terms in which schools of faith can be said to occupy the same theological space.

II

Crossings

CHAPTER 5

The art of translation

Jerusalem is a city sacred to three faiths. The city that David made his capital and where Solomon built the Temple, where Jesus celebrated Passover, was crucified and buried, is also the place where, according to sura 17, *al-Isra*, of the Quran, Muhammad made his 'night journey' to heaven. Jews make pilgrimage to the Western Wall to pray before the massive stones that are all that remains of the great Temple structure destroyed by the Romans in 70 CE. Christians come to the dark and cavernous Church of the Holy Sepulchre, the site where, according to tradition, Helena, the mother of the emperor Constantine, discovered the true cross. For Muslims, the Dome of the Rock or the Noble Sanctuary, al-Haram al-Sharif, which now stands on the Temple Mount, is the third holiest site in Islam and the point towards which Muslims turned for prayer before Muhammad established the focus or *qibla* as the Kaaba in Mecca. These are all places hallowed by the prayers of countless thousands of pilgrims and devotees from the three faiths. This extraordinarily moving and tragically divided city, a mere third of a square mile in area, concentrates the memories and the lived experience of Jews, Christians and Muslims throughout the world. If religion had an archaeology it would be Jerusalem.

As I wandered around the old city for the first time I was struck by a single thought. The silver-encrusted circular hole in the floor of the church of the Holy Sepulchre may not have been the exact spot where Jesus was crucified. The hollow set deep down under the building may not have been the place where Jesus was laid to rest. But they could not have been that far away. For Christians, of course, the only important focus of pilgrimage is Jesus himself. The Fourth Gospel makes that clear time and time again; Jesus is the one in whom the religious institutions of Judaism, including the Temple itself, all find their fulfilment. Place, it seems, is transcended and no longer religiously significant. Such an interpretation of the scriptures, however, would be to underestimate the importance of history, and of certain historical events, for the proper understanding of Christian faith.

Places preserve memories. There is nothing like a visit to the Holy Land to bring home the paradox that runs all the way through Christian history: that a universal truth is refracted through some very specific events that actually happened. The city of Jerusalem, divided by a history of conflict and tragedy, is still the 'city of peace', a place of strange inspiration. In this light, the sacramental instinct that forms Catholic sensibility is not something vague and irretrievably other-worldly. It is rooted in the power of particular signs to evoke memory and make present God's undying promise.

This immediately raises a question mark over the tendency to aggregate all religious and cultural forms to each other. To walk down the Via Dolorosa, with the sound of stallholders and bargain-hunters buzzing in the ear, is to be aware of how closely Judaism, Christianity and Islam are intertwined. Substantially this scene has not changed for over 2,000 years. Yet, for all that they share common themes, common memories and in Jerusalem and the Holy Land a common place of origins, these are very different and distinct traditions.

For decades this difference has been obscured by the tendency to speak of a single 'Judaeo-Christian tradition'. More recently the usage has been expanded to include Islam – the 'Judaeo-Christian-Islamic tradition'. Quite when these terms became part of the interreligious argot is unclear. Arthur Cohen calls it a cultural myth that began in the late nineteenth century when German Protestant Higher Criticism of the Old Testament invoked the concept in order to account for the crucially important Jewish dimension of Christian experience. It was, however, in the USA rather than Europe where it became popular. In the 1920s, the National Conference of Christians and Jews fought anti-Semitism by proposing a more liberal interpretation of the shared values of the two major religious influences on American culture. The intention, says Cohen, was to build Jewish and Christian solidarity. What happened, however, was that the 'Jewishness' of Christianity became no more than an aspect of its pre-history. Jews and Christians were driven together by a number of factors, not least the hostility of wider secular society, with fatal implications for the integrity of both traditions. 'The Judaeo-Christian tradition is an eschatological myth for the Christian who no longer can deal with actual history and a historical myth for Jews who can no longer deal with the radical negations of eschatology.'[1] There is, of course, everything to be said for once antagonistic traditions identifying points of agreement and making common

---

[1] Arthur Cohen, *The Myth of the Judaeo-Christian Tradition* (New York: Harper and Row, 1970), p. xx.

cause. Problems arise when this otherwise admirable intention leads not to communication across boundaries but to the erasure of that specificity of vision that gives a tradition its inner vitality.

Cohen's 'cultural myth' becomes, in the rather more trenchant critique of Jewish–Christian relations by Jacob Neusner, myth 'in the bad sense' – that is, a lie. For Neusner, the truth is that Jews and Christians are 'different people talking about different things to different people'.[2] He is appreciative of the enormous shifts that have taken place in Christian attitudes to Jews in the last half-century, and is also well aware that Christians and Jews work with many shared presuppositions. What he finds unacceptable, however, is any attempt to set the two traditions together as anything more than two different religions with different structures and different interests. Neusner has reservations about the intellectual presuppositions of dialogue and what he perceives as a tendency to fudge distinctions in favour of some apparent consensus. He does not want Judaism to be reduced to a part, even a highly significant part, in a Christian story. To talk, from a Protestant perspective, of Christianity as announcing a prophetic 'reform' of Judaism, or, using more Catholic categories, as a continuation or fulfilment of what has been begun in the Jewish revelation, spectacularly misses the point. The events of the first century, and particularly the destruction of the Temple in 70 CE, created two completely different religions: the Christian with its universalist belief that in Jesus the Messianic promises to Israel have been fulfilled and the 'intense inwardness' of a new piety, based on synagogue worship and Talmudic study. This rabbinic Judaism, which emerged in the first centuries and took on a form codified in the Mishnah and the Talmuds, represents a major transformation of the Pentateuchal tradition of Old Testament Judaism.[3] Christianity is not a spiritual offshoot of pre-rabbinic Israel, nor its superior improvement, but a unique and autonomous religious system in its own right. In the first centuries of the Christian era, these two traditions spoke to their own agenda and developed distinctive languages. In brief, they stopped narrating a shared story and started interpreting its common themes and symbols according to very different needs.

Neusner's vast scholarship and command of the early rabbinic period should give pause for thought. His reading of those crucial early years in which very different traditions went their separate ways raises a question mark over the familiar Christian tendency to ignore the development of diaspora Judaism in all its richness and diversity. However, Neusner is very

---

[2] Jacob Neusner, *Jews and Christians: The Myth of a Common Tradition* (London: SCM, 1991), p. 1.
[3] Jacob Neusner, *The Four Stages of Rabbinic Judaism* (London: Routledge, 1999).

far from denying the possibility of sympathetic dialogue. Richard Harries's careful and sympathetic reading of 'Jewish attitudes to Christianity', from Buber and Rosenzweig to Abraham Heschel and Neusner, shows how they all respond positively to certain perceived Christian 'resonances' in the work of the rabbis. For Neusner, the God of Israel is, indeed, ineffable. But he says:

> When I tell my stories, in which I learn how the Torah reveals God, both the stories of the prophets and what God said to them, and the stories of our sages of blessed memory and how they knew God in incarnate form, I can understand how someone else may tell stories about God in us, and about how we can become like God. And I then listen with sympathy to the Christian story of Jesus Christ God incarnate? Without doubt: I can listen with sympathy, because the Torah teaches me how.[4]

As Harries notes, Neusner is not saying that this way of thinking necessarily leads to Jesus Christ, only that it is possible 'using Jewish traditional sources' to understand something of Christian faith. Difference – even a difference developed over centuries of conflict, ignorance and misunderstanding – does not irrevocably set the two traditions apart in such a way as to refuse any possibility of interreligious learning.

The vast amount of comment and research that has been done on the early formative period, both from Christians and from Jews, makes it clear that talk of a single 'Judaeo-Christian tradition' requires considerable nuance. No doubt Neusner is right to insist that Judaism as it exists today depends for its sense of self on the 'difference' established by the rabbinic sages and is not to be reduced to some irrelevant relic. It does not follow, however, that the 'Judaeo-Christian' tradition is either cultural myth or patronising accommodation. Different traditions certainly, but held together by various shared concerns, values and theological ideas – most notably the imperative of the *Shemah*, 'listen'. What Christians share with Jews is not primarily a set of texts but a conviction that God has spoken and invites human beings into the intimacy of a loving relationship. Christians and Jews are formed as peoples in a particular way, with a common desire to be faithful to God's self-disclosing Word. That said, any talk of a 'common tradition' has to be treated critically and with care. The separate 'religions' that we now call Judaism and Christianity have a history and need to be

---

[4] From Jacob Neusner, *Telling Tales* (Louisville, Ky.: Westminster John Knox Press, 1993), p. 137. Quoted in Richard Harries, *After the Evil: Christianity and Judaism in the Shadow of the Holocaust* (Oxford University Press, 2003), p. 181.

understood as the results of historical movement and interaction – like the sediment laid down by the inexorable progress of slowly moving rivers.

The Islamic extension of the 'Judaeo-Christian tradition' I will take up in a later chapter.[5] I shall argue that what holds the three so-called 'Abrahamic religions' together are different but not incompatible responses to the divine imperative. So far my discussion of interreligious learning has centred round key themes that are central to any account of the contemporary meeting of people of faith. The 'school of schools' has been set up as an ideal meeting place, where a hospitable communication can take place and a mutually enriching wisdom grow. In such a safe space, the crucial question can be addressed: how to be faithfully anchored in a religious tradition and yet responsive to another world of discourse, able to cross linguistic, symbolic and cultural boundaries? In opening up the 'crossings' that are possible once 'meetings' have been effected, I turn now to the terms of a spirituality of dialogue. That theme will become more explicit in Chapters 7 and 8 when we turn to the dialogue between Christianity and the meditative traditions of India. In this chapter and the next I stay with the contested but formative experience of the 'Judaeo-Christian tradition'. I begin with the example of two of the most important Jewish thinkers of the last century. In their different ways, Franz Rosenzweig and Martin Buber faced questions that have occupied Jews for centuries – questions about identity and faithfulness; about religion, culture and politics; above all, about how to maintain a specifically Jewish identity without being assimilated to the secular Enlightenment culture of Europe. Their ideas can help Christians not just to develop a version of the 'Judaeo-Christian tradition' that avoids the extremes of secession and assimilation but to learn from that engagement the virtues of dialogue and interpersonal relations that I refer to as the 'art of translation'.

THE NEW THINKING

A decade before the Nazi persecution of the Jews began in earnest, Franz Rosenzweig wrote a satire on philosophy. Called *Understanding the Sick and the Healthy*, it describes the unhappy state of a poor sick philosopher stuck in a sanatorium where wise doctors are trying to find a way of curing him

---

[5] The addition of Islam is a recent phenomenon which can most probably be ascribed to the instant judgement on common features which subordinates a particular integrity to 'good will' and the demands of the common good. See, e.g., an article on the *Washington Post* website (and subsequent comments) by Robert Parham, 'Our Common Judeo-Christian-Islamic Tradition', 4 June 2009.

from his inordinate desire to grasp the grand meaning of things.[6] The sanatorium has been built at the exact geometrical centre of three great mountains – God, World, Man – which can be glimpsed through the window. What has led to the philosopher's sickness is the failure to recognise that whatever else they are these three great themes are not separate and independent ideas. How are the doctors to help him overcome his obsession with essences and grasp something of the relatedness of the three mountains, their interdependence? Rosenzweig's answer is what he calls the 'new thinking' – an approach to philosophy that commends a radical return to the origins of all philosophical enquiry in wonder.[7] Wonder arises, he says, from 'ordinary life', from the 'flow of life itself'. The purpose of philosophy is not to indulge in metaphysical speculation but to support a responsible way of living. What is new about the 'new thinking' lies 'in the need of an other and, what is the same thing, in the taking of time seriously'.[8] It means speaking *to* some one and thinking *for* someone – a very definite human being 'who doesn't merely have ears like the general public but also a mouth'.[9] Such speaking and thinking is bound by time; it does not know where it will end. It lives by virtue of another's life and is called forth by the demands of another's life.

There's something wonderfully ironic here. Rosenzweig is most famous for what did not happen to him – his 'non-conversion'. When he was studying for his Ph.D. on Hegel he was part of a circle of friends who had converted to Christianity. He eventually decided to do the same. For one last time he went to the synagogue in Berlin for the 'high days' of Rosh Hashanah and Yom Kippur in 1913. Exactly what he experienced there nobody knows. But he came out transformed. Resolving to 'remain a Jew', he embraced the orthodox tradition and turned dramatically against the Hegelianism of his early years. Later he wrote to his cousin Rudolf Ehrenberg, who had converted to Christianity: 'We agree on what Christ and his Church mean in the world: no-one comes to the Father but through him (John 14:6). No one comes to the Father – but it is different when

---

[6] Franz Rosenzweig, *Understanding the Sick and the Healthy: A View of World, Man and God*, trans. Nahum Glatzer (New York, 1953), second introduction by Hilary Putnam (Cambridge, Mass.: Harvard University Press, 1999).

[7] See Franz Rosenzweig, *The New Thinking*, ed. and trans. Alan Udoff and Barbara E. Galli (New York: Syracuse University Press, 1999).

[8] *Ibid.*, p. 87.

[9] *Ibid.* See Hilary Putnam, *Jewish Philosophy as a Guide to Life* (Bloomington: Indiana University Press, 2008), pp. 30 ff.

somebody does not have to come to the Father because he is already with him. And this is so for the people of Israel.'[10] The Jews are God's elect people. Their story, told in the Hebrew scriptures that Christians call the Old Testament, elaborated in the formal commentarial traditions of Talmudic study and practices through the orthodox round of high days and holy days, is anything but 'new'. Yet it is from this distant and disregarded cultural world that Rosenzweig seeks to engage with the German philosophical tradition of his day. And in his hands it assumes an extraordinary intellectual vitality, imbuing the orthodox Jewish tradition with a new life. His great masterpiece, *Star of Redemption*, a philosophical account of Judaism and its relationship with Christianity, is the first fruits of the new thinking, a difficult and complex work that has a very simple purpose: to *translate* Jewish thought into a modern philosophical idiom. With startling originality, *Star* brings Judaism and Christianity into a new correlation, teaching members of both traditions to think about each other in a new and different way.

Any work of translation, expressing the truths of one culture through the linguistic medium of another, is a difficult, perhaps impossible, task – but it still needs to be done. 'Translating means serving two masters,' says Rosenzweig. 'It follows that no one can do it. But it follows also that it is, like everything that no one can do in theory, everyone's task in practice. Everyone must translate, and everyone does.'[11] Rosenzweig's concern here is not the theoretical question of communication between persons but a version of philosophy as some sort of silent solipsistic monologue. The 'new thinking', by contrast, is an existential philosophy of life that reflects seriously on how speech creates and maintains relations. It stems directly from his rediscovery of a thought-world in which human beings are constituted by God's call. Clearly Christianity shares in this thought-world – and therefore in the themes of revelation and responsibility that so much engage Rosenzweig. But with an important difference. Rosenzweig speaks of Christianity as the 'eternal way', a sort of missionary extension of Judaism; Christians are called to take the 'eternal truth' of the self-revealing God, the guarding of which is properly the duty of the Jews, into a Gentile world. This is an attractive division of responsibilities, but it is not unproblematic, if only because it tends to subordinate Christian identity, and

[10] Quoted by Gareth Lloyd Jones, *Hard Sayings: Difficult New Testament Texts for Jewish–Christian Relations* (London: CCJ Publications, 1993), pp. 36–8.
[11] Franz Rosenzweig 'Scripture and Luther', in Martin Buber and Franz Rosenzweig, *Scripture and Translation*, trans. Lawrence Rosenwald and Everett Fox (Bloomington, Ind.: Indiana University Press, 1994), pp. 47–69. Quotation from p. 47.

therefore the centrality of Christ, to a Jewish perspective that denies that centrality. It also tends to reify two traditions in a way that I have criticised in earlier chapters; Rosenzweig is not completely free of the Hegelian structures he rejected after his 'conversion'. The positive point, as far as Christian–Jewish relations are concerned, is that his powerful rhetoric is nothing if not a reminder that what Christians tend to think of as an 'Old' tradition, which has been fulfilled by the 'New', has an origin and a fullness of meaning which belongs *elsewhere* – which is properly 'other' and not to be superseded or reduced to some inadequate adjunct. To adopt the Pauline metaphor retrieved by *Nostra Aetate*, Judaism is the ancient olive tree on to which has been grafted the 'wild branches' of the Gentiles.

At stake here is Cohen and Neusner's myth of the 'Judaeo-Christian tradition'. How can 'Old' and 'New' go on existing in a relationship that neither totalises nor relativises the other? To prepare the ground for a response, let us stay for a moment with Paul's example of translating an intrinsically Hebrew message into other languages. This idea dominates the early decades of the Church's life, a community of faith that found its voice on the day of Pentecost when the scattering of peoples at the tower of Babel was miraculously reversed by the Apostles' speaking in many tongues (Acts 2:1–12). Rosenzweig is right in his estimate of Christianity as a religious tradition that is charged with communicating a truth about God. The issue, so painfully recounted in the first half of Acts, is not about the scope of the revelation given in Christ, it is about the demands placed upon Gentile converts. The Good News revealed in Jesus's resurrection from the dead has a universal application. Alongside Paul's question about what has happened to those of his fellow-religionists who have failed to recognise this truth stands another: does Torah apply to Gentiles, particularly in the matter of circumcision? Essentially this is an 'intra-Jewish' debate. It is anachronistic to speak of 'Christianity' and 'Judaism' as designations for separate 'religions' before the end of the first century CE. More accurately we should be speaking of the Christian 'way' (Acts 9:2), which originated *within* rather than *after* that broad set of Jewish traditions that flourished at the time of Jesus. Luke tells us that it was at Antioch that they were called Christians (Acts 11:26) – on the borders of Jewish and Gentile worlds.

Paul's encounter with the 'unknown god' of the Athenians is symbolic of that shift. His attempt there to speak a 'new language' became a movement of adaptation and cross-cultural dialogue in the early Patristic period when the Church found itself confronted by a diffuse collection of mystery cults, religious philosophies, traditional myths, and state-sanctioned rites. Not the least important aspect of Chrys Saldanha's study of 'the religions' in the early Patristic period, is that he shows how the underlying 'style' of the writing of the Greek Apologists is distinctly kerygmatic; a 'divine pedagogy' seeks to persuade people of the truth they have themselves experienced in Jesus Christ. They are, however, dependent less on some strategy that would force the other into a self-evident form than on recognising distinct features that require a particular response. Saldanha speaks of a dialectic of continuity ('preparation') and discontinuity ('transcendence'). 'To eliminate, exaggerate or minimise either of these poles', he says, 'would amount to a distortion of Christianity or of non-Christian religions.'[12] While pagan idolatry has to be illuminated by the light of the Gospel, the best of pagan wisdom or Greek philosophy can be understood as a *preparatio evangelica* bringing other religious traditions to Christ. What holds these and so many of the early Fathers of the Church together is the conviction that the Gospel has to be *communicated*; and this involves translation – in the broad sense of the term. As David Bosch has suggested, referring to the work of Lamin Sanneh, the Gospel has translation as its 'birthmark'.[13] If the first Christians struggled to make their faith in Jesus as the Messiah a distinct feature of an essentially Jewish faith, the Fathers sought to express that faith in a different language and cultural form.

TRANSLATING THE SELF

We will return to Rosenzweig and the Jewish–Christian encounter later in this chapter. First, however, I want to focus on translation not just as a central theme in Rosenzweig's 'new thinking' and the personalist philosophy that it has inspired but as a metaphor for the spiritual life as a whole – especially a spiritual life lived in dialogue with other persons of faith. The previous chapter considered the theme of culture and the strategy of inculturation as a broadening of the challenge to a universalist creed to make itself understood by people of different beliefs and cultures. In an obvious sense the words of the Gospel have to be translated into another linguistic and cultural medium if they are to be understood. For Christians, however, the words point to the Word, to the person of Christ revealed through the liturgical and prayerful practices of reading, hearing and contemplating the text. Any work of encounter or dialogue or

---

[12] Chrys Saldanha, *Divine Pedagogy: A Patristic View of Non-Christian Religions* (Rome: Libreria Ateneo Salesiano, 1984), p. 121.
[13] David Bosch, *Transforming Mission: Paradigm Shifts in Theology of Mission* (New York: Orbis, 1992), pp. 447–8.

comparison – whether based in the reading of texts or arising from more interpersonal contact and discussion – leads through a process of inner communication to changes not just in the way we speak of our own faith tradition but, more importantly, in our *sense of self*. Such changes, I want to argue, are part and parcel of the experience of trying to communicate, to translate across boundaries. The question, of course, is how they can be managed with generosity of heart and integrity of purpose.

To reflect further on the formative effect that the other – and particularly the Jewish other – has on the Christian sense of self, I turn to Rosenzweig's great collaborator Martin Buber. This will help us to understand something of the inner process of communication, that self-reflective act of learning that is inseparable from any attempt to speak truth to another. I will then, in the spirit of the theme of this book, take up a particular example of these principles of interreligious learning in practice.

In his ever-popular work, *I and Thou*, Buber brought the insights of a typically Jewish personalism into the mainstream of Western philosophy.[14] As I noted in the Preface, in this regard he differs in an important way from the other great philosopher of dialogue, Plato. The Socratic dialogues use a particular method, the questions and answers of the wise philosopher, in such a way as to bring truth to birth in the enquirer. The implicit assumption is that truth is already there, somehow innate in the human person; all that is required is the skill of the teacher, to let it emerge 'in the other', the pupil. For Buber, truth is not a possession, something forgotten, to be retrieved. Truth belongs 'in between', to be born in the encounter itself, in the interpersonal relationship that opens up between human beings. In dialogue with the other, we human beings encounter a new potential. To be human is to learn how to move away from the goal-oriented, self-centred, instrumentalist attitudes that regard the other as 'It' and to see in the other, albeit in a fleeting and never complete fashion, a 'Thou', a unique partner in a creative endeavour.

'I–It' and 'I–Thou' sound like two types of relation, one 'bad' and one 'good'. Their interaction is rather more complicated than that. The two terms are what Buber calls 'primary words' – not compounds, but structures of reality, ways in which human beings go about constructing their world. The two 'primary words' work together: without the 'I–It' it would be impossible to survive, but without the 'I–Thou' that survival would be empty of meaning. Fundamentally, these two 'words' imply two interdependent modes of relating to the other, what Buber calls *orientation* and

[14] Martin Buber, *I and Thou*, trans. Ronald Gregor Smith, 2nd edn. (Edinburgh: T & T Clark, 1958).

realisation.[15] Most of the time is spent in the former mode, treating the other as a traveller might treat a strange city – linking the various houses and streets until a mental map begins to emerge and the city becomes an object that the traveller knows and can control. Science and technology work in this way, relating to the other as an object of usefulness for particular projects. The other invariably acts as a springboard or transition to something else. But in the middle of this work of *orientation* may come moments of *realisation*, when the individual takes in the other with all the senses – and not so much controls the other but finds him or herself being taken, being realised, identified with the other without ever surrendering their unique position. Dialogue for Buber is descriptive of this experience of a unity-in-difference, an *orientation* towards the other that makes *realisation* possible. 'Ordinary life', he wants to say, contains the potential for glimpses of another order, a life of meaning. Human beings seek to impose order on experience; that is the fundamental point made about the religious life noted earlier. Buber wants to show us how to do it successfully, in a genuinely 'creative' way, not soaking up external data, as it were, but choosing to engage with human experience in all its otherness and difference.

The distinction he is making is between two tendencies, two forces, perhaps, which seek to bring unity into the chaos of infinite possibilities that confront us. The first is content to surmount the other, to bring order by reducing the other or the unknown to a semblance of the known. The second comes with the recognition that such a unity can never be fully attained. It remains elusively 'other', only ever glimpsed in moments of 'realisation'. Nevertheless in this 'between', which both separates and brings unity into human relations, the 'Eternal Thou' is always present. For the mystic in Buber, whatever we truly encounter becomes a sort of envoy of God, a bearer of revelation, a mediator between us and the eternal Thou. 'In every sphere in its own way, through each process of becoming that is present to us we look out toward the fringe of the eternal Thou; in each we are aware of a breath from the eternal Thou; in each *Thou* we address the eternal *Thou*.'[16] There is something wonderfully imaginative, in the best sense, about the Hasidic spirit that permeates Buber's vision. As with Rosenzweig's 'new thinking', he looks at how ordinary life contains a potential that can speak to us and enable us to arrive at the I–Thou relationship; everything may be uplifted to the point at

---

[15] See Martin Buber, *Daniel, Dialogues on Realization*, trans. Maurice Friedmann (New York: Holt, 1964). For a lucid explanation, setting the I–Thou relation within the context of Buber's early philosophical development, see Shmuel Hugo Bergman, *Dialogical Philosophy from Kierkegaard to Buber* (Albany, NY: SUNY Press, 1991), pp. 217 ff.

[16] Buber, *I and Thou*, p. 19.

which it becomes the means to a relationship with God. While not without its problems, this idea does open up the possibility that in the middle of an instrumental account of the other (that is to say, one that in Buber's terms is limited to the 'orientation' mode) may be found indications of a richer and more theological account of dialogue (the 'realisation' of being addressed by God, the eternal Thou). For Buber, this says something important about what human beings are called to be. In an extraordinary passage at the end of his book on dialogical philosophy, the Jewish philosopher Shmuel Hugo Bergman quotes Buber:

Do you know that you are in constant need of God more than all else, and do you know that he also is in need of you with the whole of his eternal being? How could man come into the world if God had no need for him, and how could you come into the world? You are dependent upon God, and God is dependent on you.[17]

To appreciate what Buber is driving at, we should remember that these are the words of a genuine 'mystic of the everyday', a thinker deeply sensitised to the presence of God at the heart of human experience. To go back to my Buddhist image of the marketplace, there is more to the meeting of persons – the 'inter-human' – than a mere mode of consciousness or self-presence. There is more in the presence of my dialogue-partner than an object that I observe, determine and judge; more even than another person who regards me as a 'Thou'. For the Jewish mystic, persons-in-relation disclose something of the mystery of God who has promised to be present to his people. In an essay on 'The Faith of Judaism', Buber says:

It is the dialogical situation in which the human being stands that here finds its lofty or childlike expression. Judaism regards speech as a happening which reaches out over the existence of mankind and the world. In contradiction to the static of the Logos-idea the word appears here in its full dynamic as that which comes to pass. God's act of creation is speech; but also each lived moment is so. The world is spoken to the human beings who perceive it, and the life of man is itself a dialogue. What happens to a man are the great and the small, untransmittable but unmistakable signs of his being addressed; what he does and suffers can be an answer or a failure to answer. And thus the whole history of the world, the hidden, real world history, is a dialogue between God and his creature; a dialogue in which man is a true legitimate partner, who is entitled and empowered to speak his own independent word from out of his own being.[18]

[17] Bergman, *Dialogical Philosophy*, p. 238. He gives no reference for this quotation.
[18] Buber, 'The Faith of Judaism' (1928), taken from *Mamre: Essays in Religion*, trans. G. Hort (Melbourne University Press, 1946), repr. in Daniel H. Frank, Oliver Leaman and Charles H. Manekin (eds.), *The Jewish Philosophy Reader* (London and New York: Routledge, 2000), pp. 598–9.

Like Rosenzweig, Buber interprets human experience as a dialogue that God initiates and that is reflected in so many intimate moments of ordinary human living. As in the earlier quotation, human beings have a dignity that makes them more than creatures of God's initiating Word. Rather, they enjoy a fully responsible and creative role in the dynamic of divine revelation. This, of course, raises a massively complex theological issue – a God who is caught up, to the point of *necessity*, in the human situation. In what sense can God be said to be 'dependent' on human beings? For the moment let me just suggest that the language being used here is deliberately provocative, intending to make us think in radical terms about the power of the revealing Word. To take the prophetic experience as the most obvious example, when Isaiah is called by God he is first cleansed with burning coals and thus prepared for a mission that he knows to be beyond human power. Revelation, as Rosenzweig notes, is not a matter of message-bearing. Isaiah is empowered to participate in God's work and thus becomes the agent of God's Word. Something similar happens to the people of Israel as they prepare to enter the Promised Land – though here, of course, the struggle to be conformed to God's desires is more painful. In the book of Deuteronomy, Moses stands before them to speak to the people about what God expects of those with whom he has fashioned a Covenant. They must not forget 'the poor, the widow, the orphan and the stranger'. Those who are landless have a call on the generosity of the landed; their origins in the land of slavery should remind them that what they have now is pure gift and is not to be used to exploit and exclude those less fortunate than themselves. For Levinas, like Rosenzweig seeking to universalise or translate a Jewish truth, the passage illustrates his constant refrain, that human beings are characterised by the *responsibility* they take for the other. As so often, Levinas makes his point with a rasping rabbinic saying. In a collection of essays on Judaism he quotes a first-century rabbi: '"Why does your God, who is the God of the poor, not feed the poor?" a Roman asks Rabbi Akiba. "So that we can escape damnation", replies Rabbi Akiba.'[19]

DIALOGUE BETWEEN GOD AND HIS CREATURE

The question of how a peculiarly 'Jewish wisdom' can translate itself into Christianity and its implications for Christian self-understanding I leave to the next chapter, when I will return to this theme of the God who reveals

[19] Emmanuel Levinas, *Difficult Freedom: Essays on Judaism* (Baltimore, Md.: Johns Hopkins University Press, 1990), p. 20.

Godself in and through the act of dialogical engagement. Here I want to stay with that experience of shifting from 'orientation' to 'realisation', which, Buber would have us believe, turns the 'It' that we can control into the 'Thou' that speaks. Against the background of Jews and Christians as people of faith seeking to communicate with each other, I want to consider one recent exchange that, I suggest, opens up this theme of translation as an interpersonal exchange in which, as Buber and Rosenzweig (and maybe even Levinas in his more tortured fashion) would remind us, God is mysteriously present. Although the Vatican's *Nostra Aetate* and *Dabru Emet* (meaning 'speak truth', words taken from Zechariah 8:16, the statement – more a manifesto – published by a group of Jewish academics in 2000), are very different, they are both addressing the complex issue with which I began: the nature of the 'Judaeo-Christian' tradition. That the two traditions are intrinsically related is clear. But how to speak of that relationship within the 'grammar of humanism' that refuses assimilation or totalisation?

As a preface let me refer to some remarks of Rosenzweig in an article on the new German translation of the Bible on which he collaborated with Buber.[20] Rosenzweig is at pains to distinguish between the book and the word. Originally, he says, the book served the word, providing the form and technical structure by which the word or message of truth could be communicated. The danger is that so much attention and effort gets paid to the manner in which the word is presented – or translated – that the word ends up being subordinated to the book. Sheer artifice turns the word into an untouchable object, 'literature', an 'It', in Buber's terms. This clearly is of crucial importance when reading let alone translating the Bible. The book only comes alive when as word it is sounded in the lives of ordinary human beings, when the artifice of poetry and the mnemonic structures that allow the words to flow give way to the word that enables the soul to break free. In other words, the work of translation involves more than maintaining the exactness of meaning as one cultural and linguistic world engages with another. The book is subject to the word. To translate is to communicate. It is about establishing those human relationships that allow speech to flow, for it is only through spoken words that meaning can communicate itself. Between the word and the book, Rosenzweig is saying, comes the mediation of persons.

For Christians of all denominations, Vatican II's *Nostra Aetate* is something of an interreligious charter. The unequivocal statement that the

---

[20] Franz Rosenzweig, 'Scripture and Word: On the New Bible Translation', in Buber and Rosenzweig, *Scripture and Translation*, pp. 40–6.

Church 'rejects nothing of what is true and holy' in other faiths ends with a call to Christians everywhere to 'acknowledge, preserve and encourage the spiritual and moral truths found among non-Christians, also their social life and culture'.[21] No more than thirty sentences in the Latin original, *Nostra Aetate* marks a new step in Christian thinking about the relationship between people of faith. The original intention, of course, was more modest: to do something to redress what Jules Isaac called the 'teaching of contempt', Christian hatred for the Jews – a theme that we will return to in more detail in the next chapter. *Nostra Aetate*, of course, avoided any such reference to the Shoah, but it has still opened up a positive, if at times fractious, dialogue. Since its publication, in 1965, it has stirred up a great deal of response from other faith communities, most importantly in the shape of *Dabru Emet*. The eight short theses of *Dabru Emet*, hammered out by a group of American Jewish scholars during the 1990s at Baltimore's Institute for Christian and Jewish Studies, express key points on which Jews and Christians could agree.[22] To summarise, briefly, *Dabru Emet* states that

(1) Jews and Christians worship one God, the God of the patriarchs.
(2) Jews and Christians look to the same texts for spiritual sustenance.
(3) Christians can respect the claims of Israel to the Promised Land.
(4) Both communities accept the moral principles of Torah, especially the dignity of every human being.
(5) Despite the long history of Christian anti-Judaism, 'Nazism was not a Christian phenomenon' nor an 'inevitable outcome of Christianity'.
(6) Differences between Jews and Christians will only be resolved at the end of time, before which attitudes of mutual respect and non-confrontation need to be developed.
(7) The new relationship with Christians will not weaken Jewish practice.
(8) Jews and Christians must work together for peace and justice – guided together and separately by the prophets of Israel.

The document received a warm welcome from many Christians, but provoked a mixed response from within the Jewish community. The most powerful critical voice, Jon Levenson, objects that this is not the way to do dialogue; differences are being minimised in favour of

---

[21] *Nostra Aetate*, 2.
[22] The text was published as a full-page advertisement in the *New York Times* for 10 Sept. 2000. Given the critical response which it received from some parts of the Jewish world, it is important to set *Dabru Emet* within a developing dialogue, represented most impressively by a volume of essays which acts as further commentary on the process: Tikva Frymer-Kensky *et al.* (eds.), *Christianity in Jewish Terms* (Boulder, Colo.: Westview, 2000).

establishing some sort of common ground or area of agreement.[23] Levenson argues that since Jews and Christians do not look at the same issues in the same way it is downright dishonest to suggest a neat symmetry where there is none. For Christians, there is more to the Bible than the Old Testament and Jews do not see the New Testament as biblical in any way. The claim that 'Jews and Christians worship the same God' may be unproblematic for the latter, but Christian belief that God is a Trinity of persons is quite unacceptable to Jews. Levenson's point is that the authors are too keen to stress the continuities between Judaism and Christianity at the expense of the broader asymmetry both of language and context that must be acknowledged if proper understanding is to be attained. Cohen and Neusner's 'cultural myth' seems to hover uneasily in the background.

Whether or not Levenson overstates his case – and fails to acknowledge that *Dabru Emet* is necessarily a brief summary that is designed to get debate going and that therefore requires a great deal of further development – the controversy does furnish us with a practical example of serious inter- and intra-religious dialogue that raises important questions about what dialogue can be expected to achieve and, perhaps more importantly, how it is to be conducted. Although there are many Jews who regard the dialogue with Christians with scepticism, not to say alarm, none of the original signatories was interested in reaching some sort of lowest common denominator agreement. On the contrary, as responses to Levenson indicate, the first concern is to clarify areas of distinctness and difference yet to do so in an atmosphere of cordial acceptance that raises the possibility of learning from the relationship. *Dabru Emet* is remarkable not because it arrives at a new consensus but because its authors seek generously to open up a positive conversation about areas of common concern and deliberately avoid contentious language and a defensive mentality. Levenson and others of a conservative persuasion focus on the more neuralgic points of the relationship between Jews and Christians and are concerned not to lose a sense of the specificity of Judaism. Arguably, however, both can claim to be heirs to the influential thought of Franz Rosenzweig – the former emphasising his insistence on the dialogical reciprocity of the two traditions, the latter taking their stand on Rosenzweig's advocacy of Jewish primacy in the relationship. In broad terms, I would contend that versions of this dilemma run through every

---

[23] Jon Levenson, 'How not to Conduct Jewish–Christian Dialogue', *Commentary*, 112 (Dec. 2001), pp. 31–7. See also in response from the authors of *Dabru Emet*, with a number of letters, 'Jewish–Christian Dialogue: Jon D. Levenson & Critics', *Commentary*, 113 (Apr. 2002), pp. 8–21.

Christian–Jewish encounter – and, maybe, *mutatis mutandis*, through every interreligious dialogue.

An engagement with Rosenzweig brings out the very real sensitivities that attend the 'Jewish–Christian tradition' and the difficulty of establishing a relationship that can be acknowledged by both sides with genuine integrity. Following *Nostra Aetate*, Christians can now accept a version of Rosenzweig's guiding principle, that Jews are called to preserve the truth of God's loving act of creation revealed in history. This is the task of the people created by the Covenant with Israel that, as Pope John Paul II has stressed, 'has never been revoked'.[24] But what of the other side of the Rosenzweigian scheme of things? Christians claim that the Paschal Mystery of the Death and Resurrection of Jesus Christ bathes the whole of the biblical story in a new light. It is one thing for Christians to understand their identity within the broad sweep of God's providence as some sort of 'missionary arm' of Judaism, another to subordinate that identity to Judaism and give up claims to a specific source of spiritual life and motivation. To do so would be to replace one form of supersessionism with another.

In his objection to a dialogue that he clearly regards as evasive, Levenson is right to warn Christians, as much as his Jewish co-religionists, to take the other with full seriousness and to avoid any theory (and Rosenzweig, with his Hegelian take on the relationship of religions, does tend at times to be quite theoretical) that makes complex patterns of holiness subject to some grand universalism. This is not just a Jewish–Christian issue, even if the intensity of a shared history makes it particularly painful to resolve. The city of Jerusalem bears powerful witness to what Jews and Christians hold in common, but it also questions in its history of conflict and discord the coherence of some single overarching 'Abrahamic' tradition. The division into four quarters – Jewish, Muslim, Christian and Armenian – dates back centuries and was formalised by the Ottomans in the mid-nineteenth century.[25] Today's city is much more obviously divided, its allegiances more tragically fractured. 'Translation' – whether moving across the literal boundaries that separate one community from another or entering into a generous process of interreligious learning – is a much more fraught process. Jerusalem is only the most obvious example of a religiously contested space.

---

[24] On a visit to the synagogue in Mainz, 1980. See John McDade, 'Catholicism and Judaism since Vatican II', *New Blackfriars*, 88 (July 2007), pp. 367–84.

[25] See Bernard Wasserstein, *Divided Jerusalem: The Struggle for the Holy City* (London, Profile Books, 2001) and Michael Dumper, *The Politics of Jerusalem since 1967* (New York: Columbia University Press. 1997).

It acts as a potent reminder that all efforts at cross-religious translation are shot through with versions of Rosenzweig's dilemma. It is, of course, obvious that no work of translation is ever adequate to express the completeness of some original insight or idea. In that sense what I have called the translation of the person is never ending; there is always more to be learned, both with regard to the other and to the self. Nevertheless, the more pragmatic side of Buber's and Rosenzweig's vision, the 'new thinking', which only comes alive when talking *with* the other, rather than simply *to* them, does furnish us with some important principles and the possibility of more positive relationships between sometimes very different communities of faith.

VIRTUES OF DIALOGUE

Much of the literature that has emerged both within the academy and from the Church with regard to the experience of interreligious dialogue has focused on the contributions that faith communities can make to the common good. Panikkar, for instance, in expounding what he calls the 'dialogical dialogue', the experience of passing through or beyond the logical (*'dia ton logon'*) to confront the other as a subject who mediates meaning to the self, concludes with a heartfelt, even exasperated, plea, reminding his readers of the ethical dimension of dialogue:

> It is the cross-cultural challenge of our times that unless the barbarian, the mleccha, goy, infidel, nigger, kafir, the foreigner and stranger are invited to be my *thou*, beyond those of my own clan, tribe, race, church, or ideology, there is not much hope for the planet.[26]

Nearly two decades later, speaking in the shadow of 9/11, Jacques Dupuis said that '[a]n open and constructive theology of religions of the world is a pressing need if we wish to foster an interreligious dialogue conducive to universal peace'.[27] For Panikkar, theology follows the experience of being in dialogue. For Dupuis, theology comes first. Both would agree, however, that it is not just Jews and Christians who are committed to the practice of dialogue. Muslims, Buddhists and Hindus too have their own store of wisdom for life in the public space. Dialogue is very much the clarion call

---

[26] Raimon Panikkar, 'The Dialogical Dialogue', in Frank Whaling (ed.), *The World's Religious Traditions* (Edinburgh: T & T Clark, 1984), pp. 201–21. Quotation from p. 220.

[27] Jacques Dupuis: *The Tablet* open day lecture for October 2001, published in *The Tablet*, 20 Oct. (pp. 1484–5); 27 Oct. (pp. 1520–1) and 3 Nov. (pp. 1560–1). Quotation from p. 1484.

of our times, a theme constantly echoed within the churches[28] and by public policymakers.[29] A theology of dialogue, however, which would explore the properly religious motivations for dialogue, as well as the more contentious question of its relationship with mission, is proving slow to emerge. David Lochhead's perceptive study *The Dialogical Imperative* raises many of the important philosophical questions; in particular, he draws attention to the difference between Platonist and Buberian models of dialogue, the one focusing on the method of interrogation by the skilled teacher, which draws meaning from an encounter, the other concentrating on the value of the interpersonal encounter itself.[30] The question, however, as Lochhead would be the first to acknowledge, is how the two forms are to work together. To begin with the Buberian model, which privileges the interpersonal (the line I have been pursuing in this book), is not to deny that in every meeting of persons there arise intellectual issues about truth and meaning.

Panikkar distinguishes his 'dialogical dialogue' from what he calls the 'dialectical dialogue', which he defines as a method for passing judgement on another's opinions, based ultimately on the principle of non-contradiction. Again, the two forms are interdependent; the interpersonal conversation is always a *conversation about something*. The question that Panikkar's distinction raises is whether the move beyond the will to power (the danger inherent in the purely dialectical dialogue) – essentially a debate about truth claims proving who is right and who is wrong to enter into a trusting relationship with the other person as a source of understanding – is in some way theological. In what sense is interreligious learning saying something about God? At this point we move on from the theoretical questions about the nature of religion, faith and culture that have occupied

---

[28] The Vatican's Pontifical Council for Interreligious Dialogue (PCID) has been responsible, through its regular *Bulletin*, for publishing reports and speeches which reflect the Roman Catholic Church's commitment to dialogue. Of the major documents for which the PCID (before 1988, under the title of the Secretariat for Non-Christians) has been responsible, the most important are: 'The Attitude of the Church towards the Followers of other Religions' ['Dialogue and Mission'], *Bulletin*, 19/2 (1984), pp. 126–41 and 'Dialogue and Proclamation: Reflections and Orientations on Inter-religious Dialogue and the Proclamation of the Gospel of Jesus Christ', *Bulletin*, 26/2 (1991), pp. 210–50. Following the work of the Lambeth conferences for 1988 and 1998, the Anglican Communion has developed its own theology of interfaith relations as 'Generous Love: The Truth of the Gospel and the Call to Dialogue', published by the Network for Inter Faith Concerns (NIFCON) in 2008. Dialogue is understood in the context of the Church's mission as a whole and a distinction is developed between 'embassy' and 'hospitality', 'a movement "going out" and a presence "welcoming in"' (p. 13).

[29] In the UK, the Department for Communities and Local Government (DCLG) has published an important framework document for interfaith relations, 'Face to Face and Side by Side' (London: DCLG, 2008). The title comes from a distinction made by Jonathan Sacks in *The Home We Build Together: Recreating Society* (London: Continuum, 2007), pp. 173–82.

[30] David Lochhead, *The Dialogical Imperative* (London: SCM, 1988).

us in the first part of this book towards more practical and existential issues that arise from the life of Christian discipleship and the process of learning that it entails. For there is no answer to that last question, which is separated from the necessarily laborious business of discerning the leading of the Spirit of God. What I have called 'meetings' raises important questions about truth and meaning in dialogue. Such questions can be distinguished, but not separated, from questions about the virtues that support and give form to the principles of dialogue. This is the approach taken by Catherine Cornille, for whom, '[i]f dialogue is to include the possibility of change and growth, not only of the individuals involved, but of the religions themselves, then certain essential conditions are to be fulfilled'.[31] She lists five key virtues: a 'doctrinal or epistemic *humility*', *commitment* to a particular religious tradition, *interconnection* ('or the belief that the teachings and practices of another religion are in some way related to or relevant for one's own religious tradition'),[32] *empathy* (or the ability to enter into an intellectual and experiential understanding of the other) and finally that attitude of genuine *hospitality* that recognises that another religious tradition may be a source of enrichment for one's own.

These virtues are implicit in what follows in the further chapters of this book. If I add one further principle or dialogical virtue, it is not to contradict Cornille's sensitive rooting of the practice of dialogue within the spiritual traditions of the Christian pattern of holiness. To return one last time to the old city of Jerusalem: there can be no resolution to the issues that arise from that sadly fragmented space that does not recognise that theological and political issues are inextricably bound together. Dialogue in Jerusalem of all places must take on a hard edge if it is to be more than an exchange of bland religious pleasantries. Any city where interreligious relations have become a salient aspect of modern life brings up the political as much as ethical dimension of so much contemporary dialogue. In the traditional language made familiar from Vatican documents, 'common life' and 'common action' are as much part of the dialogue as 'religious experience and theological exchange'.[33] Some dimension of each form is necessary for a properly rooted practice *and* theology of dialogue – plus, I want to repeat, the patience that recognises that the work of translation *takes time*, indeed, is never finished. The dialogue with Judaism that has opened up since Vatican

---

[31] Catherine Cornille, *The Im-Possibility of Interreligious Dialogue* (New York: Herder and Herder, 2008), p. 4.

[32] *Ibid.*, p. 5.

[33] See the two PCID documents noted above: 'Dialogue and Mission', 29–35, and 'Dialogue and Proclamation', 42. Pope John Paul II refers to the same form in *Redemptoris Missio* (1991), 57.

II has shown how the two traditions have learned to become more sensitive to each other's concerns and questions. In the next chapter I will take up this point in more detail. There I shall seek to argue that the very closeness of Jews and Christians, while it stirs up unhappy memories and is often far from harmonious, yet has something important to teach the wider dialogue of religions. In the face of ideological secularism and the lazy eclecticism of postmodernity, the very perseverance in seeking to live out of a spirit of positive mutuality and interdependence is perhaps the most significant witness to the 'difference' that both unites and divides these two traditions.

In order to reiterate the idea that has run through this chapter and that informs everything that is to follow let the last word remain with Franz Rosenzweig. What I have called here the 'art of translation' is a practical skill that can be learned. It goes without saying that any act of communication across religious and cultural boundaries demands understanding of what 'the other' is saying as well as an ability to speak clearly and with conviction. Thus the translator who would cross into another cultural and symbolic world must pay careful attention not just to the appropriateness of the language that is used but to the broader context within which speech is uttered, and to the *holistic* nature of the culture, the framework of custom and myth and symbol that gives language its capacity to captivate and persuade. Otherwise the artifice that expresses 'the book' may only obscure rather than enhance the clarity of 'the word'. There are, however, always limits to what any practice can attain – and as important a skill in the translator consists in learning how to adjust to limitation. As Rosenzweig says:

What is intended to be of limited scope can be carried out according to a limited, clearly outlined plan – it can be 'organised'. The unlimited cannot be attained by organisation. That which is distant can be attained only through that which is nearest at the moment. Any 'plan' is wrong to begin with – simply because it is a plan. The highest things cannot be planned; for them readiness is everything. Readiness is the one thing we can offer to the Jewish individual within us, the individual we aim at.[34]

I have spoken of translation as a metaphor for the spiritual life lived in dialogue with the other. Rosenzweig's 'Jewish individual in us' is addressed to Jews. But if his own project is about translating Jewish wisdom into a more universalist frame of reference then it can be made to apply at some

---

[34] 'On Being a Jewish Person', in Nahum Glatzer (ed.), *Franz Rosenzweig: His Life and Thought*, 2nd edn. (New York: Schocken Books, 1953), p. 222. Quoted in Putnam, *Jewish Philosophy as a Guide to Life*, p. 33.

level to all those who aspire to become translators. They must possess the ability both to make an accurate and imaginative rendering of what is known *and* to wait upon what is strictly unknown but dimly discerned to be of God. For such a person 'readiness is everything'. To cross over successfully one begins in the middle of things, in particular places and situations, but moves, however tentatively, towards something more universal – even while knowing that the universal is always unlimited and can never be attained. In the next chapter I begin with the memories that both unite and divide the two very particular 'schools of faith' that are Judaism and Christianity. The 'Judaeo-Christian tradition', I want to argue, is neither cultural myth nor patronising construction but one way – a not particularly elegant shorthand – in which Jews and Christians struggle to speak of what holds them together and of the hope that they hold out for the future of humankind.

CHAPTER 6

Mending memories

The Remuh synagogue in Kazimierz, the ancient Jewish quarter of Cracow, has about it an air of silent dignity and tragic loss. The only functioning synagogue left in an area that in the 1930s boasted a population of some 60,000, its adjacent cemetery was desecrated by the Nazis at the height of the Shoah, the gravestones dug up and used to pave the streets. After the war the broken fragments were carefully collected by visitors and volunteers and crafted into the facing of the wall that encloses the cemetery. That wall forms a powerful reminder of Poland's lost Jewish heritage. Other synagogues that survived the war have been turned into museums or venues for art exhibitions, concerts and poetry readings. Since the fall of communism Kazimierz has reinvented itself. In the squares and winding streets where once a lively Jewish community flourished, tourists get a taste of a world long vanished. Careful restoration and the foundation of centres dedicated to retrieving the past ensures that what remains is more than just a collection of relics.[1] Here in the Remuh synagogue the Torah scrolls are still kept, a tangible sign of the survival of the life of prayer and study that once sustained the millions who died in the Shoah. Respectfully I take a yarmulke and sit at the back, behind a handful of silent Jewish visitors, their stillness made the more poignant by that terrible absence beyond the patched up walls.

For a Christian this is a disorientating yet strangely consoling place. If Auschwitz stands testimony to the banality of evil, this little synagogue is a sign of hope that hatred will never have the last word. When the Jewish historian Jules Isaac visited Pope John XXIII in the summer of 1960, his intervention in the lengthy process of preparation for the Second Vatican

---

[1] Perhaps most notably the Fundacja Judaica, a centre for Jewish Culture run by Dr Joachim Russek, and the Holocaust Museum begun by the British photographer, the late Christopher Schwartz, both in the centre of Kazimierz.

Council drew attention to the Christian roots of anti-Semitism.[2] In a lecture given at the Sorbonne the previous year Isaac spoke about the 'teaching of contempt'. Christian anti-Semitism, he said,

is much worse than its pagan predecessor: worse by its content – which is essentially theological – by its coherence, and by the variety of its themes more or less arbitrarily founded upon Scripture, or rather upon a certain interpretation of Scripture; but worse especially by its continuity – from the first Christian centuries right down to modern times.[3]

His words of warning began a process of reconciliation that, despite the inevitable setbacks, is now irreversible. Some four years later, the promulgation of *Nostra Aetate* changed forever the terms in which Christians regarded people of other faiths. At that point the section that Isaac inspired sat alongside references to Islam, Hinduism and Buddhism. The text was prefaced by an introduction that owed much to another new and unexpected development, the Church's engagement with the history and phenomenology of religion. As with so much of the Council's work, the process of *ressourcement* and the hidden scholarly work of decades suddenly bore rich fruit. But it was what Tom Stransky called a *Heshbon ha-Nefesh*, a 'reconsideration of the soul', which most marked this remarkable moment in the Church's history.[4] *Nostra Aetate*, especially through its reception in both Christian and non-Christian worlds, was as much a religious event as a theological text. Without the determination to redress the wrongs caused by the 'teaching of contempt', nothing would have been said – and theology of religions might have lacked its deeply ethical motivating force.

FROM ANTI-THEOLOGY TO 'FIRST THEOLOGY'

How correct was Isaac's comment that anti-Semitism is 'essentially theological'? It is true that Christianity had no positive theology of Judaism

[2] For the beginnings of *Nostra Aetate* in the remote preparations for Vatican II, see J. O. Beozzo, 'The External Climate', in Giuseppe Alberigo and Joseph Komonchak (eds.), *The History of Vatican II*, vol. i, *Announcing and Preparing Vatican II: Toward a New Era in Catholicism* (New York: Orbis/Peeters, 1995), pp. 393–7.
[3] See especially Jules Isaac, *The Teaching of Contempt: The Christian Roots of Anti-Semitism* (New York: Holt, Rinehart and Winston, 1964). Quotation from a lecture by Isaac, reprinted as *The Christian Roots of Antisemitism* (London: Council for Christians and Jews, 1965), p. 7.
[4] Tom Stransky was a member of Cardinal Bea's Secretariat for Christian Unity, responsible for the process which saw *Nostra Aetate* emerge from an appendix to the schema on ecumenism to take its final form as an independent declaration of the Council when promulgated on 28 Oct. 1965. His comment is recorded by Eugene Fisher, *Fifteen Years of Catholic–Jewish Dialogue, 1970–1985* (Vatican City: Libreria Editrice Vaticana, 1986), p. 139.

before *Nostra Aetate* resurrected Paul's agonised meditation on the fate of his sometime co-religionists in Romans 9–11. It is also true that there are plenty of 'hard sayings' recorded in the Gospels that speak of a growing antagonism towards those Jews who refused to accept Jesus as Messiah. The Gospel writers, putting their texts together in the shadow of the war that led to the destruction of the Second Temple, framed Jesus's death and resurrection against the background of an earth-shattering apocalyptic.[5] In a sense they could do little else. This was what Jesus's insistent preaching of the Kingdom as a present reality was all about: the perennial prophetic warning against the corruption of religious faith. It was inevitable that his disciples should interpret the fate of those who failed to respond as God's judgement on their obduracy.

There has, however, been very little 'logic' in the prejudice and suspicion which has settled that judgement on all Jews everywhere and poisoned Christian attitudes towards Jews for centuries. When Isaac spoke to Pope John he reminded him that the official position of the Church, according to the teaching of the Council of Trent, was that it was 'our sins', not the Jewish people, which were responsible for the death of Jesus.[6] The belief that the Jews as a whole were responsible – and were therefore *deicides* – originated with the second-century theologian Melito of Sardis, whose poetic and allusive text is blunt in its supersessionism: 'old is the law, new is the word, temporary the model, but eternal the grace.'[7] Two hundred years later this anti-Jewish polemic was expressed much more forcibly by John Chrysostom. The target of his *Discourses against the Jews* was the 'Judaising disease' affecting the Christian community. Thus he roundly denounces those who think the synagogue a holy place. 'This is the reason above all others why I hate the synagogue and abhor it. They have the prophets but do not believe them; they have the sacred writings but reject their sacred witness – and this is the mark of men guilty of the greatest outrage.'[8] It is something of a relief to get to the more measured tones of Augustine for whom Jews were no threat but an exhausted force summed up in the image of the 'wandering

---

[5] See Richard Fenn, *Dreams of Glory: The Sources of Apocalyptic Terror* (Aldershot: Ashgate, 2006), pp. 133 ff.

[6] See Herbert Vorgrimler, *Commentary on the Documents of Vatican II*, vol. iii (London: Burns & Oates, 1979), pp. 2–4.

[7] See S. G. Hall (ed.), *Melito of Sardis: On Pascha and Fragments* (Oxford University Press, 1979). His poetic and allusive text is clear in its supersessionism: 'old is the law, new is the word, temporary the model, but eternal the grace'. See summary in Graham Keith, *Hated Without a Cause? A Survey of Anti-Semitism* (Carlisle: Paternoster Press, 1997), pp. 100–2.

[8] *Discourse 1.5.2*. Quoted in Franklin T. Harkins, 'Unwitting Witnesses', in Brian Brown, John Doody and Kim Paffenroth (eds.), *Augustine and World Religions* (Lanham, Md.: Lexington, 2008), pp. 44–5.

Jew'. When he wrote his mighty theological survey of the history of the temporal city, Augustine referred to the Jews scattered throughout the diaspora as witnessing to God's judgement.[9] It is a sort of anti-theology. His point is not that Jews continue to enjoy some privileged and independent relationship with God. Rather, the Law and the Prophets that continue to guide their lives are proof of the central claim of Christian faith, that Christ is the authentic fulfilment of the Covenant. Some of Augustine's followers, most notoriously Fulgentius of Ruspe, took a much harder line with regard to the possibility of 'salvation outside the Church'.[10] But, as Harkins concludes his detailed survey of early Christian anti-Judaism, 'Augustine's doctrine of the Jews as unwitting witnesses to the truth of Christianity remained the most powerful and pervasive influence on Catholic thought and piety in the Middle Ages and beyond'.[11]

Just occasionally one finds signs that Jewish objections to Christian belief were treated with something approaching respect. St Anselm's *Cur Deus Homo*, for instance, was not written with Jews in mind but recognises that Jewish objections to the Incarnation have to be treated with intellectual seriousness.[12] Even Luther's early work was accommodating towards the Jews; the reformers' call for a return to the scriptural sources that had been obscured by a corrupt Church raised the possibility of an end to a long period of demonisation when Jews were ranked with Muslims as apostates and renegades. His tone changed later when, like some latter-day Chrysostom, he realised that Jews posed not just an economic and political threat to the new Protestant order; they were also to be feared on religious grounds for their subtle subversions of Christian faith.[13] Accused of a 'blood libel', that they murdered Christian children for the baking of the Passover bread, Jews were often in danger of expulsion. They were not always persecuted; indeed, there were long periods of tolerance and even prosperity.[14] Nevertheless, the prevailing attitude was a deep-seated antagonism that could all too easily spill over into actual violence. At best, Jews were

---

[9] 'If today they are dispersed over almost all the world, amongst almost all the nations, this is part of the providence of the one true God, whose purpose is that when in any place the images of the false gods are overthrown ... it may be proved that this was prophesied long ago; so that when this is read of in our Christian Scriptures there may be no ground for believing it a Christian invention.' St Augustine, *The City of God*, IV, 31, trans. Henry Bettenson (Harmondsworth: Penguin, 1972), p. 178.

[10] See Francis A. Sullivan, *Salvation Outside the Church: Tracing the History of the Catholic Response* (London: Chapman, 1992), pp. 39–43.

[11] Harkins, 'Unwitting Witnesses', p. 61.

[12] See Richard Southern, *St Anselm: A Portrait in a Landscape* (Cambridge University Press 1999), pp. 198–202.

[13] See Michael A. Mullett, *Martin Luther* (London: Routledge, 2004), pp. 235 ff.

[14] Keith, *Hated without a Cause?*, p. 115.

needed rather than wanted, tolerated but not respected, useful for the tasks they performed for the wider community but resented for their separateness and determination to remain different. At worst, it was all too easy for a gut-level invective to reassert itself and for Jews to be made scapegoats for the troubles of society, easy targets for revenge in troubled times.

The extent to which the Shoah fits into the melancholy history of European anti-Semitism and, more specifically, Christian anti-Judaism, is still hotly debated.[15] The Shoah took place in the middle of the secular twentieth century, and was the direct result of the racist policies of a modern, neo-pagan state. Nevertheless, without that climate of suspicion that had looked on Jews as stubborn outsiders and therefore a threat to the integrity of society, the anti-Jewish prejudice that led to genocide could not have taken hold. At the beginning of his history of the Holocaust, Martin Gilbert describes the four-tiered social structure of Eastern Europe where at the beginning of the twentieth century anti-Semitism was most deeply ingrained. At the top were Polish-speaking Catholics, followed by Ukrainian Orthodox; next were the *Volksdeutsch*, ethnic Germans, descendants of Protestant farmers; finally the Jew, 'eking out an existence as a pedlar or merchant'. 'No social mobility existed across these four divides. By profession, by language and by religion, the gulfs were unbridgeable.'[16] But whereas the first three had the advantage of being associated with some outside power for protection and support, the Jew had 'no such avenue of redress, no expectation of an outside champion'. After the First World War, with the destruction of the great empires that had dominated Eastern Europe and the emergence of new nation states, substantial Jewish minorities found themselves more and more isolated. Ancient prejudices very

---

[15] The Shoah was unique in the sense that it has a particular history that is not replicated elsewhere. But, despite the scale of a state-sponsored policy of extermination, it cannot easily be separated from a wider history of oppression of minority groups which gave rise, after the Second World War, to the term genocide as 'the planned and co-ordinated annihilation of a national, religious, or racial group'. See Arthur Grenke, *God, Greed and Genocide: The Holocaust through the Centuries* (Washington, DC: New Academic Publishing, 2005), p. 4 referring to Raphael Lemkin, who first coined the term that found formal expression in the 1948 UN Convention. For a detailed account of twentieth-century genocides, from 'An Armenian Prelude' to the Bosnian War, see Eric D. Weitz, *A Century of Genocide: Utopias of Race and Nation* (Princeton, NJ: Princeton University Press, 2003). See also Samuel Totten, William S. Parsons and Israel W. Charny (eds.), *Century of Genocide: Eyewitness Accounts and Critical Views* (New York and London: Garland, 1997). On the Church's complicity with the Nazi persecution, see Susannah Heschel's detailed account of the Jena 'Institute for the Study and Eradication of Jewish Influence on German Church Life', which shows how Nazi racist ideology had not just infiltrated much of the German Protestant Church in the 1930s but had succeeded in inventing a 'dejudaised' theology based on the argument that Jesus was 'not a Jew but rather had sought the destruction of Judaism'. Heschel, *The Aryan Jesus: Christian Theologians and the Bible in Nazi Germany* (Princeton, NJ: Princeton University Press, 2008), especially pp. 26 ff.

[16] Gilbert, *The Holocaust*, p. 21.

quickly returned, often – as Gilbert reports – with murderous results 'on a scale unheard of in the previous century'.[17]

In an earlier chapter, I concluded that the seeds of totalitarian ideology take hold whenever the desire to preserve the self takes precedence over the ethically informed and imaginative contemplation of difference. The other becomes too much to bear – and the nearest enemy becomes the scapegoat that will preserve the status quo. To invoke Buber's terminology, Jews have been turned into an 'It', made subject to a specifically Christian purpose: an 'orientation' that is no longer open to a 'realisation'. Rosenzweig himself would remind us that the labour of translation, universalising a particular language, is never complete in time; transcendence can never be totalised into a system. If that is correct, then it is the desire for premature resolution that is the problem, substituting the easy repetition of a single overarching narrative for what is always a complex and incomplete story of remembrance and retrieval. To put it in the terms noted earlier, the comprehensive account of reality for which religions strive must always somehow find ways of allowing for the other. The relationship between Christianity and Judaism exemplifies that problem as no other. Christians will always want to universalise their experience of Christ, for therein is contained a truth that is for all people and that challenges all manner of petty tribalism. In doing so, however, they run the risk of a triumphalist supersession. Jews, on the other hand, will always be concerned to preserve the truth manifested in the gift of Torah, to keep faith with a covenant formed with this particular people. The risk there is that in seeking to keep that memory alive Jews close themselves off and withdraw into a culture characterised by a strong sense of separatism and difference. When supersession and secession come too close it is usually a recipe for disaster.

It does not follow, however, that the only way to avoid some Judaeo-Christian version of the 'clash of civilisations' is to bury differences in a facile universalism. Jonathan Sacks, adding a distinctively Jewish voice to the debate about public reason, argues persuasively that the conviction that there is only one truth for all peoples at all times is a few short steps from totalitarianism – the imposition of an artificial unity on a 'divinely created diversity'.[18] When Sacks commends the 'dignity of difference' he is not expressing a sort of truculent nonconformity or demanding special treatment for Judaism. On the contrary, he feels that Judaism has an important contribution to make to

---

[17] *Ibid.*, p. 22.
[18] Jonathan Sacks, *The Dignity of Difference: How to Avoid the Clash of Civilizations*, 2nd edn. (London: Continuum, 2003), p. 52.

the public sphere.[19] He is insisting that there is a Jewish wisdom, learned from the experience of centuries, which seeks to maintain its own memories and traditions while yet engaging with the best of Western philosophy and culture. This peculiarly biblical wisdom reverses the normal order of reasoning, from the particular to the universal, by setting the experience of one particular individual, the patriarch Abraham, in the wider context of God's creative purposes. This, says Sacks, is what makes Judaism a 'particularist monotheism', commending faith in the oneness of God but not demanding one exclusive path for all. For the Jewish people the example of covenantal loyalty and responsibility for the other is their way of commending the value of difference. Each tradition has its own difference and particular virtues for living out a similar 'generosity of spirit' and commending it to others.[20]

The biblical story tells of God's commitment to a people from whom God's blessing is to be extended to 'the nations' – what Gerald O'Collins neatly refers to as 'God's other peoples'.[21] Bringing them into a correlation builds what (with a nod in the direction of Emmanuel Levinas) I am calling a 'first theology'. This is not an account of how two different 'religions' can somehow be said to share the same theological space but – more profoundly – an attempt to speak about *God's own story*, what God seeks to reveal about Godself. Rosenzweig's instinct, to hold together the two traditions as 'eternal truth' and 'eternal way', is persuasive, at least to this extent: that there is something about Jewish faith which is intrinsic to Christian faith and which cannot be erased without doing damage to both. However, not even Rosenzweig got it completely right. For him, Judaism and Christianity were the only realistic religious choices for the modern age. That idea seems decidedly quaint in a globalised world. It is not, therefore, difficult to sympathise with Alan Race's argument that the Rosenzweigian demand to read all interreligious relations through the 'Jewish–Christian filter' be set aside in favour of the common ground shared between Christianity and all other religious traditions.[22] What such a proposal leaves out of account, of course, is the recent retrieval by Christians of a sense of the *living tradition* of Judaism. The theory of the sad 'wandering Jew' may now be mercifully consigned to history. But Augustine's instinct, which refuses to regard the

[19] See also Sacks' more political writing on interreligious relations in the UK, including *Faith in the Future* (London: Darton, Longman and Todd, 1995) and *The Home We Build Together: Recreating Society* (London: Continuum, 2007).

[20] Sacks, *Dignity of Difference*, pp. 45–66.

[21] The subtitle of Gerald O'Collins, *Salvation for All: God's Other Peoples* (Oxford University Press, 2008).

[22] Alan Race, *Interfaith Encounter: The Twin Tracks of Theology and Dialogue* (London: SCM, 2001), especially pp. 43–64.

Jews as a mere irritating irrelevance, must now be put in more positive terms. In just three Latin words, *Nostra Aetate* makes plain that the Jews 'still remain very dear to God'.[23] These are the people from whom Christians receive the promises that are inscribed in that strangely compelling set of texts that they call the Old Testament and with whom they continue to share in the blessing that God pronounces on all humankind.

The question, however, is not how to read these texts alongside those of other traditions (whether Buddhist *sutras* or the more closely related material in the Quran); that is a further issue to which I will return. More immediately it is about how to generate from the growing familiarity of the interpersonal dialogue between Christians and Jews the virtues of engagement that will inform all our interreligious learning. 'First theology' is prior in the obvious sense that all Christian reflection begins with the pages of the biblical text, a Jewish text. That priority, however, is never purely temporal; as Taylor shows, social theory and social imaginary are related in complex ways. The project of an interreligious learning that is correctly sensitive to the variety of religious traditions as well as faithful to its own vision of divine truth calls for a spirituality of dialogue as much as a theology of religions. The former, I have argued, can be understood through the metaphor of translation. But the latter – the exercise of an 'interreligious intellect', to paraphrase Rowan Williams – also makes demands upon the would-be translator. In what follows in this series of 'crossings' I want to open up another complementary metaphor, Rosenzweig's 'readiness for everything'. How – to simplify somewhat – to ensure that such readiness is based in the theological virtue of hope and not the temptation to come to premature judgement over the other?

MAKING REMEMBRANCE

To address that question I want to repeat a point made at the end of the previous chapter – that to the various virtues of dialogue, from humility to hospitality, should be added a sensitivity to the ethical and political dimensions of any relationship. This I want to argue is intrinsic to the nature of the dialogical relationship and it is precisely this value that Christians go on learning from their relationship with the Jewish people. In so far as Jews and Christians share the biblical traditions of ancient Israel, they learn together how to respond to the great Deuteronomic call to remember that they were once slaves and therefore must care for the widow, the orphan and the

---

[23] '*adhuc carissimi manent . . .*'. *Nostra Aetate*, 4.

stranger. As a school of faith that has recently faced up to their complicity in the Shoah, Christians can now listen to the voice of the living tradition of Judaism and mend the memories that have for so long generated only jealousy and suspicion. For if there is one quality which characterises that tradition it is the fierce determination that nothing should be forgotten, that remembrance of those who have sought to remain faithful should continue to flourish despite the pogroms and the persecution. Such resilience, and the virtues of patience and perseverance that it breeds, turn out to be just as important for the sense of self as the 'content' of faith – for without the act of remembrance there would be nothing worth remembering. A story told by the Kazimierz-born journalist Rafael Scharf illustrates the point better than any tale of the Shoah that I know.[24]

Scharf himself escaped the Shoah by emigrating to England in 1938. He worked as a journalist writing on Polish-Jewish affairs until his death in 2003. During the war he served in the British Army and in 1945 returned to his native land as part of a war crimes investigation unit. Arriving in Warsaw he checked into a hotel and there in the lobby met an old school friend. They started talking about the old times and their reminiscence turned to a particularly influential teacher, Benzion Rapaport. Although he was deeply learned in biblical studies, Scharf tells us that it was Rapaport's after-class conversations that most impressed his pupils – occasions for pondering broad questions about God, faith and human responsibility. The teacher clearly had an amazing ability to relate to awkward teenagers. Scharf was made aware of the dangers of a 'facile faith' – but also of a 'facile rejection'. 'You can be an unbeliever', he was told, 'an iconoclast, an agnostic, if you wish. But, please, not a shallow one. In both cases it is the shallowness which is unworthy.'

As they are swapping information about mutual friends, Scharf notices an old man hovering on the edge of their conversation. He comes up to them and asks, 'You are Jews?' 'Indeed we are,' they reply. Then, taking from his pocket a bundle of papers, pages from an exercise book, covered in faded Hebrew handwriting, the old man places it carefully in their hands. With it there is a scrap of paper, written in Polish. 'Pious soul,' it says, 'this is a man's life. Give it into good hands.' They look at the manuscript and to their amazement recognise the handwriting of Benzion Rapaport. It would appear that he had thrown the manuscript out of the train taking him to the death camp at Belzec. The man standing in front of them had picked it up from a field and kept it safe, waiting to find Jews to whom he could entrust it.

[24] Rafael F. Scharf, *Poland, What Do I Have To Do With Thee ... Essays Without Prejudice* (Cracow: Fundacja Judaica, 1999), pp. 162–5, originally published in *Judaism Today*, 1 (spring 1995).

And what is the text all about? Scharf concludes this tale of an extraordinary coincidence by telling us that it was eventually published in Israel. Entitled 'Nature and Spirit' it is a collection of essays not on biblical studies, not on Judaism, but on 'the glories of German philosophy, Kant, Hegel and Schopenhauer'. Scharf finishes: 'The pity, the horror and the irony of it all . . .'

Remembrance, Scharf seems to be telling us, is not just a respectful nod in the direction of the life that is past. It is the very stuff of life itself. Memory is that most mysterious of human faculties, yet it is also what makes us most human, enabling us to form narratives out of the otherwise chaotic messiness of our hopes and fears, our emotions and yearnings. In discussing the nature of religion, I noted earlier that there is something in all of us that wants to understand, to find meaning, to make sense even of the darkness. We do it through constructing, and reconstructing, sacred places. We do it by making images and artefacts – and the simple act of piecing back together broken inscriptions. We do it through preserving records from the past – and faithfully keeping the precious trust of strangers. We do it through theology and philosophy, works of mind and intellect and generous writing that honours great thinkers. But most obviously we do it by telling stories. According to Paul Ricoeur, 'We tell stories because in the last analysis, human lives need and merit being narrated. . . . The whole history of suffering cries out for vengeance and calls for narration.'[25] The act of narration is more than an artistic imitation of the past that enables us to structure our memories; it is also an act of justice, in which human beings make themselves accountable to the past and find justification for present action. We tell stories not just to rehearse ancient truths that somehow edify and console but to find ways of structuring and giving purpose to our lives.

Scharf's story is not, therefore, a moral tale about the fate of oppressors or the tragic demise of the great hero but a simple account of the most powerful of all desires, the instinct of the survivor, the determination that something somehow is kept alive to tell the tale. At the moment of final dereliction a condemned man entrusts the record of his life to fate – and a chance encounter ensures it ends up in 'good hands'. The bundle of papers becomes symbolic not just of a 'man's life' but of a whole culture of survival that places the element of irony – the ignorance of those who claim to understand – in sharp relief. Rapoport's writings are the more valuable for the extraordinary story of their near miraculous preservation. They light up an otherwise dark landscape and stand witness to one man's fight to avoid an 'unworthy shallowness'.

[25] Paul Ricoeur, *Time and Narrative*, vol. i (University of Chicago Press, 1984), p. 75.

KEEPING MEMORY

Keeping faith with the past is an act of justice; the simple determination that the best of what human beings have lived and taught is not to be thoughtlessly tidied away – as might have happened to the broken tombstones that now adorn the walls of the Remuh synagogue. The challenge of interreligious learning is never about drawing a line under the past and thinking the future afresh; it is about rereading the past in order to bathe the future in a new light. At this point I begin to anticipate the theme of the third part of this book, what I have called 'Imaginings'. A more contemporary version of the creative dialogue between Apostolic Christianity and other religious cultures will form the backdrop for those chapters. There sacred, and not so sacred, places – and the conversations, memories and stories which they evoke – will occupy us not as interesting examples of some generic interreligious wisdom but as experiences that prompt the religious imagination. Here, however, we are concerned more with an earlier stage of calling to mind and pondering a 'word', which, as Ricoeur would remind us, is other and beyond our powers of control.[26] It is this very otherness that demands justice and respect. Interreligious relations, if it is not to lapse into a genial shallowness, has an ethical and political dimension.

There is, therefore, more to be said about that act of crossing over the threshold that enables the individual to accomplish a personal 'translation'. In using that term I have tried to argue that the aim is not to effect an exact communication, or even to practise a more sophisticated inculturation that brings faith into a dynamic encounter with a whole world of customs and social practices. The aim is to make people 'translators', formed in the skills and principles that allow them creatively to move across boundaries, both the synchronic and the diachronic. Mending the memories of a painful history is as important as any more physical crossing into a strange place of worship. Negotiating any such threshold, however, takes time – and that means being prepared to wait on the other.

I have spoken about the religions as practices that enable people to mark and, therefore, in some sense, control the passage of time. Thus, the stories that we seek to tell, whether myths and fables, histories and novels, children's adventures and sober biographies, all reflect the human desire for significance and harmony. That the desire for control has its own dangers is clear. Just as religion can become a banal timekeeping mechanism, a routine

---

[26] See especially Paul Ricoeur, *Oneself as Another* (University of Chicago Press, 1992). See also Kearney, *Anatheism*, pp. 75–6.

that loses all power to challenge and confront, so our storytelling can be so focused on the resolution, whether the 'happy ending' of a romance or the restoration of justice in a great epic, that we forget that the real power of any story lies in the unfolding of the actual narrative. The best of stories are not the ones that are neatly plotted and predictable but those where the drive for order is modified by the twists of plot and character. Their retelling, perhaps over and over again, like the performance of a familiar Shakespeare tragedy, acts as a catharsis in which the darkest and most obscure emotions are touched. In this sense the stories we preserve do not just honour what is past but form the moral hinterland on which life in the present depends.

Both Christians and Jews live out of a whole set of stories, many of which they share as a common tradition. The challenge is to go on telling those stories *together*, without totalising or patronising the other. For Christians, one story – the life, death and resurrection of Jesus of Nazareth – forms the basis of the life of faith and acts as the interpretive key to all other stories. Jesus is the model and pattern of all Christian living; for, as the Epistle to the Colossians puts it, he is the 'image of the invisible God, the first born of all creation' (Col. 1:15). The Christian story can only be narrated through reference to the Incarnation of the Word in Jesus Christ as the decisive 'moment' of God's self-revelation. Yet Christians cannot claim some sort of exclusive property rights to Jesus or afford to ignore other forms of interpretation or, indeed, other stories that Jesus has inspired. In a later chapter I will seek to explore how he has entered deeply into the devotional and moral framework of some Eastern traditions. There I want to show that it is not the 'cosmic' nature of the firstborn of creation that is attractive to people of faith but the human story that invites imitation and devotion. In this chapter, however, I want to stay with something rather different and more immediate – a story that can only be narrated alongside another story as part of a greater whole, what I have called God's story.

Jesus was a Torah-observant Jew. He lived and died, as the Gospels bear witness, within the tradition of the Law and the Prophets, seeking to vindicate God's covenantal promises to his people. It follows, therefore, that Christians cannot express their faith, the 'conviction of meaning' that they find in Jesus, without reference to the world of the Bible. Christians share with Jews the same story of God's election of a people for himself. The same conviction runs through this story, or, to be more precise, a whole series of stories that gather together different traditions about Israel's encounter with God and that, through these same stories, seek to *go on narrating contemporary experience*. Moses, Isaiah, and Benzion Rapaport are all part of the same story of heroic remembrance and faithfulness that has formed not just Jewish but Christian faith as well. Yet to wander through the once vibrantly Jewish quarter of Kazimierz is to be reminded that, in crucial respects, this is not the same story. The very ease with which Christians read the Old Testament texts, 'translating' them, to use Rosenzweig's term, into another thought world, should give pause for thought. The same inherited symbolic forms and imagery, in all their diffuseness and complexity, are interpreted very differently. Where the first Christians spoke of Jesus as Messiah, Lord and Son of God, most Jews of the time saw him as no more than the rabbi of Galilee. In Jewish terms, Jesus was but one in the long line of prophets who have struggled to bring Israel back to Covenant fidelity. This is not to say that it is impossible for Christians to read the Hebrew scriptures, just that they are read against a very different cultural and historical background. Diarmuid MacCulloch's one-volume tour de force, *A History of Christianity*, is subtitled 'The First Three Thousand Years', cleverly making the point that the beginnings and endings of any historical narrative are never that easy to define. Christianity has a whole 'millennium of beginnings' – and not all of them are Jewish. Nor are we speaking of some finished project, let alone system of thought. Christianity does not begin in a stable in Bethlehem but with 'the Word' spoken by God into a world that is, at once, Jewish, Roman and Greek – and that is to become European, Indian, Chinese, American.[27] While the Incarnation is the unique and decisive moment of God's self-revelation, the continuing work of the Spirit of Christ means that the Church exists in and through a whole range of relationships and, so to speak, 'translations'.

What gives this ever-growing series of relationships a life of dialogue with so many 'others' coherence and integrity? Strangely, it is precisely the insistence on Jewish particularity and the 'dignity of difference' that has drawn attention to the rich inner resources of a tradition that goes on challenging a chastened Christianity to think in more ethical as well as theological terms about the nourishment it takes from its Jewish roots. In his lucid summary of a lifetime of Christian scholarship on the Old Testament, Walter Brueggemann notes the influence of Rosenzweig, Buber and Levinas in forming his dialogical reading of the text. It is not just work with Jewish scholars such as Jon Levenson, he says, that has sensitised their Christian colleagues to the dangers of supersessionist readings; Jewish personalist philosophy too has made its own distinctively Jewish contribution to an account of faith as a 'dialogic transaction that

---

[27] Diarmuid MacCulloch, *A History of Christianity* (London: Penguin, 2009), p. 20.

refuses closure'.[28] For Brueggemann, the Old Testament is not reducible to an essence or scheme or set of ideas. Rather, the texts in all their variety record the divine–human 'I–Thou' interactions in which God calls and God's partners in dialogue respond. While study of the Old Testament does not demand that Christians deny their own faith, it does mean recovering a sense of the intensely *Jewish* nature of the texts. Jews recognise that all readings are provisional – 'because there is always another text, always another commentary, always another rabbinic midrash that moves beyond any particular reading'.[29] There are a number of equally important partners with which God engages: Israel, the human person, the nations and creation itself. Brueggemann makes the point (in a manner that Buber, the 'mystic of the everyday', would have heartily approved) that the dialogical tension that these relationships generate affects and changes *all* partners – including God.[30] That tension comes not from any ambivalence in the texts but more exactly from a typically Jewish sensitivity to the very nature of 'the dialogical God'. If the God revealed in the burning bush (Exod. 3:14), who calls prophets to courageous service (Isa. 6:8) and promises to restore his wandering people (Hos. 14:4), is active, engaged and demanding, then that means God's action is itself unending and never brought to a conclusion. This is the reason why the ongoing tradition of Talmudic commentary on the written and oral Torah has always refused the kinds of settled interpretation that Christian theology, under the influence of Enlightenment rationalism, has instinctively preferred.

The Old Testament is less an obscure narrative that needs a bit of Christian clarity than the story of God's engagement with humankind that is narrated by a particular people. In learning to 'translate' that story, in dialogue with the Jewish school of faith, Christians need to attend to the terms of Rosenzweig's distinction between book and word, noted in the previous chapter. There is a particular skill or sensitivity involved in what Clooney calls the 'close reading' of religious texts, especially those that belong to another religious tradition. 'In this basic learning', he says,

---

[28] Walter Brueggemann, *An Unsettling God: The Heart of the Hebrew Bible* (Minneapolis, Minn.: Fortress, 2009), p. 9. Levinas's collection of writings on Judaism, *Difficult Freedom: Essays on Judaism* (Baltimore, Md.: Johns Hopkins University Press, 1990) is made up of short but densely worded reflections on the significance of a traditional Jewish faith for the wider world. It also contains one powerful critique of Christianity: 'On Loving the Torah More than God' (pp. 142–5). For both text and a theological commentary, see F. J. van Beeck, *Loving the Torah More than God? Towards a Catholic Appreciation of Judaism* (Chicago, Ill.: Loyola University Press, 1989). A more lengthy reflection on Jewish faith in a post-Shoah world, with a much more generous reference to Christianity, is found in 'A Religion for Adults', *Difficult Freedom*, pp. 11–23.

[29] Brueggemann, *An Unsettling God*, p. 6.   [30] See above, Chap. 5, n. 18.

'reading is intimate, an understanding that occurs in close proximity to the text, inevitably involving the reader intellectually and affectively in the text and its world.'[31] The meaning of the text, the theological truth to which it points, must be allowed to emerge without being dominated by some grand overarching hermeneutical principle. Christian approaches to the theology of religions often begin with a section on the Old Testament that maps out a different sort of tension, between exclusivist and universalist perspectives.[32] This is often intended as a preliminary to a 'history of salvation' approach to religious pluralism that seeks to make space for the other within the single narrative of God's providential purposes for humankind. Admirable in its intentions, it is nonetheless covertly supersessionist, reading as if the regrettably chauvinist instincts of the people of Israel are to be balanced by some latent openness to 'the nations'. Any sense that these are the life-giving scriptures of another religious community of faith with a life of their own gets lost. The 'tension', as Brueggemann points out, is more complex; God's story encompasses a number of dialogues and it is the skills and principles entailed in their narration that the Christian translator most needs to learn.

Brueggemann's sensitive handling of Old Testament texts shows how it is possible successfully to address the question that I raised at the end of Chapter 1 – how the 'comprehensive pattern' can make allowances for the other. There is no pattern or essence detectable behind the multiplicity of narratives, only those memories that the Passover Haggadah speaks about as the story of *this* people here and now. Such memories produce a whole variety of responses – praise and lamentation, soliloquy and meditation – which mix literary genres and insinuate unexpected and surprising moments into a whole that is never whole because never fully resolved. Even the grandest of all grand narratives, the creation story of Genesis, reveals traces of a mysterious other that disrupts the flow and excites genuine wonder at the unfolding of God's purposes. For this consoling vision of the creator God was written by a people in exile, lamenting over the course of events, pondering over the disaster of defeat – and needing to understand the meaning of what had happened to them. Powerful and evocative myths – the disobedience of

---

[31] Francis Clooney, 'Christian Readers, Hindu Words: Toward a Christian Commentary on Hindu Prayer', *Theology Digest*, 53.4 (2006), pp. 303–19. Quotation from p. 304.

[32] Jacques Dupuis, *Toward a Christian Theology of Religious Pluralism* (New York: Orbis, 1997), pp. 29 ff. See also Veli-Matti Karkainnen, *Introduction to the Theology of Religions* (Downers Grove, Ill.: IVP Academic Press, 2003), pp. 36–40. The much more detailed and nuanced account of the Old Testament material in O'Collins, *Salvation for All*, pp. 1–78 still manages to end up with a 'tension' between texts and more than a hint of supersessionism.

Adam, the fratricide of Cain, the hubris of the builders of the tower of Babel –
are juxtaposed with the more intimate and small-scale story of one particular
family and their descendants. The election of Israel, in other words, has a
particular purpose. This is not about bringing the redemption of the world in
any straightforward linear sense by working for some future universal fulfilment, but, more precisely, about how to be an example of the blessing and
restoration that is possible if the remnant of the people keeps faith with God.
Jonathan Sacks puts it like this: 'God, the creator of humanity, having made a
covenant with all humanity, then turned to one people and commands it to
be different, *teaching humanity to make space for difference. God may at times be
found in the human other, the one not like us.*'[33] This, of course, is God's story,
not a triumphalist account of a tribal god who is only interested in preserving
his privileged followers, but the story of God's struggle to get a people to
respond to the ethical and theological force of what Levinas calls the 'epiphany of the face'. Maybe this is the closest we can get to a single narrative in the
Bible: a story of how the seduction of the 'comprehensive pattern' is
constantly being subverted as space is found for the other. In other words,
at the heart of God's election is not some abstract and arbitrary identity that
sets the people of Israel apart, but one practised in ethical relationship with
others – an ethic of neighbourliness and responsibility that recognises the
'Thou' of God's Word revealed in everyday human relations. God's people
maintain their 'difference' not in terms of a theoretical account of God's
universal concern for 'the nations' but through a more practical sense of
responsibility towards the other.

THE WITNESS OF FAILURE

The paradox is that the problem of the comprehensive pattern that I noted
at the end of Chapter 1 needs the other to maintain its own integrity. The
process of interrogating, and being interrogated by, the stranger is never-
ending – which means, as Scharf's teacher might have said, always being
open to other ways of life and other sources of wisdom as well as different
ways of looking at the tried and familiar. Very often it is the very provocation of the other that breaks open the complacency of the fixed comprehensive pattern. Thus the strangeness of Jewish foundational texts, with all
their lacunae, questions and puzzles, must be given as much weight as the
'plain sense' of the dominating narrative. Something similar can, of course,

---

[33] Sacks, *Dignity of Difference*, p. 53.

be said for the reading of any text, familiar or unfamiliar; to be avoided is the imposition of some generalised pattern on sometimes intractable material. However, when Christians seek to engage with their primary other, more is at stake than a reading of the Old Testament that takes account of Jewish sensitivities. If Christians are serious about understanding this first and most fraught of all interreligious relationships then they have to enter into a world that is every bit as complex as any other set of historically instantiated 'cumulative traditions'. *Nostra Aetate* made no mention of the continuing validity of Jewish witness to Christians or the wider world, let alone any account of developing and growing tradition. It was left to the publication of the catechetical 'Notes' some twenty years later for the Church to acknowledge that 'a numerous Diaspora . . . allowed Israel to carry to the whole world a witness – often heroic – of its fidelity to the One God and to exalt Him in the presence of all the living'.[34] The point being made is that Christian catechesis cannot adequately speak of the Gospel message without taking into account both past *and present* Jewish tradition.

In recent years, thanks in no small measure to the Scriptural Reasoning movement, such typically Jewish practices of prayer and study as Talmudic commentary have become a familiar feature of the interreligious experience.[35] But it is not just the work of Jewish academics like Peter Ochs and Michael Signer, nor the popularity of Martin Buber's collection of tales of the Hasidim, which have made Jewish faith and spirituality better known. The formative scriptures of Jewish Torah are now read in a very different cultural context, one dominated by the walls of the Old City of Jerusalem and the rather less imposing structures of a tiny synagogue in the centre of a once overwhelmingly Jewish district in the Kazimierz quarter of Cracow. Clearly there is no single 'meaning' to this complexity, and no resolution

---

[34] 'Notes on the Correct Way to Present the Jews and Judaism in Preaching and Catechesis in the Roman Catholic Church', published by the Holy See's Commission for Religious Relations with the Jews, 24 June 1985. This document was preceded by another from the same Commission, 'Guidelines and Suggestions for Implementing the Conciliar Declaration *Nostra Aetate*', 1 Dec. 1974.

[35] For a theological overview of the practice of Scriptural Reasoning, see an edition of *Modern Theology*, 22.3 (July 2006), reprinted as David Ford and C. C. Pecknold (eds.), *The Promise of Scriptural Reasoning* (Oxford: Blackwell, 2006). See especially Steven Kepnes, 'A Handbook for Scriptural Reasoning', Nicholas Adams, 'Making Deep Reasonings Public' and Ben Quash, 'Heavenly Semantics: Some Literary-Critical Approaches to Scriptural Reasoning'. For an account of the 'remote background' to Scriptural Reasoning in the post-liberal theology of George Lindbeck and Hans Frei and the recovery by Peter Ochs of the pragmatist tradition of Charles Sanders Pierce, see C. C. Pecknold, *Transforming Postliberal Theology: George Lindbeck, Pragmatism and Scripture* (London: T & T Clark, 2005). For a symposium dedicated to the contribution of Ochs to biblical hermeneutics, see articles in *Modern Theology*, 24.3 (July 2008), especially Nicholas Adams, 'Reparative Reading' (pp. 447–58). For a continuing record of reflection on the theory and practice of Scriptural Reasoning, see the online *Journal of Scriptural Reasoning*. http://etext.virginia.edu/journals/ssr/.

that does it justice. And maybe that is the most important lesson for the would-be 'translator' of God's story from its Jewish to a more recognisably Christian form. Not everything can or should be said. To do so would be to collude in another form of 'unworthy shallowness'. It is obvious that without the Old it would be impossible to understand the New. More subtly, however, the lesson that Jews continue to teach Christians is that understanding comes not with the recitation of moral tales or absorbing myths and legends but with the constant effort to retrieve and absorb for the present moment the experience that led to the telling of stories in the first place. In other words, two communities of faith acknowledge significant areas of difference within a shared commitment to the act of listening for God's self-revealing Word wherever it is to be heard. Such learning is an end in itself, not a step towards mastery over the other, but a commitment to stay with the other, even in the confusions and misunderstanding that dialogue often entails. To listen for that Word demands a difficult and patient waiting, something that Jews and Christians need to learn together.

No Jewish commentator has spoken of the 'difficult freedom' of Judaism with the power of Emmanuel Levinas. Levinas readily concedes his debt to Rosenzweig; at the beginning of *Totality and Infinity* he says that the *Star* is 'too often present in this book to be cited'.[36] That may be saying something about his style of writing, which, as Derrida put it, is rather like the ceaseless repetitions of waves lapping upon the shore.[37] But it is also a reference to Rosenzweig's 'new thinking' and his concern to invite the reader into an engagement with the voice behind the text. For Levinas, the human person is constituted by the summons to take responsibility before the face of the other. Throughout the essays and broadcasts collected as *Difficult Freedom* he reflects on the prophetic vocation of the Jew. In the aftermath of the Shoah the particularity of Jewish identity becomes clearer – but also its universality. Jewish monotheism is not a version of some general sense of the numinous; on the contrary, it breaks with such conceptions; it has 'decharmed the world, contesting the notion that religions apparently evolved out of enthusiasm and the Sacred', and establishing a certain type of 'atheism'.[38] By this he does not mean the denial of God but, more subtly,

---

[36] Emmanuel Levinas, *Totality and Infinity* (Pittsburgh, Pa.: Duquesne University Press, 1969), p. 28.

[37] 'Return and repetition, always, of the same wave against the same shore, in which, however, as each return recapitulates itself, it also infinitely renews and enriches itself. Because of all these challenges to the commentator and the critic, *Totality and Infinity* is a work of art, and not a treatise.' Jacques Derrida, *Violence and Metaphysics* (University of Chicago Press, 1978), p. 312.

[38] Levinas, 'A Religion for Adults', *Difficult Freedom*, pp. 14–15.

the denial of a certain type of 'theism', a refusal to reduce God to abstraction. Rather, insists Levinas, to affirm a 'God unimaginable' and available only through justice – in my relation to the other. Clearly Levinas is not keen on any form of religion that gets too close to God – or allows God to get too close to human beings. If we are to be genuinely free and responsible human beings God too has to be free to 'keep his distance'; precisely, not to come so close that our humanity is swamped by feelings of the spiritual, the numinous or the sacred. Unlike Martin Buber, about whose mystical Hasidic leanings he is deeply suspicious, Levinas keeps his distance from any version of religion or spirituality that allows inner feelings to create a quasi-pantheistic notion of God. Levinas comes from a very different tradition, the austere intellectualism of the Lithuanian *mitnagdim*.[39] The religious experience of the faithful Torah-observant Jew is precisely *not* vested in any sort of mystical awareness; it is, rather, to be found in the conviction of being commanded *despite* any such 'inner' assurance.

Levinas's strictures on religious experience and, more particularly, his criticisms of what he sees as the infantilising effects of a faith based on an 'emotional communion' with an incarnate God, makes Levinas's Judaism quite difficult for Christians to appreciate. As Hilary Putnam puts it, 'If Christianity valorizes the moment when an individual feels the charismatic presence of the Saviour entering into his/her life, Judaism, as Levinas presents it, distrusts the charismatic.'[40] There are, of course, other interpretations of the Jewish tradition, but, if I stay briefly with Levinas here, it is only to face the challenge that he makes to Christian theology and, more specifically, to the project of interreligious learning. Clearly what Levinas wants to avoid is the tendency to make God the object of experience or to anchor the 'glory of God' in the 'said' – some formula of words. In attempting to follow Rosenzweig by translating 'Hebrew' into 'Greek', bringing Jewish insights into the mainstream of Western philosophy, he is convinced that there is something in the uncomfortable religion of Judaism that tends to get forgotten or ignored – and which the world badly needs. This I am tempted to sum up very inadequately in terms of what Levinas calls a 'liturgy of study', by which he means not just the never-ending daily response that obedience to Torah demands but more specifically the Talmudic commentary that was such an important part of his own

---

[39] The story of this austere tradition of 'opposers', staunch critics of Hasidic mysticism, which forms the religious background to Levinas's Jewish formation, is told in Salomon Malka, *Emmanuel Levinas: His Life and Legacy* (Pittsburgh, Pa.: Duquesne University Press, 2002), pp. 11–19.

[40] Hilary Putnam, *Cambridge Companion to Levinas* (Cambridge University Press: 2002), p. 46.

religious practice. To bring text and contemporary context into some sort of a correlation involves more than a drawing out of new meaning; it is, in some sense, a sacred act, an obedience to a command. In referring to Judaism as a 'religion for adults', his aim is not to proclaim a self-satisfied exclusivism but to bring a Jewish sensibility to bear upon philosophy and thus show how something of this 'austere doctrine' can be shown to apply to 'every reasonable being'. 'Like Jews' he says,

> Christians and Muslims know that if the beings of this world are the results of something, man ceases to be just a result and receives 'a dignity of cause', to use Thomas Aquinas's phrase, to the extent that he endures the actions of the cause, which is external par excellence, divine action. We all in fact maintain that human autonomy rests on a supreme heteronomy and that the force which produces such marvellous effects, the force which institutes force, the civilizing force, is called God.[41]

The relationship between 'human autonomy' and 'supreme heteronomy' is set very much within the framework of what are often referred to generically as 'prophetic religions'. In the next chapter I will be turning from Levinas's focus on exteriority to the 'mystical' schools of faith and the theme of interiority, which, as I shall try to show, generates the conditions under which reasonable beings can hear the 'civilising force' of the Word of God. What I have tried to show from this reflection on the theological significance of the living tradition of Judaism is that that 'comprehensive pattern' which is Christian faith is never finished but only ever completed in the process of encounter and discernment. In this important sense the 'Jewish matrix' – the Church's originating relationship with the people of the Old Testament – goes on nourishing Christian faith. Jews and Christians form different interpretative communities and therefore read the same stories differently, yet that difference stands within a coherence of tradition which is faithful to the conviction that God is constant; the Covenant that God makes is not revoked. It is not, therefore, a matter of setting one tradition against another, still less setting them alongside a plethora of other traditions, but accounting for and working with that originating life-giving encounter with God that can be traced back to Sinai and beyond.

I am not arguing that this matrix determines all other interreligious relations. The story told in the single narrative of the two Testaments is essentially God's story of creation *and* salvation, the unfolding of the mystery of God's engagement with the world. It is not that the Christian story finds itself emerging fully formed from the end of the Jewish story, as if

---

[41] Levinas, *Difficult Freedom*, p. 11.

that story has ceased suddenly to have any further relevance; it arises from the very middle of a tradition that has its own integrity and vitality of faith. Nor does Judaism provide a neat package of 'Jewish principles' that Christianity inherits, or prophetic utterances that Christianity fulfils. Something more profound is at stake. The Gospel says something new, about what God does and what God is like, yet – crucially – this story is continuous with that story which the biblical narrative *as a whole* seeks to recount. Learning how to live with the terms of this open-ended single-yet-complex story forms the basis for developing that sensitivity to the other which is demanded by responsible Christian living in a multi-faith world.

This takes me back in conclusion to Rafael Scharf and his teacher. This is a story with typically Jewish motifs – the instinct of the survivor, the determination to remember, the interest in broader culture. Yet it has a much more universal resonance. Not the least important lesson of recent Christian and Jewish responses to the Shoah is that it is precisely the determination to honour the *truth* of history that keeps all interreligious relations honest. The transformation of Christian-Jewish understanding in recent years shows what is possible when the past is faced with integrity and the determination to place each others' stories 'into good hands'. While it might make life easier if the legacy of violence and conflict could be conveniently forgotten by all parties, it would scarcely make for that healing of memories which is the *sine qua non* for justice, let alone mutual respect and inter-faith understanding. In dialogue with the *living and continuing* Jewish people Christians learn the most important lesson of all: how the 'inner moment' of the Mystery of Christ is to be set alongside or in relationship with other possible 'moments' of God's action. From this Christians begin to discern other possibilities that this 'Jewish matrix', with its instinctive sense of responsibility for the other, brings to fruition within their life of witness and discipleship. More needs to be said about these topics and I will return to them in a later chapter. For the moment, let the idea that Christian antagonism towards Jews is as much a failure to listen for the 'Thou' of God's Word as it is the result of some deep-seated psychological mechanism stand as sentinel over the work of crossing the boundaries of faith.

CHAPTER 7

Channelling desire

The Christian ashram of Śāntivanam – the 'grove of peace' – is situated on the banks of the Kauvery river some miles from the great temple city of Tiruchirappalli, in Tamil Nadu. Founded by two remarkable Frenchmen, Jules Monchanin and Henri le Saux in the early 1950s, it is now very much associated with the memory of Bede Griffiths, an extraordinary English monk who came to India, he said, to discover 'the other half of my soul'.[1] Bede started his Indian sojourn at the monastery of Kurusumala, now a thriving community practising the Syriac style of Christian monasticism, high in the hills above Kottayam in Kerala. With the death of Monchanin and the increasing absence of le Saux (or Swami Abhishiktananda, as he came to be known), Bede moved to Śāntivanam in 1968, remaining there for some twenty-five years until his death in 1993. Bede was everybody's favourite *guru* – a teacher who had experienced the depths of the divine mystery and had an uncanny ability to communicate the truth of that inner conviction to others. The embodiment of the great tradition of the Benedictine host, he made everyone welcome, from Western searchers on the fringes of the hippy trail to local Indian Catholics who came, more out of suspicion than enthusiasm, to find out what this strange man with his eccentric ideas about dialogue with Hinduism was doing to their faith.

Bede also knew how to be a guest. When I stayed at Śāntivanam years ago I accompanied him on a lengthy bus journey to the blessing of a new temple in a distant village. We arrived to an enthusiastic welcome. As the Brahmin priests processed around the temple and water that had been taken from various sacred rivers was poured over the *śikhara*, the spire which covered the central sanctuary, Bede sat in reverent attention. When eventually we retired to the house of one of the village elders for a meal and a welcome respite from the heat of the midday sun, Bede was given the place reserved for the chief guest. He was received as a *sannyasi*, honoured with all the

---

[1] For the biography of Griffiths, see Shirley du Boulay, *Beyond the Darkness* (London: Rider, 1998).

rituals that would have been accorded to a Hindu holy man. No distinctions were made about faith. Respect was offered and received on both sides. With his long white hair, lively piercing eyes and gracious manners he seemed at times like a misplaced relic of the Raj. But he was also thoroughly at home in his adopted land. To listen to his Christian commentary on the *Bhagavad Gita* on a balmy summer evening as the sun set over the river was to be taken into the depths of a very Indian mysticism.

'Ashramic spirituality', as it has come to be known, is very much associated with places like Śantivanam and with figures like Monchanin, Abhishikta-nanda and Bede.[2] An ashram, to be exact, is not the place but what goes on in the place. The Sanskrit word *aśrama* (literally, 'striving'[3]) has connotations that cover a whole variety of activities from yoga and religious instruction to music, study and painting. The dichotomy, noted earlier in this book, between religion as a 'spiritual' activity and the wider cultural context within which faith is rooted, is not one that the traditional ashrams of India would recognise. When Bede – a classically trained Christian theologian – sat expounding the *Gita* he was not trying to put some sort of Christian gloss or correction on to a 'foreign' text.[4] Rather he was fulfilling the duty of the *guru* or *acarya*, the leader of an ashram: instructing his disciples who come for wisdom. In this context religious affiliation is secondary. The *Gita* is

---

[2] The ashramic movement within Christian spirituality in India stretches back to the efforts of the brahmin convert Brahmabandhab Upadhyay at the end of the nineteenth century. See Julius Lipner and George Gispert Sauch (eds.), *The Writings of Brahmabandhab Upadhyaya, Including a Résumé of his Life and Thought* (Bangalore: United Theological College, 1992). Jules Monchanin, a priest of the diocese of Lyons, came to India in 1939 but his hopes of setting up a contemplative community in the Indian tradition had to wait until Henri le Saux, a Benedictine monk from Brittany, joined him in 1950. For background on Monchanin's life and thought, see J. G. Weber (ed.), *In Quest of the Absolute: The Life and Works of Jules Monchanin* (Kalamazoo, Mich.: Cistercian Publications, 1977) and Françoise Jacquin, *Jules Monchanin Prêtre* (Paris: Editions du Cerf, 1996). For the life of Henri le Saux, see Shirley du Boulay, *The Cave of the Heart* (New York: Orbis, 2005). His spiritual diary has been edited and translated by David Fleming and James Stuart: *Ascent to the Depth of the Heart: The Spiritual Diary (1948–1973) of Swami Abhishiktananda. A Selection* (Delhi: ISPCK: 1998). The Kurusumala Ashram dates back to the late 1950s and the efforts of Francis Mahieu and Bede Griffiths. See the first chapters of Griffiths, *Christian Ashram: Essays Towards a Hindu–Christian Dialogue* (London: Darton, Longman and Todd, 1966). One of the best known teachers and chroniclers of the movement is Vandana Mataji. See especially her *'Living with Hindus': Hindu–Christian Dialogues, My Experiences and Reflections* (Delhi: ISPCK, 1999) and an edited collection of essays: *Christian Ashrams: A Movement with a Future?* (Delhi: ISPCK, 1993). Some commentary in the context of the emergence of an Indian theology can be found in Robin Boyd, *An Introduction to Indian Christian Theology* (Delhi: ISPCK, 1994), pp. 280–310. See also Dominic Veliath (ed.), *Towards an Indian Christian Spirituality in a Pluralistic Context* (Bangalore: Dharmaram, 1993).

[3] The root is *śram*, meaning 'to make effort, to exert oneself (esp. in performing acts of austerity)'. Monier Williams Sanskrit–English dictionary, p. 1096.

[4] Talks published as *River of Compassion: A Christian Commentary on the* Bhagavad Gita (Warwick, NY: Amity House, 1987).

sometimes regarded as an *Upanishad*, a special or secret teaching. The manner of its reading, prayerfully and reverently, with care for the meaning of each word, and in company of an enlightened teacher, reflects its content: the story of the instruction by the god Krishna of the troubled young warrior Arjuna. It is a story from which every questioning reader can benefit – and I shall have more to say about it in a later chapter.[5]

Here, however, I am interested in ashramic spirituality less as a form of spiritual practice that leads to personal enlightenment than as a certain type of theological hospitality in which the dialogue with classical Hinduism and Buddhism is brought to bear upon the Christian theological imagination. The last two chapters took as their subject-matter the relationship between Jews and Christians. Despite being arguably the most fraught of all inter-religious encounters, it is also the closest for Christians – indeed, the 'primary relationship' that is intrinsic to Christian identity. I now turn to 'secondary relationships' – those with the great religions that are further removed from historical Christianity. I call them secondary, however, not because they sit less prominently in some putative interreligious pecking order but because they do not share the same theological history – and therefore do not have the same theological significance. In that sense, Judaism will always be a special case for Christians. Nevertheless, as noted earlier, all historically instantiated 'cumulative traditions' are also schools of faith which increasingly exist in dialogue with one another. History is always being made; perceptions change; theological significance begins to emerge. The great voyages of discovery, which led to the 'Oriental Renaissance' and the construction of Buddhism and Hinduism, produced plenty of interreligious engagement but not a lot of mutual understanding. That is beginning to change. Recent scholarly work and ever-growing interpersonal contacts between Christian, Hindu and Buddhist practitioners have turned incomprehension into mutual regard. The wisdom gained from such movements as ashramic spirituality is finding its way into the social imaginary that underpins interreligious learning.

In the first set of 'crossings' described in this section of the book, I have argued that 'translation' might serve as a metaphor for the interreligious spiritual life. This second set keeps that basic model but proposes an adaptation. There is clearly a practical continuity across all dialogues. As

---

[5] For Christian engagement with the text of the *Gita*, see essays collected in Catherine Cornille (ed.), *Song Divine: Christian Commentaries on the* Bhagavad Gita (Louvain, Peeters, 2006). For an example of a comparative reading that highlights specificities and difference, see Gavin Flood, 'Reading Christian Detachment Through the *Bhagavad Gita*', *ibid.*, pp. 9–22.

engagements with persons of faith, 'primary' and 'secondary' relations differ in degree, not in kind. To that extent the relative distance between Christians and Hindus (and, more particularly, Buddhists) demands not a more subtle method but a greater intensification or perseverance in the process of learning. What is less clear is the extent to which the Christian theist can ever successfully translate him or herself into a world with very different ideas of what makes for human flourishing and even of ultimate reality itself. This brings into sharp relief the questions raised in Chapter 1. What happens to faith when it becomes 'inter-faith'? What does the engagement with the religious other do to the sense of self? In the previous chapter I gave an account of the 'Jewish matrix', which emphasised its prophetic dimension, the 'word' disturbing the neatness and order of the 'book'. I will have occasion to revisit that theme later. In this chapter I want to take further this idea that sensitive reading, listening for the echoes and resonances within the text and beyond, opens up theological questions about religious formation, conversion and commitment, as well as personal growth in faith. I argue that 'translation' should remain the guiding meta-phor for interreligious learning, but that, where boundaries are either contested or unclear and the sense of self is put under strain, it needs to be complemented by another model – a version of Rosenzweig's strictures on programmatic thinking. 'The highest things', he says 'cannot be planned; for them readiness is everything.'[6] The enthusiasm of the trans-lator needs to be tempered by the patience that waits upon the action of Word and Spirit. This particular virtue, I suggest, is what can be learned from the engagement with the contemplative traditions of India. First, however, something more needs to be said about that troublesome word 'spirituality'.

SPIRITUALITY AND 'THE SPIRITUAL'

From the soothing psychobabble of popular paperbacks to the mystical classics of the great religious traditions, 'spirituality' offers a vast selection of ageless wisdom and accessible practices for the seriously committed and the spiritually searching alike. Yet it remains one of the more infuriatingly ill-defined concepts to have emerged from contemporary Western culture.[7] It

[6] Quoted in Hilary Putnam, *Jewish Philosophy as a Guide to Life* (Bloomington: Indiana University Press, 2008), p. 33.
[7] Not the least important aspect of this discussion is the relationship between spirituality and theology. See especially Mark A. McIntosh, *Mystical Theology: The Integrity of Spirituality and Theology* (Oxford: Blackwell, 1998), especially chap. 1. See also Philip Sheldrake, *Spirituality and Theology: Christian Living*

is often said that while religion is dying spirituality lives. Various studies of religious practice show consistently that while attendance at Church services is going down belief in 'God or some higher power' remains fairly constant.[8] Thus spirituality is made to represent the interior experiential dimension of religion, to be set against the exterior institutional side, the world of ritual, doctrine, law and commentary.

There is, of course, something in the distinction. Just 100 years ago William James talked about the 'second-hand religious life' of those who simply follow worn-out forms and formulae and contrasted it with the original inspiration in 'first-hand religious experience'.[9] However, while it makes sense to trace the modern obsession with subjectivity back to James's strictures, there is nothing new about the quest for personal renewal and first-hand experience. In Christianity, the 'subjective turn' is as old as Jesus's preaching of the imminence of the Kingdom.[10] Mark's version begins with indicatives that imply imperatives: 'The time is fulfilled and the Kingdom of God is at hand; repent and believe in the gospel' (Mark 1:14). The desert fathers took this call with a radical seriousness that led, of course, to the foundation of the great and enduring tradition of Christian monasticism. Solitaries lived in community, their inner prayer nourished by liturgical celebration and the meditative study of scripture. Such an intrinsically contemplative faith finds expression not just in monks like Cassian and Benedict but in theologians as different as Augustine in the Latin West and Gregory of Nyssa in the Greek-speaking East. What holds them all together is less an account of the appropriation of the truths of faith through personal experience than the conviction, which runs through all Christian theology, that the Word which through the action of the Sprit is addressed to each and every person is deeply transformative of human living. As the Epistle to the Hebrews puts it, 'the word of God is alive and active . . . piercing to the division of soul and spirit' (Heb. 4:12). Or, in the words of St Paul to the Corinthians, 'God has revealed to us through the Spirit. For the Spirit

---

and the Doctrine of God (London: Darton, Longman and Todd, 1998) and essays collected in Sheldrake (ed.), *The New SCM Dictionary of Christian Spirituality* (London: SCM, 2005), especially Philip Endean, 'Spirituality and Theology' (pp. 74–9). Specifically on the relationship between theology of religions and spirituality, see Michael Barnes, 'Theology of Religions', in Arthur Holder (ed.), *The Blackwell Companion to Christian Spirituality* (Oxford: Blackwell, 2005), pp. 401–16.

[8] See especially the study by Linda Woodhead and Paul Heelas, *The Spiritual Revolution: Why Religion is Giving Way to Spirituality* (Oxford: Blackwell, 2005).

[9] William James, *The Varieties of Religious Experience* (Harmondsworth: Penguin, 1982), pp. 6, 337.

[10] Jesus's saying, often quoted to support the interior quest, that 'the Kingdom of God is within you' (Luke 17.21), means more exactly 'among you' or 'in your midst' (*entos humon*), and catches something of the enigmatic, even paradoxical, nature of the Kingdom which demands attention to the 'signs of the times' (Matt. 16.3) if it is to bring about that change of heart which Jesus's preaching of the Kingdom demands.

searches everything, even the depths of God.' (1 Cor. 2:10) For Paul this does not result in a distinction between soul and body, still less spirit and matter. The contrast is between those who are 'spiritual', animated by God's own Spirit, and the 'unspiritual', those who remain conformed to the spirit of the world. It is not, therefore, that the former have become conscious of their inner selfhood while the latter have not. If anything, the opposite is the case. Rather than introducing us to an inner world of personalised feelings, the Spirit leads us away from self and into a life dominated by the other, by life in God. As St Basil of Caesarea puts it in his treatise on the Holy Spirit:

Even as bright and shining bodies, once touched by a ray of light falling on them, become even more glorious and themselves cast another light, so too souls that carry the Spirit, and are enlightened by the Spirit, become spiritual themselves and send forth grace upon others.[11]

This theme of life in the Spirit will form an important dimension of the third section of this book, when I move more explicitly to explore 'imaginings', the creative inspiration of that 'school of faith' that is Christianity at its best. I anticipate it here in order to rescue the term spirituality from its association with alternative therapies and the pursuit of 'inner' personal assurance.

At no point do any of the biblical or patristic writers speak of a set of practices, let alone texts, called 'spirituality'. In these first centuries of the Church's life, when the experience of persecution was giving way to a more personal ascetical witness of faith, religious practice is not intended to cultivate interior experience but to order the spiritual life within the sum total of all those relationships, human and divine, which make up the Church. I shall, therefore, seek to argue later that a spirituality of dialogue is to be based on those formative experiences of faith and 'inter-faith' that motivate and support the practice of interreligious learning at all levels. A 'school of schools' is 'spiritual' in so far as it becomes more sensitive to the guiding light of the Spirit, wherever that Spirit is discerned. Here the role of charismatic individuals is crucial. There have been plenty of 'spiritual virtuosi' (to use Weber's title) who have sought to ground religious belief in a person-ally realised sense of self. Indeed, I have chosen to begin this chapter with the example of three of them, the *gurus* of Śantivanam. However, what makes many individuals stand out from the crowd is not the intensity of their inner experience (though clearly in many cases that is a factor) but their ability to inspire others, to be great teachers, to relate 'the interior' to 'the exterior'. That is where the peculiar genius of Bede Griffiths lay.

---

[11] Basil of Caesarea, *On the Holy Spirit*, 9.23.

One version of Śantivanam regards it as a centre for the renewal of first-hand religious experience; the 'grove of peace' is precisely that – a place where the rhythms of life can be restored and priorities reassessed. Another – what I am commending here – is more attentive to the different dimensions of dialogue, 'common life' as much as 'religious experience'. It therefore values the holistic experience of formal liturgy and personal silence, study and teaching, and the practice of a sacred hospitality. Here the issue is not whether there are different dimensions of the spiritual life, but how in particular instances they work together. Even the freest and most eclectic of New Age movements combine meditative technologies with rituals and myths that structure their vision of the harmony of creation. It is too easy for distinctions to become dichotomies, for 'spirituality' to be reduced to discrete inner feelings and altered states of consciousness, and for interiority and exteriority to be separated as the 'private' and 'public' realms of human experience.

The 'translation of the self' is never a straightforward process. In response to my question about what happens to faith when it becomes 'inter-faith', various possibilities suggest themselves, from a very postmodern eclecticism to a personal sense of double belonging to a more discerning theological dialogue that enhances faith commitment rather than destroys it. Spirituality is conceived here as intimately bound up with issues of personal formation and growth in faith. This is not to privilege extraordinary experiences at the expense of the 'ordinariness' of everyday reality. But nor is it to sideline intellectual issues about the rationality and coherence of faith. On the contrary, spirituality – now a subject worthy of academic and theological study, as Philip Sheldrake notes – refers to 'the deepest values and meanings by which people seek to live'.[12] Such a broad definition has its problems, of course, but at least is proof against a version of 'the spiritual' that finds itself limited to the pursuit of some individualistic personal assurance, with little appreciation of the intellectual and social context within which the meaning-giving work of a particular religious language finds its origins. Spirituality, I want to argue, is an intrinsically dynamic process of maturation, to be defined not by some inner essence vested in the extraordinary but by its orientation towards particular ends, the fulfilling of the human need for meaning and value. In this way it may be possible to avoid some of the wilder excesses of the modern obsession with certain discrete feelings and find a more adequate way of linking interiority with wider social and political relations and the challenge made by the 'religious other'.

---

[12] Philip Sheldrake, *A Brief History of Spirituality* (Oxford: Blackwell, 2007), pp. 1–2.

SPIRITUALITY AND RELATIONALITY

In what follows I shall be taking the dialogue with Buddhism as my major focus for reflection – but not because Buddhism is synonymous with 'meditation' and the pursuit of personal enlightenment. On the contrary, I argue that Buddhist meditation, when set within the context of the Noble Eightfold Path, betrays a concern for the other from which all people of faith can learn. The point I want to make is that despite enormous differences in language and basic concepts both traditions approach the issue in similar ways: the asceticism of practice must lead to a more contemplative path in which waiting becomes a dominant theme. This is not, however, to insist on some programmatic resolution to the tensions experienced in different ways on all spiritual paths. In due course we will need to return to the lack of resolution and the theme of 'waiting' that have important implications for the practice of interreligious learning as a whole.

To introduce this discussion I turn first to the relational concept of spirituality to be found in the work of another great proponent of theological hospitality towards the religions of Asia, the Spanish-Indian theologian, Raimon Panikkar. Panikkar is highly critical of a theology that would see the religions primarily in intellectualist terms as systems of meaning. Rather, each religious tradition is based in a certain practical wisdom, a particular way of correlating certain unifying themes, concepts, images and symbols. For Panikkar, spirituality 'represents man's basic attitude *vis-à-vis* his ultimate end'.[13] In practice, as Panikkar expands his theme, this attitude takes three forms: ritual, devotion, and mysticism – a triad that originates in the Hindu *trimarga*, the three 'ways' or *yogas*, forms of spiritual exercise.[14] According to Panikkar, these practices support and give shape to the human values of obedience, love and knowledge respectively. Each is important to an integrated and mature religious life. The danger is that an emphasis on any one to the exclusion of the others can lead to an imbalance in practice and to a very limited understanding of ultimate reality. Panikkar argues that together they configure different ways of responding to the 'cosmotheandric mystery' of World, God and Man, to use Panikkar's wonderfully gnomic neologism.[15] This term gives some indication of his intention, to correlate three forms of

---

[13] Raimundo Panikkar, *The Trinity and the Religious Experience of Man* (New York and London: Orbis/Darton, Longman and Todd, 1973), p. vii.

[14] Panikkar, *ibid.*, pp. 9–40. The term 'spiritual exercise' I take from R. C. Zaehner's translation of *yoga*. See his edition of the *Bhagavad Gita* (Oxford University Press, 1966).

[15] Panikkar speaks about 'theandrism' in *Trinity*, pp. 71 ff.; later he talks about the 'cosmotheandric experience' in, for example, *The Cosmotheandric Experience: Emerging Religious Consciousness*

religious practice with the three persons of the Trinity. This is a plausible and stimulating thesis, though it does, of course, raise awkward questions. In what sense can a very particular religious construction like the *trimarga* of classical Hinduism, let alone the Christian doctrine of God, which is the Trinity, be made to support a universal theory of religion? Can such an idealist package do justice to the development of Christian doctrine which, as Rowan Williams points out, takes its rise from very particular historical circumstances?[16] Much of the comment that Panikkar's meditation has attracted acknowledges the rich scope of his thought while expressing reservations about its coherence as an account of the Trinitarian relations.[17]

Whether or not such structures are somehow definitive of reality as such is not my concern here.[18] What I find persuasive, and wish to pursue, is Panikkar's insight that spirituality as a basic human attitude understood in terms of a number of practices is intrinsically cross-religious. In his view, spirituality has a heuristic purpose: it supports the search for meaning by channelling human desires and longings. There is, of course, a danger that we turn desire into some rather abstract term for the human orientation towards ultimate reality. For Panikkar, human desires are rather more complex. Although he does not develop the point, the three forms, rooted in attitudes of obedience, love and knowledge, raise questions about what we value most and what we are prepared to sacrifice for the sake of some greater good. They pose profound and intractable dilemmas and choices; the tragedy of human living is that we desire so much and can have so little – or that we desire the wrong things and get caught into transactions and relationships that turn out to be profoundly destructive. More awkwardly, and most obviously, desires of their very nature lie at the level of inarticulate feelings and emotions; they can be notoriously disordered, ranging from the relatively harmless but often quite corrupting pursuit of little pleasures to the murderous intent to destroy whatever gets in the way of self-interest.

To invoke spirituality at this point seems to play into the hands of those who would take comfort in the escapism of funny feelings and inner self-absorption. But Panikkar has an important point to make. The various

---

(New York: Orbis, 1993). The resemblance between Panikkar's idea here and Rosenzweig's threefold vision of World, God and Humanity, brought into a relation spelt out in *Star of Redemption*, is striking. See Panikkar, *Cosmotheandric Experience*, p. 144.

[16] Rowan Williams, 'Trinity and Pluralism', in *On Christian Theology* (Oxford: Blackwell, 2000), pp. 167–80.

[17] The most comprehensive and thorough critique of Panikkar's thought to date is Jyri Komulainen, *An Emerging Cosmotheandric Religion? Panikkar's Pluralistic Theology of Religions* (Leiden: Brill, 2005).

[18] See Michael Barnes, *Theology and the Dialogue of Religions* (Cambridge University Press, 2002), chap. 8.

forms of spiritual practice – ritual, liturgy, devotion, meditative and contemplative prayer, not to mention more 'active' practices like social engagement and the struggle for justice – do not just address questions about meaning and the existence of God; they provide much more profoundly human means by which the need for a sense of purpose, for integrity and coherence can be touched and tasted. Whether we think in terms of devotees going to the Buddha, *Dharma* and *Sangha* for refuge or the first disciples following after Jesus, spirituality begins with a movement of searching and striving. The question then is how the traditional language of religion is to support and take forward the struggle to recognise and come to terms with our deepest desires. How are they to be channelled so that the individual is brought to full enlightenment (to use Buddhist terminology) or be helped to a deeper conversion to God (to use what I take to be a suitable Christian equivalent)? The resolution that I flagged up above, asceticism leading to a contemplative way, can be taken as a shorthand for a movement of faith from a very self-centred desire to achieve the goal to a much more 'other-centred' awareness that the goal is not to be 'achieved' at all. It is given.

FIXING THE STILL POINT

How does the concept of 'gift' make sense within a pragmatic tradition like Buddhism? Buddhism is usually regarded as a product of the 'renouncer culture', the *yogic* tradition that grew up in an uneasy symbiosis with the all-dominating sacrificial ritual of the Vedic tradition. *Yoga* comes from a Sanskrit root meaning 'to join' and gives us the English 'yoke'. It is applied to all sorts of spiritual striving by analogy with the physical action of joining or harnessing oxen to a cart. In principle, as Zaehner indicates, *yoga* is about personal integration or spiritual exercise and can be distinguished from particular metaphysical understandings of the goal.[19] Thus it is possible to speak of Jain *yoga* or Buddhist *yoga* or various types of Hindu *yoga*, each distinguished by different ways of talking about the nature of *moksha* or release. More specifically the term comes to refer to an inner pilgrimage, the exploration of that interiority that gives rise to a sense of the Eternal. For the renouncers, *yoga* amounts to an interiorisation of the external ritual through a series of physical and mental techniques, from posture to breath control. The aim is to achieve a certain sense of inward isolation that is sometimes referred to, in deliberate contrast with ecstasy, as *enstasy*, a sort of interior

[19] Zaehner, *Bhagavad Gita*, pp. 227 ff.

stillness. The term is usually ascribed to Mircea Eliade who coined it to contrast Eastern inwardness of focus with a more typically Western concern for an 'ecstatic' exteriority.[20] This is helpful, at least in so far as it emphasises the basic practice of concentrating on one thing, achieving what the texts call *ekagrata* or 'one-pointedness', a still point of concentration. According to the classical or 'eightfold' *yoga* attributed to Patañjali, this is the way to overcome the naturally wandering tendency of the mind.[21] The aim is to achieve that focus of attention that overcomes all cognitive and affective 'fluctuations of the mind'. As Gaspar Koelman sums up his detailed exegesis of the text, 'the *Patañjala Yoga* path of liberation aims at reinstating the pure spiritual Self. Our present human personality is only a blind and mechanical supposit [*sic*] masquerading as a genuine person, a kind of parasite thriving on the pure Self'.[22]

Koelman, another Christian theologian who spent his life engaged in a sensitive reading of Hindu texts, describes an ascetical technique in which the practice of 'one-pointedness' prepares body and mind to enter into a prayerful stillness. As a general yogic method it works as an effective technique for the overcoming of distractions and facilitating the development of a focused contemplation, the sort of practice of attention to the present moment that is to be found in various forms of Christian 'centering prayer'.[23] In other words, it can dispose the Christian meditator for prayer. Beyond that, however, when the focus of attention is no longer tradition-neutral, problems arise. It is one thing to adapt what are, in effect, introductory ascetical methods that betray a certain commonality across religious traditions; it is another to focus the attention on symbols, ideas and formulae that are more obviously tradition specific. I can, for instance, use physical means of regular relaxed breathing or formal posture and position to dispose myself for prayer. But I can hardly substitute Krishna for the name of Jesus or the *nembutsu* mantra for phrases from

---

[20] Enstasy or enstasis is Eliade's translation of *Samadhi*, the final stage of the classical *Raja* or *astanga* ('eight-limbed') yoga. See Mircea Eliade, *Yoga, Immortality and Freedom*, 2nd edn. (Princeton, NJ: Princeton University Press, 1969).

[21] The phrase with which the *Yoga Sutra* opens states that the aim is *cittavrttinirodha*, literally the 'destruction of the fluctuations of the mind'. See Eliade, *Yoga*, pp. 36 ff.

[22] Gaspar Koelman, *Patañjala Yoga* (Poona: Papal Athenaeum, 1970), p. 257.

[23] A 'movement' associated with the teaching of Thomas Keating. See, for example, *Intimacy with God: An Introduction to Centering Prayer* (New York: Crossroad, 2009). The *mantra* meditation taught by John Main fits roughly into the same category: a concentration on a word or prayer. He has been responsible for the growth of the World Community for Christian Meditation and for its regular international interreligious seminars. See Main, *Christian Meditation: The Gethsemani Talks* (New York, Continuum: 1998), originally published in *Cistercian Studies* (1976–8).

the psalms – not, at least, without enormous and somewhat dubious intellectual contortions.

Leaving such theological issues to one side for the moment, let me concentrate on the practical problem of achieving 'one-pointedness'. While it is possible to conceive of some 'points' as neutral, completely lacking in cognitive or affective connotations, this is not so obviously the case with the actual technique of narrowing the attention. A distinction within the broad yogic tradition, which includes both Hindu and Buddhist forms of meditation, is in order. Very roughly, two contrasting forms of practice may be noted. The classical pattern noted above can be described as 'non-directive'. The most obvious example is the practice of controlling the breathing. By concentrating on a regular rhythm the meditator develops a mood of deep inner relaxation. The primary experience, isolation from all external stimuli, is very much a consciousness of the 'pure spiritual Self', to use Koelman's phrase. Everything, including the meditator's individuality, is absorbed into the single focus of attention. This is the sort of experience described in the 'great sayings' of the *Upanishads*. The central truths of what came to dominate the Vedantic tradition of philosophy – based on the 'great sayings', enigmatic phrases such as 'I am Brahman' or 'That thou art' – are concerned to overcome all particular or sectarian accounts of release or enlightenment by developing an instinctively monistic vision. To use the two key terms of the *Upanishads*, *Atman*, the essence of self and individuality is identified with *Brahman*, the ground of all Being. This essentially is the sort of experience, the ultimate 'non-dualism' of God and the Self, with which Abhishiktananda struggled all his life.[24]

Buddhism, however, rejects this universalising identification. Its tradition of yogic practice is quite different because it sets a different value on the point of attention, and more particularly on the *method of achieving it*. The Buddhist appropriation of the yogic tradition involves the same sort of focused attention, but the meditator is guided not by the isolation of some 'inner essence' but by the development of the quality of what in the early Pali texts is called *samma sati*, usually translated as right mindfulness, a careful attention to the entire contents of consciousness. Where the classical form of *yoga* seeks to bring about an absorption or coalescence of the principles that underlie the person and the universe (on the grounds that ultimately there is no distinction between them), the aim of Buddhist *yoga* or spiritual practice is negative, in the sense that absorption into the focus is to be avoided. It is important to refrain from

---

[24] See especially Abhishiktananda, *Saccidananda: A Christian Approach to Advaitic Experience* (Delhi: ISPCK, 1974).

identifying with the object. The technique is to observe the object, whether it lacks any specific 'content' or is familiar and meaningful. In practice, the meditator does not seek one focus to the exclusion of others but by simply observing manages to become sensitised to the presence and influence of others. Often the immediate focus of attention has a much more dynamic quality, something that moves or changes as it is observed; for example, the breathing, a sound, a feeling, or a relationship with another person. In other words, the meditator attends to the present moment and allows what is experienced to take its own form. Unlike the yogic method of 'breath control', therefore, the Buddhist simply watches and notes what happens. The practice is not so much concerned with attending to outer experience of the world as such but with developing a lucid awareness of what can be said to *carry* that experience. Thus the Buddha says that it is through the body that one should contemplate the body, through the mind one should contemplate mind, through feelings one should contemplate feelings. 'In what is seen there should be what is seen; in what is heard only the heard; . . . in what is sensed only the sensed; in what is thought only the thought.'[25] Attention is paid to whatever is given, *as it is given*, in the present moment, the 'here and now'. The primary experience is not absorption but detachment, a willingness to observe the stimuli that coalesce around the 'still point'. To go back to the question with which this section began: no value is put on any particular experience. Everything is accepted just as it is given.

THE TEACHING OF MINDFULNESS

Why is the distinction between 'absorptive' and 'negative' forms of *yoga* significant? And what difference does it make to my account of spirituality as the channelling of desire? While the incorporation of the classical *Patañjala Yoga* into Christian meditation is, I suggest, problematic once one moves beyond the basic and uncontroversial matter of purely moral and *physical preparation*, I want to argue that Buddhist *yoga* opens up possibilities for an inner transformation that is not at odds with Christian faith. This is not to ignore some seriously difficult questions to be faced with regard to the Buddhist view of human personhood and the nature of ultimate reality; these I will discuss in the next chapter. Here, all I want to propose is that Buddhist mindfulness opens up important horizons for the project of interreligious learning.

---

[25] *Udana*, 1.10. Quoted in the edition and commentary on the *Satipatthana Sutta* by Nyanaponika Thera, *The Heart of Buddhist Meditation* (London: Rider, 1962), pp. 33–4.

It is important first to set the practice of mindfulness within the context of those pillars of Buddhist teaching – the Four Noble Truths and the Noble Eightfold Path – that are laid out in the Buddha's First Sermon.[26] It has often been said that the Buddha's teaching is best understood by analogy with medical practice. The First Noble Truth diagnoses the human condition in terms of suffering, impermanence and insubstantiality. The root of suffering is stated in the Second Noble Truth to be that 'thirst which reproduces re-existence and re-becoming, bound up with passionate greed'. The third truth identifies a cure – the unconditioned state of *Nirvana*, while the fourth truth prescribes the cure – the practices that make up the Noble Eightfold Path itself. These include elements that would not be out of place in the classical *Yoga*, such as right speech, right action, right livelihood and right concentration. Right mindfulness, however, is typically Buddhist: that lively attention to the myriad stimuli observed in the here and now.[27] There is something paradoxical here, of course: Buddhist 'one-pointedness' of concentration comes from opening up to stimuli, not by shutting them out and withdrawing into oneself. What makes this possible is another paradox – the insight behind the second noble truth which teaches that desire can only be overcome by desire itself, more exactly by *right* desire.

What makes desire right? Desires, as already noted, can be ambiguous. The word translated as 'thirst' in the Second Noble Truth means all forms of craving and desire, including the more subtle attachment to personal ideas, ideals and beliefs that may inhibit true freedom.[28] The descriptions of the cause of suffering vary considerably, from thirst and ignorance to the popular triad of greed, hatred and delusion. Even when directed towards Ultimate Reality, desire is suspect; for the capacity of human beings to fool themselves is enormous. The Zen tradition is full of instructive stories about the dangers of the misdirected zeal for enlightenment. 'How long will it take?' asks the eager pupil. 'Maybe ten years', says the master. 'But if I work really hard?' asks the pupil. 'Then it will probably take twenty years', comes the acid reply. The

---

[26] *Dhammcakkappavattana Sutta*, or 'setting in motion the wheel of truth', *Samyutta Nikaya*, LVI, 11.

[27] The major Pali text on the 'setting up of mindfulness' is the *Satipatthana Sutta*, *Majjhima Nikaya*, I. 55–63, with an expanded version *Mahasatipatthana Sutta*, *Digha Nikaya*, II. 305–15. There are also shorter treatments in other canonical Pali texts. See detailed commentary in Analayo, *Satipatthana: The Direct Path to Realization* (Birmingham: Windhorse Publications, 2003).

[28] The word in the Pali is *tanha* (Sanskrit *trsna*). Walpola Rahula renders it as 'desire, greed, craving' and then notes that 'it should not be taken as the first cause, for there is no cause possible as, according to Buddhism, everything is relative and interdependent.' Walpola Rahula, *What the Buddha Taught* (London: Gordon Frazer, 1967), p. 29.

Buddha was too wise to think that effort is enough. The sixth stage of the eightfold path, coming just before right mindfulness, is right striving – *samma vayama* in the Pali. Buddhism may commend a very particular form of yogic discipline, but it still insists on all sorts of practices that bring the senses and emotions under the yoke of the mind. Indeed, the *Vinaya*, the code of discipline of the monastic community or *sangha*, is a detailed elaboration of a way of life that is regarded as the *sine qua non* of enlightenment. The very last words of the Buddha are recorded as 'decay is inherent in all component things! Work out your salvation with diligence!'[29] This is not an invitation to ascetical self-absorption. If enlightenment is bound up with restraining the senses, then – as the Buddha points out – the deaf and the blind would be enlightened. There is an important wisdom here. Desire cannot be obliterated, ignored or eradicated; like any form of unfettered energy it can only be shaped or directed by ethical behaviour, by disciplined spiritual practice, and by careful and thoughtful discernment.

The wisdom of Buddhism teaches that true ascetical discipline has to acquire a contemplative quality. To put it another way, the practice of the prudential moral life and the physical practices of right posture and restraint of the senses go hand in hand with a discerning attitude to life in the world that learns *to see things as they really are*. All practice begins with right effort – here meaning mental energy and perseverance – which is not an end in itself but a necessary predisposition for the final stages of the Way. Effort is made 'right' by being tempered by mindfulness; mindfulness is made 'right' by being orientated towards concentration. And what makes concentration 'right' is the acquisition of certain qualities, the first of which is indifference or equanimity. The word used here, *upekkha* in the Pali, means something like 'looking on'.[30] It is the last stage before *Nirvana* that can be described. For *Nirvana*, of course, is beyond description. This is the fruit not just of right effort or right mindfulness but of the whole of the Noble Eightfold Path. It is built up through a complex meditative effort into a discriminating understanding of the phenomenal world, a detached objectivity. Eventually one learns to 'look on' with total awareness and clear comprehension, a complete lack of disturbance not just from all negative emotional states, such as anger and ill-will, but also from what may be considered more positive ones. Even emotions of joy and happiness impose their own

---

[29] *Mahaparinibbana Sutta, Digha Nikaya,* XVI. 156.
[30] 'Looking on, hedonic neutrality or indifference, zero point between joy and sorrow, disinteredness, neutral feeling, equanimity. Sometimes equivalent to *adukkham-asukha-vedana,* feeling which is neither pain nor pleasure'. *Pali–English Dictionary* (Pali Text Society), p. 150.

limitations and can act as distractions from the proper apprehension of the present moment.[31]

The ultimate soteriological value is given to a purified consciousness in which the mind has become freed from its dependence on all sensory objects – *and yet* sees them and values them for what they are. It does not follow, however, that 'ultimate reality' can only be grasped by a consciousness somehow 'different' from everyday awareness. On the contrary, the ordinary processes of cognition have to be purified from limitation and distraction so that the characteristics of reality are known with perfect clarity and equanimity. Whatever is good or bad, helpful or unhelpful does not disappear but is seen for what it is – a temporary state that cannot disturb an inner clarity of vision and purpose. Buddhist meditators who have practised the wisdom taught by the *Vipassana* (insight) or Zen schools speak of achieving a sense of heightened awareness that is still very much 'in touch' with everyday stimuli. Unlike the yogic consciousness, the Buddhist form has a distinctly 'this-worldly' or, following the comparative analysis described by William Johnston, 'incarnational' feel to it.[32]

WISDOM AND COMPASSION

This allows a certain dialogue with Christianity to take place and may explain why so many Christian monks and priests like Johnston have managed to practise Buddhist meditation so fruitfully.[33] Desires are to be channelled not controlled, discerned not destroyed. More importantly, perhaps, the desires that make us most human, from desires for sensual gratification all the way to that most sublime reaching out which takes us into the very depths of the divine, are all of a piece. Like Buddhism, Christianity begins with the relationship established between teacher and disciple. That willingness to be led, to be open to the *givenness* of a teaching, allows for growth and learning – for conversion or enlightenment. Following Panikkar, we

---

[31] See *Samaññaphala Sutta, Digha Nikaya*, II. 74.

[32] William Johnston, *Silent Music: The Science of Meditation* (London: Fontana-Collins, 1974), especially pp. 32 ff.

[33] The number of Jesuit priests living out of the Ignatian school of Christian spirituality who are also deeply committed to Zen practice is intriguing. The reflections of William Johnston on the practice of Zen retain their popularity. See especially *The Still Point* (New York: Harper and Row, 1970) and *Christian Zen* (Dublin: Gill and Macmillan, 1979). Other significant guides are Hugo Enomiya Lassalle, *Zen Meditation for Christians* (La Salle, Ill.; Open Court, 1974) and *The Practice of Zen Meditation* (Wellingborough: Aquarian, 1988). For writing with a more literary and poetic bent, see Robert Kennedy, *Zen Gifts for Christians* (New York: Continuum, 2000) and *Zen Spirit, Christian Spirit* (New York: Continuum, 2001). Writing out of an Indian experience of Zen is Ama Samy. See especially his *Zen: Waking to your Original Face* (Thiruvanmiyur, Chennai: Cre-A, 2005).

might call this the necessary 'basic attitude' towards our ultimate end. Panikkar talks about a triad of obedience, love and knowledge. In the eagerness to experience the last two the first is easily overlooked. Yet it is also the most difficult to get right. In the Ignatian tradition followed by Johnston and Enomiya, to be able to hear the revelation of God in Christ it is first necessary to gain the right disposition, an openness to what God may ask. Hence the demand that Christian living means learning a certain 'indifference' to all created things – meaning not that what God has given is to be ignored or demeaned, out of some misplaced sense of self-denial, but that all things are to be valued *precisely because God has given them for a purpose.*[34] They are there to be used wisely. Tangible things, like wealth, or the more illusory, such as power and fame: all excite human desire but not all are useful. Only through a careful, responsible attention to the value of things, and their significance in any particular situation, is it possible – to use the Buddhist term – to get it 'right'.

What such indifference or equanimity builds is very far from the narrow obsession with interior states discussed earlier. In fact, very much the opposite. Mindfulness of the present moment, as taught by the Buddha, develops a heightened awareness of the presence and value of material things. This may give a clue to the interaction of the two great Buddhist values of *praja* and *karuna*, wisdom and compassion. Buddhism is often misrepresented as a religion of stolid self-seeking – and there are no doubt plenty of versions of Buddhist practice that do, indeed, play into this caricature. Yet even in the ancient Theravada school, with its emphasis on enlightenment achieved through formal meditation and scholastic analysis, are to be found forms of meditative practice that are based on the development of qualities of loving kindness and compassion. The meditator can pick a variety of starting points for developing mindfulness, from death and decay to the qualities that give rise to enlightenment such as equanimity or loving kindness. If mindfulness genuinely is focused on the present moment and whatever is given in the present, then it soon becomes impossible to draw any distinction between this object and that, this quality and that, or, indeed, this person and that. Mindfulness builds from an attention to objects to an awareness of persons and their needs. To see things as they really are is to become sensitive to all sentient beings, building up the qualities of the *bodhisattva*, the saint who vows to work for the well-being and enlightenment of all people.

---

[34] See St Ignatius of Loyola, *The Spiritual Exercises*, especially Principle and Foundation, para. 23.

The commentary of the Theravadin scholar Walpola Rahula on the ox-herding pictures with which I began this book is concerned with the nature of enlightenment, how practice purifies the person and leads to that realisation of things as they really are. He does not, as I remarked earlier, bring us back to the life of the marketplace as the Mahayanists tend to do. Something seems to be lacking here, and certainly there are forms of Theravada practice that border on an arid intellectualism. In an earlier chapter, I noted how Aloysius Pieris in his own dialogue with Theravada Buddhism proposes that the Buddhist 'gnostic idiom' needs to be complemented by the 'agapeic idiom', which is typical of Christianity at its best. The question I have been discussing in this chapter is not about metaphysics; that is still to come. Here I have been concerned with Buddhist practice as a type of spirituality that is concerned primarily with human transformation and enlightenment. The Buddha himself in his famous answer to the inquisitive searcher Malunkyaputta insisted that he did not preach speculative truth. Like the good physician he did the one thing necessary – provide the cure for *this* person's needs now.[35] Such sage advice is reminiscent of Rosenzweig's attack on the absurdity of a philosophical pursuit of the 'essence of things'. Neither the Buddha nor the great Jewish philosopher is being awkwardly anti-philosophical. They just want to give practical or 'common sense' questions their proper place, restoring the humanity of the religious or philosophical search. Which takes us back to my opening point that spirituality is not about the cultivation of extraordinary states of consciousness but, more prosaically, about getting order into the confusion and chaos of life. The yogic tradition tells us to concentrate on one thing only; the Buddhist gloss on this is to commend a type of mindfulness of the present that learns to face reality – and the human relations that are its very heart – with equanimity.

What can the Buddhist gnostic idiom add to the Christian agapeic? The latter, of course, gives Christian prayer its specific quality of response to God's initiative. Love cannot be commanded, as if it is the necessary result of a mechanical process. It depends on the action of grace. In that sense, prayer is always the work of the Spirit. Hence Paul's conviction that since we do not know how to pray as we ought the Spirit prays in us, interceding 'with sighs too deep for words' (Rom. 8:26). In this sense, the Spirit does not just dispose the meditator to listen but more positively enables the Word of God to be heard and a response of faith to be made. This too is the work of

[35] Rahula, *What the Buddha Taught*, pp. 13–14.

the Spirit, forming in human beings that primary attitude of obedient faith which acknowledges that there is, indeed, an all-loving God whose desires for human beings exceed all that can be known or taught. I will return to this topic in my penultimate chapter. Here I am concerned with that experience of openness and equanimity which takes delight in the sheer givenness of things. The primary aim of Buddhist meditation is not the ruthless process of self-conquest, still less some single-minded quest for the *summum bonum* of Nirvana, but the cultivation of a quality of mindful attention to the present without which it is impossible to see things as they really are. This is why the great modern Burmese teacher of *Vipassana*, or insight meditation, S. N. Goenka, commends the Buddha's words, that mindfulness is the 'one and only way'.[36] This is not, he says, a sectarian claim but a 'law of nature': without an awareness that has penetrated to the very depths of one's being, understanding and, more particularly, change and growth are impossible. Christian meditators can learn from this practice that God is not to be encountered simply because that is what is desired – for 'God' all too easily becomes a projection of our unacknowledged desires. Christian prayer is always dependent on God's prior act of loving self-communication. The Buddha's reticence in speaking of Ultimate Reality is nothing if not a warning to Christians to listen to the Word, not to be seduced by 'mere words'. This is why the model of Christian prayer is the Lord's Prayer; not the 'heaping up' of empty phrases, but the act of humble submission that puts God first. The praise and thanks commended by Jesus, and the traditional prayer of the Church centred round the regular recitation of the Psalms and Canticles of the Bible, express that dependence on God. But so does the act of wordless contemplation that silently takes delight in the source of all things.

OPENNESS TO THE OTHER

This chapter has critiqued a version of spirituality as the pursuit of a certain type of interiority, with a fixation on the personal assurance of inner experience. I have argued instead for a different approach, one that takes its rise from the practice of a theological hospitality embodied in the lives of three sages of Śantivanam. Good Benedictine that he was, Bede Griffiths welcomed travellers and searchers to his ashram. The very practical openness and warmth he always showed them was born of a sensitivity to the

---

[36] S. N. Goenka, *Satipatthana Sutta Discourses* (Seattle, Wash.: Vipassana Research Publications, 1998), p. 96.

echoes and resonances of the one whom Christians refer to as the Spirit of Christ. And therein lies the real value of Buddhist mindfulness for Christians. Jesus preached the coming of the Kingdom, the imminent arrival of God's judgement and mercy. Paradoxically, the abundance of God's promise lies with the God who is revealed in the *here and now*, the present moment. The Gospel points not to some other-worldly reality, the life of a heavenly realm, but to the God-revealing power of the 'signs of the times'. It is this growth in sensitivity to what God is doing, to what the 'seeds of the Word' may well reveal of God's providential purposes in the world, which forms the virtues necessary for the searcher to become a *translator* and makes possible what I have called interreligious learning.

This work of translation, however, demands a certain healthy reticence that expects meaning to emerge but is prepared to wait patiently – for this is *God's* work. I started with an account of religion as the 'comprehensive pattern' of living that is supported by the practices of faith. My contention is that every religious community is formed or socialised by the traditions that make it a 'school', a centre of teaching and learning, committed not just to the passing on of memory and wisdom but to an engagement with the other that tempers the tendency to totalise and overwhelm. If it is true, as I have argued, that all human beings are guided by the 'conviction of meaning' and need some inner sense of the ultimate harmony of experience and the unity of things, then the crucial question is not about the crafting of some intellectually coherent theory but to do with the living out of a particular pattern of holiness in the context of a plurality of opinions. The former may be a necessary condition, but, without the latter, no theory can ever be sufficient to meet the demands of life in a secular and multi-faith society. Thus Hick is quite right to defend his pluralist hypothesis from the accusation of relativism by developing a theory of religious experience that brings different versions of religious phenomena into a correlation with the single overarching divine *noumenon*. Whether this makes sense philosophically is not my concern; I have noted my doubts earlier in the book. My interest lies elsewhere. What the normative pluralist thesis does not do is provide any support for the much more arduous business of living with the lack of finality while yet maintaining an integrity of religious commitment.

The skill of the translator is to be able to mediate between cultural wholes, to communicate truth from one to another – in that sense to practise an interreligious learning. Equally important, however, is the humility and patience that remains content with the impossibility of resolution. The experiment that European contemplatives began in the 'grove of peace' by the side of the Kauvery River has become emblematic of the move towards a contemplative inculturation of Christian faith in India. Latterly it has given way to forms of Dalit theology, with their overt commitment to justice for oppressed low caste tribes and peoples.[37] The two may seem far removed – mystic detachment and prophetic action pulling in opposite directions. Maybe, however, they should be seen as two sides of the same coin – what Pieris would call Christian 'gnostic agape' in practice. I have spoken of spirituality as the right channelling of desire. To get any serious action right takes time and patience; the more so when we are speaking of that generous response to God's Word which is the life of Christian discipleship. Christian spirituality, as I have described it in this chapter, has its own forms of asceticism and contemplative awareness that are intended to encourage careful discernment of the workings of God's Spirit. That Christian faith can be enhanced by practices which still the restless mind is clear. But it is not so obvious that all forms of Eastern meditation are equally valuable in tempering the movement of translation with a healthy reticence. Theological hospitality does not mean entertaining, still less translating, everything. For the Christian, interreligious learning is not a matter of developing a broader account of the interconnectedness of things. It is, rather, about sharpening a moral vision of a universe in which personal desires and feelings are made subject to the other – to God. In the next chapter I want to open up the issues that such a disconnect seems to raise. Staying with the dialogue with Buddhism, I want to raise a version of the question with which I began: what happens to the sense of self when desires are governed by the concept of 'no self'?

---

[37] The movements are tied together in Michael Barnes, 'From Ashrams to Dalits: The Four Seasons of Inculturation', *The Way* (Jan. 2001), pp. 61–71. The standard history of Dalit Christianity is John Webster, *The Dalit Christians: A History* (Delhi: ISPCK, 1992). For social and cultural background, see Michael Amaladoss, *Life in Freedom* (Anand: Gujarat Sahitya Prakash, 1997). For excellent commentary and comprehensive bibliography, see Peniel Rajkumar, *Dalit Theology and Dalit Liberation* (Farnham: Ashgate, 2010).

CHAPTER 8

Waiting on God

This chapter begins in an unlikely *zendo* – in a condominium in Jersey City, an unfashionable neighbourhood that lacks the glitz and naked power of downtown Manhattan on the other side of the Hudson river. The pace of life here is slower, the surroundings more prosaic, the religiosity less whacky. All the more intriguing to find in such an area a place dedicated to a traditional religious practice. Zen Buddhist centres can reflect the carefully cultivated simplicity of a Japanese garden or embody the wisdom reflected in masterpieces of calligraphy. To a great extent that is to do with atmosphere, with creating an aesthetic of place which provides the right conditions for meditation. This particular *zendo* is a bare room decorated with a few flowers, the odd joss stick and a large head of the Buddha standing on a table. Around the walls black mats and cushions are laid out. A temple gong stands ready to mark the periods of meditation. Only the view out the window and the sounds from off the street remind me that this is Main Street, USA.

A group of local people gather here early each morning to meditate in silence for a couple of hours. The basic form of the meditation follows a pattern set by the tradition of centuries, sitting meditation or *zazen*, broken by *kinhin* or walking meditation, and ending with the chanting of the *bodhisattva* vows in Japanese. Religiously the members of the group are mixed, but 'religious affiliation isn't an issue', I was told by one of them. What quickly becomes clear is that this is no religious hybrid, a pick 'n' mix affair for a few disaffected spiritual nomads. The practice is rooted firmly in the ritual and formalities of the Japanese Zen tradition. I will return to this theme at the end of the chapter, for, despite this cultural form (or maybe because of it), people from different faith traditions find something that, through the power of mindfulness, enables them to sharpen their individual commitments. I have been asking a question about interreligious learning, about how the sense of self grows through dialogue with the other. If, however, Christian life is about communicating a deeply felt truth – and not just contemplating it in some secure spiritual fastness – then any cross-religious practice, from study to conversation to meditation, must raise a further question. What does this say about God?

As a Christian I have practised simple forms of Zen meditation for years and have always been struck by how the combination of sitting and walking returns the incipient wandering of the mind to the everyday. No doubt that has something to do with the act of walking itself, which, as I argued earlier, is the most elementary practice by which a strange city is encountered and mapped on to consciousness. In Zen the practice of *kinhin* is designed to break the pent-up monotony of silent sitting and provoke that moment of inner awakening or *satori*. It often comes as a relief when the gong is gently struck, the meditators get up, bow reverently and process round the *zendo*. Aching knees are slowly unwound and the inner rhythms of the body find a different equilibrium. The same quality of pure attention to the present moment, the essence of all Buddhist meditation, is maintained through-out – but now it is the feeling of foot on floor that concentrates the mind. In this sense *kinhin* is a variation on a theme.

The Vietnamese Zen teacher Thich Nhat Hanh quotes a little story. 'The Buddha was asked, "What do you and your disciples practice?" and he replied, "We sit, we walk, and we eat." The questioner continued, "But sir, everyone sits, walks and eats." The Buddha told him, "When we sit, we know we are sitting. When we walk, we know we are walking. When we eat, we know we are eating."'[1] To see things as they really are, such is the aim of Zen. There is, however, something more, something that does not so much change the nature of mindful concentration but sets it in a different perspective. From focusing on breathing and the inner rhythms of the body, one becomes sensitised not just to outer movements but also to the presence of others who share the experience and in an important sense make it live. Meditation is, of course, possible on one's own; indeed, the attraction of Zen and forms of yogic practice to the fragmented Western mind is precisely that it makes room for the recovery of a life-giving interiority. But the right channelling of desire is not a private enterprise that sees the relationship with the other as a distraction to be transcended or a temporary stage on the path to other-worldly bliss. It is intrinsic to the practice, even if it is all too easy to get carried away into a detached reverie that avoids the messiness of life on the streets. To stress the ordinariness of the everyday is not to play down the significance of contemplative experience for interreligious learning. On the contrary, it takes

---

[1] From Thich Nhat Hanh, *Essential Writings*, ed. Robert Ellsberg (Darton, Longman and Todd, 2008), p. 147.

us through the middle of things where mindful attention takes on a very specific meaning.

Zen does not abstract from the real; it plunges the meditator into the middle of things. Thus, in *kinhin* one concentrates not on the feet nor on the floor but on the interaction between the two and the movement it makes possible. To focus on the finer points of footfall may sound mildly obsessive. But strangely it opens up a sensitivity to *this* place and *this* moment. It may be what I called earlier the incarnational quality of Zen meditation that makes Zen so powerfully attractive for Christians – as if, at some level, the two traditions share an important dynamic. That claim does, however, require some justification. In the previous chapter I distinguished between two types of meditative experience, the 'absorptive' and the 'negative'. Both come from the great yogic tradition but raise different theological issues. Whereas the former engages with non-dualistic Vedantic metaphysics, the latter deliberately avoids any such commitment, charting instead the Buddhist Middle Way between extremes. How can such an uncompromising critique of all metaphysical constructions be a source of interreligious learning for Christians? In this chapter I want to consider in more detail the claim – largely implicit in the sort of groups who do their daily *kinhin* in tune with the movements of Western cities – that Christianity and Buddhism, for all their manifest differences, do share a certain inner affinity. So far from suppressing questions about the reality of God and the substantiality of human flourishing, Buddhist meditation sounds echoes of the Word of God in sometimes startling ways.

JESUS AND BUDDHA

Let me begin on the other aside of the religious divide. Thich Nhat Hanh is not just a much loved spiritual guide, and perhaps the most important exponent of Engaged Buddhism,[2] but a popular teacher who has reflected

---

[2] 'Engaged Buddhism' is the title for a relatively new development with roots set deep in the ancient commitments of Buddhism. The term is usually ascribed to Thich Nhat Hanh and his teaching of 'interbeing', a version of the theory of *pratityasamutpada* or conditioned origination. Nhat Hanh defines interbeing as 'the Buddhist teaching that nothing can be by itself alone, that everything in the cosmos must "inter-be" with everything else'. *Living Buddha, Living Christ* (London: Rider, 1995), p. 203. Engaged Buddhism is the correlate of this teaching – its practical outworking. On Nhat Hanh, see Patricia Hunt-Perry and Lyn Fine, 'All Buddhism is Engaged: Thich Nhat Hanh and the Order of Interbeing', in Christopher S. Queen (ed.), *Engaged Buddhism in the West* (Boston, Mass.: Wisdom, 2000). The essays collected in this volume are a useful survey of modern developments. See also Christopher S. Queen and Sallie B. King (eds.), *Engaged Buddhism: Buddhist Liberation Movements in Asia* (New York: State University of New York Press, 1996) and Christopher [S.] Queen, Charles Prebish and Damien Keown (eds.), *Action Dharma: New Studies in Engaged Buddhism* (London:

generously on the influence of Jesus on his religious practice. He writes in his most popular book that 'When we look into and touch deeply the life and teaching of Jesus, we can penetrate the reality of God. . . . God made Himself known to us through Jesus Christ.'[3] If an appreciation of the values of Jesus the enlightened teacher is not unusual, this frank use of theistic language by Buddhists certainly is. Some of the stereotypical disjunctions between Buddhism and Christianity have been noted. That there are enormous conceptual differences needs to be admitted. Christians and Buddhists disagree profoundly about the doctrine of creation. While for Christianity creation is the pure expression of God's self-gift, in Buddhism it is an unanswerable question that distracts from the central purpose of life, the gaining of enlightenment. Where Christians respond to the God-given imperative to listen to the Word wherever it is spoken in the world, Buddhists are content to follow a Middle Way that rejects all speculative theory as unnecessary. Something similar can be said about human flourishing and perfectibility. For Christians, human beings are made in the image and likeness of God and, in Christ, are called back to that life-giving relationship. Buddhist anthropology, on the other hand, is dominated by the concept of *anatmavada* – the teaching that human being lacks a substantive self or 'soul'. However, the most important difference is epistemological. Christianity is irretrievably historical, bound up with the particularity of God's self-revelation in time. Buddhism seeks to transcend all historical contingencies. At best the sort of theism for which Christianity stands, with its focus on the God who enters into time and transforms time, is a preparatory stage to the realisation that all things, including systems of belief and metaphysical theories, are transitory and insubstantial.

That may seem to make any sort of dialogue impossible. The reality, as Thich Nhat Hanh's disarmingly direct use of theistic language makes clear, is often rather different. Underlying such disjunctions – which often

Routledge-Curzon, 2003). As an example of a politically and, particularly, ecologically committed form of Engaged Buddhism in the West, see the work of Ken Jones, especially *The New Social Face of Buddhism: A Call to Action* (Boston, Mass.: Wisdom, 2003) and Joanna Macy, especially *World as Lover, World as Self* (London: Rider, 1993). Macy speaks of a number of developments, both in modern 'Western' Buddhism and more traditional forms ('Sarvodayans in Śri Lanka, Ambedkarite Buddhists in India or Dharma activists in Tibet, Thailand or South East Asia') as 'the third turning of the wheel'. Perhaps the most influential teacher of this form of socially committed Buddhism in the ancient Theravada tradition is the Thai monk Buddhadasa. See Donald K. Swearer, *Me and Mine: Selected Essays of Bhikkhu Buddhadasa* (Delhi: Śri Satguru Publications, 1991) and Buddhadasa, *Dhammic Socialism*, ed. and trans. Donald K. Swearer (Bangkok: Thai Inter-Religious Commission for Development, 1986).

3 Thich Nhat Hanh, *Living Buddha, Living Christ*, p. 35.

owe as much to expectations of the dialogue as they do to attitudes towards theological language – lies a more significant, if infuriatingly diffuse, correlation. Wherever its formal beginning, dialogue between Buddhists and Christians almost always finds its way towards the exploration of the experience that the language of tradition seeks to describe. From this rooting in spiritual practice something else begins to grow and provoke the religious imagination. To put it another way, the very 'space' that opens up between Buddhist non-theism, with its profound suspicion of the power of language, and Christian theism, with its foundation in the central image of God as generative and life-giving Word, is big enough to keep these two traditions at a respectful distance yet small enough to encourage creative thinking that is prepared to move beyond the usual stereotypes.

A remark by Rowan Williams points the way forward. In a discussion of the postmodern fixation with 'absence', he notes that Christianity refuses Buddhist reticence by giving what he calls a 'pivotal place' to the 'language of *gratitude*'. 'The absent other in language is there-and-not-there', he says, 'because we are always already spoken *to*.'[4] Gratitude, the response of a loving faith, is the correlate of givenness – the theme of the previous chapter. In other words, the language of 'creation out of nothing', which is so central to Christian theology (and so taken for granted), is saying something about the nature of God as self-giving, about creation itself as the expression of that gift and of human beings as called to a life of gratitude for what has been given. Buddhism, of course, is suspicious of the power of language to reify and reduce. That does not, however, make a dialogue with Buddhism fruitless. My suggestion is that it can actually enhance our understanding of Christian theism – not by providing some alternative 'model' but by enabling us to explore the *conditions that make the acceptance of God's self-gift possible*. Instead, therefore, of asking how different ideas about ultimate reality, creation and personhood can somehow be made compatible, the question to ask is why particular ideas emerge in the first place. What is the broad religious and cultural context that frames the central Buddhist teaching of 'selfless persons'?[5] And what part does this account of human being play in the various ethical and meditative practices that make enlightenment possible?

[4] Rowan Williams, *Lost Icons* (Edinburgh: T & T Clark, 2002), p. 182.
[5] From the title of Steven Collins's important contribution to the history of ideas, *Selfless Persons: Imagery and Thought in Theravada Buddhism* (Cambridge University Press, 1982).

AVOIDING THE EXTREMES

To answer such questions we might begin with the guiding concept of Buddhist life and practice that is described in the First Sermon as the Middle Way between extremes. These are played out in the Buddha's own life-story with its juxtaposition of the extreme of the early life of the *bodhisattva* as a pampered prince and his searching for *Nirvana* through the extreme of rejection and withdrawal from the world represented by various forms of asceticism. This personal progress is mirrored by what can be called a metaphysical Middle Way between the extreme of 'annihilationism' (the desire for utter quiescence) and that of 'eternalism' (striving to realise the eternity of the self). This latter position is best understood in terms of the *atmavada* of the *Upanishads*, the teaching that fundamentally the essence of the universe and the essence of the person are one. This is embodied in the non-dualistic Vedanta that I described above as the fruit of an 'absorptive' form of meditation. This is what Buddhism rejects. Instead of commending the isolation of some substantive inner essence of the human person, Buddhism teaches an analysis of the human subject in terms of the five *skandhas*, literally 'aggregates' or constitutive factors, none of which has any ultimate value in itself. Any account of 'the human' that would isolate some sort of essential *atman* is vigorously resisted. Instead of appearing as an eternal essence clothed in material reality, Buddhism sees in the human person a flux of ever-changing psycho-physical 'energy' that leads to a further same-yet-different re-expression of states of being. Metaphysically, there is only a temporary collection of elements, which are held together, as it were, by the glue that is ignorance. The Buddha's teaching is that we must first understand the truth about human being and achieve a right view and true detachment from the desire to cling to things if we are to achieve true freedom or *Moksha*. This appears, as I have said before, counter-intuitive, but *anatmavada* has its own logic. What the Buddha is saying is that it is contradictory to hold that the person can be regarded as some sort of amalgam of eternal and insubstantial elements. The First Noble Truth, that everything is suffused with 'suffering', is worked through to its logical extreme. Not only the world 'out there' that we observe is suffused with suffering; *you too*, the observer, is suffering – every element. This is what makes the human person strictly *anatta*, lacking an unchanging 'soul', in the Theravada tradition, or – to use the Mahayanist formulation – *śunya*, empty of 'own being' or essence.

This can sound like the other extreme that the Buddha rejects, namely 'annihilationism'. But Buddhism is not nihilist, just suspicious of the easy language that canonises various putatively eternal entities. To that extent the Middle Way, which is worked out with enormous subtlety in the scholastic and philosophical literature, is not to be interpreted in terms of a postmodern rejection of an identifiable substantive self. More exactly, as I tried to explain in the previous chapter, Buddhism shows how human living as a striving for enlightenment is a never-ending process in which even the most high-minded of desires, the desire for enlightenment itself, has to be scrupulously observed – and sublimated. In this sense what has to be overcome is the *ego*, which is more concerned with self than with what can draw the self away from its own isolation. This account of the person as essentially insubstantial is nothing if not a reminder that Christianity too is based on a sense of personhood that is only ever found by being lost. As Roger Corless points out, in his juxtaposition of the two parables of spiritual progress from Julian of Norwich and the *Lotus Sutra*, spiritual progress is only ever made by confronting sin or ignorance, not by denying its reality.[6] In both traditions the fundamental 'problem' of the human condition is the transience of all things. The paradox is that in understanding that truth correctly lies the solution. For the Christian, it means the embrace of death, after the manner of Christ; for a Buddhist, it entails a quite radical denial of 'soul-theories' in imitation of the Buddha's enlightenment experience of seeing things 'as they really are'.

To accept very different concepts of true personhood, ideals of what makes for human destiny or fulfilment, does not mean that there is not a roughly similar *strategy* of achieving true human personhood at work. As noted earlier, with regard to the 'asceticism-contemplation' tension, by confronting truth in the 'here and now' and deliberately avoiding any would-be escape into a 'safe haven', a comfortable 'beyond', Buddhists and Christians ask the same questions – even though the philosophical and cultural roots from which they spring mean that they come up with radically different answers. For the Theravadin, the person is a linguistic construct that is analysed in the course of thorough introspective medita-tion; in the Mahayana, liberation comes not through such 'personless' self-effacement, but by working for a vision of the personal as always 'interpersonal', in which the 'I' can only be said to exist in so far as it exists in relationship with the other. In both schools there seems to be very little by way of an individual self; there is only the interconnectedness of persons.

---

[6] Roger Corless, 'The Dramas of Spiritual Progress', in *Mystics Quarterly*, 11.2 (1985), pp. 65–75.

In Christianity, of course, the concept of person emerges more directly, and more strongly, from the biblical image of a humanity made 'in the image of God'. Human beings are essentially made for an eternal relationship with God. It may be possible to distinguish roughly between a more ecclesial or communitarian Catholic sense of how God's grace is 'at work' in the world, and a more individualistic Protestant sense of personhood formed in response to God's Word. Yet both have their validity, reflecting two sides of Christian faith in that God calls each person 'by name' and has formed a people for Godself. 'Human flourishing' is both personal and communitarian. As Rahner points out, 'even in his most personal history man is still a social being whose innermost decisions are mediated by the concreteness of his social and historical life, and are not acted out in a special realm which is separate'.[7] How to express this truth about humanity – which is also, of course, a truth about the self-communicating God?

In the Buddha's first sermon, he teaches a Middle Way between the extremes of 'eternalism' and 'annihilationism' – belief in the survival of some eternal soul-essence and a more subtle, yet equally destructive, death wish. In a remarkable study that seeks to bring out the complementarity of the Buddhist teaching of *anatta* and the Christian concept of *pneuma*, the Śri Lankan biblical theologian Lynn de Silva constructs a different sort of Middle Way, a dialectic of personal and communal accounts of human flourishing that are rooted in a mindful contemplation of graced existence, life made whole in and by the Spirit of Christ.[8] In Buddhism, the self-perception formed by mindfulness takes one out of the obsession with seeking an unchanging ultimate or essence of things and develops the 'counter-perception' of *pratityasamutpada*. Often translated as the 'nexus of conditioned origination' (or, invoking Thich Nhat Hanh's term, 'inter-being'), this refers to the Buddhist vision of the relatedness of all things and all sentient beings.[9] In Christianity, as de Silva shows, human destiny is understood not as the survival of some separable 'soul'-essence but in terms of *resurrection*, in imitation of the one whom God raises from the dead. In 1 Corinthians 15, for instance, Paul is attacking an early form of Christian 'eternalism', some sort of Platonist belief in an enduring if not transmigrating 'soul'. He stresses how much Christian faith makes a radical challenge to such assumptions. The Resurrection is not just a demonstration of God's power over death and therefore a *motive for faith*; it is, more exactly,

[7] Karl Rahner, *Foundations of Christian Faith* (London: Darton, Longman and Todd, 1978), p. 314.
[8] Lynn de Silva, *The Problem of the Self in Buddhism and Christianity* (London: Macmillan, 1979).
[9] Thich Nhat Hanh. See above, n. 2.

the self-revelation of God himself and therefore an *object of faith*. In other words, Christians believe in a God who has raised Jesus from the dead and now promises to do the same for all who believe and are therefore incorporated by the Spirit into Christ. The form that that incorporation takes is a new way of embodiment. This is the belief that makes Christians more than just another religious community whose identity lies in following a particular teaching. For Paul, they are a new creation, the 'Body of Christ'. As the people of Israel were themselves called by God 'from among the nations', so the disciples are constituted as Church, the beginnings and sign of what the world is to become. They find themselves 'embodied in Christ' through the life-giving action of his Spirit. In Paul's terms what was once a 'physical body' into which God breathed life is now recreated anew through the Spirit of Christ and made a spiritual body (1 Cor. 15:44).

There is at least one way in which the Buddhist concept of *pratityasa-mutpada* reinforces rather than contradicts the Christian conviction of being called by the imageless God out of darkness. Everything exists 'in dependence'. Putting it in very un-Buddhist terms, there is never a self that can be set apart from the other. Rather, the self is a self precisely *because of* the other. In Christianity, the individual receives eternal value from responding to the call to enjoy a filial relationship with God. This call, as noted above, is always mediated through social and historical forms. God does not pluck human beings out of this world but engages with them where they are, inextricably bound up with a whole series of relations, as individuals who are yet fathers and mothers, brothers and sisters, as members of communities, as a people related to and dependent on other peoples, as bound up with, and responsible for, the rest of God's creation. The God of the Old Testament, to recall Brueggemann's evocative phrase, is a 'dialogical God'.[10] In the manner in which God calls a people for himself is grounded the possibility of harmony in human relationships. Dialogue in this Buberian sense becomes a worthy end in itself because it reflects the very nature of the 'new creation' brought about in Christ. Christians meet in Christ whose members they become and whose fellowship they seek to communicate to others. Indeed, without that act of communication – a Christian version of the Buddhist *karuna* or compassion – there is something crucially lacking to the practice of Christian faith. Christians are always being called to learn how to become

---

[10] Walter Brueggemann, *An Unsettling God: The Heart of the Hebrew Bible* (Minneapolis, Minn.: Fortress, 2009), pp. 1–17.

persons who are not 'mere' individuals but individuals who exist in relation to each other because they always exist in relation to God.

Buddhism, of course, refuses to ascribe human relationality to God's act of calling a people together. The Buddha's silence can be interpreted in a number of ways: as sheer agnosticism, in apophatic terms as a type of *via negativa* or as a nihilistic insistence that language is only a source of mystification. However, the Buddha does not claim that he does not know; it is much more that words cannot contain everything that can be said.[11] More specifically, he refused to answer questions that he considered unhelpful. Immediately, of course, the Buddha was reacting against the religion of the brahmanical sacrifice, its sheer 'wordiness' and the human desire for hard and fast answers that it embodied. All too easily, words, images and symbols can become idols. This is not to say that the Buddha denies 'God' or Ultimate Reality. Rather, he attempts to overcome the tendency to idolise some symbol or image of God by awakening people to a sense of their own contingency. That is the point of beginning with an account of 'selfless persons'. The so-called positive way or way of analogy and images gives way through skilful practice and discernment to a sort of *docta ignorantia* – literally, of course, a 'learned ignorance', but in the light of Buddhism it might almost be translated as 'enlightened silence'. It seeks to follow the example of the Buddha himself who, according to the mythology, only decided to speak about Dharma out of compassion for suffering sentient beings and at the specific request of the god Brahma.[12] It is worth noting in passing that traditional Buddhism does not deny the existence of the Vedic gods or *devas*, only their *ultimate* significance; they are all part of the great continuum of creation.[13] The risk in speaking of God is that words disfigure, they turn the Ultimate into an object. To guard against this, the Buddha speaks not of the goal itself but only of the *way* to the goal. This gives us another clue to the interpretation of the Middle Way. It is not just a *via media* between extremes of practice or theory but an

---

[11] On the relationship between Buddhism and the Christian mystical tradition, see John Keenan, *The Meaning of Christ: A Mahayana Theology* (New York: Orbis, 1989).

[12] *Mahapadana Sutta, Digha Nikaya*, II. 36 ff.

[13] See John Bowker, *The Religious Imagination and the Sense of God* (Oxford University Press, 1978), especially pt. 4. On how the distinction plays itself out in terms of 'popular Buddhism', see Aloysius Pieris, *Prophetic Humour: Doing Inter-religious Studies in the Reverential Mode* (Colombo: EISD, 2005).

encouragement to equanimity with regard to the goal. To be 'in the middle' is enough.

There is, however, another way of considering the issue, one which opens up the creative space for dialogue referred to above. According to Panikkar, the Buddha's silence can only properly be understood within the context of meditation.[14] To put it again in Christian terms, theology is not speculation but a response to God that begins in contemplative wonder about the 'dialogical God'. Panikkar is thus undoubtedly right that it is only within the silence of the heart that this peculiarly Buddhist quality of 'equanimity' (which leaves one, as it were, on the threshold of *Nirvana*) can be experienced. But he also wants to point out how silence can assume a constructive role within all ritual, a role that sets it in a dialectical play with 'word', the language that in some sense can be said to 'command' or 'control' the sacrifice. Ritual is, of course, based on a response that is expressed in words – through the liturgical action itself, hymns of praise, formal prayers etc. But it relies for its effectiveness on the silence that it encourages and to which ultimately it leads. No religion, as Panikkar reminds us, can afford to ignore the religious significance of silence.

Even in a tradition like the Judeo-Christian, in which praise is very often the dominant element in ritual, the observance of silence cannot be dispensed with when one comes face to face with God. And of course the tool par excellence of the contemplative life is the silence that not only hushes word, but also, and especially, thought. Silence regards mystery.[15]

The Buddhist way is not normally thought of as a ritual. But it is impossible to ignore many ritual-like elements in the practice of the Noble Eightfold Path: not just the central practice of meditation and such ritual-like movements as *kinhin* walking meditation but the formal taking of the refuges and precepts. What is being developed, however, through these formal elements, is not some sort of speculative intellectual structure of faith but the silence which stills the restless mind. Through 'skilful means' the meditator discerns how the two levels of truth – conventional truth (*samvrtisatya*) and ultimate truth (*paramarthasatya*) – are continually interacting, leading the meditator towards that level of mindfulness that sees things 'as they really are'. If there is a Christian parallel, it is probably there in Anselm's mode of theology as a prayerful dialogue with God or, more fundamentally, Augustine's direct address to God in the *Confessions*. These are words of love,

---

[14] See, in particular, Raimundo Panikkar, *The Silence of God: The Answer of the Buddha* (New York; Orbis, 1989), pp. 148–56.

[15] *Ibid.*, p. 156.

typically born of the 'agapeic' idiom of Christianity. But in a certain sense the outcome is similar to what we noted in the Zen practice with which I began. There is a stillness generated by constant practice of sitting and walking that is also a gathering of tension. This, to use Pieris's distinction, is in the 'gnostic' idiom. Just as Zen subversion of the verbal or the Mahayana dialectical process clarifies what it is possible to say, so in Christian theology everything that comes from God is returned to its source in God; all speech *about* God gives way to a contemplative silence *before* God. It is this quality of faithful *waiting* upon the Word that typifies not just Christian eschatology but all sacramental and liturgical practice. All words issue from silence and must return to silence. Putting the point in the terms of Christian Trinitarian theology, the Word is spoken out of the silence of the Father and returns in the Spirit that is love. In more Buddhist terms, Silence and Word are always 'dependently co-arisen', interrelated; they depend on and enfold each other. For the Christian, of course, the key question is Christological. How to speak of Christ the Word – perhaps, more properly, how to allow the Word to speak – in the middle of 'the words'? There can be no answer to that question outside the contemplative experience in which learning and loving are two sides of the same coin. Not unlike the Buddha's insistence that one can speak only of the Middle Way, not of the goal itself, so the Christian remains always 'on the way', only ever *with Christ* in God. This is what makes the 'naming' of the Word as 'Emmanuel', God with us, of crucial significance for Christian faith.

RESONANCES OF THE FORM OF GOD

Our reflections on the nature of a Christian faith that enters into serious engagement with Buddhism almost inexorably raise questions about the theological value of *relationality* itself. Where – to oversimplify somewhat – is God Emmanuel in the Christian's relationship with the other? As far as the Buddhist–Christian dialogue is concerned, the suggestion already advanced is that the mystery of the self-revealing God is to be discerned not in some common metaphysical essence hanging around mysteriously in the background but in the unfolding story of the dialogue itself, especially in what Buddhists and Christians may learn *together* about the nature of humanity. In other words, is it not possible, however tentatively, to suggest that the *story that is Buddhism itself* may reveal aspects of the practice of Christian faith – albeit in the form that Levinas would refer to as a 'trace of the other'? To repeat Panikkar's point, if there is to be a dialogue between Buddhists and Christians, it must be at the level not of 'mere dialectic and subtle lucubrations' but in terms of contemplation. 'Buddhism is purely and simply a school of prayer ... All that the Buddha has said gains its significance and beauty when we understand it from the viewpoint of contemplation.'[16] The challenge here, in the spirit of the comparative theology project, is to read the Christian and the Buddhist stories together – to let them develop echoes of each other, or what, following some suggestive remarks of Christopher Brown, might be called 'resonances'.[17]

In this regard it is not unhelpful to seek out *vestigia Trinitatis*, or Trinitarian 'resonances', in the Buddhist experience.[18] With the *parinirvana* or final enlightenment of the Buddha questions began to be asked about the nature of one who lived as a human being yet also transcended the human condition. The apotheosis of the Buddha is, of course, a lengthy and complex process, but Paul Williams is surely right to remind us that within the context of Indian religion with its strong sense of the divine at home in the familiar and prosaic this is not a radical or unusual move. 'It was natural', he says, 'to refer to the Buddha in terms also used of gods. Such indicated little more than an attitude of deep respect and humility on the part of his followers.'[19] The earliest form of 'Buddhology' seems to have recognised a distinction between the Buddha's *Rupakaya* or 'form-body' and the *Dharmakaya* or 'transcendent body', the former focusing on the cult of relics, embodied in the burial mounds or *stupas*, and the latter on the Buddha's teaching. The two bodies can be understood as ways in which the Buddha's memory or influence can be said in some sense to continue. As speculation developed, especially under the influence of the Mahayana practice of glorifying the *sutras* (understood as 'further' teachings of the Buddha taught by enlightened *bodhisattvas*), a threefold division emerged: the *Nirmanakaya* or 'apparition body' by which the Buddha appears in human form and preaches the Dharma to human beings; the *Sambhogakaya* or 'enjoyment body', which the Buddha assumes to preach to the heavenly *bodhisattvas*; the *Dharmakaya*, the unmanifest form or 'transcendent body', which is the ultimate truth shared by all Buddhas.

Naturally the seductive 'threeness' of this distinction resonates with Christian theology. And it is impossible to ignore the intriguing parallels between this emergent Buddhology and the way in which Christology and the doctrine of Trinity develop within Christianity. The Resurrection

---

[16] *Ibid.*, p. 155.
[17] Christopher A. Brown, 'Can Buddhism Save? Finding Resonance in Incommensurability', *Cross Currents* (1999), pp. 164–96.
[18] On Buddhism and Trinity, see Keenan, *Meaning*, pp. 240 ff.
[19] Paul Williams, *Mahayana Buddhism: The Doctrinal Foundations* (London: Routledge, 1989), p. 170.

narratives express a similar quandary: the Risen Lord is now exalted to be with the Father yet continues to bear the marks of crucifixion and his earthly life. A Christian will, however, see in the *Trikaya* Buddhology a Docetism that makes the 'historical' Buddha, Siddhartha Gotama, just one example of a projection into the world on the part of some sort of transcendent principle. Parallels or 'resonances' are bound to appear as we cross over into another world and seek to make sense of its concepts and symbols. But what may at first seem like a common strand may turn out, on closer inspection, to hide a greater dissimilarity. The art of translation is not an exact science. To that extent any purely speculative attempt to draw hard and fast analogies between the Buddhadharma and the Christian doctrine of the Trinity is bound to be misleading.

Bearing in mind the cautions of the Buddha himself, it may be that metaphysical speculation is not the best place to begin. Buddhist doctrine is not the elaboration of some philosophical conundrum but is to be understood primarily in terms of the concept of *upaya*, the 'skilful means' by which the *Dharma* is taught. And, however much Christian theology may have been formed by the dialogue with Hellenistic culture, faith in the triune God is – to repeat – essentially a response to the call of the one who experienced God as Father and promised the coming of the Spirit of truth. If the context of a spiritual discipline (in Buddhism) and the life of discipleship (in Christianity) is borne in mind then a suggestive, if somewhat inchoate, comparative 'resonance' between the two traditions emerges. In Buddhism, consciousness is formed by a discipline that moves from hearing the *Dharma*, through practices inspired by the memory of the enlightened one, to enlightenment itself. In Christianity, the new identity of the disciples is formed by the action of the Spirit, in whom they confess that Jesus is Lord – the one whose life, death and resurrection manifests the God he calls Abba (Father). But in neither instance is the *summum bonum*, the ultimate truth about human nature and destiny, reducible to some sort of esoteric wisdom.

The fundamental point, to go back for a moment to my practice of *kinhin* in that New Jersey *zendo*, is that for both traditions truth is not to be identified as some 'transcendent essence' but is always *embodied or incarnated* in some form. Truth, as I said in an earlier chapter, can never be limited to culture but is, nevertheless, *inseparable from* culture. Hence the need to find a way of differentiating between form, which implies limitation of some kind, and the unlimited or unconditioned to which form points or leads. Classical Christian theology has always used the concept of analogy to speak about God, always recognising that however much God may be thematised in human language, and thus be said to be 'like' some human form, the 'unlikeness' is always greater. This is why *Pneuma* must complement *Logos* – not so much to allow God somehow to function in two interdepend-ent ways but, more profoundly, to remind us that *form can never be exhausted by the consciousness of form.*[20] Thus when Jesus calls God Abba he is not turning God into some comforting icon or talisman. Rather, in Jesus is heard God's Word, the voice that speaks out of the silent depths of God. Jesus thus introduces us into a *relationship* that itself expresses the very nature of God. At the same time, as Buddhists would remind Christians, to name that which is beyond all names is to risk idolatry. Silence, as Panikkar describes it, is not an empty lack but the space within which the Spirit enables us to hear the Word of God. That is why it is only 'in the Spirit of Christ' that we are able to speak of that relationship, because the Spirit witnesses not just to the 'naming' of God that takes place 'in Christ' but to the wider context of a discipleship that leads the one who dares to use that name Emmanuel further and further into the infinity and inexhaustibility of the self-giving God. Putting it another way, the Spirit is the Spirit of Christ because the Spirit is always the Spirit of love whose very nature is to go on witnessing to the continual unfolding of the mystery that is God.

POINTING TO THE OTHER

In a later chapter, I will expand on this theme of the life-giving Spirit, with the suggestion that the Spirit points in 'two directions'. As the combination of sitting and walking meditation juxtaposes two ways of relating to a particular place, becoming anchored in the moment and moving through it, so the Spirit is always pointing back, as it were, to the one whom Jesus called Father while at the same time initiating and ordering the life of discipleship, leading the Christian community into the depths of the Paschal Mystery. Buddhism does not, of course, use the language of the Spirit. Yet something of that elusive 'inner affinity' between Christianity and Buddhism, which has so much intrigued the likes of Pieris and de Silva, is to be discerned through the dialogue of spirituality or religious experi-ence. Words like readiness, openness, waiting and equanimity abound, and give something of the flavour of that quality of mindful attention to what is given in the present moment, *both* memory of what is past *and* hope-filled anticipation of what is to come, which Christians might well understand as

---

[20] Thus Rowan Williams, commenting on Panikkar's *The Trinity and the Religious Experience of Man*, in 'Trinity and Pluralism', an essay in *On Christian Theology* (Oxford: Blackwell, 2000), pp. 167–80.

the work of the Spirit. What I have tried to explore in these last two chapters is how it is possible for Christians, in practising Buddhist meditation with integrity, to sense something of the spirit of mindfulness. At stake is not the acquisition of a few helpful relaxation techniques but the learning of a Christian *upaya* – practical skills of engagement that under the guidance of God's Spirit build up the 'spiritual body'.

This section of the book has juxtaposed the 'primary' relationship of Christianity – with the Jewish people – with a 'secondary' relationship – with Buddhism. This relationship is arguably the most other for Christians, which is why I have paid more attention to the translation of the person than to constructing a theology of Buddhist–Christian relations. Buddhism and Christianity have much in common: perhaps most importantly, as I argued earlier, that both are traditions that only *come alive* when engaging with and transforming the spirit of a culture. That is not to say that faith and culture cannot be distinguished, but rather that the former can only be apprehended as it is refracted through the latter. Indeed, the strangest paradox of Buddhism is that it relativises all cultural forms while working through them. Something similar can be said for Christianity; the Word becomes incarnate in the world and faith must therefore 'become culture', but that is not to sanctify any particular cultural form. The Buddhist would say that culture passes just as the flower fades and all things must die. There is, therefore, no essence of Zen any more than there is an essence of Christianity. *Dharma* is not to be equated in any purely speculative way with God, nor Buddha with Christ, nor *Nirvana* with the beatific vision. Not that there are no 'resonances' here. Clearly there are. My point, however, is that an account of these two traditions that extracts from place and culture starts in the wrong place – with the search for word or concept equivalents. If the Buddhist teaches the Christian one thing it is that mindfulness involves attention to all that is given in the everyday. 'All' here means precisely *all* – learning to come to terms with every experience, whether of joy or pain. And all this is *given* – it appears not as some purely contingent entity which is to be manipulated or used, but precisely as that gift which inspires the language of gratitude.[21]

This is why in the dialogue with Buddhism it makes more sense to begin with the Spirit and the life that the Spirit inspires; not, that is, with preconceived notions about Ultimate Reality that have to be painfully and systematically deconstructed but with the glimpse of the mysterious *śunyata* of the everyday. By this I do not mean that the Spirit is to be regarded in Buddhist

---

[21] Williams, *Lost Icons*, p. 182.

terms as the *Sambhogakaya* – some sort of principle of joy or delight, to be set in relationship with Jesus's more 'explicit' human role as the *Nirmanakaya*, the 'manifestation body' (or, as Christians might be tempted to say, the Epiphany of God). Nor is this to turn the Spirit into some more dynamic form of the concept of *Pratityasamutpada*, the principle of the ultimate interrelatedness of things. Suggestive though these 'resonances' are, they go against the inner spirit of both Buddhist and Christian faith by feeding into the speculative and neglecting the practical and experiential. I therefore warm to the intriguing suggestion of von Balthasar, who, in a perceptive account of the dialogue with Buddhism, says that 'the Spirit does not wish to be seen but to be a *seeing eye of grace in us*'.[22] In the context of the Buddhist–Christian relationship – and maybe this applies to all interreligious relations – the Spirit points to the other, bringing to mind all that is ignored, or forgotten, or maybe never considered before.

SOUNDING THE WORD

Again, this points us forward to some ideas that I want to develop in the last section of the book, under the heading of 'Imaginings'. Before concluding this section, let me venture one final thought about 'crossings' and the spirituality of dialogue.

By bringing Christianity's 'primary' and 'secondary' relationships into a correlation I do not want to suggest that one automatically leads to or implies the other. Rather, I am arguing for an account of dialogue that forms and supports the practice of an ever-deepening learning. Whatever the truth in the 'spirituality/religion' dichotomy as a phenomenon of the postmodern age, it fails to explain how the personal and interior goes on renewing the communal and exterior. If spirituality, following Panikkar, can be defined as the 'right channelling of desire', attention needs to be given not just to the experience of being 'inter-faith', of crossing a threshold into another world, but to the terms of its motivation, how interior and exterior are to be related and how the Word is sounded in Silence.

When the term 'spirituality' first makes an appearance in the Christian tradition (in a fifth-century letter once ascribed to Jerome, according to Philip Sheldrake) it maintained the Pauline moral sense of life in the Spirit.

---

[22] From Hans Urs von Balthasar, 'Der Unbekannte jenseits des Wortes', *Spiritus Creator* (Einsiedeln: Johannes Verlag, 1967), p. 100. Quoted by Hans Waldenfels, in 'Buddhism and Christianity in Dialogue: Notes on the Intellectual Presuppositions', *Communio* 15 (1988), pp. 411–22. Quotation from p. 421.

Gradually, however, the focus on interiority takes on a life of its own and begins to divorce itself from the broader communal context from which it takes its rise. By the twelfth century, with the advent of scholasticism, 'spiritual' finds itself opposed to 'corporeal' – the beginning of 'that disdain for the body that sometimes appeared in later spiritual writing'.[23] Sheldrake traces this pejorative sense of spirituality into the late seventeenth century when quietist movements emerged with an emphasis on inner dispositions and refined states of consciousness. The need to categorise the stages of the individual's inner journey of faith led in turn to a type of 'mystical theology' that took the process of inner transformation as its proper object and in so doing separated it from the more systematic accounts of the Christian life to be found in fundamental and dogmatic theology. The contemplative dimension of Christian life became all too neatly distinguished from the intellectual – with deleterious consequences for the coherence of both. While theology turned itself into the ordering of metaphysical entities with precious little anchorage in the daily practices of people of faith, spirituality became detached from what Mark McIntosh calls any 'stable communal goal or reference' and became 'susceptible to the idols, compulsions, or fears of the individual'.[24]

It is this dichotomy of formal institution and more free-flowing personal quest that the contemporary obsession with interior experience claims to identify. Thus, in the study of the 'spiritual revolution' noted in the previous chapter, Woodhead and Heelas draw a distinction between what they call 'life-as', according to which one lives in tune with particular social expectations, and a more authentic 'subjective life', in which one connects with one's own unique and deepest experiences.[25] In fact, as Sheldrake and McIntosh show, versions of the 'life-as'/'subjective-life' distinction were anticipated at least as early as the Church–State splits that resulted from the seventeenth-century European wars of religion. In his writing on mysticism, Michel de Certeau draws attention to one enduring dimension of this cultural shift. He argues that the turbulence of the post-Reformation period led not just to a realignment of intra-ecclesial political allegiances but to a more profound change within Christian discourse about the nature of the human person – more exactly, *about where the truth of that nature is to be learned.*

---

[23] Philip Sheldrake, *Spirituality and History: Questions of Interpretation and Method* (London: SPCK, 1991), p. 35.

[24] Mark A. McIntosh, *Mystical Theology: The Integrity of Spirituality and Theology* (Oxford: Blackwell, 1998), p. 14.

[25] Linda Woodhead and Paul Heelas, *The Spiritual Revolution: Why Religion is Giving Way to Spirituality* (Oxford: Blackwell, 2005).

Thus in his reflections on the mystical writings of St Teresa of Avila, de Certeau shows how personal experience takes the place of canonical scripture as the source of authenticity. Teresa's writing, he says, is 'undoubtedly part of a long Socratic and spiritual tradition of the "know thyself", but it displaces that tradition from the outset in translating it into two other questions: "Who else lives inside of you?" and "To whom do you speak?"'[26] The self who was constituted by the single seamless web of pre-Reformation religious and civil life has gradually given way to a different sort of awareness of the origins of speech about God. Mystical writings, claiming the authenticity of their own experience, begin to make an appearance, resulting in various forms of pietism, born of attention to the 'voice within', which anticipate the contemporary turn to the spiritual subject. William James, with his return to 'first-order' experience, noted earlier, is only the most prominent example of a supposedly modern trend – the search for solid foundations – that can be traced back as far as Augustine and Gregory of Nyssa.

What is new is less the discovery of interiority than a more complex notion of *how interiority relates to exteriority*. For a religion that is always focused on the Word that God speaks in the world, the crucial question is always about how and where that Word is spoken. In that sense there is clearly a continuity between the more 'modern' mystical writings of St Teresa of Avila and St John of the Cross which preoccupy de Certeau and the earlier tradition, whether we are talking about the stark apophaticism of the Pseudo-Dionysius or the much more image-laden work of St Bernard of Clairvaux, St Bonaventure and the followers of the *Devotio Moderna*. The point is made in texts as different as the sermons of Meister Eckhart, which are intended to bring about the 'birth of the Word' in the soul, or the far more practical and mission-orientated *Spiritual Exercises* of St Ignatius of Loyola, with his vision of all things coming down from God and suffusing the world with God's grace. They do not just act as records *of* experience; they are also (and more significantly) calls *to* experience. In the Christian school of faith which takes its rise from Jesus's preaching of the Kingdom the Word is always spoken in the imperative mode, calling Christians both to discern the signs of God's action incarnated in the world *and* to become actively engaged with what is strictly God's own work, the *Missio Dei*. In short: the cultivation of interiority cannot be understood apart from the conditions that constitute exteriority.

I have used two metaphors to describe a spirituality of dialogue. 'Crossings' from one school of faith to another can be understood as

[26] Michel de Certeau, *The Mystic Fable* (University of Chicago Press, 1992), p. 195.

translations, but if echoes and resonances are not to be missed, translators must also learn to wait in hope upon the prior action of the Spirit. I have made Buddhism the most important of Christianity's 'secondary others' not because I think the *Buddhadharma* is somehow complementary to the Gospel or provides some paradigm for other interreligious relations. My point is rather that if the object of any dialogue is learning then the very contestation of religious language, which is central to the Buddha's critique of the brahmanical tradition, asks for a similar sensitivity to the way Christians, and other theists, give voice to the leading of the Spirit – or, to put it another way, use words to speak God's Word. This is not to say that the Paschal Mystery of the Death and Resurrection does not reveal the very nature of the self-communicating God, only that that revelation comes from another, from God, and must be accepted as pure gift. In language derived from Christianity's Jewish other, we may speak of God because we are addressed by God. In more Buddhist terms, everything we know about God is *śunya*, 'empty of own being' because it has no independent existence of its own but belongs only to God.

These two great traditions, sometimes distinguished as prophetic and mystical, share a common sensitivity towards the ineffability of Holy Mystery. But they put a very different valuation on words, and how words are to be used. Christianity differs from Buddhism because it dares to name God – indeed, is bound to name the God who is revealed as the Father of Jesus. Hence the Christian is committed not just to an interreligious learning, which is forever probing into the depths of God, but to the dual responsibility of discipleship. The disciple needs to learn the skills of translation (above all of translating the self) across frontiers while at the same time waiting and listening for the guidance of God's Spirit. If the former recognises that all Christians are called to participate in the *Missio Dei*, God's action of sending the Son and Spirit into the world, the latter warns of the danger of premature closure, the temptation to substitute for God's Word a facile resolution that does not allow God to be God. Together these two responsibilities show us how the spiritual life is to be lived, a life at once active in responding to Christ's proclamation of the Kingdom and contemplative in discerning the signs of the Spirit already at work in the world. Studying the texts or listening to the wisdom of another tradition, sharing in meditative practices, being present at worship or ritual, are not exercises in the religiously bizarre and esoteric. Nor are they acts of spiritual plagiarism: gathering up new insights and ideas to bolster an impoverished tradition. In so far as they bring about a deeper understanding of the truths and values of another tradition and a more perceptive sensitivity to the demands and responsibilities of one's own, they may be considered a participation in the 'seeing eye of grace' that is the Spirit of love. The Spirit reminds the Church that its faith is rooted in the Word that issues from the silence of God, inspiring words of praise and thanks. And the same Spirit goes before the Church, opening up new vistas for the spiritual imagination to contemplate. To that double challenge to the religious imagination we must now turn.

III

Imaginings

CHAPTER 9

The divine imperative

When Pope Benedict, in the safe recesses of a German university, began an academic lecture by quoting an obscure medieval text on holy war, he can scarcely have expected the uproar that ensued.[1]

After an amiable word of thanks to his old university colleagues, the pope referred to a set of dialogues, probably held in the winter of 1391, between the emperor of Byzantium, Manuel II Paleologus, and an 'educated Persian'. Their subject was the truth of Christianity and Islam. The emperor, speaking with what the pope called 'a startling brusqueness ... that we find unacceptable', raises a question about the relationship between religion and violence, arguing that violence is incompatible with the nature of God and the nature of the soul.

God is not pleased by blood – and not acting reasonably is contrary to God's nature. Faith is born of the soul, not the body. Whoever would lead someone to faith needs the ability to speak well and to reason properly, without violence and threats. ... To convince a reasonable soul, one does not need a strong arm, or weapons of any kind, or any other means of threatening a person with death.[2]

---

[1] Meeting with the Representatives of Science, University of Regensburg, 12 Sept. 2006. The text of the lecture is published along with a commentary in James V. Schall, *The Regensburg Lecture* (South Bend, Ind., St Augustine's Press, 2007).

[2] According to the footnote appended to the published version of the lecture (Libreria Editrice Vaticana, 2006), Theodor Khoury published the seventh 'controversy', with footnotes and an extensive introduction on the origin of the text, on the manuscript tradition and on the structure of the dialogue, together with brief summaries of the 'controversies' not included in the edition. The Greek text is accompanied by a French translation: 'Manuel II Paléologue, Entretiens avec un Musulman. 7e Controverse', *Sources Chrétiennes*, 115 (Paris, 1966). In the meantime, Karl Förstel published an edition of the text in Greek and German, with a commentary, in *Corpus Islamico-Christianum* (*Series Graeca*): 'Manuel II. Palaiologos, Dialoge mit einem Muslim', 3 vols. (Würzburg-Altenberge, 1993–6). As early as 1966, E. Trapp had published the Greek text with an introduction as vol. ii of *Wiener Byzantinische Studien*.

The pope does not associate himself with these comments – and in the published version of the lecture explicitly distances himself from them.[3] But by then the damage had been done and a highly complex set of references and citations that set the emperor's disparaging remarks about the prophet Muhammad in strong relief was enough to enrage Muslim opinion.

Two days later I was taking part in a phone-in on the BBC's World Service and the questions and comments ranged from the mildly aggrieved to the downright vitriolic. How dare the leader of the Catholic Church with the blood of crusades on his hands criticise Islam for nurturing violence? If he wants to talk about religiously inspired violence, why not choose something closer to home? Surely the point of interreligious dialogue is to promote peace and reconciliation, not stir up criticism and argument? Not all were from angry Muslims. There were a few angry Christians only too ready to applaud the pope for standing up for Christianity in the face of the 'Muslim menace'. As some sort of moderating influence in the middle of the storm, my task was to steer a course between total endorsement and reasoned criticism of what had – and had not – been said. Few callers, of course, had actually read the lecture. If they had, they would have noticed that Pope Benedict used the text of the dialogues not to attack Islam but to introduce a theme that is dear to his heart – the relationship between faith and reason.[4] Not a wise course of action, perhaps, in the febrile atmosphere of Muslim–Christian relations post 9/11, but not quite the vicious attack on all things Islamic that some commentators claimed to have heard.

It is not my purpose to enter into the controversy that the lecture ignited. I start in this particular middle of things to illustrate the sensitivities that surround not just the engagement between Christians and Muslims but any dialogue that carries the freight of an unhappy history. Memory, as I have already tried to indicate, refuses to be suppressed and, even though time does its own healing work, the traumas of the past are never erased from human experience. The answer, therefore, is not to privilege comfortable topics that generate predictable outcomes but – at some point – to face the reality of hatred and misunderstanding head on. While growing in awareness of the depth of feeling aroused by ancient memories and more current

---

[3] See Schall, *Regensburg Lecture*, p. 147 n. 3: 'In quoting the text of the Emperor Manuel II, I intended solely to draw out the essential relationship between faith and reason. On this point I am in agreement with Manuel II, but without endorsing his polemic.'

[4] The context of the university lecture is easily overlooked. See *ibid.*, especially pp. 18–40.

hurts, it is important that dialogue maintains its own appropriate level of robustness. The response to a polemical approach to the other cannot be a retreat into some mealy-mouthed victim mentality.

I take the dialogue with Islam as my example here because the practical dilemma – when to listen, when to speak; how to listen, how to speak – is starker here. In recent years, Muslim sensitivities have been inflamed by scurrilous cartoons, provocative films and crass criticisms of Islamic dress and culture in the popular press. Many Muslims have overreacted; many have exercised a commendable self-control. But it is undeniably the case that to be a Muslim in 'the West' brings with it a public prominence that for the majority is unwelcome. Philip Lewis, speaking at a conference soon after 9/11, tried to find a way through what he called an 'avalanche of materials' coming from the media. The left, he said, tends to blame Western and specifically American economic and cultural hegemony for the continuing humiliation of traditional Muslim societies. For the right, the real villain is a religious extremism that has been allowed to flourish in the West due to liberal immigration policies and a sentimental multiculturalism. For at least some Christian pressure groups the problem is simply Islam, which 9/11 showed in its true colours as a tribalistic regression. For doctrinaire seculaists, the issue is just as simple: religion – *all* religion – if it has any place in the modern post-Enlightenment world, is a purely private affair and should have no role whatsoever within the public polity. Lewis notes that there are insights buried in all of these perspectives. The challenge is to relate them to the very real 'confusion and perplexity' that many Muslims feel. If Islam is the final and perfect revelation of God for humankind how can it be that the Muslim world is in such turmoil?[5]

Whether that is a fair assessment of how 'many Muslims' feel is a moot point. The result of the intense media scrutiny is that Islam now sets the interreligious agenda, provoking a variety of responses, ranging from the sympathetic to the darkly suspicious. Paul Weller, for instance, ends his thoughtful and thorough survey of multicultural Britain twenty years after 'the Rushdie Affair' with a series of judicious principles for dialogue that are prefaced by the laconic statement that 'words matter'.[6] Muslims, he says, should be quick to censor their own dissident voices but, equally, politicians have to be careful about handing down lordly solutions that only inflame

[5] Philip Lewis, in a contribution to a symposium in London, Oct. 2001.
[6] Paul Weller, *A Mirror for our Times: 'The Rushdie Affair' and the Future of Multiculturalism* (London: Continuum, 2009), pp. 200 ff.

passions further. The distinguished Middle East scholar Bernard Lewis makes no such concessions to neutrality. He begins his brief but provocative survey of the current crisis in Islam by quoting Osama bin Laden for whom the last eighty years have been full of 'humiliation and disgrace'.[7] Muslims are guided by a strong sense of God working out his purposes for the community of the *umma*. The collapse of the Caliphate and the eclipse of the ideal of a single people gathered under a unified spiritual and political authority raise strong emotions that warn of interreligious turmoil for years to come. Philip Jenkins questions such doom-laden prophecies. In his study of the new religious configurations in Europe, he finds talk of a 'Eurabian nightmare' premature.[8] Certainly the number of Europeans originating in the Middle East or the Indian subcontinent is on the rise, but the 'religious tone' of the resulting mix and the level of accommodation to European cultural norms remains an open question. Jenkins has got at least some statistics on his side. A Gallup survey, comparing various attitudes of the Muslim and general population of France, Germany and the UK, found that, by and large, British Muslims feel more comfortable with many of the institutions of the state than the majority of the population – the media, the judiciary, the press, the police, government – even banks and financial institutions (the one exception is the army). Asked what was necessary for 'integration' into British society, 84 per cent of Muslims ticked 'celebrating national holidays'.[9]

Overcoming the media stereotypes is only the most obvious task for any constructive dialogue with Muslims. While monolithic accounts of what has always been a diverse tradition have in recent years been replaced by a more nuanced sense of a range of schools and strands, from the 'safe' Islam of Sufi poets to the 'angry' Islam of the popular press, discerning the truth behind contemporary perceptions of Islam remains problematic. I do not

[7] Bernard Lewis, *The Crisis of Islam: Holy War and Unholy Terror* (London: Phoenix, 2004), p. xv.
[8] Philip Jenkins, *God's Continent: Christianity, Islam and Europe's Religious Crisis* (Oxford University Press, 2007), pp. 1–25.
[9] *The Gallup Coexist Index 2009: A Global Study of Interfaith Relations* (Washington, DC: Gallup and CoExist Foundation, 2009), pp. 22–3. The study examines interreligious relations and community integration with special reference to the presence of Islam in the UK, France and Germany. Opinions from the general public are set together with opinions from the Muslim communities themselves. Perhaps the most interesting finding concerns differences of perception. For instance, as the Executive Summary notes, with regard to questions about the compatibility of religion and national identity, 'While British, French and German Muslims are more likely than the general population in those three countries to identify strongly with their faith, they are also as likely (if not more likely) than the general public to identify strongly with their countries of residence. Additionally, majorities in France, Germany, and the United Kingdom either do not think Muslims in their respective countries are loyal to their countries of residence or they are unsure. However, strong majorities of European Muslims surveyed think Muslims are loyal to their respective countries of residence in Europe' (pp. 8–9).

intend to chart a path through a testy debate.[10] Rather than engage with some question-begging form of 'moderate' Islam, I prefer to take up what Chris Hewer detects as a growing tendency among younger British-born Muslims. Whether through the influence of such British converts as Timothy Winter (Abdal Hakim Murad) or more traditional scholars like Zaki Badawi, a new tradition is beginning to emerge, a 'way of being Muslim as a minority in non-Muslim countries (*fiqh al-aqalliyat*)'.[11] The middle section of this book was concerned with the theme of 'crossing', that tentative movement across interreligious boundaries that I have characterised in terms of the complementarity of the 'art of translation' and the attitude of 'attentive waiting'. This final section I have called 'Imaginings', a series of reflections on the engagement between persons of faith in all their 'confusion and perplexity'. Again, my argument is that underlying the practice of dialogue is the inspiration of the virtues that underlie all holy living – the theological virtues of faith, hope and love. Opening up the realms of the imagination, so as to bring faith, hope and love to bear upon the sometimes fraught relationships between religious communities, does not mean playing about with a few wistful dreams of a better future. It means anchoring dreams in the messy reality of the present. Which is why I begin this section not in any sort of sacred site but in a very different sort of place – a radio studio, where all the ambiguities of a globalised media-saturated world are immediately apparent.

The dialogue between Buddhists and Christians that occupied the last two chapters has a relatively benign history that creates a great deal of space for exploration. With Islam it is the other way round. The history of that engagement is fraught and the space already tainted by polemic and caricature. Nevertheless, any interreligious engagement, discerned with generosity and integrity, can lead to a deeper interreligious learning. If I stay now with the pope in Regensburg it is not to give a detailed analysis of the subsequent process of engagement between Muslim and Christian scholars, theologians and authoritative figures. The topic of this chapter is a version of Cantwell Smith's '*Bhagavad Gita* question', which challenges the Christian imagination in a very particular way. If talk of a

[10] In addition to material already referred to, the following give some indication of the variety of responses to Islam in 'the West'. John Esposito, *Unholy Wars: Terror in the Name of Islam* (Oxford University Press: 2002); Hamid Dabashi, *Islamic Liberation Theology: Resisting the Empire* (London and New York: Routledge, 2008); Tariq Ramadan, *Western Muslims and the Future of Islam* (Oxford University Press, 2004); Bat Ye'or, *Eurabia: The Euro-Arab Axis* (Madison, NJ: Fairleigh Dickinson University Press, 2005); Christopher Caldwell, *Reflections on the Revolution in Europe: Immigration, Islam, and the West* (New York: Doubleday, 2009).

[11] C. T. R. Hewer, *Understanding Islam: The First Ten Steps* (London: SCM, 2006), p. 209.

single 'Judaeo-Christian tradition' is contested, the extension to include Islam is even more problematic. It seems plausible to extend a theology of revelation that is based on a continuity between Old Testament prophecy and the person of Christ to include a tradition that, however it may differ in its interpretation of the Word that God speaks in the world, does set enormous store by the significance of Jesus as one of the prophets of Allah. But what sense to make of a tradition that emerges centuries *after Christ?* Or does such a question begin with the wrong premises and make misleading assumptions about the nature of prophecy and revelation – and, indeed, of Islam itself?

A COMMON WORD

Within a month of Regensburg, an 'open letter' was written to Pope Benedict by thirty-eight Muslim scholars and leaders. In some ways it is a model of respectful interreligious dialogue: thanking the Catholic Church for the inspiration of *Nostra Aetate*, aware of how much good has been done to build good relations, the leaders gently but insistently point out the mistakes in the pope's interpretation of Islam. The Vatican's official response was muted, but the pope's visit to Turkey where he prayed respectfully in a prominent mosque was nothing if not symbolic of his desire to calm the passions that the lecture had unwittingly aroused. On the anniversary of the latter a rather bigger group of 138 signatories, from all parts of the Muslim world, wrote to the pope and to Christian leaders of all the prominent churches – from the patriarchs of Constantinople and Alexandria to the General Secretary of the World Council of Churches 'and leaders of Christian churches, everywhere'. Called *A Common Word*, this document is a call to Christians to join with Muslims in working for peace and understanding in the world. The summary and abridgement begins:

Muslims and Christians together make up well over half of the world's population. Without peace and justice between these two religious communities, there can be no meaningful peace for the world. The future of the world depends on peace between Muslims and Christians. The basis for this peace and understanding already exists. It is part of the very foundational principles of both faiths: love of the One God, and love of the neighbour. These principles are found over and over again in the sacred texts of Islam and Christianity. The Unity of God, the necessity of love for Him, and the necessity of love of the neighbour is thus the common ground between Islam and Christianity.[12]

---

[12] The text of the open letter of 13 Oct. 2006 and the expansion that was issued as *A Common Word* (published 13 Oct. 2007), plus background, reactions, commentary and subsequent responses from

What is remarkable about this text is that it exists at all. If nothing else, it witnesses to the desire in many parts of the Muslim world constructively to engage with Christians at a theological level. The choice of theme – love of God and love of neighbour – looks beyond typically Islamic forms of discourse in order to show how a coherence, if not a correlation, can be discerned between the central testimonies of the two faiths. The long list of quotations from Old and New Testaments betrays a careful attention to Christian ways of thinking. Christian responses have been many and varied, including a full-page advertisement in the *New York Times* (reminiscent of *Dabru Emet*) based on a consultation by the Yale Center for Faith and Culture (18 November 2007) and a lengthy rejoinder entitled *A Common Word for the Common Good* written by the Archbishop of Canterbury following an international conference of the Anglican Communion (14 July 2008). The dedicated website lists more than fifty Christian responses, including a letter from Pope Benedict's Secretary of State to Prince Ghazi bin Muhammad bin Talal of Jordan, who has been one of the most enthusiastic initiators of the project. In that letter Cardinal Bertone quotes the pope who said in an address to Muslims in Cologne (20 August 2005):

I am profoundly convinced that we must not yield to the negative pressures in our midst, but must affirm the values of mutual respect, solidarity and peace. The life of every human being is sacred, both for Christians and Muslims. There is plenty of scope for us to act together in the service of fundamental moral values.[13]

The energy released by these exchanges has opened up a number of areas for dialogue and co-operation between Christians and Muslims. Indeed, if ever proof was needed that dialogue is no longer the preserve of a few spiritual groupies, that far more serious issues are at stake, the very public dialogue begun unhappily at Regensburg and carried on through the *Common Word*

Pope Benedict XVI and the Archbishop of Canterbury, can be found on the official website www. acommonword.com. For a summary of the development of the process, see Yvonne Yazbeck Haddad and Jane I. Smith, 'The Quest for "A Common Word": Initial Christian Responses to a Muslim Initiative', *Islam and Christian–Muslim Relations*, 20.4 (2009), pp. 369–88. The most substantial contribution to the continuing dialogue comes from the essays by both Christian and Muslim thinkers, edited by Miroslav Volf, Ghazi bin Muhammad and Melissa Yarrington, *A Common Word: Muslims and Christians on Loving God and Neighbor* (Grand Rapids, Mich.: Eerdmans, 2010).

[13] The Regensburg lecture was what provoked the letter of the 38 Muslim scholars, but the 'Common Word' initiative itself was preceded by two major documents that emerged under the auspices of King Abdullah of Jordan and the Royal Aal al-Bayt Institute for Islamic Thought: the 'Amman Message' (2004) and the 'Amman Interfaith Message' (2005). The former was the result of a conference of some 180 Muslims scholars from 45 countries, covering the major schools of Islamic thought; it makes the point that 'more exists in common between the various schools of Islamic jurisprudence than there is difference between them'. The latter was intended more precisely to build up relations between Muslims, Jews and Christians and includes prominent reference to the Quranic injunction 3.64, which gives *A Common Word* its central theme.

process has provided it. Not that the theme of 'attentive waiting' discussed in the previous chapter is no longer important. Arguably, patience and humility are just the virtues necessary for what has become a much more politically charged dialogue.

According to the website, the purpose of *A Common Word* is to provide a 'common constitution' for dialogue, a 'starting point for co-operation', based on 'the most solid theological ground possible: the teachings of the Quran and the Prophet, and the commandments described by Jesus Christ in the Bible'. This it does by making the 'common word' the single unifying theme of love.

> Say: O ye people of the Scripture, come to a common word between us: that we will not worship other than God and associate anything with him, and that none of us shall take others for lords besides God. (sura 3.64)

The two great commandments are traced back to a single 'Divine Origin' and great play is made of the same 'Abrahamic heritage' that is shared by Christians and Muslims. Every effort throughout the text is made to communicate in an accommodating style, and the range of sources quoted is admirable. Nevertheless, it is not altogether surprising that divergences of interpretation, as much as points of continuity, quickly make themselves apparent. Even the term 'love of God' is understood in very different ways. For Muslims, it is, strictly speaking, love *for* God, the expression of perfect submission.[14] For Christians, on the other hand, the love of God is first and foremost God's love for us, what is experienced in Christ and therefore made possible through his example.[15] Even the initial theme of a 'common word', phrased as a divine imperative addressed to both Muslims and Christians, turns out to have a very specific, and very Islamic, meaning, as becomes clear from a brief examination of the context.

It comes from sura 3, *Al Imran*, revealed, say the commentators, on the occasion of a visit by Christians from Yemen to the prophet in Madina.[16] God's call to the *Ahl al Kitab*, the people of the book, is preceded by a

---

[14] See, e.g., suras 5.54, 2.165 and 3.31–2, which makes it clear that Allah loves the righteous but not those who 'reject Faith'.

[15] See, most obviously, Jesus's 'new commandment', John 13.12–35.

[16] Mahmoud Ayoub describes the context as polemical (quoting al-Tabari, one of the foremost early commentators, as saying that the Najran delegation 'manifested unbelief in God'). See Mahmoud Ayoub, *The Quran and its Interpreters*, vol. ii (Albany, NY: SUNY Press, 1992), pp. 1–6. Ayoub refers to the debate about whether the verse applies just to the Christians of Najran or to Jews and Christians generally (*ibid.*, pp. 202–8). Jane McAuliffe adds the line of interpretation from Ibn al-Jawzi, which sees those addressed as Jews alone. There are also questions about what precisely the 'common word' refers to – whether it is something which the three revealed books *Tawrat, Injil* and *Quran*, agree on. According to Maududi, 'The invitation here is for the two parties to agree on something which is

lengthy section that speaks of the birth of Mary, the annunciation and birth of Jesus and true and false belief in Jesus. Jesus is a creature of God like Adam; this is the truth that comes from God, about which there can be no doubt. There is a simple logic at work here: God's Word is spoken through the prophets, reminding humankind of God's demands, promising protection and judgement, and guiding those who will listen to a heavenly reward. The prophecy of Jesus restores what the Jews have ignored; the prophecy of Muhammad returns humankind to the right way that Christians have subverted. The problem, as Muslims see it, is not just that God's revelation is not heard, but that human beings in their ignorance tamper with it and change it. Christians have turned the messenger into the message, ignoring Jesus's preaching of God's will for humankind and substituting the false doctrine of the Trinity for the sublime monotheism of Islam. None of this is stated explicitly in *A Common Word*. Indeed, it is possible to detect a different strand of reasoning at work, that which, as Jane Dammen McAuliffe notes, sits awkwardly alongside the accusation of *tahrif* or corruption, namely efforts to find in the biblical text prophecies of the coming of Muhammad.[17] Nevertheless, if the spirit of ancient polemic is refreshingly absent, the opening imperative does spell out an invitation or *da'wa* to Christians to submit to God's will for humankind.[18] This is hardly surprising. Islamic orthodoxy demands that Muslims witness to their faith, just as Christian faith is inseparable from the mission with which God, through the Son and the Spirit, has charged his Church. It is only honest – as with any dialogue – to recognise the differences and disparities, sometimes quite enormous, which exist between communities of faith.

At the end of this chapter I will return briefly to the dialogue that *A Common Word* has provoked. At that point I shall restrict my comments to this issue of mission – arguably the most contentious division between the two faiths. I wish to approach that question, however, through the difficult, but still rewarding, experience of Muslim–Christian dialogue. When critical voices are raised about the limitations of 'joint texts' or proposals for common action, it sometimes seems that 'dialogue' is fruitless. If people are not prepared to listen, understand, and make some accommodation to the other which significantly affects the presentation of their faith, does this

believed in by one of them, the Muslims, and the soundness of which could hardly be denied by the other party, the Christians'. S. A. A. Maududi, *Towards Understanding the Quran* (Leicester: Islamic Foundation, 1988), vol. i, p. 262. I am grateful to Chris Hewer for this reference.

[17] Jane Dammen McAuliffe, 'The Quranic context of Muslim Biblical scholarship', *Islam and Christian–Muslim Relations*, 7 (1996), 141–158 and McAuliffe, 'Is There a Connection between the Bible and the Quran?', *Theological Digest*, 49 (2002), pp. 303–17.

[18] On *da'wa*, see David Marshall, *God, Muhammad and the Unbelievers* (London: Curzon, 1999).

not entrench them more deeply in their carefully defended positions? It depends, of course, on our expectations of dialogue. Throughout this book I have been working with a model of religious community as a school of faith and used metaphors for the practice of dialogue such as translation, reading, attention and waiting. This works well, I have argued, for the encounter between Jews and Christians, where the relationship is historically so close, and for the dialogue with Buddhism, where the traditions are so different. With Islam the challenge to the Christian theological imagination is that much greater.

This is not just because creedal confessions and testimonies are in many ways diametrically opposed, but because Christianity is built into the Muslim narrative. This need not imply a total abrogation of Christianity in favour of Islam; indeed, there are verses in the Quran that can and should be read with an inclusivist rather than exclusivist meaning.[19] The Shi'a theologian, Muhammad Legenhausen, argues for what he calls a 'non-reductive pluralism'. He agrees that Christian theology needs to be rewritten in favour of the message of the *original* forms of *Tawrat* and *Injil* as God delivered them.[20] But this is not to say that Islam relativises all the previous prophets. On the contrary, the perfection of revelation given in the Quran validates and, indeed, protects all that has gone before; Islam is not commending an indifferentism towards religious commitment. Strictly speaking, Islam does not 'need' Christianity or Judaism; the Quran is enough. Nevertheless, both traditions are implicated in the Quran and, whether one takes a strict supersessionist line or some version of Legenhausen's non-reductive pluralism, with its distinctly more generous (and more Catholic-sounding) sensitivity to the workings of grace in the human heart, the Muslim narrative will always include some reference to Christianity and Judaism as intimately bound up with what is revealed in the Quran, God's revelation of his will for the whole of humankind.

Christians, however, are not bound by any particular account of the 'Muslim other'. Islam emerges historically several centuries after the death of the last apostle, the point at which, according to Christian tradition, revelation is said to be closed. What possible prophetic message can Muslims offer to Christians? If dialogue is primarily about *learning* from

---

[19] See, e.g., sura 2.62: 'Those who believe (in the Quran), and those who follow the Jewish (scriptures), and the Christians and the Sabians, and who believe in God and the Last Day, and work righteousness, shall have their reward with their Lord: on them shall be no fear, nor shall they grieve'. (Repeated in a slightly shorter form in sura 5.69.) According to many scholars, these are late Medinan suras – which means that they are not open to abrogation. My thanks to Ahmad Achtar for this point.

[20] Muhammad Legenhausen, *Islam and Religious Pluralism* (London: Al-Hoda, 1999).

the other something of the ways of God with human beings, then for the Christian partner this question must be kept clearly in view. In what follows, while accepting that there can be no theological correlation that smoothes out the different estimates that Christians and Muslims give to each other, I want to argue that there is great scope for developing a more interpersonal dialogue. Christians and Muslims may not agree about the theological content of our respective scriptures nor how they are to be interpreted, but that does not make the effort to read together a fruitless exercise. To invoke Rosenzweig's distinction, comparative theology in Islamic mode, perhaps more than any other dialogue, depends not on the commonalities of scripture (the 'book') but on what I shall call the logic of spiritual practice – meaning by this a version of Rosenzweig's 'word', what can be heard in and through a sometimes sharp and demanding debate – which opens up between the participants.

CHRISTIAN REACTIONS TO ISLAM

The exercise does, however, need care and preparation. If Islam remains at the present time a puzzle, and even a threat, an integrity to the tradition of faith that sustains Muslims has to be acknowledged. All the more reason to pause to consider the history of engagement. The origins of Islam in the seventh century CE had a profound impact on the Christianity of the time. Hugh Goddard draws our attention to three different reactions.[21] The earliest was to interpret Islam in the light of Old Testament stories about the descendants of Abraham. In the book of Genesis, Abraham has two sons, Ishmael born of the slave girl Hagar, and Isaac, born of Sarah, Abraham's wife. God makes a promise to Abraham: 'I will make a nation of the son of the slave woman also, because he is your offspring' (Gen. 21:12–13). Later, when the descendants of Abraham are listed, Ishmael's sons are placed before Isaac's; they make up twelve tribes, appearing somehow to parallel the twelve tribes of Israel. In this light Islam is a recrudescence of Old Testament prophecy. Very quickly, however, this interpretation was challenged by the self-perception of the early Muslims themselves, that their faith was not a refounding of an ancient tradition but a direct challenge to the corrupt practice of Christian and Jews. What made the Muslims' case so persuasive was that the Christian world in which Islam emerged was itself

---

[21] Hugh Goddard, *A History of Christian–Muslim Relations* (Edinburgh University Press, 2000), pp. 34 ff. The same issues are discussed by Norman Daniel, *Islam and the West: The Making of an Image* (Oxford: Oneworld, 2000), especially pp. 35–99.

fragmented and divided. Islam, with its disarmingly simple monotheism, brought unity. It is not altogether surprising, therefore, that a Christian apologia emerged which saw Islam as God's judgement on churches that were responsible for causing Christian disunity. A third reaction shifted attention back to the Muslims themselves. This made Islam a Christian heresy. John of Damascus (675–*c*.750) is the first and most prominent exponent of this interpretation. Islam is a dangerous concoction of the Old and New Testaments, full of 'laughable revelations', a 'forerunner of the Antichrist' that leads people astray.[22] In Armour's opinion, 'John had several things right' about Islam, including the ancestral link back to Ishmael and the well-known story of the recognition of Muhammad's prophethood by the Syrian monk Bahira.[23] John, however, was quick to make Bahira an Arian Christian and condemn the Islamic phenomenon as a mix of Arianism and Nestorianism.

These three responses – fulfilment, judgement, heresy – cannot be neatly separated out from one another. They developed against a background of growing political and theological antagonism which ensured that any positive insight into the nature of this new phenomenon was quickly lost. Rolland comments that if Islam was a heresy then 'it had no independent revelation and should come under the authority of the Church'.[24] Further ammunition was needed to attack what, with the extraordinary flowering of Islamic civilisation in Spain and the beginning of the Crusades at the end of the tenth century, was beginning to appear as a major religious and political threat. The focus of attack shifts to the person and, more particularly, the character of Muhammad himself. If Muslims claimed that Jesus was 'only a prophet', then the Christian riposte had to be that Muhammad was not just less than a prophet but a human being of dubious character: violent, sensuous, untrustworthy, who – crucially – did no miracles and passed off his own fantasies as the revelations of God. Such polemics have lasted up until the present day, creating a theological atmosphere in which the person of the prophet Muhammad himself has become a major issue.[25] *Nostra Aetate*, for all that it made such promising overtures towards the Muslims, commending their worship of the one true God, their reverence for Jesus

---

[22] See Andrew Louth, *St John Damascene: Tradition and Originality in Byzantine Theology* (Oxford University Press, 2002), pp. 76–83.
[23] Rollin Armour, *Islam, Christianity and the West: A Troubled History* (New York: Orbis, 2002), p. 42.
[24] *Ibid.*, p. 52.
[25] A clear and straightforward version of Christian polemic against Muhammad as a pseudo-prophet is to be found in Daniel, *Islam and the West*, pp. 100–30.

and his mother Mary, avoided even naming Muhammad. A rather more constructive response to the question is beginning to emerge, helped in no small measure by historical scholarship that has retrieved the 'public culture' of language and philosophy shared by Muslims and Christians in the formative period of Islamic history. The question – what status can be given to this new religious phenomenon? – is not in itself new. Whatever the perceptions that have driven the two faiths apart over the centuries, there was a point, as Sidney Griffith remarks, when 'there really was in some measure a community of discourse about religion between Muslims and Christians in spite of the clash of their theologies, and in spite of the civil and social disabilities under which the Christians, together with the Jews and other religious minorities, lived'.[26] Maybe it is time, suggests Griffith, for the Church to listen to the voices of Christians who have done their philosophy and theology in Arabic and Syriac for centuries. The history of relations between Christians and Muslims is capable of a very melancholy interpretation, and usually gets it. Nevertheless, the story is not all negative, and positive theological comment has always been possible – as the researches of scholars and the experience of a handful of interreligious pioneers show.

Despite the polemics, it is recognised that, in some sense, we are talking about a common intellectual tradition. But how precisely are these commonalities to be handled? First, let me make a couple of brief reflections. What holds the two traditions together is not the Muslim concession that makes Christians people of the book, *Ahl al-Kitab*, but, more subtly, the theological issue that the reliance of *both* on a textual tradition raises. The infinite and mysterious God is made manifest in the world by speaking a word. In Christianity, of course, the Word is *made Flesh*; in Islam the Word is *made Book* – the Holy Quran. The temptation is twofold, *either* to make the incarnate Word or the 'enbooked' Word something less than the fullness of God's revelation – God *truly* present – *or* to turn the 'form' taken by the self-limiting God into an idol. Just as Christians have developed a whole mode of discourse to explain the Incarnation, so Muslims have sought to show how God can be 'made book', how God can speak God's Word and still remain God. To that extent Christians and Muslims labour at very similar theological tasks. Christ is not a creature who carries out God's salvific will, but the creative Word through whom all that is comes to be. Similarly, Muslims ask whether the Quran is created or uncreated – the first

---

[26] Sidney Griffith, *The Church in the Shadow of the Mosque* (Princeton, NJ: Princeton University Press, 2008), p. 156.

of God's works or eternally existing as an attribute of God?[27] The Quran refers to the original foundation of eternal Scripture, the 'mother of the book' (*umm al-kitāb*, Quran 13:39; 43:4), which is to be distinguished from the forms – *Tawrat, Zabur, Injil* and finally the Quran itself – revealed to the prophets. God's Word is 'sent down' upon the Prophet Mohammad who receives it without intellectual or creative engagement.

A rather abstract debate about the nature of the eternal and beginningless Word that yet appears in time is resolved for most Muslims by a practice of faith that is deeply rooted in continued 'recitation' of the sacred text. The prophet is but a mouthpiece; he does not interpret the Word but acts as its channel to human beings. Thus the continuing performance of the 'event' of the Quran is everything. At this point the debate begins to shift away from the polemics of interpretation to the 'logic of practice'. As a Muslim friend once put it to me, 'God loves to hear God's Word'. God takes delight in the praise of the people God has created. Although so often reduced to a compendium of commands, warnings and judgements, the Quran is primarily a liturgical text that forms a community of faith as well as providing a guide for human living. In this sense we are talking of the revelation of *God's will* rather than a manifestation of God's self. The Quran makes possible a way of life for those who submit; through the discipline of faith that teaches self-control and just relations with the rest of human society the individual achieves a measure of integration and inner harmony.

Naturally there is an anthropological issue here. Islam has a generally positive attitude to human nature. There is no doctrine of the Holy Spirit to explain how the mystery of God's Word can be heard, let alone spoken, by human beings – because there is no need. Muslims will always say that they have no doctrine of Original Sin, that every human being is capable of practising Islam, submission to the will of God. Although the questions of human freedom and predestination are important, more awkward questions

---

[27] For Christianity, says Esposito, the 'appropriate question is "What do Christians believe?" In contrast, for Islam (as for Judaism), the correct question is "What do Muslims *do?*"'. Nevertheless, the emphasis on orthopraxy rather than orthodoxy 'has not precluded the importance of faith or belief'. Islamic theology (*kalam*, speech or discourse) may not have been developed with the thoroughness or intensity of its Christian counterpart, but it addressed similar questions and responded to similar debates, most obviously the dispute about God's attributes between the rationalist Mu'tazilites, for whom the Quran is to be interpreted allegorically and is therefore created, and the mainstream Sunni response of the Asharite school, where the emphasis is more firmly on the Quran as the revealed yet eternally uncreated Word. See John Esposito, *Islam: The Straight Path* (Oxford University Press, 1998), pp. 68–74. The terms of this controversy, and the parallels which it finds in Christian debates about the nature of God's self-revealing Word, are discussed at length in the classic study by Harry Austryn Wolfson, *The Philosophy of Kalam* (Cambridge, Mass.: Harvard University Press, 1976).

about grace and necessity and the sheer tragedy of lives that fail to recognise the reality of God are much more difficult to raise. As we shall see in the next chapter, the theme of redemptive suffering is not entirely alien to Islam; the Shi'a tradition, with its 'martyr myth' stemming from the battle of Karbala, is dominated by what Yann Richard calls 'this agony which is at one and the same time a revolt and a sign of hope'.[28] There are important 'resonances' here with the Servant motif of Judaism and Christianity (points to be explored in the next chapter). But they have to be set against the fundamental thrust of the mainstream of the Sunni tradition in which God speaks and works directly with human beings and needs no intermediary. The exemplary status of Jesus's suffering as free submission is one thing. To give him some sort of redeemer status *on behalf of others* quite another.

In dialogue, the 'room for manoeuvre', let alone translation, is limited. In so far as we are speaking about traditions that share a single yet complex and contested history, it seems entirely plausible to find the meeting point between our two traditions within the doctrine of revelation. For Muslims Jesus speaks the *Injil* in the same way as Muhammad speaks the Quran. For Christians, however, the Word of God revealed in Christ is an invitation to human beings to participate in the very life of God. The Word is not a Word *about* God, but a revelation of Godself that sanctifies the whole of creation. The specificity of Christian faith is always to be understood in terms of a particular narrative of God's engagement with a people who are formed after the manner of Christ. For Muslims, of course, this leads to a mistaken identification of the Word with the person of the prophet Jesus. At stake here, I feel, is not the unanswerable question of how Christian and Muslim accounts of revelation can be made to cohere (unanswerable not just because what is revealed is quite different but because the Christian version is openly contested by the Quran itself); it is, rather, to do with how the Christian narrative can maintain its focus on the Incarnation as the decisive 'moment' of the action of the self-revealing God while yet granting some substantive value to properly Muslim accounts of prophecy and revelation.

A PROPHETIC WORD OF PRAISE

This is where we need to shift tack and to ask a different sort of question, one that takes us back to the neuralgic question of the status of the prophet Muhammad. The early idea that Muhammad was a prophet in the line of

[28] Yann Richard, *Shi'ite Islam* (Oxford: Blackwell, 1995), p. 29

Abraham has been developed most famously in Louis Massignon's account of Muhammad as a 'negative prophet'. This is not a comment on the value of Muhammad's utterances. Massignon is making the point that the Quranic revelation does not add anything radically new but points back to the single prophetic tradition that guides all God's people. Islam is 'The faith of Abraham revived with Muhammad'.[29] This is a welcome shift away from the tradition of Christian vilification of Muhammad as, at best, insincere and, at worst, a cynical manipulator. The idea of 'negative prophecy' has, however, received different interpretations, among them the interesting suggestion that it should be understood in apophatic terms as drawing attention to the insufficiency of language about God and, therefore, the danger of idolatry.[30] Some ambiguity is inevitable. Massignon's theological problem is how to address Muslim concerns that Christians should give some positive role to Muhammad as a prophet (and to express their own admiration for the person and teaching of Muhammad) while remaining true to the Christian faith that nothing more can be added to what has been definitively given in Christ. Both words are important. Muhammad is a *negative* prophet because he warns of the dangers inherent in Christian language about the Incarnation of Jesus. But he is a negative *prophet* because he continues to uphold the prophetic vocation of Israel that recognises the utter transcendence of God and the demands that God makes on his people.[31] Massignon, therefore, takes the emphasis away from any 'message' that Muhammad might actually be saying and gives the Quran itself an interpretation that Christians can understand in Christological terms. In other words, despite the structural similarities, the Quran is not a further collection of 'inspired words' that can be made to stand alongside those of the Old and New Testaments. But it can still be understood – through the 'logic of practice' as *a word of prophecy*. Through interpersonal engagement, in which ideas about the great themes that connect Jewish, Christian and Muslim faith, familiar echoes are often heard. These may well turn Christians back to Christ, reminding them perhaps of some forgotten or unexpected meaning. Some version of this movement of retrieval is present in any interreligious encounter. In the dialogue with Islam, however, something more crucial is at stake.

---

[29] See, e.g., Sidney Griffith, 'Sharing the Faith of Abraham: The "Credo" of Louis Massignon', *Islam and Christian–Muslim Relations*, 8 (1997), pp. 193–210.
[30] *Ibid.*
[31] I am grateful to Christian Crokus for this insight (unpublished Ph.D. thesis, Boston College, 2009). The formulation here is, however, my own.

Christianity does not 'need' Islam for its sense of self. On the other hand, the very contestation of Christian claims (albeit in the benign terms of Legenhausen's non-reductive pluralism) does raise a serious challenge to the Christian confession that in the Paschal Mystery of the Death and Resurrection of Christ God's providential purposes for the whole of humankind are definitively revealed. The question, therefore, is how very different accounts of revelation can be developed so that the continuity between the economy of creation and the economy of redemption is heard by both parties. It is arguable that the dynamic of the Christian narrative moves naturally from the latter, the 'moment' of divine entry into the world, to the former, the overarching mystery of God's self-giving. It is because of the Church's experience of God revealed in Christ that the language of Trinity is developed. What I have called the Islamic 'logic of practice' works the other way round. To repeat: what is revealed is God's will rather than God's own self. The sovereignty of God demands recognition and the glory of humanity lies in being made capable of giving praise to God through service and submission. That is what human beings are created for: not somehow to retrieve what has been lost but faithfully to recite God's own words which bring to mind the single divine truth that holds all things in being. This leads Kenneth Cragg to remark that 'When they are wisely alert both Islamic and Christian theologies make for human doxology with the natural order as its ground and theme.' He then goes on, perhaps surprisingly, to say that '[h]owever differently they proceed, they both mean that the human experience is everywhere sacramental'.[32] Cragg's point is that both traditions, albeit in different ways, recognise that human beings are hallowed in and through the world of everyday experience – whether we can be said to enter into this experience through 'the flesh' or through submission to the divine command. The meeting point lies in a doctrine of creation or, to be more precise, in a doctrine of revelation that makes God's act of creation its central theme.

The ease with which Muslims refer everything to God is both intriguing and disturbing. And maybe that is the point. The *Shahada*, the confession of faith, is apophatic discourse of a peculiarly radical kind. It starts with a negative: '*La ilaha illa Allah*: there is no god save Allah.' This is very far from asserting that God is the one God among many, still less that the God of *this* people is somehow supreme over all. It is a statement about the utter incomparability of God. To understand what is being said here it is necessary to enter into the sort of Semitic rhetoric that comes from a

---

[32] Kenneth Cragg, *The Christ and the Faiths* (London: SPCK, 1986), p. 42.

community deeply aware of living in *the very presence of God* yet also partaking of a space contested by others – pagan Arab tribes as well as Jews and Christians. The *Shahada* has to be understood against the background of the cleansing of the Kaaba and its rededication to Allah. 'None is worthy of worship except Allah.' For Christians this is a strange type of rhetoric, born from a particular experience of God and the idolatrous denial of the divine relationship, *Shirk*, which is its opposite. But, as noted earlier, it is not an alternative narrative to Judaism and Christianity so much as a deliberate critique of all other narratives. Such is Islamic universalism: a reassertion of what was given by God in the act of creation.

The status of Muhammad as prophet – and therefore the very nature of the Quran as in some way revelatory of divine reality – is the most avoided question in Muslim–Christian relations. A purely Abrahamic perspective would see Islam as a revival of an ancient covenantal tradition, a version of the 'oldest theology' of Islam noted earlier. Islam is basically a recrudescence or return of a form of Old Testament prophecy in which God's promises to make a people for himself are played out through a vast dialectic of peoples and nations none of whom is left without God's Word. This is all very plausible but can leave us mired in a form of supersessionism – made quite explicit in the familiar image of the three 'Abrahamic' traditions as a series of oases refreshing the weary traveller on the journey through the desert. Christians have only just learned to avoid supersessionist accounts of Judaism; all the more reason to avoid buying into similar versions of Islam that would reduce Christianity to no more than a failed tradition which needs radical overhaul. Hence my argument that Christians and Muslims seek to establish a wider framework for understanding the great theme of revelation – a doxological *Adamic* perspective in which human beings are called to give glory to their maker. In Islam, God's Word is described as acting in the world in different ways, speaking to different peoples, until the final revelation given through Prophet Muhammad. Nevertheless, Christians can still accept an account of Islam as celebrating God's creative Word – and the power of that Word to go on reminding all people everywhere of God's absolute demands and responsibilities.

RESPONSES TO GOD'S IMPERATIVE

According to my 'logic of practice', it is the pattern of faithful living that both keeps communities of faith apart and – strangely – holds them together. Judaism, Christianity and Islam have many religious phenomena in common; the God of revelation and prophethood most obviously. They are also very different; the status assumed by the canonical texts is only the most obvious point of divergence. Yet it is incontrovertible that all three traditions are based in responses to the creative and loving initiative of God. It is, therefore, entirely understandable why *A Common Word* should choose to open up a dialogue based on the theme of the two great commandments; texts on common themes can be set together and compared and contrasted. What is not so obvious, as my opening illustration was intended to show, is that the broad context within which texts must be read differs – sometimes enormously. Again, this does not make dialogue impossible. But it does demand attention to the history of a tradition's development and its engagement with wider culture, as well as with other religions. Christians have tended to set themselves apart from Judaism – and from Islam as a 'reversion' to Judaism – by invoking the distinction between 'law' and 'love'. Recent scholarly work on the Pharisee tradition of the first century has changed all that.[33] Jesus's 'second commandment' is not foreign to Judaism. On the contrary. Franz Rosenzweig, in his extraordinary account of the practices of Jewish faith, notes that the Passover service includes a reading from the Song of Songs. In the middle of the sacred recitation of the most ancient of Jewish memories about salvation and freedom comes this deeply erotic love poem. Rosenzweig's point is that the love that binds 'I and Thou' is 'stronger than death'. God's self-revelation, before it ever takes the form of a series of commands, Torah, is expressed in the imperative mood, 'Love'.

A downpour of imperatives descends on this evergreen pasture and vitalises It. The imperatives sound different but always mean the same thing: 'Draw me after you, open to me, rise, come away, hurry – it is always the same imperative of love.'[34]

Does it make sense to understand these three great traditions as embodying different but complementary responses to the divine imperative to love as God loves? Or, better, different versions of that *one* imperative that is revealed in God's act of creation? In Judaism the central imperative is the *Shemah*: 'Hear, O Israel' – Moses' great call to the people to remember what the God of the Covenant has done for them. For Christians, of course, there are many imperatives. The Gospels are shot through with imperatives, from the 'repent and believe' of Jesus's first preaching of the Kingdom to the 'do this in memory of me' spoken over bread and wine at the Last Supper.

---

[33] See particularly E. P. Sanders, *Paul and Palestinian Judaism: A Comparison of Patterns of Religion* (Minneapolis, Minn.: Fortress, 1977).
[34] Franz Rosenzweig, *The Star of Redemption*, trans. William W. Hallo (Notre Dame, Ind.: University of Notre Dame Press, 1985), p. 202.

There is the invitation to the tax-collector to 'follow me', the command to the fishermen to 'put out into the deep', the intriguing counter to the question of John's disciples, 'come and see'. Why so many? Perhaps because we human beings in all our pride and perversity require a good deal of probing and cajoling if the Word of God is to make a home in our hearts. If Judaism is based on the people's obedience, their acceptance of Torah, their willingness to live out the Covenant relationship, Christianity is through and through based on the personal relationship that is established between Jesus and those whom he calls to a life of discipleship.

And Islam? In arguing for an Adamic rather than an Abrahamic perspective on the relationship of the three traditions I want to foreground the theme of creation, and humanity's responsibility to witness to God's creative gift. David Burrell begins his contribution to the Yale symposium on *A Common Word*: 'where we all begin, and where Jews, Christians and Muslims all concur: the free creation of the universe by the One God'.[35] Creation is itself the act of the loving Creator and to respond to that love is what makes for the dignity of human beings. The Quran begins with another imperative, the command to the prophet 'Recite'. To recite as the prophet himself obediently repeated God's command is not just to speak but to do, to be faithful to God's Word in all aspects of one's life. Muhammad is the 'seal of the prophets' who is called to be the mouthpiece of God's Word to humankind. His task is to speak again the ever-demanding Word of God: 'there is no god but God'. There is a unity, a completeness perhaps, in God's self-revelation that sanctifies the whole of human living and that promises human beings the peace that comes only through a self-denying submission. That is not the same as fatalism; a Muslim would say that to put God first and to acknowledge limitation and creatureliness is the beginning of true human freedom. The creature is made with a dignity and a task; Adam is the first Muslim, created to give glory to God, for, as my friend put it, 'God loves to hear God's words.' Human beings only become free when we accept our vulnerability and acknowledge our dependence on God from whom all good things come.

COMMON WORDS AND GOD'S INVITATION

In conclusion, let me return briefly to where we began, to *A Common Word* and the questions it raises about dialogue and mission. I began with an example of a robust engagement between Muslims and Christians. Both are

---

[35] David Burrell, 'Transforming Love', in Volf, Muhammad and Yarrington, *A Common Word*, p. 153.

missionary traditions, with a universal message and certain non-negotiable truth claims. Muslims and Christians disagree on some important fundamentals, and a bluntly straightforward manner of self-presentation will go on characterising their relationship for the immediate future. The divine imperative of sura 3.64, 'come to a common word', is glossed by the authors as 'love' and leads to discussion of the two great commandments as the unifying theme between Christianity and Islam. Whatever else needs to be said about the very real differences that such a theme covers over, the fact is that *A Common Word* has started a conversation that takes seriously the mutual responsibility owed by both traditions to each other and to the wider pluralist and secular world of which they are part.

A common word is quite different from a final word. The purpose of interreligious dialogue is not some sort of treaty that keeps everyone quiet. Rather it is to open up conversations in a spirit of mutual regard and respect that allows the integrity of tradition to go on generating meaning and understanding. This is where the close textual study commended by comparative theology and such important movements as Scriptural Reasoning has an important practical purpose. Originating in the Jewish commentarial tradition, Scriptural Reasoning now involves both Christians and Muslims who come together in a variety of settings to learn from the communal study of specific texts.[36] The practice is intended to bring out the inner logic of the three traditions, drawing on the abundance of meaning from the 'plain sense' of the text, and introducing readers into their inherited prudential wisdom. In principle, such a shared reading makes for an attractive and easily regulated form of interreligious engagement. In practice, it can be as demanding as Clooney's painstaking comparison of Hindu and Christian texts – but for a different reason. If what I have argued above is correct, then whatever the similarities between the themes or wording of Jewish, Christian and Muslim canonical scripture, the correct Christian analogy for the Quran is the person of Christ, the Incarnate Word of God, not the New Testament. In terms of theological status the New Testament is closer to the *Hadith*, the collection of sayings and reports about the prophet that provides the model or *Sunna* for the Muslim way of life.[37] Like is not being compared with like. Does that reduce the exercise to a patronising nod in the direction of irredeemable strangeness? Only if the purpose of interreligious engagement is taken to be the negotiation of agreement

---

[36] On Scriptural Reasoning as an interreligious practice, see above, Chap. 6, n. 35.
[37] See Paul L. Heck, *Common Ground: Islam, Christianity and Religious Pluralism* (Washington, DC: Georgetown University Press, 2009), p. 18.

rather than the work of bringing people of faith together in an atmosphere of friendship and trust.[38] What Talmudic commentary, Bible study groups and Quranic exegesis all share is a conviction that a meaning is to be found in the text and that meaning is only to be discerned through a practice that begins and ends in prayer. For the Christian, what is being heard is not another message, still less a supplement to what has already been given in the pages of the New Testament, but echoes of that single imperative, to love, that is incarnated in the person of Christ. Into that mystery there can be no end of invitations.

It is, of course, perfectly possible to interpret Islam and Christianity as being in competition with each other – as many of the responses to my radio broadcast indicated. Yet what I have tried to show is that contestation of some sort of shared revealed tradition is not the only way to regard what has, of course, been a relationship replete with polemic and at times almost visceral hatred. Religions are not a set of more or less similar answers to the same question. Rather, they ask different questions and make different responses to what I have called in the title of this chapter the 'divine imperative'. Dialogue is less about debating truth claims than about creating the conditions within which the *questions themselves* can be heard and understood. Christians, Jews and Muslims are only at the beginning of this process, and have a long way to go. But it may be a mark of some progress that through texts like *Nostra Aetate*, *Dabru Emet* and now '*A Common Word*' persons from these three similar-yet-different traditions have begun to acknowledge at least the possibility that God's imperative speaks through the voice of the other, to 'us' through 'them'.

It has become a commonplace since the Second Vatican Council to speak of the Church as missionary of its very nature.[39] The Church does not *have* a mission but, more accurately, participates in *God's* mission, in God's action of sending the Son and the Spirit into the world. The Church exists in order to co-operate in this mission by witnessing to the truth that is Christ. This is not to say that the only legitimate form of mission for Christians is preaching. Indeed, it opens up myriad other possibilities for giving witness to life lived in and through the Spirit of God. In calling this section of the book

---

[38] Thus Peter Ochs, its 'philosophical god-father', speaks about Scriptural Reasoning as 'a laboratory, rather than as an effort to test only a single hypothesis, and as a process of comparing notes rather than generating a consensus.' Important here is the refusal of an 'either/or' dichotomy; for Ochs, Textual (and therefore Scriptural) Reasoning has its own form of rationality, one which mediates between or seeks to overcome the inevitable tensions thrown up by textual traditions. See Peter Ochs, 'Response: Reflections on Binarism', *Modern Theology*, 24.3 (July 2008), p. 496.

[39] See especially the Vatican II Decree on the Church's Missionary Activity, *Ad Gentes*, 2.

'Imaginings' I am drawing attention to the *sine qua non* of any successful act of translating the self into another cultural world. Clearly an imaginative approach to mission, which actively discerns the ways in which God's Spirit always goes ahead of the Church, is nowadays more necessary than ever. By imagination, however, I am not talking about the facility to exercise the power of the mind to consider things that are not directly present to the senses, still less to envisage what is not real. I am concerned with establishing a version of Taylor's 'social imaginary', which responds to the complex demands of life in a pluralist multi-faith society.[40]

In the next chapter I want to take up the challenge that Islam raises for any such Christian 'social imaginary', especially with regard to the demands of justice, and in the final chapters I will press this point further by returning to the theme of the Spirit. Here I close with a final word on the theme of mission and with a brief reference to St Francis of Assisi, whose personal mission to the Egyptian court of Al-Malik al-Kamil, the nephew of the great Muslim leader Saladin, makes him an admirable patron of interreligious dialogue and whose mission was a delicate business.[41] His commitment to finding an alternative to a belligerent engagement is prophetic of our situation today when the Church finds itself living side by side with people from very different cultures and faith traditions who have their own vision of truth. Once the other was expected to soak up a manifest truth; now the other takes a more active role and presumes to answer back. Proclamation has always had a privileged place in the missionary's armoury. But there are other ways of communicating truth – not least the witness of a life that speaks of deeply held values. To paraphrase the admirable sentiment of St Francis of Assisi, 'preach always, and sometimes use words'.

---

[40] Taylor, *Modern Social Imaginaries*, p. 23.
[41] The example of St Francis as an 'interreligious patron' is noted in the document from the Vatican's Secretariat for non-Christians: 'The Attitude of the Church Towards the Followers of Other Religions' ['Dialogue and Mission'], *Bulletin*, 19/2 (1984), pp. 126–41.

CHAPTER 10

Passion for justice

A few years ago I was part of a small delegation of Catholic theologians visiting the Iranian holy city of Qom, some 100 miles south of Tehran. It is a city that beats to the pulse of tradition. Holy sayings are inscribed in mosaic and traced in neon lights. The unmoving face of the Imam Khomeini glowers from posters. Women, young and old, fresh-faced students as well as aged grannies, bustle around, all dressed top-to-toe in black widow's weeds. Yet it is also a place with a rich and diverse religious culture of its own. Qom has been likened to an Islamic Oxford with its array of academic institutes and study centres. Libraries proliferate, some the benefactions of much-loved local teachers, others carefully husbanded collections of religious and philosophical literature from different parts of the world. The scholarly pursuit of truth is part of the atmosphere. On every street corner, mullahs, dressed in the full-length flowing robes of the Shi'a cleric, seem to be engaged in one never-ending seminar – or maybe just haggling over the price of the books.

In such an atmosphere, where religion is such a live issue, interreligious conversations can suddenly happen in unlikely places. I have a vivid memory of the hair-raising bus trip back to Tehran. The driver clearly thought that careering along a narrow crowded road with headlights blazing at the oncoming traffic was some sort of virility test. In order to distract myself from the prospect of instant oblivion I got into conversation with my companion, a Shi'a theologian who was our host in Qom. Shouting over the constant blare of horns, he explained that Shi'a Islam is based on three principles – spirituality, rationality, and justice. The life of prayer and intellectual enquiry together support a life dedicated to the cause of truth and justice in the world. Putting it another way, he went on, the Shi'a account of the religious life is vested in three aspects of the divine–human relationship, what God reveals about God's will for human beings.[1] Human beings find their purpose in life by bringing the three into some sort of a correlation – to pray sincerely, to think clearly, and to do what is right. What he had to say impressed me, as much for the cogency of his presentation as for the craziness of the situation in which we found ourselves. I cannot, to be honest, remember much of the detail with which he justified the Shi'a version of interdependence of the three principles. It was, however, clear from the thoughtful way in which he expounded his thesis that the Shi'a tradition he represented was light years away from the popular stereotype of the self-flagellating masochist – or from the distinctly irrational behaviour of our driver.

In the previous chapter I used a certain 'logic of practice' as a point of entry into the dialogue between Christianity and Islam. I was concerned there to expand the scope of the Christian religious imagination to embrace a tradition that remains an enigma, seemingly a recrudescence of the prophecy so familiar from the Old Testament yet expressed in a form that speaks less of revelation as Christians would understand the term than of sheer delight in the beauty and order of God's creative purposes. The divine imperative that human beings should 'recite' God's Word is, however, more than a demand to engage in some never-ending ritual of prayer. It is also a demand to act justly. And therein, of course, lies a huge risk – what I spoke of at the end of my very first chapter. Religion as a 'comprehensive pattern' has to give space to the other; when it does not, conflict almost inevitably follows. It is relatively easy to imagine how things might be different, much more difficult to temper the imagination with the truth of everyday tragedy and suffering.

Later that evening, after we had arrived in Tehran at the grandly titled Ministry of Culture and Islamic Relations, I listened to an old man recounting his experience of the Iran–Iraq war of the 1980s. He was not in a forgiving mood. From what he told me, I could not blame him. It was a chance meeting, a reality check that set the urbane spiritual conversations I had enjoyed in Qom in stark relief. The task of harmonising the claims of spirituality, rationality and justice is complex. However much we human beings may seek that ideal patterning of things that gives meaning to our experience, however carefully we may measure our actions against the canons of reason, however faithfully we may seek to put into practice the

---

[1] In this chapter I freely acknowledge my debt to various Shi'a friends, particularly to Mohammad Ali Shomali, who has written copiously on aspects of Shi'a religious practice. See his *Shi'i Islam: Origins, Faith and Practices* (London: ICAS, 2003), especially pp. 123–50 and *Discovering Shi'i Islam* (Qum: Jami'at al-Zahra, 2003), especially pp. 39–51.

teachings of tradition, we are always in the middle of things, never hovering majestically above the mess. There is always a limit to what we can see, always the loose strands that cannot be neatly tidied away, never the perfect resolution of ideals and desires. It may be a subtle violence, but it remains violence nonetheless – to impose order where none at this precise moment is possible. At times it is almost as if we are too afraid of falling into the trap of that 'unworthy shallowness' that Rafael Scharf's teacher complained about; we think only a strong response will do. Order, however, is not the same as justice. The risk is that the desire for justice spills over into a lust for vengeance.

THE PATHOLOGY OF RELIGION

At its best, spirituality and the wisdom of tradition channel human attitudes, instincts and feelings and enable a community to structure its social and cultural life. But religion is not always 'at its best'; it can go toxic and lead to violent excesses. In seeking to give some account of the pathology of religion – its dark and destructive side – it is the sheer power of conviction, that these actions are right or even commended by God, which demands attention. The problem with appeals to some transcendent authority is that they can justify almost anything – a whole spectrum of responses, from peace movements to terrorist outrages.[2] Bernard Lewis notes that most Muslims are not fundamentalists and most fundamentalists do not resort to terrorism. But a few do and are proud to do so in the name of Islam.[3] Not that this is a peculiarly Islamic problem – even if, since 9/11, it is in Islam that the fatal ambiguities of motivation are most apparent. At the beginning of his frightening yet fascinating survey of the rise of religiously inspired violence in recent years across a whole range of religious traditions, from anti-abortion Christians in the USA to Sikh separatists in Panjab, Mark Juergensmeyer admits to a certain bemusement: 'What puzzles me is not

[2] The capacity of religion to inspire deeply felt yet very different responses is the opening theme of Scott Appleby's excellent study of religiously inspired violence, *The Ambivalence of the Sacred* (Lanham, Md.: Rowman & Littlefield, 2000). Since 9/11, the debate about the relationship of violence and religion has run in various directions. Working within 'new genocide studies' and seeking to trace the origins of violence as 'constitutive of the human condition', John Docker links the ancient Greek world and the Old Testament to the Enlightenment in *The Origins of Violence: Religion, History and Genocide* (London: Pluto Press, 2008). For a strong version of the link between genocide and religion, see Steven Leonard Jacobs (ed.), *Confronting Genocide: Judaism, Christianity, Islam* (Lanham, Md.: Lexington, 2009). For a counter to the thesis that religion is the single most significant cause of intercommunal violence, see William T. Cavanaugh, *The Myth of Religious Violence: Secular Ideology and the Roots of Modern Conflict* (Oxford University Press, 2009).

[3] Bernard Lewis, *The Crisis of Islam: Holy War and Unholy Terror* (London: Phoenix, 2004), p. 117.

why bad things are done by bad people, but rather why bad things are done by people who otherwise appear to be good . . . by pious people dedicated to a moral vision of the world.'[4] The piety of the devout, the righteousness of the prophet, the suffering of the hero, the zeal of the aggrieved victim, all in their own way are admirable. But, as Juergensmeyer's melancholy portraits illustrate so powerfully, unmediated, uncritical religion can be dangerous. These are difficult and murky areas that have spawned an ever-proliferating literature, from studies of particular instances of inter-community conflict to more theoretical accounts of the links between religion and violence.[5] That this is a global phenomenon, affecting international relations as much as theology, is set out with enormous erudition in Samuel Huntington's celebrated book about the coming 'clash of civilizations'. The central theme of the book is that 'culture and cultural identities . . . are shaping the patterns of cohesion, disintegration, and conflict in the post-Cold War world.'[6] In the wake of 9/11, it seemed eerily prophetic. Huntington argues that the world is now entering an era of 'identity politics' in which the most important groupings of nation states will be determined not by the bipolar antagonisms of the 1960s but by 'fault lines' laid down by centuries of cultural growth and interaction. Huntington names eight civilisations: Western, Confucian, Japanese, Islamic, Hindu, Slavic-Orthodox, Latin American 'and possibly African'. The hesitation over the last is nothing if not an indication that religio-cultural fault lines are never easy to draw. Not that it is just Africa which turns out on closer inspection to be an awkward addition to the new 'multi-polar, multi-civilizational' world map. In the last decade, it has not been the strength of some sort of Islamic power block that has appeared as a threat to the West but the very opposite.

In the previous chapter I drew attention to Philip Lewis's comment about the 'confusion' that so many young Muslims feel in today's world. A similar point was noted in an essay some years back in which Marshall Hodgson speaks about the collapse of self-confidence in the Muslim world.[7] Caught

---

[4] Mark Juergensmeyer, *Terror in the Mind of God* (Berkeley: University of California Press, 2003), p. 7.
[5] On the phenomenon of fundamentalism, see the five volumes of Martin Marty and R. Scott Appleby (eds.), *The Fundamentalism Project* (University of Chicago Press, 1993–2004): *Fundamentalisms Observed, Fundamentalisms and Society, Fundamentalisms and the State, Accounting for Fundamentalisms, Fundamentalisms Comprehended.*
[6] Samuel Huntington, *The Clash of Civilizations and the Remaking of World Order* (London: Simon and Schuster, 1997), p. 20. The central thesis behind the book appeared in an article 'The Clash of Civilizations?', *Foreign Affairs* (summer 1993).
[7] 'Modernity and the Islamic Heritage', in Marshall Hodgson, *Rethinking World History: Essays on Europe, Islam, and World History*, ed. Edmund Burke (Cambridge University Press,1999).

between Western achievement and the failure to renew traditional means of self-identification, contemporary Islam is institutionally weak. While Huntington's distinction of monolithic blocks does have a certain plausibility, it begs too many questions – about what is meant by 'civilisation' and 'religion', let alone how geographical distinctions like 'Western' or 'Latin American' can be put on the same plane as 'Confucian' or 'Hindu'. I have argued by contrast that no 'religion' is monolithic; we are speaking about internally diverse communities of persons who are themselves the products of diffuse historical forces. That alone makes the marking of boundaries between supposedly unique 'religious civilisations' sometimes quite problematic. The issue is not about maintaining some sort of West-dominated universal values that can be applied across the board of religious diversity but about understanding how difference and sameness can coexist *within* the same broad traditions of faith. 'Religion', to repeat an earlier point, is not a universally applicable term. If there is a universal, we are speaking about an instinct that is deeply rooted in the human psyche: what I have called the 'conviction of meaning', that ultimately life makes sense. The danger, as I have argued, is that faith can become reduced to 'mere' culture or radicalised into 'pure' ideology (a failing, ironically, to which Huntington himself is prone). To put it another way, the desire for transcendence can be subverted or given a premature resolution.

What I have called a spirituality of dialogue is a matter of reflecting on the implications of living in Buber's 'inter-human', listening to the other and seeking to discern through the interrogation of themes and ideas the signs of the Spirit at work in the world. If there is an answer to the problem of religiously inspired violence (and I am not sure that there can ever be one 'answer', for so much depends on particularity and context), it lies with the constant practice of returning to the marketplace, if not transformed then better informed and more resolved to stay with the problems of a broken world.[8] This section of the book I have called 'Imaginings', the third and arguably the most important dimension of the social imaginary that underpins interreligious learning. Recalling Taylor's words once again, we need to distinguish between the 'intellectual schemes' that people think about when in 'disengaged mode' and the 'deeper normative notions and images' that

---

[8] The image of the 'broken middle' comes from the book of that title by Gillian Rose (Oxford: Blackwell, 1992) and is taken up in Michael Barnes, *Theology and the Dialogue of Religions*. For a philosophical critique of Rose's work, set against her biography and reception into the Anglican Church, see Andrew Shanks, *Against Innocence: Gillian Rose's Reception and Gift of Faith* (London: SCM, 2008).

give shape to their expectations.[9] The point I am arguing is that we are often too much in a hurry to bring the two together – usually to the detriment of the latter. There can, however, be no purely 'rational' response to problems of inter-communal violence without first taking time to attend to the underlying affective as much as cognitive issues that foster suspicion and prejudice. To go back to what my Shi'a friend was saying, the proper channelling of desire that is spirituality is as important as the demands to do justice and act with reason.

In continuing the dialogue between Christians and Muslims, I do not intend to come up with some magic formula for bringing spirituality, rationality and justice into some sort of neat correlation. I want rather to extend the range of a spirituality of dialogue by considering the part rituals and religious practices of all kinds play in structuring traditions and religious practice. By anchoring ourselves into the secure structures that the wisdom of the school of faith hands down, we learn how to practise imaginative improvisations on the various imperatives that are constantly sounded by the Word of God. What follows is just one such variation on a constant, if elusive, theme. After a brief comparison of Ramadan and Lent, I move on to the Shi'a tradition in order to bring a different perspective to bear upon the question of religious agency. This will take us back to the fraught issue of religiously inspired violence. Throughout, I am concerned less with what people do than with *why* they do it. In asking how Christians and Muslims can learn from a dialogue of religious practice and experience, is there some insight to be gained into the pathology of religion? How does practice form the religious imagination? And is this something *we* do – or what we somehow allow God to effect in us?

PRAYER AND COMMUNITY

There are, of course, many similarities between Christianity and Islam in terms of actual religious practice. Each of the 'five pillars of Islam' – *shahada*, the statement of belief, *salat*, prayer, *zakat*, almsgiving, *sawm*, fasting and *hajj*, pilgrimage – has its parallel and a similar purpose in Christianity. Prayer in both traditions is an act of remembrance and praise, putting God first and returning all God's favours to their ultimate source. Fasting is intended to promote a proper sense of priorities and develop self-discipline. Almsgiving redresses the balance in God's creation and reminds people of the needs of the poor. Even statements of belief and pilgrimages, for all that

[9] Charles Taylor, *A Secular Age* (Cambridge, Mass.: Harvard University Press, 2007), p. 171.

they differ in many particulars, have certain fundamental points in common. In both Islam and Christianity religious life begins with the initiation of a public commitment which then takes the form of a sometimes arduous journey. In both, that journey is punctuated by moments of withdrawal for prayer, for acts of self-discipline and not least for remembering that God expects a faith that does justice.

Once we probe a little deeper, subtle and sometimes more obvious distinctions make themselves felt. Prayer in Islam conjures up images of serried ranks of worshippers all bowing in the direction of Mecca. This, however, is no act of mindless regimentation. For the Muslim, prayer is a public exercise that brings the entire *umma*, the community of faith, into a very physical submission to God. In conversation with Muslims I have noted a certain sense of what Catholics would call the 'communion of saints'. Prayer, even when practised alone, is never a solitary effort. Muslims experience a solidarity in faith – not just with their fellow-believers but with the spiritual universe of protectors and prophets. Muslims pray with the body, standing, bowing and prostrating. God is the centre of prayer but the act of turning the head to each side establishes bonds with one's companions and acknowledges the support of guardian angels.

Almsgiving, formalised as a sort of tithe or wealth tax, is a further dimension of public commitment – this time to the less fortunate members of the community. Muslims are expected to give 2.5 per cent of their surplus wealth each year to those in need – in addition to more informal acts of charitable giving. Underlying *zakat* is the principle of *sadaqah*, translated by Hewer as 'bearing one another's burdens'.[10] As in Judaism, giving to the poor redresses the social balance that has been skewed by accumulated wealth; in this sense the motivation is rooted less in 'charity', a free giving away of an over-abundance, than in a recognition that all assets are held as a trust from God. In the Quran it is said that 'They will question you concerning what they should bestow voluntarily. Say: "whatever good thing you bestow is for parents and kinsmen, orphans, the needy and strangers and whatever good you do God has knowledge of it"' (2.211). Like everything else in Islam, almsgiving has a primarily *theological* purpose. However much it may sound like legal prescription, it is the motivation – to align one's every act and desire with the will of Allah – which counts.

The breaking of the fast or *iftar*, performed at dusk on each day of Ramadan, brings the community together to celebrate and give thanks. Prayers are said, a single date is eaten and a sip of water drunk, a welcome

[10] C. T. R. Hewer, *Understanding Islam: The First Ten Steps* (London: SCM, 2006), p. 106.

respite after hours of restraint. Then food and drink are dispensed to all present. As with the rhythm of the prayer, fasting is a public not a private matter – and so is the thanksgiving celebration that marks the end of each day. People act together, rising at the same time, observing prayer times and keeping the fast, then together offering all back to God as the night closes in. Once when I attended the *iftar* the imam told us that prayer and self-denial and almsgiving have one purpose only – to increase *taqwa* or 'God-consciousness'. The word has connotations of being known to God, becoming deeply anchored in God's love. The fasting month of Ramadan builds up a communal solidarity that witnesses to the unity of God. As I noted in the previous chapter, Islam is a tradition that celebrates the God of creation, God as the first and last enlivening force that holds the whole of that creation in being and invites human beings to participate in and be responsible for the fruits of God's generous love. Ramadan is essentially a daily round, a ritual that marks time and measures the rhythms of life. At the end of each day the process is repeated, until the entire spiritual and physical universe is gathered around a single point of time and creation is restored to a new harmony.

This cosmic dimension to Muslim practice puts any public/private distinction in perspective. The familiar Gospel reading for Ash Wednesday has Jesus preaching the Sermon on the Mount.

> 'When you give alms, do not blow a trumpet before you, as the hypocrites do in the synagogues and in the streets to win the praise of others. . . . When you pray, do not be like the hypocrites, who love to stand and pray in the synagogues and on street corners so that others may see them. . . . When you fast, do not look gloomy like the hypocrites. They neglect their appearance, so that they may appear to others to be fasting.'

Rather, almsgiving, prayer and fasting are to take place away from the public gaze – 'and your Father who sees what is hidden will repay you' (Matt. 6:1–7). I have yet to meet a Muslim who blows a trumpet or anoints his face to make it look miserable. On the contrary, the humility exhibited in the manner of praying is quite palpable. While it is always possible that ritual can become ritualism – a reliance on form for its own sake – Jesus is not criticising the public nature of formal liturgy as such. It is, rather, the pride of 'the hypocrites', their concern to have their virtue advertised in the public sphere, which excites his ire. To that extent his words are addressed to everyone, whoever makes a show of 'my' prayer and 'my' good works. The pious Muslim anxious only to develop *taqwa* would agree. Just as Christians put their faith in the Father who 'sees what is hidden', so Muslims are guided by the conviction that, as the Quran puts it, 'whatever you give, God knows of it' (3.86). For both traditions human beings receive from God an extraordinary dignity that makes them capable of responding to God. In so far as it is treated as pure gift, this transforming power of God remains eternally creative.

This dignity we may, of course, abuse. Juergensmeyer's remark alluded to earlier is that pious people can do all sorts of ghastly things under the delusion that they are doing good. Let me therefore pursue a little further the question of motivation, how prayer and asceticism form certain typically Muslim and Christian ways of being and acting. I first want to argue that for Christians the various practices of prayer, fasting and almsgiving always have an intensely personal dimension because they are done *in imitation of Christ*. This suggests another point of comparison, one that finds its analogue more in the Shi'a tradition of Islam, and opens up further possibilities for considering themes that engage both traditions – especially about the tragedy of mis-directed good intentions.

PRAYER AND DISCIPLESHIP

Lent is like Ramadan in the obvious sense that several weeks of prayer, fasting and almsgiving build up the community of faith. However, this is an annual rather than a daily rhythm. The map of time that Christians seek to draw is more complex, less about some sort of cosmic renewal than projecting the act of faith into an unknown future. Lent intensifies the Christian's relationship with God, working like an inner pilgrimage in which, through personal companionship with Jesus, moving with him from the moment of baptism to the moment of crucifixion, we are drawn more deeply into the intimacy of God's act of self-communication. The metaphor of the journey brings together the many different dimensions of the human relationship with God. We begin with the well-meaning assent to 'repent and believe' and end with the desolation of 'sit here while I pray'. From the sober self-confidence of Ash Wednesday to the poignancy of Holy Week, there is an intrinsic stillness, even a loneliness, about Lent. Discipleship can be a painful business, not because of any asceticism we may practise, but because the very unpredictability of the journey may make us feel uncomfortable. Repentance is risky; it calls for difficult choices to be made. What makes it all possible, however, is not the grim determination to succeed but another imperative, the words that follow the Gospel reading for Ash Wednesday. 'Pray like this.' Jesus's own prayer, his relationship with the one he calls Father, is the heart of all Christian living, the lifeline of

Lent. To pray in these words is not a preparation for the way; it is, more exactly, prayer *on the way* – a prayer in company with the one who is himself the Way.

Companionship is clearly central to Christian faith. As noted in the previous chapter, what is specific to Islam is the revelation of God's Word as text, the Holy Quran. In Christianity God's Word is made flesh; God is revealed as person. Decades of Christological speculation and argument eventually clarified the parameters of orthodox Christian faith, but the result, almost inevitably, was a distancing from the historicity of the Christian story and a loss of the sense of Jesus's true humanity. Only in the high Middle Ages did the balance shift and a passionate devotion to the person of Christ reassert itself. Mark McIntosh quotes Hadewijch, writing to younger Beguines and protesting:

'O beloved, why has not Love sufficiently overwhelmed you and engulfed you in her abyss? Alas! When love is so sweet why do you not fall deep into her? And why do you not touch God deeply enough in the abyss of his Nature, which is so unfathomable? Sweet love, give yourself for Love's sake fully to God in love!'[11]

Love of the suffering Christ, so characteristic of the *Devotio Moderna*, finds its way into the *Spiritual Exercises*, where St Ignatius of Loyola proposes to his exercitant not just an intellectual understanding of the divine truth incarnated in Jesus but an affective intimacy in following him.[12] The imagination is brought to bear on Gospel scenes and carefully constructed 'considerations' of spiritual truths that are intended to move heart and will and develop a sense of mystical devotion to the one who embodies God's love in and for the world. Something similar can be found in the highly emotional *bhakti* traditions in Hinduism – a topic I will pick up in the next chapter. Here, however, I am more concerned with a less familiar, and rather less obvious, parallel.

Jesus is, of course, a prophet of Islam – indeed, the most important after the prophet Muhammad, the 'seal of the prophets'. As noted earlier, it is

---

[11] Mark A. McIntosh, *Mystical Theology: The Integrity of Spirituality and Theology* (Oxford: Blackwell, 1998), pp. 174–5.

[12] One of the few books which Ignatius recommends for spiritual reading during the Exercises is Thomas à Kempis's *The Imitation of Christ* (see Michael Ivens, *Understanding the Spiritual Exercises* (Leominster: Gracewing, 1998), pp. 86–7). According to Melloni, the christocentric spirituality of Ignatius has demonstrable links with the *Devotio Moderna*. See Javier Melloni, *The Exercises of St Ignatius Loyola in the Western Tradition* (Leominster: Gracewing, 2000). The 'new devotion' of the fifteenth century has its roots in the Franciscan and Cistercian spirituality of the Middle Ages, and in works by Bernard, Bonaventure, Suso and the Carthusian, Ludolph of Saxony, whose *Life of Christ* famously inspired Ignatius. See John H. van Engen, introduction to *Devotio Moderna* in the Classics of Western Spirituality series (Mahwah, NJ: Paulist, 1988).

difficult to see how the different estimates of Jesus in Islam and Christianity can be reconciled; indeed, it is by no means clear that at this point the two traditions are speaking the same religious language. Terms that are so familiar to Christians, such as redemption and sacrifice, are not easy for Muslims to hear. Thus for Christians to respond adequately to the distinctly docetic account of Jesus's crucifixion and death in the Quran and an eschatology that sees him ushering in the final judgement can be distinctly problematic. Nevertheless, whenever the person of the suffering Jesus is mentioned, a certain resonance is found in the person of Hussein, the grandson of the prophet Muhammad and the third of the twelve Shi'a imams who have given that tradition its particular character.

Hussein became a martyr at the battle of Karbala on the tenth day of the month of Muharram in the year 680 CE fighting against the Ummayads who had, he claimed, usurped the position of the true successors to the prophet. The battle that was fought near the banks of the river Euphrates and the martyrdom of Hussein and his handful of faithful followers provides Shi'a Islam with its founding narrative. At one extreme this has resulted in a martyr cult that has inspired a number of radical groups, such as Hezbollah and Hamas. At the other, however, is the deeply moving intensity of the day of Ashura, when Hussein's martyrdom is remembered with grief and mourning for a fallen hero and the ideals of justice and truth for which he stood. Despite the fact that the stories are in so many ways quite different, it is impossible not to notice the echoes of themes and ideas in the life of Jesus. Both stood for the cause of truth and justice; both acted as prophets against a corrupt political elite; both found themselves deserted at the last by erstwhile friends; both died lonely and violent deaths; and most importantly both began a movement that would fight for the powerless against the forces of oppression. Few would want to argue that these are versions of some universal myth, a common truth for all humankind. Nevertheless, many Shi'a are quick to commend the commonalities in any conversation or more formal dialogue. At the very least, Christians and Shi'a share common values. What is at stake is the power of an idea to give hope to a shattered people. Faith, as noted earlier, is the conviction of meaning, or, to put it in the terms that the Shi'a would recognise, that overriding hope that God's will for humankind will triumph. But any resolution will not be easy or straightforward; both Christians and Shi'a Muslims know that there is no triumphant way that avoids the path of pain and loss. In Gethsemane, Jesus prays that he may not have to endure the passion. Yet at the end he puts everything into the hands of God: 'Not my will but yours be done.' Whether Hussein prayed in some similar way before Karbala is the stuff of pious speculation – especially from a Christian. But, according to Shi'a orthodoxy, which believes that the Twelve Imams are all in some way 'righteously guided', Hussein knew exactly what he was doing. To do battle with an overwhelming enemy seems the height of folly, and hardly the sign of infallibility. For the Shi'a, however, it is indicative of a clarity of purpose and calm resolve that puts everything into the hands of God. Thus, on the eve of the battle Hussein commends his companions to God. 'May God reward you all, I think tomorrow will be the end of us . . . Go, all of you. I will not keep you. The night will cover you. Use it as your steed.'[13]

The last words attributed to Hussein just before his death – 'Is there any one to help?' – could be interpreted as a sign of final despair, or as an experience of the 'dark night' that overwhelms the soul in moments of crisis. Neither seems appropriate. Where the Christian is reminded of the words of Jesus on the cross, 'My God, my God why have you forsaken me?', the Shi'a hear an urgent rallying cry, not the voice of dereliction in face of final oblivion but a moral call to arms that sounds down the centuries. Strangely – because, after all, we are talking about a defeat – the memory of Karbala is every bit as inspiring for the Shi'a as the memory of the Exodus is for the Jews. Not only does it form a people with a profound sense of their own destiny, it roots the thirst for justice deep in the religious psyche. It is almost as if each of the Shi'a hears those final words as addressed to him or herself personally, words that challenge the entire community of faith never to allow evil to triumph again but to live lives that will vindicate the courage of the imams – all of whom, according to tradition, have died martyrs' deaths. Yet here an awkward question arises – the one anticipated earlier. The piecing together of a narrative that would keep faith with a distant, and ever elusive, past risks substituting a romantic ideal for reality – even, perhaps especially, when that vision is hung about with images of tragedy and loss. Is memory not selective and partial – at best a resort to nostalgic consolations, at worst a dangerous playing into the victim mentality? Is the 'Karbala story' no more than a prophetic denunciation of evil and an exhortation to take power and meet violence with violence?

The story is certainly an inspiration; but the very fact that it celebrates heroic failure makes it much more than the source of a steely determination to destroy the enemy.

There is something else at work here, something implicit in the mood of grief and sorrow that suffuses Ashura. Shi'a Islam is founded on the family

---

[13] Quoted in Yann Richard, *Shi'ite Islam* (Oxford: Blackwell, 1995), p. 29.

of the prophet. God's revelation comes through Muhammad, but after his death his authority is vested in his son-in-law Ali and Muhammad's direct descendants. Each of the imams after Ali shares his destiny, most obviously Hussein. The twelfth imam lives on in 'occultation', awaiting a final return to bring justice upon the earth. In that sense, Hussein has not died – or, rather, his death is the prelude to a new life in God. Meanwhile his memory is kept alive by the mourning that treats his death, as it must treat any death, as the tragic inevitability of all human living. In this present moment life is always about enduring loss, the threat of oblivion that challenges all human hopes and desires. Death is the one thing that is absolutely sure about our lives, yet none of us knows what death is like. Not the 'how' or the 'when' or the 'where'; only the 'that'. For the Shi'a those final words of Hussein – 'is there any one to help?' – are intended as a reassurance that although death means letting go of everything the love which is passed on through the ancestral tradition, forming a people as companions in faith, does not die. The Shi'a 'school of faith' is like an extended family that traces its line back to the prophet of Islam and his descendants. Yet family does not mean protected domestic cosiness. As a school, the Shi'a family is, in a very obvious sense, about teaching people how to come to terms with otherness, the unknown. That is to say that as in any family growing up is a matter of growing apart, learning to be oneself, not a mere clone of one's parents. The very closeness of parents and brothers and sisters makes their relationship just as tricky to negotiate as that with strangers. Which is why, when Jesus is told that his mother and brothers are outside he retorts with the rhetorical question: 'Who are my mother and brothers? Whoever does the will of God is my brother, and sister, and mother' (Mark 3:31–5). Jesus radicalises and challenges a narrow focus on blood relations. Family, friends, neighbours, acquaintances, strangers: the circles of closeness and the differences of relationship are a matter of degree not kind. Success in negotiating that awkward if generally benign otherness of relationship with the family may lead to success in living alongside strangers and those with whom one has no natural bond.

If that is correct, it is not fanciful to bring Jesus and Hussein together at this point. They may have died painfully heroic deaths. But they did not die alone. They had the assurance of companionship – friends and family who stayed with them, even if in Jesus's case it was a fearful remnant who for the most part observed from afar. The point is that neither narrative – certainly not the Gospel – is a tale of clarity and instant understanding. The Gospels begin with the imperative to follow; the disciples answer a call to a marvellous destiny, to become co-workers in building a Kingdom of justice. But it took time, a story of misunderstanding and the tragedy of loss, for them to become properly transformed into real companionship with Jesus. In this sense Jesus's 'seventy others' sent out to preach the Word among 'wolves and serpents' resemble Hussein's tiny band of warriors holding the line against far superior forces. They learn not despite adversity but through it. In the Resurrection narratives there is never any sense that Jesus's appearances herald a restoration in which family and friends are brought back together. What is revealed is something new – an anticipation of God's work of bringing about the new creation. While it would be fanciful to see this new creation played out in terms of Islamic visions of the paradise that rewards the righteous, there is something of it reflected in that great Shi'a theme of hope vested in the twelfth imam. He will eventually appear – a promise of the risen life to come. And such a hope changes the way the present is conceived. In both traditions the 'risen life', a transformation of this world, is anticipated in the here and now.

TRANSCENDENCE, TRANSFORMATION AND TIME

So much for my example of how religious practice motivates action. Images of the transcendent, in their different ways, contribute to the transformation of the individual. So much is uncontroversial. Nevertheless, if the balance between a future and present transformation is not kept, it can subvert the best of intentions, leading otherwise pious and godly folk to do dreadful things in the name of religion. The moral resources implicit in any 'social imaginary' find themselves superseded and subverted by the desire for immediate order and control. The stranger is turned into an alien – and worse. This is the theme with which I began and to which we must now return in the last part of this chapter.

While it is tempting to classify all examples of religious conflict in Huntington's 'multi-civilizational world' as the results of 'fundamentalism', the reality is rather more complex. The term comes, of course, from a movement in early twentieth-century American evangelical Christianity. At one level there is nothing remarkable here. All religions go through periods of revival and reform when it is natural to look to ancient stories and traditions to establish a way of life and deal with practical questions. That might make religion a naturally conservative force, but it does not follow that it is intrinsically uncritical, irrational or given to violent excess. What makes the original phenomenon interesting is that it is a peculiarly modern development, driven by the quest for firm foundations in the face of a destabilising external threat. Certain texts are given a more exalted status and subjected to a more rigid process of interpretation with the aim of making a much sharper distinction between insiders and outsiders – or those on the fringes. To put it in what are undoubtedly rather crude semi-psychological categories, a sense of weakness and insecurity is projected outwards on to the modern, secular, anti-religious – or at any rate areligious – world. The result is a rapid retreat into a self-defining religious enclave and a strident antagonistic polemic. In the case of the Hindu chauvinism of the Viśva Hindu Parishad the threat is identified as Muslim and Christian; in the case of Wahhabi-inspired puritan Islam it is Western liberal modernity and the decadent 'infidels' who no longer merit the title Muslim. In these cases, and many others, the 'comprehensive pattern' has no way of dealing with the other than through a more or less violent exclusion.

As far as it goes this analysis is helpful. However, motivations for action vary considerably, just as the status of the texts that provide stimulus or justification for action varies from tradition to tradition; the New Testament is not on a par with the Quran nor is the *Bhagavad Gita* the Hindu equivalent of the Buddhist *sutras*. Recourse to some generic explanatory scheme, let alone one based on a very particular movement, needs to be treated with care. It rather assumes that all forms of 'fundamentalism' are characterised by some sort of textually based justification – whether a choice of Quranic verses in the case of some Islamist groups or a nationalist proto-myth in the case of the Indian *hindutva* phenomenon. Even the most revered of sacred texts have to be related to context – and the practice of reading or enactment by a community. Easily overlooked in the rush to shore up the rapidly disintegrating structures of faith is the time and effort it takes to relate the present need to the wisdom of tradition. Rich and complex commentarial traditions can be sidelined in favour of some question-begging 'return to sources'. Left out of account is the broad context of ritual and prayerful reading, which, through a process of repetition, gives *these* particular texts a significance in the first place. As I argued in an earlier chapter, the reading of texts re-enacts memory, putting people back in touch with key formative experiences.[14] The question that needs to be addressed, therefore, is not about what scriptural principles are to be used to justify human action or even how scripture is to be brought into dialogue with modernity. It is about the relationship between the ideals that the life of faith as a whole inspires and the actions that it demands. In other words,

[14] See Paul J. Griffiths, *Religious Reading: The Place of Reading in the Practice of Religion* (Oxford University Press, 1999), especially 'Conclusion', pp. 182 ff.

Juergensmeyer's puzzle – how good people can do bad things – is not a straightforward issue about finding chapter and verse for a particular action. That is not to ignore the fact that there are many 'fundamentalists' who resort to scriptural quotation to justify their actions. Clearly there are. But, even here, I want to argue, something else is at work – a more subtle and more exactly theological issue.

Rituals are not magic, promising instant solutions to human hurt and the deep longing all people share for answers, resolution and security. The month of Ramadan and the period of Lent, Muharram and Good Friday are constant reminders of the past that is gone and the future that is promised. They are all full of prayers and practices that of their very nature need to be repeated. This is not because they did not 'work' the first time, but because the *work* or performance itself is central. In this sense rituals do not point to or symbolise *something else*; they are an end in themselves. This is what people *do* – a people with a particular culture, a way of making sense of things. However much they differ, rituals (whether Hindu *puja*, Islamic *salat*, the Christian Eucharist or the secular liturgies played out on hundreds of football fields on Saturday afternoons) have at least this much in common: they return people to the marketplace of reality and anchor them in the everyday. Each one, or each set of patterned actions and responses, builds a certain framework within which the desire for meaning can be shaped and justified.

I suggest that this may give us an insight into the vexed issue of what I called earlier toxic religion. Once we stop thinking of religion as belief in other-worldly entities but as rooted in the human desire for meaning it is not difficult to understand where it all goes wrong – how 'pious people dedicated to a moral vision of the world' can do dreadful things. For René Girard, with his Freudian take on human nature, we are creatures of passion, trusting too readily in a capacity to understand and oblivious to a deeper irrationality that always risks getting out of control. The realist in Girard recognises that society is shot through with potentially murderous instincts because human beings all desire the same things. Before society is ever formed, and even when some harmonious *modus vivendi* has been adopted, human beings are in competition with one another. Things appear as objects of desire by being mediated to us by others. We do not desire something because it has some sort of intrinsic value in itself. Rather it becomes desirable because others make it so.

The other can be a role model, the source of something we desire, but very quickly can become a rival when that good is not forthcoming – or is jealously withheld. 'Two desires converging on the same object', says Girard, 'are bound to clash. Thus mimesis coupled with desire leads automatically to conflict."[15] To put it in the terms that I tried to develop earlier, such a relationship can become pathological – that is to say, tend towards violence – when desire becomes overly focused on myself and my own perceived needs over against those of the other. In biblical terms, the Cain–Abel story illustrates the point: the harmony that any society needs to function is always in danger of being undermined by a deep-rooted acquisitive instinct.

There is a powerful insight here. The great merit of Girard's work is that he writes as a literary critic with a deep sense of the power of story, giving a fresh reading of the essential truth of the Gospel. God is revealed as the loving father who in Christ brings to light the source of the latent aggression at the heart of all interpersonal relations.[16] This is the revelation that challenges the 'scapegoat mechanism' in which, according to Girard, communities unite behind a mutually agreed substitute or victim who acts as a sort of lightning conductor for communal anger. As Girard puts it, in characteristically gnomic fashion,

The qualities that lend violence its particular terror – its blind brutality, the fundamental absurdity of its manifestations – have a reverse side. With these qualities goes the strange propensity to seize upon surrogate victims, to actually conspire with the enemy and at the right moment toss him a morsel that will serve to satisfy his raging hunger. The fairy tales of childhood in which the wolf, ogre or dragon gobbles up a large stone in place of a small child could well be said to have a sacrificial cast.[17]

The positive point is that, while religion may on occasion sharpen what turns out to be a deeply *human* problem, it also contains the seeds of a solution. Once seen for what it is, the worst aspects of mimetic rivalry can be overcome. The counter-violence of the 'scapegoat mechanism' can never bring an end to the cycle of violence until it is itself set in a new light by the love revealed in Christ.

Whether or not such a potentially totalising account of the relationship between Christianity and 'other religions' ends up not defusing violence but deflecting it back on to them is not a question I intend to pursue here.[18]

---

[15] René Girard, *Violence and the Sacred* (London: Continuum, 2005), p. 146.

[16] Although not writing as a theologian, Girard's fundamental insights into mimetic theory do lead in a theological direction, as is demonstrated by one of his most lucid interpreters, Raymund Schwager. See especially *Must There be Scapegoats? Violence and Redemption in the Bible* (Leominster: Gracewing, 2000).

[17] Girard, *Violence and the Sacred*, p. 4.

[18] For an excellent discussion of the issues, see the chapter entitled 'Girard and the Religions', in Michael Kirwan, *Girard and Theology* (Edinburgh: T & T Clark, 2009), pp. 120–31.

I prefer to stay with the point with which I began this chapter: the demands of spirituality, rationality and justice, which – as Girard makes only too plain – can lead not to harmonious resolution but to violent imposition. What I have sought to describe are two contrasting, but perhaps complementary, 'logics of practice' in which *time* adds an additional regulating element to what otherwise can appear as an abstract configuration of principles. To temper spirituality as the 'right channelling of desire' with reason is only half a solution. The problem is that passions remain; violence is not always controlled or sublimated, still less directed towards the practice of justice. Thus Juergensmeyer suggests a different understanding – a more Durkheimian account – of the role that religion plays in forming and controlling human relations. 'Religion', he says, 'must deal with violence . . . because religion, as the ultimate statement of meaningfulness, has always to assert the primacy of meaning in the face of chaos.'[19] If religion is understood as giving a community a sort of *language* with which to talk about the world, to articulate the hope of resolution and the ultimate triumph of order over disorder, and justice over amorality, then that language is almost bound to develop narratives of conflict, myths of triumph and powerful symbols of battle, martyrdom and the like. But the process of applying any set of religious concepts to reality requires care and discernment. As Juergensmeyer puts it, with reference to the *dharmic* religions of India, it is very easy for a metaphorical cosmic war to get confused with a struggle in the social world – and when that happens religious violence becomes savagely real. The *time* that it takes to form and channel desires of all kinds is forgotten.

This is what rituals do: they anchor a community in time and teach it to take time. It is the lack of attention to the time it takes to recognise and come to terms with all too human passions and jealousies that characterises so much religiously inspired violence. When traditional rituals fail to make a difference, the temptation is always to short circuit the process, as it were, to act out the 'great conflict' between the forces of good and evil in the middle of the world. Strangely there is a logic or rationality at work here – but one which is dominated by the comprehensive system that has totalised the other. Juergensmeyer sees in terrorist violence a mirror image of religious ritual – a distorted mirror, to be sure, but one that uses religious forms and motifs in order to bring about *now* what traditional rituals only promise in the future. His analysis of religious violence asks how 'three things – religious conviction, hatred of secular society, and the demonstration of

---

[19] Mark Juergensmeyer, 'Sacrifice and Cosmic War', in Juergensmeyer (ed.), *Violence and the Sacred in the Modern World* (London: Frank Cass, 1992), p. 108.

power through acts of violence' come together. He makes great play of the last and uses an evocative image to illustrate the spectacular nature of so many terrorist acts: the 'Theater of Terror'. Such 'spectaculars' have a symbolic rather than strategic significance – that is to say, they impress by the magnitude of the drama they enact. In Don DeLillo's words, terrorism is 'the language of being noticed'.[20] It is not just a matter of killing but of making sure that people *observe* the killing – and are terrified by it. Such public acts, with their television audience of millions, function as symbolic acts that define a sort of social 'space'. In other words, whatever form of words is used to justify or explain what is done – (mis)using scriptural quotation or constructing some 'modern' discourse of alienation and victimhood – violent acts are rooted in a parody of the actions that form a community of faith. Just as Christians find support for their everyday lives by following Jesus in the pilgrimage of Lent, and the Shi'a find similar support in the story of Hussein's martyrdom at Karbala, so 'fundamentalists' in all religions mark their world by acting out their own story in a distinctively public way.

I began and now end with 'three things'. One way of understanding toxic religion – 'religious conviction, hatred of secular society, and the demonstration of power through acts of violence' – is to see it as the obverse of practices of spirituality, rationality and justice. Spirituality without reason and the claims of justice can be self-absorbed; rationality without the right channelling of desire and a proper regard for the other can be obsessively critical; and a desire to do justice that is not anchored in an intellectually and affectively balanced inner life ends up as ill-directed anger. To that extent my Shi'a friend is right. Three principles act as a sort of shorthand for the most important of all cross-religious ethical demands. If they are not to be turned into a cheap substitute for the transformative practices of faith I have tried to describe in these pages – study and asceticism, contemplative prayer and sensitive listening to the voice of the other – then we have to learn *in any particular situation* how to put them together wisely and imaginatively. I have argued that religion goes toxic when this necessarily lengthy process of careful discernment is subverted by a short-term passion for justice. There is, however, another way in which passion has been used in this chapter. When Shi'a look at the aftermath of Karbala, when Christians look at Jesus on the cross, we both contemplate what human beings are capable of, the darkest forces in human nature, the way human beings suppress the greatest of God's demands – justice, faithfulness and peace – because they are difficult. But we also see what human perseverance and trust in God can create.

---

[20] Don DeLillo *Mao II* (1991), p. 157. Quoted in Juergensmeyer, *Terror in the Mind of God*, p. 141.

Tragedy and loss

Decorating one of the walls of the Jesuit dialogue centre of Tulana outside
Colombo is a moulded terracotta sculpture by the Buddhist artist, Kingsley
Gunatilleke. His subject is the finding in the Temple. Various characters,
from Greek philosophers to Jewish prophets (and including a relief of an old
woman to depict the suffering poor), surround the central figure of the
young Jesus who, with his parents hovering anxiously in the background, is
listening intently to the wise elders. Among them are prominent teachers
from different religious traditions: Krishna, Muhammad, Confucius. But
this is no manifesto for normative pluralism. We are in Śri Lanka – and
Jesus is looking directly at the figure of the Buddha.

The frieze is a beautiful act of homage by a lay Buddhist to the tradition
for which he has developed great respect and no small understanding. For
the observer it brings together two moments of truth, one Christian and one
Buddhist. Luke's story marks a point of transition when the child Jesus
leaves 'home' and must be about 'my Father's business' at the very centre of
the Jewish world. Luke finishes the infancy narrative by telling us that
Jesus's parents failed to understand, though Mary 'kept all these things in
her heart'. Jesus meanwhile 'increased in wisdom and in stature, and in
favour with God and man' (Luke 2:52). The other story is related by
Walpola Rahula in his version of the ox-herding pictures. The Buddha,
taking a lotus blossom, enacts a moment of wordless communication. None
in the assembly understood what the Buddha had done except the elder
Maha-Kaśyapa. The holding up of a flower symbolises the perfect relationship of teacher and pupil that is so central to the Zen tradition. 'I have the
True Dharma Eye, marvellous mind of Nirvana', says the Buddha. 'This
now I commit to you, Maha-Kaśyapa.'[1]

---

[1] Rahula relates the story of the traditional origin of Zen. 'One day, while preaching to the assembly on
the Vulture peak, the Buddha held up a golden lotus flower. None in the assembly understood the
meaning of his act except Maha-Kaśyapa, the great elder, who looked at the Buddha and smiled.'

The intriguing image depicted in the sculpture, which implies that Jesus becomes learned not just in the wisdom of Moses and the prophets but in the teachings of other religious traditions, is an exercise of the interreligious imagination. Much the same can be said for another work at Tulana by Gunatilleke – this time an enormous pair of sculptures of Jesus and the woman at the well. It depicts a moment that never happened, or, at any rate, a moment never described in John's text, when the woman pours water over the hands of Jesus. John gives us the details of a conversation about 'living water' that brings the woman to faith in the Messiah. He receives nothing from her except puzzled questions. As always in the Fourth Gospel he is not just the source of divine revelation, but its very incarnation. Perhaps it takes a Buddhist, mindful of the minor details that are also a source of insight into the way things are, to fill out the human side of the story. Did she ever give him 'something to drink'? We do not know. But Gunatilleke's sculpture of Jesus stooping to take the water from the pitcher carried by the woman is marvellous in evoking the gracious condescension by one human being to another. A Christian cannot but be moved by such a figure of the infinity of God's self-gift refracted through such simple gestures of giving and receiving. Like the figure of the boy gazing into the eyes of the Buddha, this sculpture too is a powerful example of the religious imagination at work. The question, of course, is whether this is just idle fancy for the spiritual voyeur or genuinely a work of interreligious learning.

There can be few cultures that have not in some way been touched by the Gospel story and the person of Jesus. Mahatma Gandhi was famously influenced by the Sermon on the Mount. The values of the Gospel inspired Hindu reformers like Ram Mohan Roy. In India especially, signs of Christian influence are everywhere. Pictures of the Sacred Heart pop up in Hindu household shrines alongside the elephant-headed Ganesa and the flute-playing Krishna. One is also likely to find thoughtful hagiography, such as I noted earlier in the writings of Thich Nhat Hanh, or in the meditation *The Man Who Never Died*, by the Sikh statesman Gopal Singh.[2] Interpretations vary. The neo-Vedantin universalism of

---

Rahula concludes coyly that '[t]he whole episode is of doubtful origin'. See Walpola Rahula, *Zen and the Taming of the Bull: Towards the Definition of Buddhist Thought* (London: Gordon Fraser, 1978), p. 19.

[2] Gopal Singh, *The Man Who Never Died* (Honesdale, Pa.: Himalayan International Institute of Yoga Science and Philosophy, 1990). For a collection of classical passages and commentaries on the person of Jesus from a non-Christian perspective, see Gregory A. Barker and Stephen E. Gregg (eds.), *Jesus Beyond Christianity: The Classic Texts* (Oxford University Press, 2010). A number of similar accounts are to be found in a volume of the Oxford Readers series: David Ford and Mike Higton (eds.), *Jesus* (Oxford University Press, 2002).

Swami Vivekananda makes Jesus a docetic symbol of deified humanity. In Islam, Jesus is a prophet of God, second only in importance to Muhammad himself, the one on whom the Word of God is said to 'descend'. While Jesus is refused the title Son of God, there are those Muslims who regard him as Messiah, due to return at the end of time. And many Shi'a Muslims, as I indicated in the previous chapter, are happy to find resonances between the story of Jesus and the martyred imam Hussein.[3] These are hardly examples of orthodox Christian faith but that should not demean their value as examples of how human beings are always alive to the traces of God's presence in unexpected places.

Christian faith can be said to begin with the episode at Caesarea Philippi when Jesus asks the disciples: 'Who do you say that I am?' From Peter's confession arise various titles that form the basis for the Creeds and the Christological orthodoxy of Chalcedon with its account of Christ 'in two natures ... concurring in one person and one subsistence (*hypostasis*)'. These, of course, are Greek and Latin categories; given the Mediterranean focus of a missionary faith they could hardly have been anything else. But what would have happened if the apostles had all followed St Thomas to India rather than scattered in the opposite direction? If Christian faith had established itself in another cultural milieu than that dominated by Greece and Rome, would the Church have learned to speak of that faith in a different theological key, with metaphors of *guru* or *bodhisattva* to answer Jesus's Christological question and Buddhist-inspired distinctions between *samvrti* and *paramartha satya*, conditioned and unconditioned truth, to speak of the coalescence of divine and human natures? These may be discounted as mere speculation, but that should not take away from the worth of some fascinating interreligious discussions that have been provoked by the challenge to think about the significance of Jesus in another cultural idiom.[4] Like Gunatilleke's sculptures, Christ in the guise of the Gandhian *satyagrahi*[5] or embodying the qualities of detachment and wisdom so beloved of the Sufi sheikh[6] witness to the power of symbols to give rise to thought.

---

[3] At least one Shi'a theologian, in gathering together *hadith* from the Shi'a imams, thinks it is time for 'an Islamic Christology'. See Muhammad Legenhasen, *Jesus Through Shi'ite Narrations* (Qum: Ansariyan Publications, 2004).

[4] On the dialogue between Hinduism and Christianity, see, e.g., Michael Amaladoss, *The Asian Jesus* (New York: Orbis, 2006); on that with Buddhism, see John Keenan, *The Meaning of Christ: A Mahayana Theology* (New York: Orbis, 1989) and Leo Lefebure, *The Buddha and the Christ* (New York: Orbis, 1993); while the works of Kenneth Cragg command a special status with regard to the dialogue with Islam: see especially *Jesus and the Muslim: An Exploration* (Oxford: Oneworld, 1999).

[5] Amaladoss, *The Asian Jesus*, pp. 86–104.   [6] Ford and Higton, *Jesus*, pp. 153–4.

To that extent they stretch the limits of the religious imagination, providing endless variations on a story that speaks to all people of faith.

The Chalcedonian definition is, however, not a Greek answer to a Jewish question. It is, rather, a framework within which all possible answers, and all possible speculations, are to be tested.[7] The theological 'trajectory' that is established in the confessions of the New Testament, where the disciples' experience of the person of Jesus introduces them to a new life of participation in God, arises from a particular Jewish theological sensibility. That is why, as I argued earlier, the nature of the 'Jewish matrix' is so crucial for Christian self-understanding. Christian orthodoxy is an expression of the inner logic of the Church's confession that Jesus is Emmanuel, 'God with us'. The Church is charged with confessing Jesus as the Christ or Word or universal Wisdom, the source of salvation who holds the whole of creation in being. It is one thing, however, to say that Christ will always go on challenging the limits of human language, another to turn him into a single totalising symbol that brings all human meaning and human relations into a single correlation. Both within the Church where discipleship in the name of Christ is lived out, and outside the Church, in our pluralist world where Christ is not unknown, what the early Fathers referred to as 'seeds of the Word' is primarily an expression of the eschatological hope of the Jewish people. The language of faith has to find a home in other idioms and cultures; such is the nature of a tradition that has translation as its 'birthright'.[8] But whether we are working diachronically, adapting the Gospel to new eras and new ways of thinking, or synchronically, looking for different religious forms on which to speak cross-culturally, any dialogue that encounters the boundaries of orthodoxy must be related back to the formative matrix of Jewish faith and culture if it is to be spoken with real Christian integrity.

In this chapter I do not want to argue for some sort of 'inter-faith Christology' – spelling out the meaning of Christ in the language of anther faith. Still less do I intend to fill in the inadequacies of the responses of other people of faith to Jesus's Christological question. Rather, I commend once again the principles that have inspired the sort of dialogical comparative theology that runs through this book and the turn to 'imaginings' that sets the tone for this final set of reflections. I have already spoken about the 'art

---

[7] For Oliver Crisp, the Chalcedonian definition is 'theologically normative' in the sense that the first Creeds and Confessions act as a 'sort of hermeneutical bridge between Scripture and the church'. Oliver Crisp, *God Incarnate: Explorations in Christology* (London: Continuum, 2009), pp. 12–13.

[8] David Bosch, *Transforming Mission: Paradigm Shifts in Theology of Mission* (New York: Orbis, 1992), p. 447.

of translation' as the primary metaphor for a spiritual life committed to communication across religious boundaries. To repeat the point made above, the Church in its *very being* embodies and lives out the conviction that the Holy Spirit is already bringing to fruition that transformation of culture that has been initiated through God's act of creation. This is what the Church 'proclaims' and 'manifests' through a variety of activities – from prayer and worship to work for justice and interreligious dialogue.[9] In other words, living and working across cultures is what it means to be Church. If the first Christians struggled to make their faith in Jesus as the Messiah a distinctive feature of an essentially Jewish faith, the early Fathers sought to express that faith in a different language and cultural form. This is, to repeat, not to make Christianity a cultural or philosophical hybrid in which Jerusalem is forever warring with Athens but a school of faith that derives its very life from the crossing of borders and the desire to explore other worlds in the conviction that they too say something of the mystery of the God revealed in the person of Christ.

I began with images of teaching and recognition and I continue now with another story in which familiar and unfamiliar are seen to overlap. My aim is to take further the theme of contemplative discernment of the world of the ordinary and everyday – not so much a repetition of earlier themes but a glance, as it were, from a different angle, refracted through the ever-popular figure of Krishna. The previous chapter looked at a particular version of the comprehensive account that is religion through the lens of Shi'a Islam; this one does the same through one of the major traditions of *bhakti* Hinduism. In the second part of the chapter I want to relate this engagement back to the theme outlined above, the formative matrix of New Testament faith. I begin, however, with the Krishna story as an example of how the 'resonances' discerned in the dialogue of faiths inspire the imagination and lead to a questioning of the often unexamined assumptions behind the project of interreligious learning.

STRUGGLING WITH A STRANGE GOD

Krishna is the most popular manifestation or *avatar* of God in the Hindu pantheon. He is the mischievous child who delights parents, the dependable

---

[9] The distinction between (Protestant) 'proclamation' and (Catholic) 'manifestation' is taken from an important article by William Burrows, 'A Seventh Paradigm? Catholics and Radical Inculturation', in Willem Saayman and Klippies Kritzinger (eds.), *Mission in Bold Humility* (New York: Orbis, 1996), pp. 121–38. Burrows himself draws on the work of David Tracy, *The Analogical Imagination: Christian Theology and the Culture of Pluralism* (New York: Crossroad, 1981).

hero who strengthens warriors, and above all the ideal lover who seduces the soul with his passion and beauty. In the popular *Rasalila* episode from the *Bhagavata Purana* he plays his flute late at night and the *gopis*, the milkmaids from the village, leave their husbands' side and follow him into the moonlight where they are caught up in a dance of ecstatic love.[10] Out in the forest so transfixed are they by Krishna's presence that each one finds herself dancing with Krishna alone; in his overwhelming generosity he has multiplied his form so that they are all conscious of being the centre of his attention. For the author of the *Purana* that is what God is like – the source of abundant love. Then, at the height of the dance, Krishna disappears – and the *gopis* are left to lament his absence, the God whose tangible presence is no more. That also is what God is like – the source of a love that is often painfully strange and incomprehensible. At the moment I feel most comfortable and at home with the God who has suddenly and unexpectedly drawn us out of ourselves, it all appears to go wrong. The almost tangible presence of the divine lover appears to set me apart from the others – at that moment of ecstasy I lose it all. That the joy of the moment never lasts is part of the tragedy of human living, of being creatures who are bound in time and only ever given a glimpse of the eternal. However much the experience is bound up with and explained in the esoteric language of mysticism, there is something very ordinary and deeply human here.[11] The story says something about everyday human relationships, about pride, jealousy and selfishness. So often our desires remain confused and disordered. I may want it all – but I cannot have it.

In Hinduism, worship of Krishna belongs within that form of spirituality which Panikkar refers to as 'personalism'.[12] The Hindu term *bhakti* has connotations of loyalty and sharing and participation. It refers to a selfsurrender to the love of God that is all-enveloping and, in the emotional or

[10] One of the great compendiums of ecstatic *bhakti* in honour of Krishna, which has given rise to many vernacular versions. See the English translation of the Sanskrit by G. V. Tagare (Delhi: Motilal Banarsidass, 1976). On the Rasalila performance, see G. M. Schweig, *Dance of Divine Love: The Rasa Lila of Krishna from the Bhagavata Purana, India's Classic Sacred Love Story* (Princeton, NJ: Princeton University Press, 2005).
[11] On the theme of Krishna as divine lover, I am indebted to the seminal study by Friedhelm Hardy, *Viraha Bhakti: The Early History of Krsna Devotion in South India* (Oxford University Press, 1983), especially pp. 569 ff, where Hardy makes some astute comparisons between the experience of 'emotional *Krsna bhakti*' and the Christian mystical tradition of the 'dark night' in the Rhineland mystics and St John of the Cross. On the same theme of 'cosmic desire' and the experience of separation from the divine lover, see Hardy, *The Religious Culture of India: Power, Love and Wisdom* (Cambridge University Press, 1994), especially pp. 274–95.
[12] Raimundo Panikkar, *The Trinity and the Religious Experience of Man* (New York and London: Orbis/Darton, Longman and Todd, 1973), pp. 19–24.

ecstatic form found in the *Bhagavata Purana*, often quite disturbing. Another, rather more technical term, *prapatti*, comes from a root meaning to take refuge and reminds us of the act of searching out and seeking the protection of a teacher or *guru* that is found in the ascetical or renouncer traditions of India. More exactly, *prapatti* is a term appropriate for theistic traditions such as Vaishnavism that manage to touch the heart while at the same time raising subtle and sophisticated philosophical issues to do with grace, necessity and freedom. This is where the loving relationship with Krishna properly belongs. To practise *prapatti* is to give oneself completely, without reserve, having lost all inhibitions and forsaken all self-centred calculation. This is not some irrational plunge into the unknown. On the contrary, surrender is the outworking of the 'conviction of meaning', born of that faith which trusts that meaning is to be found in certain texts and in the thought world which texts create. Thus, at the end of his study of a ninth-century Tamil devotional text, the *Tiruvaymoli* of Śatakopan, Francis Clooney observes that

perhaps the ideal reader can be described as one who reads like a *prapanna* – like someone who does *prapatti*, who surrenders completely, somewhat desperately, having run out of strategies and plans: surrendering to the text and its meaning after attempting and abandoning every skilful strategy by which to make something certain and safe of it. This *prapanna* would then speak and write from this simple, clear, unadorned learning.[13]

To understand the exacting work of textual reading by analogy with the story of Krishna and the *gopis* may seem far fetched. But the experience of separation and distance from the strangely absent God on which the story turns bears some resemblance to what I have described as interreligious learning. A different example was alluded to in an earlier chapter: Paul's pained meditation on the fate of his own people in Romans 9–11, which issues in an extraordinary outburst of praise for the 'depth of the riches and wisdom and knowledge of God!' (Rom. 11:33). It is almost as if the intellectual tension that has been built up as Paul wrestles with a profound theological problem suddenly cracks and he bursts forth in an unexpected moment of enlightenment. He begins with careful reasoning but learns how to abandon the desire for any purely rational solution by placing everything back into the providence of God. This is not to give up on hope but, as Clooney remarks, to cultivate the virtues that are necessary to the vocation of the theologian/scholar turned *prapanna*. Once soaked thoroughly in the

---

[13] Francis X. Clooney, *Seeing Through Texts: Doing Theology among the Śrivaisnavas of South India* (Albany, NY: SUNY Press, 1996), p. 310.

language and symbolic world described by the texts, one learns how to interpret a wider world – and to live with the lack of resolution in confidence that '[e]verything gets included, eventually'.[14]

There is, in other words, much more to a 'personalist' spirituality than the cultivation of a private communion with one's favourite image of the Divine. That is the lesson of the *Rasalila* story. It is also the warning that Panikkar gives about a self-indulgent *bhakti* that trades personalism for anthropomorphism.[15] Eventually, in God's good time, comes understanding and vindication of the 'conviction of meaning'. Meanwhile, there are some hard lessons to be learned by those who would seek to possess and protect their moment of communion with the divine. The virtues of learning include intellectual integrity, patience and willingness to wait for coherence to emerge, but also imagination, courage and openness to the strange and risky. What holds them together, according to the wisdom of *bhakti* spirituality, is the companionship of the teacher or friend. This shift from the isolation of a purely intellectual struggle to a shared conversation with another person is the underlying theme of what is generally acknowledged to be the originating text of the whole *bhakti* movement, the *Bhagavad Gita*. Here Krishna appears as the charioteer, a wise *guru* and counsellor of the young warrior Arjuna. The *Gita* is a relatively short and concise section from the great epic of India, the *Mahabharata*. Yet its importance in the day-to-day lives of countless millions is out of all proportion to its brevity. It stands at the beginning of a movement that transformed the ancient Vedic tradition and has not left other religions, including Christianity, untouched. The truth the *Gita* teaches about the way things are makes it a devotional version of what we considered in an earlier chapter with reference to the Buddhist 'gnostic agape'. Paradoxically, the way of love and devotion is inseparable from the struggles and conflicts of life in a world shared with limited and selfish human beings. This is as radical a discovery as anything that is taught in the more emotional narrative of the *Bhagavata Purana*.

THE GOD OF THE *GITA*

What makes the *Gita* such a fascinating text is that it is a work that combines a number of traditions and practices.[16] The author is familiar

---

[14] *Ibid.*   [15] Panikkar, *Trinity*, p. 24.
[16] For Sanskrit text with translation, introduction and substantial commentary, see R. C. Zaehner, *Bhagavad Gita* (Oxford University Press, 1966).

with theistic strands, most especially Krishna, originally a popular god hero of a local tribe from north India, and Vishnu, originally a minor deity from the hieratic Vedic cult. These he combines with various non-theistic philosophical currents, the classical *Upanishads*, the dualistic *Samkhya* philosophy, and Buddhism. Wrestling with the intractable problem of how God can be both immanent and transcendent, he comes up with a synthesis of monistic, quasi-pantheistic and theistic ideas that are weaved together into a text of sometimes confusing complexity. This is not to say, however, that there is no logic to be discerned in the account the author gives of the spiritual life. What holds it all together is the dominating theme of *Dharma*, with its connotations of right, justice and truth. *Dharma* refers to everything that is solid and dependable, but more specifically it is also bound up with right teaching and the duties and responsibilities of life in a highly stratified society. In theory there is a way of behaviour appropriate to one's particular place in society. This is outlined in the classical Hindu system of *varnaśramadharma*, the 'duties of class and state', which apportion the tasks and responsibilities that are appropriate to particular groups at different stages of life. In theory everyone knows their place and the appropriate duties – their *svadharma* – on which the wise functioning of society depends. In practice, of course, nothing is ever that straightforward. Duty and desire inevitably come into conflict. While recognising one's duty may not be that difficult, the very human problem of finding the courage and motivation to do it is another matter.

The metaphor for the spiritual life that the *Gita* invites us to explore is made explicit at the beginning of the text. Faced with the appalling prospect of exterminating those he knows and loves, 'fathers, grandsires, teachers, uncles, brothers, sons, grandsons and comrades' (1.26), Arjuna refuses to fight. He cannot see how the purposes of *Dharma* can be served by engaging in mortal combat with his own kin. Krishna's purpose is to get the young hero to fight, persuading him to set aside his scruples for the sake of a greater good. To that extent, the battle is no more than a backdrop, the particular setting against which a moral dilemma is debated. Krishna's first argument focuses on the inevitability of death. To the one who properly understands, the self is indestructible, moving through the stages of one life and into another, beyond the power of weapons, fire and water. Krishna's second line of argument is that Arjuna should fight because that is the duty of a warrior; the protection of *Dharma* or 'right order' is a noble cause that is not to be shirked. This is a 'just war'; the warriors drawn up opposite Arjuna may be family but they are also his enemies. The cause he stands for must be respected and evil resisted. A third line is more visionary, and takes us into the peculiarly religious motivations of the *Gita*. Krishna tries to set Arjuna's dilemma within the framework of eternity. All things emerge from an originating first principle, God who plants the seed of creation in the womb of nature. This is what the wise know. If all comes from God and returns to God, then everything which one perceives, is equal (5.18), God in all beings and all beings in God (6.29). This is the mark of the one who is a genuine ascetic or *yogi*, one completely pervaded by the awareness of the truth that everything is one in *Brahman* (5.7, 19).

This, of course, begs the question: who is ever wise? How does one perceive this truth for oneself – instead of merely taking it on trust from the beneficent teacher? If Arjuna's dilemma cannot be solved by exhortation to do his duty as a warrior or by intellectual arguments about the nature of ultimate reality, maybe the solution is to become an ascetic, to renounce the world and follow the way of the lonely self-denying *sannyasi*, the wandering renouncer? Arjuna is wise enough to see that action cannot be avoided. If I try to restrain myself and withdraw from all activity I only succeed in isolating myself, not in becoming detached. I drew attention to this in the discussion about Buddhist meditation earlier. All activity has results, effects that carry on through life – and pervade even the relative passivity of the ascetic. However, the *Gita* does not teach fatalism. Again, as in Buddhism, the effects of action or *karma* can be avoided if one develops that contemplative capacity to see what makes the process function; that is to say, not to see *karma* as the inevitable result of a process in which the human being is inexorably caught up, but to understand that desire is more basic than action. A different sort of *yoga* or spiritual exercise is commended, a practice which in the *Gita* is transformed by the more 'popular' theistic religion with its roots in the cult of Krishna. The main practice is the same, the developing of 'one-pointedess' of concentration, but now the person of Krishna himself is made the central focus of attention. As Krishna says to Arjuna: 'sit, integrated (*yukta*) intent on me' (2.61). Strictly speaking, of course, any theistic focus could have been co-opted into the yogic practice, any moral exemplar with the power to fix the attention and channel the confused desires of the devotee-meditator. The brilliance of the move that the *Gita* makes, however, comes from the mythology that is built up around this particular hero. Krishna comprises in himself all the perfections of the *Upanishadic* principles. He is the origin and meaning of all things, embodying in himself the model of how work should be done. The Supreme Lord is perfectly involved in creation, yet perfectly detached from it. The lesson is clear. Krishna has no need to act but is always involved in activity so that the world continues in being. So must Arjuna help to maintain world order by fulfilling his own *dharma* and acting dispassionately after the manner of Krishna.

THE BLESSED LORD

What is radical about the *Gita*'s new development of *bhakti-yoga*, learning detachment by keeping the attention fixed on the person of God, is that it reinterprets both the orthodox Vedic sacrifice and the renouncer traditions. The yogi who retires from society to devote his life to meditation performs an 'interior sacrifice' through the practice of asceticism and attains *moksha* or release. The theistic conception of the personal God who periodically becomes incarnate for the sake of suffering humanity introduces a different vision of God's nature and a different way of realising that truth. The notion of a personal God who freely manifests himself to save is foreshadowed in the later *Upanishads* but in the *Gita* this is made quite explicit.[17] However, it is not that *bhakti-yoga* is an easier way, an alternative for those less hardy souls who baulk at the thought of all that meditating while standing on one leg deep in the forest. The revolution lies with the power of an image and the realisation that God is not some distant mystery, but *Bhagavat* – usually translated 'blessed' but from the same root as *bhakti*, 'participation', and therefore meaning the God whose very nature is to 'take part' in the world of human affairs. This is the transcendent one now immanent in creation, participating in the world as an enlivening principle, but not to be identified with it. As a special grace to Arjuna, Krishna reveals

his highest sovereign form, a form with many a mouth an eye and countless marvellous aspects; many indeed were its divine adornments, many the celestial weapons raised on high. Garlands and robes celestial he wore, fragrance divine was his anointing . . . If in bright heaven together should arise the shining brilliance of a thousand suns, then would that perhaps resemble the brilliance of that God so great of Self. (11.10–12)

In this ecstatic vision Arjuna learns the truth about himself – he cannot die – and about the Universe – all things subsist in God. This is the final argument, a magnificent explosion of divine power, intended to destroy Arjuna's hesitation and inspire him with the courage to be faithful to his *dharma*. Instead he is terrified. He is full of praise for the God he has experienced in this moment of ecstasy, but rather than grabbing his spear for the fight he begs Krishna to revert to his original form. It takes time for the warrior to

---

[17] See especially the theistic *Śvetāśvatara Upanishad*, with its focus on the person of Śiva. See Hardy, *Religious Culture*, pp. 289, 348.

understand what God wants of him. The revelation of God as pure love is more subtle – as Arjuna comes gradually to understand.

In the meantime he is sustained by a principle that Krishna embodies. The *Gita* teaches that actions as such have no effect provided one acts without desire for a particular result. As Krishna says to Arjuna: 'Hold pleasure and pain, profit and loss, victory and defeat to be the same: then brace yourself for the fight. . . . Work alone is your proper business, never the fruits' (2.38, 47). The principle of disinterested action or *nishkama karma* means literally 'work that has no desire'. Arjuna is told to work without being anxious for the results of work.[18] This is not to say that the *Gita* promises an informed programme which will cover all the exigencies of life in a complex world. Rather, the one who sincerely trusts in the guidance and care of God comes to realise that *bhakti* is not a matter of entering into some state of self-transcendence but of finding that the transcendent is already there in the everyday. This is the dawning truth that comes with practice. Thus at the end of the *Gita* Krishna delivers his most important message that yet appears almost like an after-thought, a sort of reminder of the truth that has been there all along. 'Give ear to this my highest word, of all the most mysterious: "I love you well" . . . so will you come to me, I promise you truly, for you are dear to me' (18.64–5). Mysteriously, the one who has shown devotion to God by constant attention through 'desireless action' to doing what is necessary with diligence and dedication finds that God is devoted to him. This is the real religious revolution effected by the *Gita* – a shift away from the concern to achieve *Moksha* in some dim and distant future to the benefits of an immediate loving relationship with the deity in the here and now.

Even this brief overview should be enough to show that this extraordinary text consists of rather more than pious exhortation, a moralising response to the dilemmas of human living. The form of the *Gita*, as I noted above, is that of the typical instruction of a pupil by his *guru* – a scheme of graduated instruction that leads the pupil from the simplest of truths to the more difficult and 'highest secret of all'. Thus it is often regarded as an *Upanishad*, a secret teaching in which Arjuna is initiated into the deepest of truths – the love of God incarnate that alone enables men and women to make sense of the manifest contradictions and paradoxes of

---

[18] These ideas are developed through a dialogue with Ignatian spirituality in Michael Barnes, 'With God in the World: A Dialogue between the *Bhagavad Gita* and the *Spiritual Exercises* of St Ignatius of Loyola', in Catherine Cornille (ed.), *Song Divine: Christian Commentaries on the Bhagavad Gita* (Louvain and Grand Rapids, Mich.: Peeters/Eerdmans, 2006).

life. But, for all that the text is at times repetitive and even bewildering in its complexity, the *Gita* does have its own originality. It is easy to underestimate the role played by the questioning pupil who refuses to take the traditional answers without an argument. It is through honest yet supportive dialogue that truth begins to emerge and learning takes place. The central principles of Krishna's teaching are clear: accept what is given in the present and learn indifference to the final fruits of work. But what makes this more than some sort of secret *gnosis* (which would really belong in the more rarified philosophical world of *jñana-yoga*, the '*yoga* of knowledge') is the truth revealed in the imaginative constructions that surround the person of Krishna: those who are open and generous towards God will find God open and generous towards them. Through contemplating this narrative of God at work in the present moment comes true conversion of heart.

LOVE FOR GOD AND THE GOD OF LOVE

How does this tradition of a God whose 'desireless work' and personal love for the devotee overcomes the dilemmas and tensions of human living speak to Christian faith? Jesus's 'Christological question' with which I began is not calculated to induce a mood of peace and equanimity. Indeed, very much the opposite. The Jesus story contains no blazing theophany, nor does it lead directly to a straightforward statement of faith. Instead we get conflict, confusion and betrayal. Something of this is reflected in the *Gita* story and, of course, in the sense of terrible loss experienced by Krishna's *gopis* in the *Bhagavata Purana* as their carefully constructed spiritual world collapses about them. Underlying two very different ways of talking about the love of God made manifest in the world is another, very human, drama, that of the devotee, the one called to struggle with the mystery of God's love. If this is what interreligious learning is about then what bears further investigation is the position of the pupil rather than the teacher, the struggle to learn rather than the act of teaching. The focus, therefore, is not on Jesus or Krishna but on Peter and Arjuna.

The episode at Caesarea Philippi is placed right at the centre of the Gospel narrative, a sort of fulcrum around which the whole dynamic of the self-revelation of God revolves. Peter answers Jesus's question with the confession that he is the Messiah, the anointed one of Jewish expectation; Jesus is the very presence and promise of God. But Peter, of course, only gets the answer half-right, as it were. Jesus confides in the disciples that he must suffer and be killed, that on the third day he will rise from the dead. Peter, of course, will have nothing of this and protests vehemently.

Whereupon Jesus rounds on him: 'Get behind me, Satan!' The violence of Jesus's words are incomprehensible until a conversation is opened up about what the Jewish people expected of the Messiah – and what we human beings want our heroes to be like. A Saviour who must suffer and die is certainly counter-intuitive. The Jesus who wanders through the land, teaching and healing, even Jesus the prophet who criticises the status quo, is an attractive and comprehensible figure who sits neatly within most religious frameworks. The Jesus who is left hanging on the cross, beaten and rejected, is much more difficult to take: not the sort of theophany anybody expects or wants. But somehow the story has to be told – the story not just about how those, like Peter and the first disciples, eventually came to understand the meaning of it all, but a more profound story about how God challenges human pretension. At the end of Mark's Gospel it is not Peter who 'gets it right' at last; it is the Gentile, the foreign centurion (Mark 15.39). Jesus is the Messiah but a very different Messiah from what his followers expect or want. There is a continuity between what God reveals through Torah and what God speaks through Jesus the Christ. But there is also a discontinuity, something new and unique about what he stands for. Only at the end of the story, when we get the entirely different but still very disconcerting theophany of the Risen Lord, is it clear that this historical figure is the touchstone by which their sense of God is now to be reckoned.

There is, of course, a paradox here. The story of understanding is also the story of misunderstanding; indeed, it is only the confusion of shattered faith that makes more mature and settled faith possible. This gives the story an improbable 'interreligious element': Peter and Arjuna share similar experiences. The conversation that Jesus begins at Caesarea Philippi challenges the comfortable conviction that faith is about having the right answer. Right in the middle of the Gospel story, a quite dramatic question mark is raised over all human claims to know God. In this way the story speaks to all people of faith. If nothing else, it is a salutary reminder that hard and fast distinctions between those who understand and those who do not are difficult to make. What Paul rejoiced in as the 'scandal of the cross' is not, therefore, a claim to some esoteric intuition into the problem of suffering, still less some apophatic version of the nature of God. Rather it is a reminder that at the heart of all faith lie doubt and hesitation; in Christian terms, one must lose a sense of self in order to find it. The advice of the *yogis* to the searcher for enlightenment is to concentrate on the one point. In practice it is never that easy. The spirituality of *bhakti* arises in the Indian traditions because myths, epics and stories give a different sort of structure to human existence. When Krishna becomes the focus of concentration Krishna's own life begins to take over. There is, very simply, a humanity in the devotion of the heart that touches us on many levels. That is not proof against crisis and confusion. Indeed, it may take a real crisis to provoke an understanding that is proof against doubt and confusion. Anyone who reads the *Gita* will empathise with the position of Arjuna. And anyone who listens to the Caesarea Philippi story and its aftermath with an open mind will be perplexed, but also strangely consoled. Peter's earlier brashness and ignorance give way eventually to a rather more humble and self-effacing confession of faith: 'Lord, you know everything. You know that I love you' (John 21:17). Peter is made the first of the Apostles not because he has attained some special enlightenment or been initiated into the Ultimate Mystery but, quite simply, because he has learned how to love.

THE CHRIST OF FAITH

I began this chapter with an image of Jesus in the Temple reaching out to the figure of the Buddha. It could have been any other religious teacher – and, indeed, they are present in Gunatilleke's frieze, a penumbra of 'religions' present at that decisive moment when Jesus, in the spirit of Malachi's prophecy, enters and takes possession of the Temple (Mal. 3:1). In terms of their respective narratives, in their general outline the stories of Gotama and Jesus are strikingly similar: birth surrounded by heavenly portents, the experience of harassment by a devil figure, the gathering of disciples and the peripatetic preaching of a message of salvation, death attended by earthquakes and triumphant visions.[19] Some parts of the story – most obviously the visit of Asita the ascetic who seems to mirror the prophetic role played by Simeon in the Temple – have led some to speculate about mutual influence.[20] This is clearly possible but remains unproved. Nor should parallels be emphasised at the expense of difference. Gotama is at times highly critical of the Brahmin 'establishment' but he is not betrayed and killed; Jesus is depicted as in prayer to the Father but he does not seek personal enlightenment. In Buddhism, the human condition is subjected to a complex diagnosis in which various causes are minutely analysed; for Jesus, on the other hand, sin is the breakdown of a personal relationship with a loving God. And behind the 'wise sayings' in the Gospel and such

[19] See especially Lefebure, *The Buddha and the Christ*, pp. 28–56.
[20] See, e.g., the summary of parallels between the story and teaching of Buddha and Christ in Edward J. Thomas's classic, *The Life of the Buddha as Legend and History* (London: Routledge, 1996 [1927]), pp. 237–48.

Buddhist scriptures as the *Dhammapada* are very different visions of what human beings are saved *to*, the *summum bonum*. Perhaps where these accounts converge is less in the content of teaching than in the manner of its realisation. Jesus preaches a breaking in of the Kingdom into the present, the truth that 'God reigns'. For the Buddha, enlightenment is only achieved through constant attention to the present, by being 'mindful' of what is here and now.

Some such dialectic of similarity and difference can be played out in all forms of comparative theology. More important, however, than attending to points of contact in the respective narratives is to consider the interaction of canonical text and contemporary reading. To stay with the dialogue between Christianity and Buddhism for a moment longer, the two traditions can only be properly understood as responding to some version of the question: how can what Pieris calls the 'core liberative experience' be said to go on inspiring the life of the community?[21] This search for a continuity of faith is the foundation of both Christology and Buddhology; Jesus is confessed as the Christ, Gotama recognised as the Buddha, because they are identified not just as pointing to a truth but in some way actually *embodying* it. If religious learning can be said to consist in making explicit what is contained within the social imaginary of a tradition, then *interreligious* learning is about allowing the dialogue with the other to enhance that understanding and to see things in a different way. For the Christian learner the life-giving relationship of Jesus to the Father that brings about a new creation is seen to include not just all aspects of experienced reality but all sources of spiritual wisdom. Not that this can ever be a straightforward process.[22] The point of my lengthy discussion of the Krishna story in Hinduism was to ground this vision in the reality – so often a painfully difficult process – that is the life of faith in a less than perfect world. The questions with which I began this book – about what happens to faith when it becomes inter-faith; essentially about how faith changes and grows – indicate that the interreligious learning which comparative theology demands is often arduous and both intellectually and affectively demanding. The aim is not to set up religious equivalents but to let the faith formed by the Christian story be challenged and informed by other stories. Thus my commentary on the Krishna stories told in the *Gita* and the *Bhagavata*

---

[21] See Aloysius Pieris, 'Christianity in a Core-to-Core Dialogue with Buddhism', *Love Meets Wisdom* (New York: Orbis, 1988), pp. 110–35.

[22] For a comparative account of Christianity and Buddhism as paths or journeys, see Michael Barnes, 'Way and Wilderness: An Augustinian Dialogue with Buddhism', in Brian Brown, John Doody and Kim Paffenroth (eds.), *Augustine and World Religions* (Lanham, Md.: Lexington, 2008).

Purana is intended not so much to provide an alternative to that idealised Zen moment of instant communication as to root it in the everyday experience of a growth in faith that is always achieved in the middle of tragedy and loss.

At stake throughout this book are the terms of a Christian discipleship lived in dialogue with the other. The Gospel is shot through with imperatives, most obviously to follow Jesus, to share his company and imitate his life. The call is met by generosity and an initial willingness to follow. However, if Peter's own experience can be regarded as somehow emblematic of the journey of faith, the disciple goes through crisis and perplexity as God's own questions are raised in the words of Jesus and, more obviously, in the profoundly disorientating moments of the Passion. In that sense arguably the defining moment of Christianity is Jesus's experience of dereliction and abandonment in Gethsemane. Here Jesus himself has to face God's own question, risking himself before the unknown: 'not my will but yours be done'. Christian life mirrors Jesus's own example of self-giving and seeks to commend that truth so that it is mirrored in the lives of others too. The interreligious learning that I have spoken about does not just happen by a process of genial osmosis, picking up insights from the other and insinuating them into some revised account of faith as if all that is at stake is developing a cast-iron system of meaning. Dialogue involves listening and being taught but it also demands the responsibility of actively teaching and challenging. The Christian Word is nothing if not a prophetic Word that must sink into and change the terms set by culture as well as resist the corrupting elements of its homogenising power. Jesus's 'Christological question' – 'who do you say that I am?' – is not an intellectual conundrum put to Peter's naivety but involves a denunciation of the direction being taken by a religious establishment that was all too content with a comfortable status quo. The context of the story is important; if Tom Wright is correct that the theme of prophetic judgement on the current direction being taken by Israel's leaders is to be traced to Jesus himself, then Christian discipleship must itself share in that call to prophetic responsibility.[23] Dialogue may not be the same as denunciation, but it does involve some measure of critique.

Chalcedonian orthodoxy, I said at the beginning of the chapter, mediates between Scripture and the life of the Church; it thus forms a framework within which responses to Jesus's question are to be tested. In Christ is found the definitive and decisive moment of God's act of self-revelation; in

---

[23] N. T. Wright, *Jesus and the Victory of God* (London: SPCK, 1999), especially pp. 320 ff.

him God's very being is glimpsed and the invitation is made to participate in God's life. Against this background the suggestion that Jesus's question can be answered in a Hindu world by referring to Jesus as the *avatar* of God or that in a Buddhist world we can speak of Jesus as the *bodhisattva*, the 'being for enlightenment', misses the point. Clooney's account of comparative theology is predicated not on the desire to 'get the right answer' but to learn from and with the other; to be more precise, to learn about our learning, how it is possible with integrity to participate in the mystery of Godself. The conversation may *begin* with the comparison of titles and the expressions of faith but cannot rest content with the trading of verbal equivalents. Otherwise we risk making 'Christ' some universal symbol that gathers together all God-given meaning. Apart from evacuating Christian faith of its own specificity, to argue in this way would be to turn Krishna and Buddha and other figures into versions of some great cosmic reality – and thus empty them too of all really human significance. The alternative, however, is not to make the Christian story one among many purely contingent accounts of the human search for God. What Christians propose, as Rowan Williams so neatly sums up, is Jesus as God's question.[24] In this sense Christ is the norm by which all human presumption to know and understand the ways of God is to be judged.

LEARNING FROM THE OTHER

So how are Christians to learn from the dialogue with the other? Let me finish with four brief points. The first is that any sort of engagement with the other is itself an act of faith. The greatest challenge is to recognise how the stories that people of other faiths tell – even the stories they tell of Jesus – do not conflict with, but positively enlighten, the Christian story. There are plenty of indications that the faith of Muslims, Buddhists, Sikhs and Hindus has been touched by the Gospel; the new conversation does not take place in a religious and cultural vacuum.

Secondly, what is needed is not a theology that corrects or fulfils these responses but one that builds a spirituality of engagement and inculturation, supporting the life of faith that keeps the conversation going. If the liturgy is the heart of Christian faith, then it will always be necessary to use artistic and musical forms so that the life of the Church grows not just from ancient scripturally based forms of prayer but also from the local

[24] Rowan Williams, 'The Finality of Christ', in *On Christian Theology* (Oxford: Blackwell, 2000), pp. 93–106.

culture in which it becomes rooted. That is where encounter with persons of faith, where dialogue comes alive, has to begin. Biblical language and symbols develop a capacity to see meaning and make connections; in imaginative engagement with other texts, artefacts and practices they generate a deepened awareness of another symbolic world, if not an adequate understanding.

Thirdly, by living in the Spirit of Christ Christians learn how to become sensitive to the 'seeds of the Word' as they are glimpsed elsewhere. The aim is not to patronise inadequate or immature versions of the Christian creeds, but to read another faith tradition with an eye to identifying those elements of truth that can speak to the Christian imagination.

Finally, the fruits – such as they are – of the encounter need to be taken back into the inner life of the Church. Prayerful reflection on the significance of Jesus's words and actions, both within the Church and in that more open-ended conversation with others to whom Jesus is not a stranger, is itself a continuation of a life lived out in response to the question that God-in-Christ goes on asking. In an obvious sense there can be no final and complete answer to that question. Rather than produce answers the Church is committed to repeating, for itself and for others, Jesus's own question. Thus the Church *learns to live in the presence of God* who is revealed in Jesus's life, death and resurrection. Strictly speaking, of course, this is the work of the Spirit whose task is to form people after the manner of Christ, reproducing in them Jesus's experience of loss and dereliction and the birth in him of a sense of God as the compassionate Father. Ultimately it is this Trinitarian account of God in terms of the vulnerability of relationship that the Church seeks to translate into other languages and other cultures.

Towards the end of his great study of tradition in the Church, Yves Congar notes that there is no such thing as the pure Word of God, 'only a translation of this Word in the preaching of the Church in time, in which is embodied its living response to God's initiative'.[25] In a multi-faith world the Church remains responsible for working that translation, whether through evangelisation and dialogue, or in the many ways in which human beings share their lives and deepest desires. When Peter was asked by Jesus '*Who do you say that I am?*' he was led into an extraordinary journey of faith that had its moments of darkness as well as light. In Peter, perhaps, we can see a model of the Church that lives not by producing the right theological formula but by entering into and learning to live in the presence of the God who is revealed in Jesus's life, death and resurrection. As Jesus himself

---

[25] Yves Congar, *Tradition and Traditions* (New York: Macmillan, 1966), p. 474.

has to face the darkness of faith in Gethsemane, risking himself before the unknown, so the Church has to *live in faith* before understanding what faith implies. My point is that we can respond to Jesus's question '*Who do you say that I am?*' only when we have ourselves made some attempt to understand the story and the experience which provokes it and which leads the Church to make its confession of faith in Jesus as the Christ, the one in whom God's purposes for the world are revealed. What this implies is that wherever we find 'God-with-us' leading God's people not perhaps through literal deserts but through 'desert-experiences' of loss and perplexity in face of various others *Christ can be said to be there*. Even, perhaps, especially, in the darkness of faith, when we find a lack of understanding and more questions than answers. Such an account of the Paschal Mystery as God putting his question to our presumption to possess 'the answer' will encourage a certain healthy reticence, a theological humility which accepts that we do not know everything about God's purposes. It will also open up the conviction that others are touched by the Spirit of Christ and that this is a cause of joy and consolation. The role of the Spirit in confirming this 'new creation' is the last topic to which we must now turn.

CHAPTER 12

Spirit of wonder

Anandpur is a small Indian town nestling in the foothills of the Himalayas on the eastern fringes of the state of Panjab. Dominating the town is an elegant *gurdwara*, the second most important Sikh religious site after the Golden Temple complex at Amritsar. Here in the month of Vaisakhi, 1699, Gobind Rai the tenth *guru*, founded the *Khalsa*, the Sikh 'community of the pure'. Not for the first time the Sikhs were facing a crisis. The story goes that Gobind called a great meeting. Depictions of the event show him standing before a vast crowd, gesturing with a drawn sword. He challenges the crowd to give their lives in sacrifice. One man volunteers and is taken behind a curtain. A moment of silence, a sudden swish, a dull thud. The *guru* comes out, the sword dripping with blood, and demands another sacrifice. Five times the challenge is repeated, until finally Gobind draws back the curtain and there stand the five men, alive and well. The story is eerily reminiscent of God's command to Abraham to sacrifice his son Isaac on the mountain of Moriah (Gen. 22:1–18) and is usually interpreted as a test of loyalty and courage. How free are Gobind's would-be followers to give everything for the cause they believe in?[1]

Whatever actually transpired that day has resonated through the Sikh community ever since. Gobind Singh – the lion, as he then styled himself – decreed that the leadership of this new community should henceforth be vested not in any human *guru* but in the Holy Book, the *Guru Granth Sahib*, the collection of hymns that can be traced back to the teachings of the first *guru*, Nanak – and, indeed, beyond, for Sikhs proudly include the hymns of other *sants*, Hindu and Muslim holy men, in the *Granth*. Why Gobind Singh made this move is unclear. Possibly he wanted to avoid the weakness inherent in the dynastic style of leadership that bedevilled similar *sant* communities. More likely, as Harjot Oberoi puts it, he wanted to 'end

[1] See Louis E. Fenech, *Martyrdom in the Sikh Tradition* (Delhi: Oxford University Press, 2000), pp. 39–40.

the ambiguities of Sikh identity'.[2] It was, however, the work of a religious genius, transforming what began as a development within the *bhakti* traditions of northern India into a coherent, organised community that was prepared to fight and face death to defend its interests. Prominently displayed in the *gurdwara* in Anandpur is a collection of gleaming steel weapons. On the wall opposite are inscribed the names of the first five men to answer Gobind's call to arms, the *panj piare*, or 'five dear ones'. According to tradition they came from five different cities and five different castes, the first and most powerful witness to the Sikh belief that God's love is there for all people and no distinctions are to be made between individuals on grounds of age, gender, caste or religion. All are equal in the sight of God. With the institution of the *Khalsa*, the two dimensions of Sikh tradition, the spiritual and the temporal, are harmonised in the ideal figure of the soldier-saint, totally dedicated to the love of God and the welfare of humanity. On that first Vaisakhi day *Guru* Gobind declared: 'I am the son of the immortal God. It is by his order that I have been born and have established this form of initiation. They who accept it shall henceforth be known as the Khalsa. The Khalsa is the Guru and the Guru is the Khalsa. There is no difference between you and me.'[3] When he died in 1708 the guruship was held to lie with God alone.

On the annual commemoration of Vaisakhi, 14 April in the modern calendar, Sikh communities throughout the world take to the streets. In the town where I live five barefooted men, representing the *panj piare*, robed in saffron and carrying drawn swords, precede the *Guru Granth* as it is processed from one *gurdwara* to another. During the day fireworks are exploded, hymns chanted and above the hubbub can be heard the shouting of *Waheguru* – 'wonderful God!'[4] It is a word that punctuates Sikh prayer – a word of praise, an exclamation born of joy and delight. Whether muttered by old women in silent corners of a *gurdwara* or shrieked loudly by young people at the height of the Vaisakhi celebrations, the word sums up the inner spirit of Sikhism. *Sikhi* – 'discipleship', to give the tradition its proper designation – reminds us that Sikhs are committed to performing a simple uncomplicated devotion to God that transforms the whole of reality and builds an intensely practical attitude to life in the world. To utter that word *Waheguru* is to cry out with an act of faith that stirs the heart and touches the soul.

[2] Harjot Oberoi, *The Construction of Religious Boundaries: Culture, Identity and Diversity in the Sikh Tradition* (Delhi: Oxford University Press, 1994), p. 59.
[3] Quoted in W. Owen Cole and Piara Singh Sambhi, *Sikhism and Christianity* (Basingstoke: Macmillan, 1993), p. 85.
[4] Usually found in the form: *Waheguru ji ka Khalsa! Waheguru ji ki Fateh!* ('Hail to the *Guru*'s Khalsa! Hail to the victory of the *Guru*!').

'It is almost impossible', says Birinder Singh Kharbanda, 'to reflect on the vastness of the Lord as giver. How far He extends His control is beyond the imagination of any human being.'[5] The final chapter of this book is neither repetition nor, strictly speaking, conclusion. My aim, following those suggestive remarks of Charles Taylor, has been to build up the 'social imaginary' appropriate to the school of faith that is Christianity. In a world of many faiths all theology is comparative, at least in the sense that the beliefs and practices of other communities play some part in the articulation of Christian faith. That is not to say that a community's sense of self depends on what others say about it, only that the act of communication and response has some effect on how the content of faith is formulated. I began with the textual version of comparative theology and, in so far as I have touched upon the dialogues raised by *Nostra Aetate*, *Dabru Emet* and *A Common Word*, the intra-textual engagement between faiths has been an important aspect of the version of comparative theology that I have sought to develop. I have, however, been concerned to stretch the sense of textuality to include all manner of statements – from casual oral conversation to those that are inscribed in religious culture, particularly buildings and artefacts. Interreligious learning describes a form of faithful living which recognises that the integrity of Christian faith is maintained not through defensive strategies that place the neighbour at a comfortable distance but in an engagement that seeks to learn *about* the neighbour as well as *from* and *with* the neighbour.

That there is always more to be said is obvious – and not just because 'the vastness of the Lord' exceeds the capacities of the human imagination. This book has been constructed around particular episodes, meetings and stories in order to show that the principles of dialogue, if not the content and particular issues discussed, cross the boundaries that human beings are always setting up and taking down. To the extent that I write from a Christian perspective, I have done no more than indicate how Christians can learn to reflect on the truths and insights of other faith traditions. But, with each act of meeting, crossing or imagining I hope I have managed to show how the social imaginary that is built up by learning gives flesh and practical import to genuinely cross-religious virtues, what Catherine Cornille describes as humility, commitment, interconnection, empathy and hospitality.[6] How these, or analogous, features are to be drawn from

---

[5] Birinder Singh Kharbanda, *One with God: A Sikh View* (Delhi: First Edition, 2005), p. 78.

[6] Catherine Cornille, *Im-Possibility of Interreligious Dialogue* (New York: Herder and Herder, 2008), pp. 1–8.

the accumulated wisdom of other traditions is not for me to say. My final task in this book is to return to the questions about human growth and transformation with which I began. Having given some practical illustration of the vicissitudes of interreligious learning at a variety of levels, let me reformulate them now in a way that takes us back into the mainstream of Christian theology. How does the Spirit of Christ inspire that vision of the vastness of God's generous love which generates the virtues essential for respectful interreligious learning?

WORD AND WORDS

I have chosen to consider that question through the dialogue with Sikhism and the palpable sense of delight that Sikhs take in the name of God. This is not because Sikhism fits a preordained pattern of response to the divine initiative such as is exemplified by the more familiar monotheistic traditions. It is, rather, that Sikhism at its best very consciously and deliberately seeks to cross boundaries while, at the same time, manifesting a social and cultural distinctiveness that has been shaped, more than most Indian traditions, by the contingencies of history. That distinctiveness is no more evident than in the spirit of hospitality that extends an invitation to everyone, regardless of rank or religion, to share food after worship and prayer. Together the *darbar* or prayer hall and the *langar* or communal dining area, the two major public areas in any *gurdwara*, have a single purpose, to witness to the unity and equality of all human beings before God. Such apparently small acts of gracious welcome have enormous symbolic import.

Sikhi is built upon evocative words and phrases such as *Waheguru*, for this is the tradition of the poet-mystic. From words of praise that express a personal commitment has developed Sikh religious practice, the *rahit* or precepts for moral and spiritual life, and more developed forms of symbolic discourse.[7] The *Mul Mantra*, the 'root text', the brief and near untranslatable statement of faith that is placed at the head of the *Guru Granth*, witnesses to Sikh monotheism:

> He is the Sole Supreme Being; of eternal manifestation;
> Creator, Immanent Reality; Without Fear;
> Without Rancour; Timeless Form; Unincarnated;
> Self-Existent; Realised through Divine grace.
> In primal Time, in all Time, was the Creator;

---

[7] For the *rahit-namas*, the manual of code of conduct, see Oberoi, *Construction*, pp. 62 ff.

Nothing is real but the Eternal.
Nothing shall last but the Eternal.[8]

These words are not intended as an exact definition of God any more than *Waheguru* is a metaphysical treatise that would serve as an explanation of things. What Nanak records are certainly terms that describe and clarify Sikh faith, but, however venerable and exalted, the meaning that they bear emerges from the context of devotional prayer and finds its proper setting within the life of true holiness that the words support. To appreciate the connection between an exclamation like *Waheguru* and the more extended hymns of the *Guru Granth* that celebrate the majesty and beauty of God demands attention to the nature of devotional language which, in the first place, gives voice not to statements *about* God but to inner emotions that are inspired *by* God. Birinder Singh writes: 'While accepting that the Sikhs have a focus point in the word "Waheguru", it must also be remembered that this is not the only Name. Any other equivalent word in any other religion used to focus on God has the same importance and value as we value the word "Waheguru" in the Sikh world.'[9] The value of that particular word is that it enables *simran* – 'remembrance' of God. Through rhythm and cadence and phrasing as much as the powerful metaphor that hints at meaning, such words evoke an affective response. This is not to reduce the language of faith to 'mere' poetry. In many religious traditions the most inspiring of utterances give way to vast commentarial traditions – not because they are inadequate guides for a way of life but precisely because they *make it possible*. Such language of the heart, in other words, opens up the desire for understanding, but the 'inner logic' that builds a tradition of interpretation is based not on the desire *for* meaning but, more exactly, on the conviction that meaning has, indeed, *been given*. God's imperative is spoken, demanding a response of faith, and that response, expressed so often in words of praise and thanks, forms the bedrock of a religious culture.

The Sikh spiritual and social ideal of the 'soldier-saint', the contemplative devotee who is yet committed to prophetic justice for the oppressed, was formed during a critical period in which the *panth* experienced violent opposition from the Mughal emperors. The fifth *Guru*, Arjun, who had been responsible for the compilation of the *Guru Granth* and the building of the Golden Temple at Amritsar, was executed in particularly gruesome

---

[8] The *Japuji* or *Mul Mantra* forms the opening invocation of the *Guru Granth Sahib*, the Sikh holy book, compiled by the fifth *Guru* Arjun. The English text here is from the translation by Gurbachan Singh Talib (Patiala: Punjabi University, 1988).
[9] Birinder Singh Kharbanda, *One with God*, p. 24.

fashion in 1606. According to Harbans Singh, that event 'marked the fulfilment of Guru Nanak's religious and ethical injunctions. Personal piety must have a core of moral strength. A virtuous soul must be a courageous soul. Willingness to suffer trial for one's convictions was a religious imperative.'[10] If Gobind, the last of the Ten *Gurus*, formalised the commitment of Sikhs to a public witness to their faith on that momentous Vaisakhi day in 1699, he was only underlining an inner spirit that had been growing for decades. *Guru* Arjun's martyrdom was recorded by Jerome Xavier, Jesuit priest and great-nephew of the missionary St Francis Xavier.[11] Himself part of the Jesuit mission to India in the early seventeenth century, Xavier reported back to his superiors in Rome in a letter that concluded: 'In that way their good Pope died, overwhelmed by the sufferings, torments and dishonours.'[12] Jerome Xavier's instinctive appreciation of the courage of the *guru* – the first recorded historical contact between Sikhs and Christians – says something about the inner affinity of two otherwise quite distinct traditions that are prepared to go to extraordinary lengths in order to maintain spiritual and social integrity in a violent world.

Now talk of inner affinity does not imply some common essence or sacred core dimly discerned like a precious orchid struggling to escape the encompassing spiritual undergrowth. To revert to the more familiar Patristic metaphor, 'seeds of the Word' are less an undeveloped growth 'out there' than reflections of a *process* of growth already happening 'in here'. Making it possible to engage with the other in this more affective way is what Simone Weil calls 'the miraculous virtue of sympathy'.[13] Xavier would, of course, have been familiar with the meditations of the *Spiritual Exercises* that so inspired his great uncle some seventy years earlier, and particularly with that quality of compassionate openness to the other that they teach. The Call of the King, which acts as a sort of fulcrum for the dynamic of the Exercises, and the Two Standards, with its evocation of a titanic battle between the forces of good and evil in the world, are often read as if they are intended to galvanise all sorts of heroic desires for the service of God and humanity.[14] Ignatius is more subtle than that. The *right channelling* of desire takes time and requires a freedom from disordered emotion. The first

---

[10] Quoted by Patwant Singh, *The Sikhs* (London: John Murray, 1999), p. 39.

[11] For detailed discussion of the sources, see Fenech, *Martyrdom*, pp. 116 ff.

[12] Quoted in many accounts of Sikh history. See Amandeep Singh Madra and Parmjit Singh (eds.), *'Sicques, Tigers or Thieves': Eye-Witness Accounts of the Sikhs (1606–1809)* (New York and Basingstoke: Palgrave Macmillan, 2004).

[13] Simone Weil, *Waiting for God* (New York: HarperCollins, 2001), p. 118. Quoted by Catherine Cornille, *Im-Possibility of Interreligious Dialogue*, p. 138.

[14] *Spiritual Exercises of St Ignatius*, paras. 91–100, 136–48.

enemy that needs to be conquered is always the ego, by which I mean that disordered tendency in all human beings that makes us think we are serving some grand purpose when we are serving no one but ourselves. The celebration of Vaisakhi is marked by outpourings of joy. At first sight this seems far removed from the mood of openness and indifference that Ignatius demands of his exercitant (or which, to pick up a point from an earlier discussion, typifies the Buddhist quality of equanimity). My point, however, is that the delight expressed in that word *Waheguru* is a making present of a foundational memory, a memory of loss transformed. Vaisakhi celebrates not the manipulation of a submissive people by an unscrupulous demagogue but a moment of unexpected grace. *Guru* Gobind did not stir up the crowd to some fever pitch of emotion. There is an element of shock in the story, but it is more akin to the manner in which Jesus teaches through parables, turning expectations on their head and subverting fixed ideas about the nature of God. Gobind taught through such a parable-in-action. The miracle of that day in Anandpur lay not with the restoration of the dead but in the power of an act of courage to disturb and change irrevocably the mood of a people.

This is where the theme of the central section of this book, 'crossings', meets with the 'imaginings' that have held this third section together. At stake here, I want to suggest, is the nexus between joyful moments of shock and surprise and Weil's 'miraculous virtue of sympathy'. For Levinas, it is the proximity of the 'face of the other' that jolts me out of my self-centred complacency and becomes the locus of the revelation of God's Word. There is, however, nothing automatic about this process for, as Levinas is at pains to point out, the face is not a phenomenon to be mutely observed but, more exactly, a *way* of appearing that sounds a command from an 'immemorial past, which was never present'. As he puts it:

The face of a neighbor signifies for me an unexceptionable responsibility, preceding every free consent, every pact, every contract. It escapes representation; it is the very collapse of phenomenality. Not because it is too brutal to appear, but because in a sense too weak, non-phenomenon because less than a phenomenon.[15]

What Levinas seems to be concerned with is a primordial consciousness that is not – strictly – a consciousness at all because it is not a consciousness *of* anything. It is not, in other words, a personal experience that I can be said in some way to control and enjoy for myself but a graced moment that takes

[15] Emmanuel Levinas, *Otherwise than Being or Beyond Essence* (Dordrecht: Kluwer Academic Publishers, 1991), p. 88.

me out of myself not despite the other but precisely *because* of the other. In the terms I used earlier to talk about Buddhist meditation and the 'attentive waiting' that it can be said to develop, the contemplative path is not an inoculation against reality but the necessary moment of preparation that makes prophetic engagement with that reality possible. The context that I have described in this chapter is quite specific – theistic devotional spirituality rather than the intensely personal interiority of meditative prayer. Yet, even if the application may be different, we are talking about a similar dynamic of progress: in Levinas's elliptical terms, the proximity of the other turns me elsewhere and makes me think otherwise. As Buddhist meditation on the brute fact of suffering opens up the more subtle and elusive sensitivity to the suffering of other human beings, so parables – Jesus's homespun teaching, Ignatius's carefully constructed meditations, or Gobind's staged event – disturb the status quo and open up the possibility of a different sort of life in God.

Whatever else they may or may not share in terms of a history of persecution and struggle for justice, Sikhs and Christians are guided by delight in the one God who has come close to human beings and inspires lives of service. What Sikhs call 'Naam' and Christians speak of as God's Logos is not dogma to be experienced but the truth about the self-manifesting God that is prior to all experience. In what follows as conclusion to this book I want to probe further into the relationship between the prayer of praise and the life of faith, between that outburst of joy that expresses a response to God's loving call and the expressions of discipleship to which they give rise. I do this in two stages, first considering the relationship between doxology and theology, and then opening up a question that, I want to argue, faces the practice of interreligious learning, namely how it is possible to speak of God and ultimate truth at all.

THE LANGUAGE OF FAITH

Traditional statements of faith like the Sikh *Mul Mantra* do not exhaust meaning. On the contrary, they are intended to generate meaning, to nourish faith and enhance one's vision of a world shot through with the traces of God's presence. Christians quite rightly look to the Creeds for a clear statement of the essential truths of Christian faith. But they are much more than that. Not only do they help us to understand what scriptural texts are saying about such and such a doctrine, they act as records, so to speak, of how the Holy Spirit goes on guiding the Church into God's truth. It would, therefore, be a travesty to treat these great records of Christian reflection on the mystery of God as if they are merely a list of propositions. They are rooted in a history of patient discipleship and need to be understood not as the timeless residue of centuries of debate and dispute but as baptismal formulae that give shape to the primary act of Christian initiation. In the contemporary liturgy of the Church the Creed is the formal response to the Word of God. It defines who these people are. It is impossible, in other words, to understand human language about God – whether Christian or Sikh or whatever – if it is sundered from the life of faith. There is a directness to the language that Sikhs use to speak about God. Yet simplicity does not mean naivety. Nanak's hymns combine what in the Indian religious tradition are known as *saguna* and *nirguna bhakti* – devotion to God 'with qualities' and God 'without qualities'. This reflects something of the distinction found in Christian theology between the kataphatic and apophatic. It is, however, easy to miss the point here. The 'negative way' is often understood as reflecting the conviction that God is beyond grasping by human intelligence and therefore by human language. Put like this, it implies the *remoteness* of the Ultimate. That scarcely seems fair to the Christian mystical tradition where the foundational experience is not distance but *closeness*.[16] The celebrated passage in Exodus where Moses approaches the burning bush is less an awesome theophany than a person to person encounter, marked by curiosity and wonder as Moses opens up a conversation with God.[17] As Janet Martin Soskice reminds us, 'God has given himself to be named'. She quotes Augustine at the beginning of the *Confessions*, 'My faith, Lord, calls upon you. It is your gift to me. You breathed it into me by the humanity of your Son, by the ministry of your preachers.'[18]

So-called negative theology does not spring from a cool conviction that language is inadequate to describe the experience of God and must

---

[16] For a fascinating discussion of the terms of the emerging Christian mystical tradition, here set in dialogue with the Mahayana Buddhist tradition, see John Keenan, *The Meaning of Christ: A Mahayana Theology* (New York: Orbis, 1989), chap. 5: 'A Mysticism of Darkness: Gregory of Nyssa and Pseudo-Dionysus' (pp. 86–119).

[17] In *The Life of Moses* Gregory asks how Moses can be said to have entered darkness and then seen God. His response is to speak of a 'yearning for understanding [which] gains access to the invisible and incomprehensible'. St Gregory of Nyssa, Life of Moses (Classics of Western Spirituality), ed. Abraham J. Malherbe and Everett Ferguson (Mahwah, NJ: Paulist, 1978). Quoted in Keenan, *The Meaning of Christ*, p. 94. The idea that the spiritual life is not about the pursuit of some state of inner being but about progress and growth is brought out in the introductory section where Gregory seeks to redefine the meaning of 'perfection in virtue'. Taking up the Pauline theme of *epektasis*, 'reaching out' (Phil. 3.13), Gregory surmises that 'The perfection of human nature consists perhaps in its very growth in goodness' (1.10).

[18] Book 1.i, as quoted by Janet Martin Soskice in 'The Gift of the Name', in Oliver Davies and Denys Turner (eds.), *Silence and the Word* (Cambridge University Press, 2002), pp. 61–175.

somehow be transcended; it arises from wonder at the sheer awesomeness of God – who has condescended to engage intimately with human beings. Moreover, in the light of the *gurus'* hymns of praise and delight, this depiction of the remote God also seems untrue to the way the *saguna/ nirguna* distinction is understood by the Sikhs. The word 'God' is invoked to describe the object of people's concern, the aim of their searching and striving. But it is easy to forget that God knows us and our every action better than we know ourselves, and without God's loving initiative such a searching would be impossible.[19] For the Sikh, God is given a number of names but remains always the 'timeless one', beyond all names. Kabir, an older contemporary of Nanak, some of whose hymns appear in the *Guru Granth*, writes with a 'rough rhetoric' that often seems crude and overly direct.[20] But he is also passionate and personal, yearning to impart something of his conviction that God has come so close that all titles, all manner of address, all names and certainly all religions, are irrelevant. Only a naked waiting on God's goodness is necessary.

> Yogis, ascetics, hermits, mendicants,
> and all those who roam in pilgrimage,
> those who wear ropes
> and pluck, shave or mat their hair –
> all in the end must die.

> Then why not worship Ram?
> What can Yama do, if your tongue loves Ram?
> Those who know the Shastras
> the Vedas, astronomy,
> and all the grammar;
> those who know spells, mantras, medicine –
> all in the end must die.

> Those who revel in empires, canopied thrones,
> countless alluring women,
> betel, camphor,
> and sandalwood's sweet fragrance –
> all in the end must die.
> I have searched all the Vedas,

---

[19] See, e.g., Birinder Singh Kharbanda, *One with God*, p. 36.
[20] 'Rough rhetoric' is the term applied to Kabir's style by Linda Hess in her introduction to the Bijak, the sacred book of the Kabir Panth. See Linda Hess and Shukdeo Singh (eds.), *The Bijak of Kabir* (Oxford University Press, 2002). For Kabir's hymns included in the *Guru* Granth, see *Songs of Kabir from the Adi Granth*, ed. Nirmal Dass (Delhi: Śri Satguru Publications, 1991).

the Puranas, the Smriti –
salvation lies in none.
Kabir says, 'So I repeat Ram's name –
He erases birth and rebirth'.[21]

For Sikhs and Christians alike God takes the initiative in taking human beings into the mystery of God's own life and therefore enabling them to speak *out of* that mystery. Both traditions here share in a love mysticism, a sense of being caught up in, or seduced by, God's attractive power. *Bhaktas* like Nanak and Kabir insist that God comes close to human beings because that is what God is like. Their point – what brings them so close to the spirit of Christian devotion – is that God can only be spoken of in such relational terms. They are profoundly suspicious not just of ascetical excess but more particularly of the ritualism of the 'official' cult that validated the caste system and the injustices that it caused. God is not an object, to be appeased by sacrifices and sacred acts, but to be found in the relationship that God alone establishes.[22]

In this sense the language of faith is not some alternative – supposedly 'religious' – account of the way things are. It is what is made possible when the imagination is opened up to the wonder of creation and is stimulated to find words that express joy and delight at the vivifying and transforming power of God. This is *saguna bhakti* or the kataphatic way to speak of God: not using words that in their inadequacy and excess need to be corrected and negated by another type of language, the *nirguna* or apophatic way of the mystics, but rejoicing to name God with the words that God has inspired. Although the classical Christian Creeds are very different in form from the effusions of Hindu and Sikh *bhaktas*, my point – to repeat – is that, in dialogue with other faiths, they need to be rooted in the lived experience of the community of faith. Their painfully honed phrases can be traced back to the titles given to Jesus in the New Testament, especially to the Pauline confession that 'Jesus is Lord'. In their properly developed form, of course, Creeds betray a triadic or, more appropriately, a Trinitarian form that issues from the baptismal formula of Matthew 28:19 and the act of faith that it expresses. Thus they begin with the utter stillness of God the Creator, the source of all; they move into the historical narrative of God's loving gift of himself through the revelation of God's Word in Jesus Christ; they proclaim that life of hope which the Church seeks to share with the world under the guidance of the Spirit.

---

[21] *Songs of Kabir from the Adi Granth*, p. 128.   [22] Birinder Singh Kharbanda, *One with God*, p. 34

This, of course, is not a linear or temporal pattern; each 'moment' of God's self-presence is contained within the others. Spoken together they shape experience and provide a way of speaking about it. When Christians say that 'we believe in God, the Father, the Almighty', what is being expressed is a commitment, an intention to trust *in* God, to rely utterly *on* God. Similarly, with 'we believe *in* Jesus Christ'; 'we believe *in* the Holy Spirit'. The grammatical form is curious – but important. To illustrate the point Nicholas Lash quotes Augustine. 'What is it to believe in him? It is in believing to love, in believing to delight, in believing to walk towards him, and be incorporated amongst the limbs or members of his body.'[23] In this sense the Creeds that summarise the Christian doctrine of God do not just accompany prayer; they *are* prayer. They generate that recognition of the traces of God which leads to acts of praise and thanksgiving for what God has done and goes on doing. To put it another way, what the Creeds do is distil the meaning of the words of scripture which as the living record of God's Word inspire in Christians a sensitivity to the great sweep of faith.

Interreligious learning here is not a process of losing the integrity of two traditions in some 'higher' *tertium quid* but a growing awareness of the 'vastness of the Lord' who alone can form the 'school of schools'. Particular moments of 'reading' generate habitual practice and habits open up questions and insight. When Easter and Vaisakhi are celebrated within days of each other in the same crowded area of multicultural West London, two very different sets of beliefs mingle and interpenetrate – almost despite themselves. Themes of hospitality, justice and prophetic witness cross boundaries, sounding resonances and echoes of the familiar in the unfamiliar, the known in the unknown, and reminding people of the defining moments of faith. They turn us back to founding memories to find new ways of expressing familiar truths. Thus, with Sikh traditions in mind, I find myself attending to what I like to call, all too crudely, the Christian '*Waheguru* moment'. Experiences of conversion and insight abound in the pages of the New Testament, often provoked by miracles or parables or a saying of Jesus. Thus, in the penultimate chapter of John's Gospel, we hear how Peter and John, having heard the extraordinary news from the women, run to the tomb. Peter goes in first and sees the cloths with which they had wrapped the body of Jesus lying on the ground. Then John goes in. 'He saw and believed.' We are not told *what* John believed. In fact the evangelist makes the point that 'as yet they did not know the scripture that

---

[23] Nicholas Lash, *Believing Three Ways in One God* (London: SCM, 1992), p. 20 (quoting Augustine's *Commentary on John*, xxix).

he must rise from the dead' (John 20:9). It is enough that John puts his trust in God, that he continues – despite the mystery of what has happened – to keep faith with what has gone before. It is part of a pattern. Throughout the Gospel we come across people who express their confidence in the person of Jesus. In the story of the man born blind, for instance, Jesus works a miracle not as a response to faith but in order to provoke it. 'Do you believe in the Son of Man?' asks Jesus. 'Who is he that I may believe in him?' Jesus says that it is he. The man replies 'Lord, I believe.' And the evangelist adds – 'he worshipped him' (John 9:35–6). It is as if the power of God, which has been simmering unnoticed beneath the surface, suddenly bursts forth. The man sees for the first time. The steadfastness and constancy of God – for that is what God is, the utterly reliable source of all, who gives energy and dynamism and meaning to existence – is revealed in the person of Jesus. The Fourth Gospel is full of 'signs', miracles and healings, but, properly speaking, there is only one sign – and that, of course, is the Risen Lord himself. The disciples put their trust in him; they express their complete dependence on the one who proves himself dependable. That is why he is given the title Lord, a statement of faith certainly, but, in the first instance, a doxology, an outburst of wonder that gives glory to God.

For Christians, the story of the death and resurrection of Jesus Christ is, of course, paradigmatic. But that is not to say that it totalises, reduces or even accommodates all other stories – for it is not the story itself that questions and supports other stories but the Word to which it points and of which it is the primary sign and sacrament. What is translated, to go back to Rosenzweig's insight, is not in the first place a message but the school of faith that is taught by God's grace and embodies the Spirit of delight.

Earlier I spoke about the three great monotheistic religions as different responses to God's single imperative – to love. Three different schools of faith hear the Word spelled out in a particular way and form their ways of life accordingly. To put it another way, the divine imperative develops a *culture* of religious expression which is rooted in ritual, liturgy and formal worship. But what of the individual's place in that communal act? One of the questions to which the theme of doxology gives rise – particularly pertinent in the context of the dialogue with a love mysticism like Sikhism – is the nature of revelation itself, or, to paraphrase Levinas's words above, the *way* in which the Word can be said to speak and be heard by human beings. To go back to the initial Sikh experience of becoming personally accountable to the *Satguru*, faith is not faith until it is confirmed by the power of God that turns fearful individuals into confident individuals and confident individuals into a community characterised by the ideal of courageous service in pursuit of ideals of justice and truth. The act of faithful trust is transformed by the recognition that one is, indeed, loved and capable of love. As Panikkar puts it, speaking of *bhakti* – in his terms 'personalism' or the spirituality of devotion – 'God is an "I" who calls me and names me "thou", and in calling me gives me my being and my love, i.e. my very capacity to respond to him'.[24] It is undoubtedly the case, as Panikkar indicates, that *karma-marga* and *bhakti-marga* form complementary spiritualities, but more is at stake here than some sort of dialectic between communal and personal experience. The question that I have not touched upon is the nature of interreligious learning as itself *religious experience*. This is what I want to consider briefly in the final section.

FAITH AND THE SPIRIT

I have spoken of the typically Sikh sense of being transformed by the loving God that issues in hymns of praise. To learn from this experience is to discern there the resonances of a similar pattern of self-making. In Christian Trinitarian terms human transformation into the image of God is the work of the Spirit. There is no language of the Spirit in the school of faith that is Sikhism. The Old Testament imagery of *ruah*, the 'wind' or 'breath', with its connotations of mysterious movement and promise of new life, seems far away. This is hardly surprising. There is something very particular about the prophecy of Isaiah, with its contrast between the Word of God that stands firm for ever and the grass that withers when 'the breath of the Lord blows upon it (Isa. 40:7–8), and Ezekiel's extraordinary image of the valley of dry bones where God is depicted recreating his people by breathing life into otherwise empty shells (Ezek. 37:1–14). God's Spirit is that inner vitality in human beings which can be manifested in different ways, particularly as gifts of prophecy and leadership (e.g., Gen. 41:38–9; Exod. 35:31; Deut. 34:9; 1 Sam. 10:6). All of this is bound up with the Covenant promise and says something about how God works with his people.

Nevertheless, there is at least one quality of the Spirit that finds a ready resonance with the Sikh tradition. I have spoken of how the immanence of God's word, the closeness of God to his devotees which makes it possible for Sikhs to speak of God as teacher, father, mother, brother and sister, issues in words of praise. This is what God does – and what God is like: God enables speech. Thus in the *Guru Granth Sahib* it is said:

---

[24] Panikkar, *Trinity*, p. 24.

None has encompassed your bounds, so how can I describe you using my single tongue? Whoever meditates on your true word is united with you. God's word is a shining jewel which reveals the divine by its light . . . One understands oneself and merges in the Truth through God's instruction. (*Adi Granth*, 1290)

In both the Old and the New Testaments (where the Spirit is always closely linked to what God accomplishes in and through Christ) the Spirit is a principle of life. But it is, in an important sense, thoroughly foreign to human beings: it belongs to *God* and is always God's gift that disturbs and surprises. This suggests an answer to the question of interreligious learning: how anyone – whether Christian or non Christian – can recognise and point to that which is beyond words, beyond categories, beyond form. Christians will answer by saying that the Spirit works within us; we experience the 'first fruits' that the Spirit is always bringing into being. Without the Spirit we could not make our confession of faith. Without the Spirit we could not know Christ, or speak of his Word, for – as St Paul says – 'we do not know how to pray as we ought' (Rom. 8:26). The Spirit is the Spirit of Love, the 'excess' that flows from the mutual giving and receiving of Father and Son – a revelation in which the whole of humanity is caught up and transformed. In this regard Congar quotes Aquinas, who, commenting on Jesus's insistence that the Spirit leads 'into all the truth', says:

The Son gives us his teaching since he is the Word, but the Holy Spirit makes us able to receive that teaching. He therefore says: 'He will teach you all things'. Man may try to learn externally, but this labour will be in vain if the Holy Spirit, from within, does not give understanding.[25]

According to Congar, the Word of God is not some sort of 'explanatory principle' of the rational nature of the world. Rather, the Word is spoken as a voluntary personal decision of God that makes known God's plan for human beings. In this sense the Spirit does not impart 'information' about Jesus – the Spirit as some divine teacher. In biblical terms, the Spirit is a God-given force that disrupts all attempts to force the life of faith into neat and straightforward language. For Christians, the archetypal passage is Emmaus (Luke 24:13–35). The disciples' world is shattered and only the unexpected stranger on the road enables them to put it back together again. They recognise Jesus over a meal, in a borderline between ordinary and extraordinary experience, between the prosaic sharing of bread and the

---

[25] Yves Congar, *The Word and the Spirit* (London: Chapman, 1984), p. 12 (quoting Aquinas's *Commentary on the Gospel of John*, 16.6).

moment in which the broken pattern mends itself and forms again. How do
they understand? Perhaps that is the ultimate mystery. But it would not
have happened without both the stranger made visible to them, the 'outer
Word', and the stranger's 'inner Word', which provokes memory and
recognition.

If, as Vatican II teaches, the Church is 'missionary of its very nature' (*Ad
Gentes*, 2) because it participates in the *Missio Dei*, the sending by the Father
of the Son and the Spirit into the world, then the enterprise to which the
Church is committed is nothing less than God's own work of transforming
the whole of reality. It is to the truth of this 'new creation', being brought to
light in the middle of things, to which the Church points: 'a truthfulness',
says Rowan Williams, 'that exposes the deepest human fears and evasions
and makes possible the kind of human existence that can pass beyond those
fears to a new liberty'.[26] This is what the Church goes on painfully learning
and, in the power of the Spirit, seeks to communicate. Thus the Emmaus
passage looks forward to the experience of the Church in Acts, where the
disciples are continually led by the Spirit into new ways of exploring and
explaining to others what is always *God's* mission. Paul's encounter with the
Areopagites (Acts 17:16–34) is in many ways the story of a flop; many of the
Athenians laughed when Paul mentions God raising Jesus from the dead.
But it is also one of the first examples of the Christian responsibility to
'inculturate' the Gospel, an experiment in speaking the truth in a new
language. Paul was not just translating Jewish terminology, finding word
equivalents in another language. More obviously he was acting like the Jesus
of the Emmaus story – bringing the conviction that the Spirit is forever
inspiring new encounters and raising new questions into line with the 'given
story', the concrete historical form or memory of the Christ event. At work
here is the experience of interreligious learning in the earliest experience of
the Church. The Spirit enables the Apostles to look in *two directions* at once.
The Spirit always goes ahead of the Church and is always unseen and
therefore beyond our 'imaginings'; in that sense the Spirit expresses the
abundance of God's grace towards human beings. But, as the 'Spirit of
Christ', the Spirit always points back to Christ, reminding the Church of
the form, the shape, the character, which Christian living and discipleship
take – the following of Jesus of Nazareth. Christians will always seek to do

---

[26] Rowan Williams, 'Postmodern Theology and the Judgement of the World', in Frederic B. Burnham
(ed.), *Postmodern Theology: Christian Faith in a Pluralist World* (San Francisco, Calif.: Harper and
Row, 1989), pp. 92–112. Quotation from pp. 95–6.

that – to relate the strange, unknown and unexpected to what is revealed in Christ.

A sense of both 'directions' is necessary if the Spirit is to be more than some all-too-vague mysterious divine presence in the world of the other. There is, to repeat, something intrinsically indefinable about the Spirit. Like the wind it blows sometimes with devastating power through the landscape; like human breath it is the sign of life, an outward sign of the most intimate of divine gifts. Such imagery is wonderfully enriching, making it plausible to ascribe everything that overwhelms and challenges, everything that cannot be understood, everything that does not fit into available categories, to the realm of the Spirit. Thus, when faced with the mystery of holiness discerned in the lives and practices of people of other faiths, holiness apparently unconnected to any formal mediation through Christ, the action of the Holy Spirit may be invoked. When in witness to Christ, through dialogue, conversation and co-operation, we find ourselves struck by deep similarities and not so hidden traces of the Good News, we discern the Spirit already at work.

As far as it goes, such a pneumatology is helpful: the Spirit energises, leading us across strange boundaries, consoling us with what is familiar and challenging us with the unfamiliar. The problem is that such functionalism tends to dichotomise the action of 'God in Christ' and 'God in the Spirit'; God is present to and saves Christians through the concrete and recognisable form of the Gospel of Jesus Christ, while others are led by the much more mysterious and unknown processes that we ascribe to the Spirit. Plausible though this sounds, it compromises the 'unicity' or continuity of God's creative-and-salvific action.[27] While such a scheme allows for the difference between Christians and non-Christians, and provides a very simple solution to the old conundrum of the salvation of the unbeliever, it relies upon a set of temporal categories that makes God do two different things and enact different dispensations, one for Christians, another for non Christians. More subtly, in drawing so strong a divide between Christianity and other religions – deliberately holding them apart, as it were – it allows no positive role to the faith of others and the insights and questions that they may well bring to the dialogue. They are simply set neatly to one side, the problematic preserve of a 'secondary' Spirit, a sort of 'divine afterthought' that has nothing substantial to say to the 'primary' work of Christ within the Church. Is there not a more central role that the Spirit

---

[27] The point is made with some sharpness in the Vatican's 2001 statement, *Dominus Iesus*.

can be said to play within the 'school of schools' created by interreligious learning?

DOUBLE LEARNING

It is always possible to invoke the action of the Spirit to explain what we do not know about God's action; hence the plausibility of the apophatic or *nirguna* account of religious language. But how is such language to be related to what we *do* know, to kataphatic or *saguna* categories? To put it another way, how is an interreligious learning that is also a *double learning* – learning about the self and learning about the other – inspired by the *same Spirit*? How does the Spirit enable us to enter more deeply into the mystery of God's own Word *and* to learn more from the 'seeds of the Word' that may be present elsewhere?

Irenaeus's famous image of the Word and the Spirit as 'the two hands of the Father' suggests a way forward. Jacques Dupuis asks how they can be said to combine 'endowing the religious life of persons with truth and grace' – how, in one and the same revealing action of God, both Word and 'seeds of the Word', the 'saving values' enshrined in the religious traditions, can be said to coexist.[28] Congar, referring again to Aquinas but also invoking Augustine, talks about a learning that goes on as the 'inner master' inspires understanding.[29] Irenaeus's 'two hands' work together not to provide 'objective information' nor to create a set of answers to the question of the other but to point us away from purely theoretical constructions towards the only arena within which any sort of answer is possible, namely to the *practice of prayerful discipleship*. Through the myriad practices that faithful discipleship involves – from formal worship and praise to the struggle for justice and interreligious dialogue – we gain that sensitivity which enables us to discern the echoes and resonances which reflect what *Nostra Aetate* calls a 'ray of that Truth' that is Christ. There can be no Christology without pneumatology, and vice versa. Without the Spirit, our understanding of Christ would be a static representation: the revealed image of God certainly, but more a great cosmic symbol than the *living* presence of

---

[28] Irenaeus *Adversus Haereses* III, 11.8. See Jacques Dupuis, *Toward a Christian Theology of Religious Pluralism* (New York: Orbis, 1997), pp. 195, 321.

[29] Yves Congar, *The Word and the Spirit*, p. 22. Congar says that the fact that in Augustine this theme comes from Neoplatonism 'does not make it any less profound or true in Christianity. In a homily he cites 1 Jn 2:27: "You have no need that anyone should teach you, as his anointing teaches you about everything and is true ..." For Augustine this is the Holy Spirit.' Quotation from Augustine, *In Epistolam Ioannis ad Parthos tractatus decem*, III, 13.

God's love incarnate in today's world. And without Christ the Word that God speaks in the world, the Spirit would be reduced to the level of some sort of 'spiritual' experience, a rather vague generalisation that has very little purchase on what is most deeply and concretely significant for humanity. To quote Congar again, this time on the continuity of tradition:

The Holy Spirit and Christ do the same work, but different aspects of the work are appropriated to them in different ways. The Incarnate Word reveals the Father and establishes the new and eternal covenant in its full reality: he institutes the sacraments, the apostolate, and founds the Church. The Holy Spirit gives to this structure its vitality, the inner movement of its life, and interiorizes in men the gifts which Christ has acquired for them.[30]

For Christians, the Spirit is always the Spirit of Christ. The Spirit works within the Church to reveal the Word of God just as the same Spirit inspires the conscientious right living of other persons of faith. And yet there is also a specificity to the nature of Spirit that cannot be subsumed within the 'grammar' appropriate to God as Father and Son. The Spirit is also pure gift – and a sometimes surprising one at that. As Rowan Williams notes, the Spirit does not simply reproduce the words and actions of Jesus, or act as the principle behind certain charismatic experiences that convince us of the power and presence of God. More exactly, the Spirit guarantees the 'translatability' of the paradigmatic Word of God into the diversity of history, ensuring that God's action maintains the form given by the life, death and resurrection of the Son but is always free and uncircumscribed. The grammar appropriate to the Spirit, says Williams, is that of spirituality – 'in the fullest sense of that emasculated word, the grammar of interplay in the human self between the given and the future, between reality as it is and the truth which encompasses it; between Good Friday and Easter.'[31] In the midst of confusion and even doubt, the gift of the Holy Spirit becomes the very centre of Christian living, not because it is somehow different and separable from every other experience but precisely because it brings them all into a new correlation.

Thus, to come back to the opening remarks of this chapter and the '*Waheguru* moment': speech about God is primarily a word of praise and thanksgiving that is inspired by the revelation of God's Word. To learn how to speak about God it is necessary to listen to what *God says* about God – however inchoate or ill-understood that Word may be. Which is why the Christian narrative is inescapably Trinitarian: God as the silent source from

[30] Yves Congar, *Tradition and Traditions* (New York: Macmillan, 1966), p. 265.
[31] Rowan Williams, 'Word and Spirit', *On Christian Theology* (Oxford: Blackwell, 2000), pp. 107–27.

whom all things proceed, God as the Word who gives form and intelligibility to things, and God as the animating power or Spirit who draws all created reality together and inspires words of praise in human beings.[32] To say anything less would be to compromise the fundamental principle that must underlie any responsible Christian account of interreligious learning: that there is a *single economy of the Word and the Spirit*. The Christian tradition sees the Spirit as creative, the source of an inspiration and a hope that points us towards the future. But where we go and what we see will always be given a certain 'shape' by our discipleship, by the following of Jesus of Nazareth that is made possible by the action of God's Spirit. What this builds is a sensitivity and a critical generosity that is prepared to learn how the mystery of God's self-revealing love – Father, Son united in the Spirit of love – is often to be discerned in the many ways we find ourselves interacting with persons of different faiths.

Let me repeat, finally, that as a work of the Spirit guiding the 'school of faith' that is the Christian Church, interreligious learning is not an act of theological colonialism, a step towards mastery over the other, but a commitment to stay with the other, even in the confusions and misunderstanding which dialogue often entails. Something of that experience – not the retrieval of a sense of origins as such but the recovery of the excitement and delight that goes with any significant encounter – is to be found in moments that turn 'meetings' into 'crossings' and 'crossings' into 'imaginings'. In careful reading of texts, or thoughtful contemplation of rituals, artefacts and sacred places – above all, in theological reflection on what is actually said – I may well learn something about the other that intrigues, questions and delights, and points me back to my own '*Waheguru* moments'. To that extent I may also learn more about my own faith. But to say that I 'learn more' is only to stress that I enter more deeply into the Trinitarian mystery; I become more sensitive to the way the Spirit always seeks to impart the form – the form revealed in Christ – which embodies and manifests the 'vastness of the Lord'.

---

[32] A version of this formulation of the Trinitarian relations is implicit in Panikkar's *Trinity*. See the appreciative critique by Rowan Williams, 'Trinity and Pluralism', *On Christian Theology*, pp. 167–80.

Postface

Spirituality and difference

This book began with an overview of theology of religions and has sought to develop a spirituality of dialogue. I have spoken of theology as the 'work of religious intellect', spirituality as the 'right channelling of desire'. Both are necessary for interreligious learning. Without being anchored in the life-giving if sometimes diffuse wisdom of the great religious traditions, theology risks turning itself into an intellectualist system that totalises 'the other'. Without proper attention to the reasoned critique of faith and religious practice, spirituality is always in danger of splitting experiences of interiority from the broad context of social and ethical relations. In Christian terms, *Logos* and *Pneuma* – the givenness of form and the endless generation of meaning that is properly the work of the Spirit – reinforce and support each other.

Interreligious learning, as I have tried to describe it in this book, is not, therefore, a variation on the threefold paradigm that locks Christian thought into predictable categories but a more self-reflective account of Christianity-in-dialogue, a school of faith that responds to God's imperative to give and receive love by forever moving across boundaries and translating its faith into forms that others can understand. My aim has been to construct a Christian 'social imaginary' and to offer a Christian contribution to a 'school of schools'. In choosing to focus on particular experiences of interreligious encounter I have tried to account for a life of dialogue in which moments of insight and glimmers of understanding enhance Christian learning about the ways of God's Spirit.

This is not, however, a straightforward journey. The movement between faith and 'inter-faith' is marked as much by the joy of discovery as by a perplexity that can at times be thoroughly disarming. Moments of personal illumination go hand in hand with a growing sense of the dark ambivalence of so much human religiosity. In a thoroughly pluralist world the truth that faith commends has to grapple not just with other accounts of truth but also with the agnosticism and anti-religion of secular society. There may have been moments in this book when the reader has been conscious not of learning

261

and growth in faith but of the possibility of a postmodern fragmentation. To which I can only reply that there have been moments when the writer too has been well aware that the invitation to cross the interreligious threshold and expand the Christian imagination raises a distinct challenge to the limits of Christian integrity. Some might say that what I have mapped out is plausible but elitist, the preserve of those equipped with the linguistic and theological resources to cope with the intellectual complexities of life in another cultural and religious world. Others might object that interreligious learning, like all dialogue, risks a syncretistic self-indulgence that blunts the edge of Christian mission. Certainly there are many conceptual as well as practical issues raised by the life of faith in a massively complex multi-religious world – and I do not presume to have dealt with them adequately. All I have done is mark a beginning, attending to what is given in 'the middle of things' and to the stimulus that everyday interreligious encounter and face-to-face conversation gives to thoughtful theology.

There is no such thing as a final word that can tie up all the loose ends. At the end of the book I propose neither an epilogue nor a conclusion but a 'postface', which reiterates my basic conviction that the more one learns about the other the more one learns about the self. I have not tried to prove that conceptual point; I have used records of experience to make a cumulative case for understanding religious traditions as schools of faith, centres of teaching and learning, and for interreligious learning itself as building up a school of schools. I began by speaking of dialogue and learning as necessities not luxuries. There is no need to repeat what was said earlier about shifts in religious culture, especially about how, under the influence of the globalising force of postmodernity, religion is becoming more pluralist, more eclectic and more ambiguous. Religion may have a more prominent ethical and political face in the post 9/11 era, but that only makes it more contested – with some uncomfortable consequences for secular society and rather more destructive ones for those communities that find their traditional security structures under threat. At stake for so many people of faith is how the integrity of faith, commitment to visions of truth, can be maintained in a sometimes strange and hostile world. The enterprise of learning, refusing to homogenise values and turn the richness of difference into a few all-encompassing certainties, is more than a lifestyle choice for the leisured and learned. It has claims on all persons who take the 'conviction of meaning' seriously.

Clearly not everyone will be ready to engage in a sophisticated exploration of Quranic exegesis or feel ready to debate the finer points of Vedantic meta-physics. Nor should they feel so compelled. I hope that, if this melding of theology and spirituality has shown one thing, it is that there are many starting points for interreligious learning. Just as there are a number of forms of dialogue, so there are many ways of exploring the world as mapped out by another religious tradition. I could have developed other themes in other ways, with a focus on bilateral rather than multilateral dialogue or on particularly evocative cross-religious themes. My chosen topics could have been less personal, and attended more to classic theological concepts such as Rosenzweig's celebrated trio of creation, revelation, and redemption. I have, however, focused on places for a very practical, as much as theological, reason.

It may sound obvious but if dialogue and learning are imperatives for modern living then we have to start somewhere. The ideal place does not exist, nor the ideal time; there is only *this* place and *this* moment. We begin in particular situations where people live out their patterns of holiness, keeping faith with precious memories and seeking to pass them, as Scharf's teacher implored, 'into good hands'. Places can, of course, be ambiguous. They root us in the middle of things, providing security for the host and a refuge for the guest; they may also be places of danger, borderlands that belong to no one, or even sources of threat and terror. But in all such places a living context is given to the face of the other. Difference becomes palpable; it can be acknowledged, explored and faced. Once a meeting with the other has been effected, any place can become a point of crossing and a catalyst for the imagination. There are, of course, and always will be, 'outsiders' and 'insiders', guests and hosts, seekers and initiated, learners and teachers, people in the know and people aspiring to know. Interreligious learning as I have sought to describe it is not a matter of the one fading into the other, as if the object of the exercise is to elide all difference. The process is never-ending, a 'reaching out' in faith that only ever ends in God's good time. The paradox is that the more we learn the less specific the outcomes turn out to be; the less we worry about specific outcomes the more learning becomes an unconscious habit. In this way interreligious learning, as I noted in the Preface, becomes almost an end in itself.

Almost but not quite. Conversations and collaboration may build up those qualities of empathy and respect which the school of schools needs and which will, no doubt, be good for the cause of social cohesion. But for the Christian theologian the integrity of the Christian tradition is paramount – just as, for each school of faith the truths and values people hold dear continue to provide the touchstone against which other patterns of life are to be measured. In other words, Christian experience of the other in recent decades may have retrieved the crucially important form of interpersonal Buberian dialogue but it cannot ignore the demands of the Platonist dialogue of ideas. Just how the two are to be brought together in conceptual terms is not a subject I have chosen explicitly to pursue. I have chosen to work with examples of practice – not in order to postpone theoretical reflection but to ground it in the middle of things where the workings of God's grace are to be discerned.

Let me finish, therefore, not by presenting some dubiously neat answer or even a few rules of thumb but by repeating a couple of the questions that have guided my reflections through this book. First, can the vision of people of faith learning about, and from and with each other be more than a pragmatic response to everyday necessity? The 'school of schools' that I am commending is not trying to construct a fuzzy universalism, still less reduce complex wisdom to bland spiritual slogans. It is about building up the virtues of religious living that make interpretation, communication and translation possible. That is not to say that all the schools need to do is subordinate the content of faith to a process of interaction. The point I am trying to make is that both are necessary – theology and spirituality have to work together. Each school of faith has its own contribution to make, its own insights and traditional wisdom, its own skills of engagement. Each will be different – and it will be precisely in the honouring of difference that the schools are most likely to safeguard their own integrity and, in so doing, to become sensitised both to the echoes and resonances of the known in the unknown *and* to those elements of strangeness that may (or may not) be an invitation to a move beyond the short-term scramble to find points of agreement. If there is a universalism at work here, it is vested less in common themes and concepts than in a critical awareness of what human beings can *do* together once they have learned how to face each other in honesty and truth. At that point, it becomes possible to speak of a 'we'. While remaining members of very different religious traditions, we – interreligious learners – witness not just to the particular truths and values sedimented in our funds of ancient wisdom but – more profoundly – to the action of that Holy Mystery, however it be understood, which has made the life of faith possible.

This takes me to a second question, about how Christian faith in dialogue with other faith traditions can develop a 'social imaginary' that still bears faithful witness to the Gospel. How can the Christian 'school of faith' maintain its own specificity and not end up sunk in some genial pan-religious melange? Earlier I talked about the 'art of translation' to describe the spirituality appropriate to the Christian school of faith – a quality embodied in the likes of Justin and Aquinas and Ricci whose creative brilliance spoke for a Church that has always been charged with bearing public witness to the hope that is within it. As their extraordinary experiments in communicating across philosophical and cultural worlds remind us, the work of translation is not an exact science; it requires linguistic skills and discerning leaps of the imagination if what is understood in one set of symbols and concepts is to be understood through the medium of another. Translation, as Rosenzweig says, is a project that is almost doomed to fail. But it has to be done – for communication is what Christian mission is all about. The alternative is an ethnocentric refusal to translate that leads inexorably to some sort of risk-averse fundamentalism – a Christian subculture that has lost its capacity to teach because it has lost the appetite to learn. This is what makes dialogue, in both its Buberian and Platonist forms, an essential expression of what it is to be Church in a postmodern world. While learning more about 'them' we also become more responsibly 'us' – not because such encounters fill us with some consoling sense of spiritual togetherness but because, more profoundly, they act as persistent invitations once again to 'come and see' and to engage with Jesus's question: 'who do you say that I am?'

The answers which respond to that question, from New Testament titles to the balanced protocols of Nicaea and Chalcedon, have become the bedrock of Christian theology – and will remain so. It does not follow, however, that different ways of expressing and explaining that truth are not possible – or, indeed, desirable. Such will be the work of translation. Moving across strange frontiers can be arduous and demanding, but it can also be creative and energising, especially when 'traces of the other' sound some echo of a familiar truth. The Christian school of faith teaches a comprehensive vision that is formed in response to the God who is revealed in the person of Christ. God is intrinsically relational. If, therefore, the interpersonal is the primary analogue for the Christian understanding of what God is like, then it will be through learning how to live in companionship with Christ that the skills necessary for discerning the work of the Spirit will be learned. Comprehensive visions only become totalising of the other when the time it takes to learn – ultimately, of course, God's own time – is subsumed into a concept of time that values the immediacy of the present over the painstaking work of shaping events and experiences. That this moment, here and now, in the middle of things, can be understood to speak of God is clear – but only if it is related to all that has gone before and whatever is yet to come, the full span of the movement of grace. Rather than being locked into our own world, the horizons of that world are expanded, so that an element of the other ends up elusively embedded in our primary vision. Being returned to the middle of things is not a matter of routine and repetition but, as the Zen master might have said, discovering how extraordinary is the ordinariness of everyday relations.

What holds this book together is the experience of the stranger become guest: the other become familiar, revealed in places and artefacts, conversations and chance encounters, the one who opens up a glimpse of something different yet mysteriously familiar. It is always the living communities of faith that lift the experience of learning beyond the intellectual and aesthetic to something that is both ethical and properly theological, speaking somehow of Godself. By focusing on interreligious dialogue precisely as *learning* I have sought to draw attention away from the search for cross-religious universals and on to the much more open-ended question of how one responds to truth, what impact it makes, what one *does* to realise truth. This is, of course, a work of the religious imagination, a learned capacity to listen for resonances, build hypotheses and search out possible meanings. But that is only to say that it is, in Christian terms, the work of God's Spirit who always goes ahead of the Church.

Bibliography

Abhishiktananda, *Saccidananda: A Christian Approach to Advaitic Experience* (Delhi: ISPCK, 1974).

Ascent to the Depth of the Heart: The Spiritual Diary (1948–1973) of Swami Abhishiktananda. A Selection, ed. and trans. David Fleming and James Stuart (Delhi: ISPCK, 1998).

Addiss, Stephen, 'The History of Ox-Herding Poems and Paintings', in Stephen Addiss, and Ray Kass, *John Cage: Zen Ox-Herding Pictures* (Richmond, Va.: University of Richmond Museums, 2009).

Alberigo, Giuseppe, and Joseph Komonchak (eds.), *The History of Vatican II*, vol. i, *Announcing and Preparing Vatican II: Toward a New Era in Catholicism* (New York: Orbis/Peeters, 1995).

Almond, Gabriel A., R. Scott Appleby, and Emmanuel Sivan (eds.), *Strong Religion: The Rise of Fundamentalisms around the World* (University of Chicago Press, 2003).

Amaladoss, Michael, *Life in Freedom* (Anand: Gujarat Sahitya Prakash, 1997).

The Asian Jesus (New York: Orbis, 2006).

Analayo, *Satipatthana: The Direct Path to Realization* (Birmingham: Windhorse Publications, 2003).

Anselm, St., *Anselm of Canterbury: The Major Works*, ed. Brian Davies, and G. R. Evans (Oxford University Press, 1998).

Appleby, Scott, *The Ambivalence of the Sacred* (Lanham, Md.: Rowman & Littlefield, 2000).

Arendt, Hannah, *Eichmann in Jerusalem: A Report on the Banality of Evil*, rev. edn. (New York: Viking Press, 1965).

The Life of the Mind (New York: Harcourt Brace Jovanovich, 1978).

Armour, Rollin, *Islam, Christianity and the West: A Troubled History* (New York: Orbis, 2002).

Arnold, Matthew, *Culture and Anarchy*, ed. R. H. Super (Ann Arbor, Mich.: University of Michigan Press, 1965).

Augustine of Hippo (St Augustine), *The City of God*, trans. Henry Bettenson (Harmondsworth: Penguin, 1972).

Ayoub, Mahmoud, *The Quran and its Interpreters*, vol. ii (Albany, NY: SUNY Press, 1992).

Ballantyne, Tony, *Between Colonialism and Diaspora: Cultural Formations in an Imperial World* (Durham, NC and London: Duke University Press, 2006).

Balthasar, Hans Urs von, 'Der Unbekannte jenseits des Wortes', *Spiritus Creator* (Einsiedeln: Johannes Verlag, 1967).

Banchoff, Thomas (ed.), *Religious Pluralism, Globalization and World Politics* (Oxford University Press, 2008).

Barker, Gregory A., and Stephen E. Gregg (eds.), *Jesus Beyond Christianity: The Classic Texts* (Oxford University Press, 2010).

Barnes, Michael, *Religions in Conversation* (London: SPCK, 1989).

'From Ashrams to Dalits: The Four Seasons of Inculturation', *The Way* (Jan. 2001), pp. 61–71.

Theology and the Dialogue of Religions (Cambridge University Press, 2002).

'Theology of Religions', in Arthur Holder (ed.), *The Blackwell Companion to Christian Spirituality* (Oxford: Blackwell, 2005), pp. 401–16.

'With God in the World: A Dialogue between the *Bhagavad Gita* and the *Spiritual Exercises* of St Ignatius of Loyola', in Catherine Cornille (ed.), *Song Divine: Christian Commentaries on the Bhagavad Gita* (Louvain and Grand Rapids, Mich.: Peeters/Eerdmans, 2006).

'Way and Wilderness: An Augustinian Dialogue with Buddhism', in Brian Brown, John Doody and Kim Paffenroth (eds.), *Augustine and World Religions* (Lanham, Md.: Lexington, 2008).

'Religious Pluralism', in John Hinnells (ed.), *The Routledge Companion to the Study of Religion*, 2nd edn. (London and New York: Routledge, 2010).

Batchelor, Stephen, *The Awakening of the West* (London: Thorsons, 1994).

'The Other Enlightenment Project', in Ursula King (ed.), *Faith and Practice in a Postmodern Age* (London: Cassells, 1998).

Baumann, Gerd, *Contesting Culture: Discourses of Identity in Multi-Ethnic London* (Cambridge University Press, 1994).

Beattie, Tina, *The New Atheists: The Twilight of Reason and the War on Religion* (London: Darton, Longman and Todd, 2007).

Bergman, Shmuel Hugo, *Dialogical Philosophy from Kierkegaard to Buber* (Albany, NY: SUNY Press, 1991).

Bhagavata Purana, trans. G. V. Tagare, 5 pts. (Delhi: Motilal Banarsidass, 1976).

Biggar, Nigel, and Linda Hogan (eds.), *Religious Voices in Public Places* (Oxford University Press, 2009).

Blechler, James E., and H. Lawrence Bond, *Nicholas of Cusa – Interreligious Harmony: Text, Concordance and Translation of* De Pace Fidei (Lampeter: Edwin Mellen, 1991).

Bosch, David, *Transforming Mission: Paradigm Shifts in Theology of Mission* (New York: Orbis, 1992).

Bowker, John, *The Religious Imagination and the Sense of God* (Oxford University Press, 1978).

Boyd, Robin, *An Introduction to Indian Christian Theology* (Delhi: ISPCK, 1994).

Brown, Brian, John Doody, and Kim Paffenroth (eds.), *Augustine and World Religions* (Lanham, Md.: Lexington, 2008).

Brown, Christopher A., 'Can Buddhism Save? Finding Resonance in Incommensurability', *Cross Currents* (1999), pp. 164–96.

Bruce, Steve, *Fundamentalism* (Cambridge: Polity, 2000).

Brueggemann, Walter, *An Unsettling God: The Heart of the Hebrew Bible* (Minneapolis, Minn.: Fortress, 2009).

Buber, Martin, *Mamre: Essays in Religion*, trans. G. Hort (Melbourne University Press, 1946).

Tales of the Hasidim: The Early Masters (New York: Schocken Books, 1947).

The Later Masters (New York: Schocken Books, 1948).

The Origin and Meaning of Hasidism, ed. and trans. Maurice Friedman (New York: Horizon Press, 1960).

I and Thou, trans. Ronald Gregor Smith, 2nd edn. (Edinburgh: T & T Clark, 1958).

Daniel, Dialogues on Realization, trans. Maurice Friedmann (New York: Holt, 1964).

Hasidism and Modern Man, ed. and trans. Maurice Friedman, 2nd edn. (Atlantic Highlands, NJ: Humanities Press, 1988).

Buber, Martin, and Franz Rosenzweig, *Scripture and Translation*, trans. Lawrence Rosenwald, and Everett Fox (Bloomington, Ind.: Indiana University Press, 1994).

Buckley, Michael, *At the Origins of Modern Atheism* (New Haven, Conn.: Yale University Press, 1987).

Buddhadasa, *Dhammic Socialism*, ed. and trans. Donald K Swearer. (Bangkok: Thai Inter-Religious Commission for Development, 1986).

Burrows, William, 'A Seventh Paradigm? Catholics and Radical Inculturation', in Willem Saayman, and Klippies Kritzinger (eds.), *Mission in Bold Humility* (New York: Orbis, 1996).

Caldwell, Christopher, *Reflections on the Revolution in Europe: Immigration, Islam, and the West* (New York: Doubleday, 2009).

Cavanaugh, William T., '"A Fire Strong Enough to Consume the House"', *Modern Theology*, 11.4 (Oct. 1995).

The Theopolitical Imagination (Edinburgh: T & T Clark, 2002).

The Myth of Religious Violence: Secular Ideology and the Roots of Modern Conflict (Oxford University Press, 2009).

Cheetham, David, *John Hick: A Critical Introduction and Reflection* (Aldershot: Ashgate, 2003).

Clarke, J. J., *Oriental Enlightenment* (London and New York: Routledge, 1997).

Clooney, Francis X., *Theology after Vedanta* (Albany, NY: SUNY Press, 1993).

'Comparative Theology: A Review of Recent Books, 1989–1995', *Theological Studies*, 56 (1995), pp. 521–50.

Seeing Through Texts: Doing Theology among the Śrivaisnavas of South India (Albany, NY: SUNY Press, 1996).

Hindu God, Christian God: How Reason Helps Break Down the Boundaries between Religions (Oxford University Press, 2001).

Divine Mother, Blessed Mother: Hindu Goddesses and the Virgin Mary (Oxford University Press, 2005).

'Christian Readers, Hindu Words: Toward a Christian Commentary on Hindu Prayer', *Theology Digest*, 53.4 (2006).

'Comparative Theology', in John Webster, Kathryn Tanner and Iain Torrance (eds.), *The Oxford Handbook of Systematic Theology* (Oxford University Press, 2007).

Comparative Theology: Deep Learning across Religious Borders (Chichester: Wiley-Blackwell, 2010).

The New Comparative Theology: Interreligious Insights from the Next Generation (London: T & T Clark, 2010).

Cohen, Arthur, *The Myth of the Judaeo-Christian Tradition* (New York: Harper and Row, 1970).

Cole, W. Owen, and Piara Singh Sambhi, *Sikhism and Christianity* (Basingstoke: Macmillan, 1993).

Collins, Steven, *Selfless Persons: Imagery and Thought in Theravada Buddhism* (Cambridge University Press, 1982).

Nirvana and other Buddhist Felicities (Cambridge University Press, 1998).

Congar, Yves, *Tradition and Traditions* (New York: Macmillan, 1966).

The Word and the Spirit (London: Chapman, 1984).

Corless, Roger, 'The Dramas of Spiritual Progress', in *Mystics Quarterly*, 11.2 (1985), pp. 65–75.

Cornille, Catherine (ed.), *Song Divine: Christian Commentaries on the* Bhagavad Gita (Louvain: Peeters, 2006).

The Im-Possibility of Interreligious Dialogue (New York: Herder and Herder, 2008).

Cragg, Kenneth, *The Christ and the Faiths* (London: SPCK, 1986).

Jesus and the Muslim: An Exploration (Oxford: Oneworld, 1999).

Crisp, Oliver, *God Incarnate: Explorations in Christology* (London: Continuum, 2009).

Crockett, Clayton, 'On the Disorientation of the Study of Religion', in Thomas A. Idinopulos and Brian C. Wilson (eds.), *What is Religion? Origins, Definitions and Explanations* (Leiden: Brill, 1998), pp. 1–13.

D'Costa, Gavin, *Theology and Religious Pluralism* (Oxford: Blackwell, 1985).

'"Extra ecclesiam nulla salus" Revisited', in Ian Hamnett (ed.), *Religious Pluralism and Unbelief: Studies Critical and Comparative* (London: Routledge, 1990).

'The Impossibility of a Pluralist View of Religions', *Religious Studies*, 32 (1996), pp. 223–32.

'Theology of Religions', in David Ford (ed.), *The Modern Theologians*, 3rd edn. (Oxford: Blackwell, 2005).

Christianity and World Religions: Disputed Questions in the Theology of Religions (Chichester: Wiley-Blackwell, 2009).

Dabashi, Hamid, *Islamic Liberation Theology: Resisting the Empire* (London and New York: Routledge, 2008).

Daniel, Norman, *Islam and the West: The Making of an Image* (Oxford: Oneworld, 2000).

Dass, Nirmal (ed.), *Songs of Kabir from the Adi Granth* (Delhi: Śri Satguru Publications, 1991).

Davies, Oliver, and Denys Turner (eds.), *Silence and the Word* (Cambridge University Press, 2002).

Dawkins, Richard, *The God Delusion* (London: Bantam, 2006).

de Certeau, Michel, *The Practice of Everyday Life* (Berkeley: University of California Press, 1984).

The Mystic Fable (University of Chicago Press, 1992).

de Giorgi, Maria, *Seimeizan* (Bologna: EMI, della cooperativa Servizio Missionario, 1989).

de Silva, Lynn, *The Problem of the Self in Buddhism and Christianity* (London: Macmillan, 1979).

de Vries, Hent, *Religion and Violence: Philosophical Perpsectives from Kant to Derrida* (Baltimore, Md. and London: Johns Hopkins University Press, 2002).

Derrida, Jacques, *Violence and Metaphysics* (University of Chicago Press, 1978).

Devotio Moderna: Basic Writings (Classics of Western Spirituality), ed. John H. van Engen (Mahwah, NJ: Paulist, 1988).

Docker, John, *The Origins of Violence: Religion, History and Genocide* (London: Pluto Press, 2008).

du Boulay, Shirley, *Beyond the Darkness* (London: Rider, 1998).

The Cave of the Heart (New York: Orbis, 2005).

Dumper, Michael, *The Politics of Jerusalem since 1967* (New York: Columbia University Press, 1997).

Dupuis, Jacques, *Toward a Christian Theology of Religious Pluralism* (New York: Orbis, 1997).

Christianity and the Religions: From Confrontation to Dialogue (New York and London: Orbis/Darton, Longman and Todd, 2002).

Durkheim, Émile, *Elementary Forms of Religious Life* (London: Allen and Unwin, 1915).

Eagleton, Terry, *The Idea of Culture* (Oxford: Blackwell, 2000).

Eliade, Mircea, *Yoga, Immortality and Freedom*, 2nd edn. (Princeton, NJ: Princeton University Press, 1969).

Elshtain, Jean Bethke Elshtain, *Augustine and the Limits of Politics* (Notre Dame, Ind.: University of Notre Dame Press, 1998).

Endean, Philip, 'Spirituality and Theology', in Philip Sheldrake (ed.), *The New SCM Dictionary of Christian Spirituality* (London: SCM, 2005), pp. 74–9.

Enomiya Lassalle, Hugo, *Zen Meditation for Christians* (La Salle, Ill.: Open Court, 1974).

The Practice of Zen Meditation (Wellingborough: Aquarian, 1988).

Esposito, John, *Islam: The Straight Path* (Oxford University Press, 1998).

Unholy Wars: Terror in the Name of Islam (Oxford University Press, 2002).

Faivre, Daniel, *Glimpses of a Holy City* (privately published, 2001).

Fenech, Louis E., *Martyrdom in the Sikh Tradition* (Delhi: Oxford University Press, 2000).

Fenn, Richard, *Dreams of Glory: The Sources of Apocalyptic Terror* (Aldershot: Ashgate, 2006).

Fisher, Eugene, *Fifteen Years of Catholic–Jewish Dialogue, 1970–1985* (Vatican City: Libreria Editrice Vaticana, 1986).

Flood, Gavin, *An Introduction to Hinduism* (Cambridge University Press, 1996).

Beyond Phenomenology: Rethinking the Study of Religion (London: Cassells, 1999).

Ford, David (ed.), *The Modern Theologians*, 3rd edn. (Oxford: Blackwell, 2005).

Ford, David, and Mike Higton (eds.), *Jesus* (Oxford University Press, 2002).

Ford, David, and C. C. Pecknold (eds.), *The Promise of Scriptural Reasoning* (Oxford: Blackwell, 2006).

Frank, Daniel H., Oliver Leaman, and Chares H. Manekin (eds.), *The Jewish Philosophy Reader* (London and New York: Routledge, 2000).

Fredericks, James L., 'A Universal Religious Experience? Comparative Theology as an Alternative to a Theology of Religions', *Horizons*, 22 (1995), pp. 67–87.

Faith among Faiths: Christian Theology and Non-Christian Religions (Mahwah, NJ: Paulist, 1999).

Friedman, Maurice, *Martin Buber's Life, and Work: The Later Years, 1945–1965* (New York: E. P. Dutton, 1983).

Frymer-Kensky, Tikva, David Novak, Peter Ochs, David Fox Sandmel, and Michael A Signer (eds.), *Christianity in Jewish Terms* (Boulder, Colo.: Westview, 2000).

Geertz, Clifford, *The Interpretation of Cultures* (London: HarperCollins, 1973).

Gilbert, Martin, *The Holocaust: The Jewish Tragedy* (London: Fontana, 1987).

Girard, René, *Violence and the Sacred* (London: Continuum, 2005).

Glatzer, Nahum (ed.), *Franz Rosenzweig: His Life and Thought*, 2nd edn. (New York: Schocken Books, 1953).

Goddard, Hugh, *A History of Christian–Muslim Relations* (Edinburgh University Press, 2000).

Goenka, S. N., *Satipatthana Sutta Discourses* (Seattle, Wash.: Vipassana Research Publications, 1998).

Gomez, Luis O., 'The Avatamsaka Sutra', in Takeuchi Yoshinori (ed.), *Buddhist Spirituality, vol. i, Indian, Southeast Asian, Tibetan, Early Chinese* (London: SCM, 1994), pp. 160–70.

Gorringe, T. J., *Furthering Humanity: A Theology of Culture* (Aldershot: Ashgate, 2004).

Gray, John, *Black Mass: Apocalyptic Religion and the Death of Utopia* (New York: Farrar, Strauss and Giroux, 2007).

Gregory of Nyssa, St., *Life of Moses* (Classics of Western Spirituality), ed. Abraham J. Malherbe, and Everett Ferguson (Mahwah, NJ: Paulist, 1978).

Grenke, Arthur, *God, Greed and Genocide: The Holocaust through the Centuries* (Washington, DC: New Academic Publishing, 2005).

Griffith, Sidney, 'Sharing the Faith of Abraham: The "Credo" of Louis Massignon', *Islam and Christian–Muslim Relations*, 8 (1997), pp. 193–210.

The Church in the Shadow of the Mosque (Princeton, NJ: Princeton University Press, 2008).

Griffiths, Bede, *Christian Ashram: Essays Towards a Hindu–Christian Dialogue* (London: Darton, Longman and Todd, 1966).

River of Compassion: A Christian Commentary on the Bhagavad Gita (Warwick, NY: Amity House, 1987).

Griffiths, Paul J., *Religious Reading: The Place of Reading in the Practice of Religion* (Oxford University Press, 1999).

Halbfass, Wilhelm, *India and Europe: An Essay in Understanding* (Albany, NY: SUNY Press, 1988).

Hall, S. G. (ed.), *Melito of Sardis: On Pascha and Fragments* (Oxford University Press, 1979).

Hamnett, Ian (ed.), *Religious Pluralism and Unbelief: Studies Critical and Comparative* (London: Routledge, 1990).

Hardy, Friedhelm, *Viraha Bhakti: The Early History of Krsna Devotion in South India* (Oxford University Press, 1983).

The Religious Culture of India: Power, Love and Wisdom (Cambridge University Press, 1994).

Harkins, Franklin T., 'Unwitting Witnesses', in Brian Brown, John Doody and Kim Paffenroth (eds.), *Augustine and World Religions* (Lanham, Md.: Lexington, 2008).

Harries, Richard, *After the Evil: Christianity and Judaism in the Shadow of the Holocaust* (Oxford University Press, 2003).

Harrison, Peter, *'Religion' and the Religions in the English Enlightenment* (Cambridge University Press, 1994).

Heck, Paul L., *Common Ground: Islam, Christianity and Religious Pluralism* (Washington, DC: Georgetown University Press, 2009).

Heschel, Susannah, *The Aryan Jesus: Christian Theologians and the Bible in Nazi Germany* (Princeton, NJ: Princeton University Press, 2008)

Hess, Linda, and Shukdeo Singh (eds.), *The Bijak of Kabir* (Oxford University Press, 2002).

Hewer, C. T. R., *Understanding Islam: The First Ten Steps* (London: SCM, 2006).

Hewitt, Harold (ed.), *Problems in the Philosophy of Religion: Critical Studies of the Work of John Hick* (Basingstoke: Macmillan, 1991).

Hick, John, 'The Non-Absoluteness of Christianity', in John Hick, and Paul Knitter (eds.), *The Myth of Christian Uniqueness* (London: SCM, 1987).

Higgins, John (ed.), *The Raymond Williams Reader* (Oxford: Blackwell, 2002).

Hinnells, John (ed.), *The Routledge Companion to the Study of Religion*, 2nd edn. (London and New York: Routledge, 2010).

Hitchens, Christopher, *God is not Great* (London: Atlantic, 2007).

Hodgson, Marshall, *Rethinking World History: Essays on Europe, Islam, and World History*, ed. Edmund Burke (Cambridge University Press, 1999).

Holder, Arthur (ed.), *The Blackwell Companion to Christian Spirituality* (Oxford: Blackwell, 2005).

Huntington, Samuel, *The Clash of Civilizations and the Remaking of World Order* (London: Simon & Schuster, 1997).

Hunt-Perry, Patricia, and Lyn Fine, 'All Buddhism is Engaged: Thich Nhat Hanh and the Order of Interbeing', in Christopher S. Queen (ed.), *Engaged Buddhism in the West* (Boston, Mass.: Wisdom, 2000).

Isaac, Jules, *The Teaching of Contempt: The Christian Roots of Anti-Semitism* (New York: Holt, Rinehart and Winston, 1964).

The Christian Roots of Antisemitism (London: Council for Christians and Jews, 1965).

Ivens, Michael, *Understanding the Spiritual Exercises* (Leominster: Gracewing, 1998).

Jackson, Roger, and John Makransky (eds.), *Buddhist Theology* (London: Curzon, 2000).

Jacobs, Steven Leonard (ed.), *Confronting Genocide: Judaism, Christianity, Islam* (Lanham, Md.: Lexington, 2009).

Jacquin, Françoise, *Jules Monchanin Prêtre* (Paris: Éditions du Cerf, 1996).

James, William, *The Varieties of Religious Experience* (Harmondsworth: Penguin, 1982).

Jenkins, Philip, *God's Continent: Christianity, Islam and Europe's Religious Crisis* (Oxford University Press, 2007).

Johnson, Kristin Deede, *Theology, Political Theory and Pluralism: Beyond Tolerance and Difference* (Cambridge University Press, 2007).

Johnston, William, *The Still Point* (New York: Harper and Row, 1970).

Silent Music: The Science of Meditation (London: Fontana-Collins, 1974).

Christian Zen (Dublin: Gill and Macmillan, 1979).

Jones, Ken, *The New Social Face of Buddhism: A Call to Action* (Boston, Mass.: Wisdom, 2003).

Juergensmeyer, Mark (ed.), *Violence and the Sacred in the Modern World* (London: Frank Cass, 1992).

Terror in the Mind of God (Berkeley: University of California Press, 2003).

Karkainnen, Veli-Matti, *Introduction to the Theology of Religions* (Downers Grove, Ill.: IVP Academic Press, 2003).

Kearney, Richard, *Anatheism (Returning to God after God)* (New York: Columbia University Press, 2010).

Keating, Thomas, *Intimacy with God: An Introduction to Centering Prayer* (New York: Crossroad, 2009).

Keenan, John, *The Meaning of Christ: A Mahayana Theology* (New York: Orbis, 1989).

Keith, Graham, *Hated Without a Cause? A Survey of Anti-Semitism* (Carlisle: Paternoster Press, 1997).

Kendall, Daniel, and Gerald O'Collins (eds.), *In Many and Diverse Ways* (New York: Orbis, 2003).

Kennedy, Robert, *Zen Gifts for Christians* (New York: Continuum, 2000).

Zen Spirit, Christian Spirit (New York: Continuum, 2001).

Kharbanda, Birinder Singh, *One with God: A Sikh View* (Delhi: First Edition, 2005).

Kiblinger, Kristin Beise, *Buddhist Inclusivism: Attitudes towards Religious Others* (Aldershot: Ashgate, 2005).

King, Ursula (ed.), *Faith and Practice in a Postmodern Age* (London: Cassells, 1998).

Kirwan, Michael, *Girard and Theology* (Edinburgh: T & T Clark, 2009).

Knitter, Paul, *No Other Name?* (London: SCM, 1985).

(ed.), *The Myth of Religious Superiority* (New York: Orbis, 2005).

Koelman, Gaspar, *Patañjala Yoga* (Poona: Papal Athenaeum, 1970).

Komulainen, Jyri, *An Emerging Cosmotheandric Religion? Panikkar's Pluralistic Theology of Religions* (Leiden: Brill, 2005).

Lash, Nicholas, *Easter in Ordinary* (Notre Dame, Ind.: University of Notre Dame Press, 1988).

Believing Three Ways in One God (London: SCM, 1992).

The Beginning and the End of 'Religion' (Cambridge University Press, 1996).

Theology for Pilgrims (London: Darton, Longman and Todd, 2008).

Lefebure, Leo, *The Buddha and the Christ* (New York: Orbis, 1993).

Legenhausen, Muhammad, *Islam and Religious Pluralism* (London: Al-Hoda, 1999).

Jesus Through Shi'ite Narrations (Qum: Ansariyan Publications, 2004).

Levenson, Jon, 'How not to Conduct Jewish–Christian Dialogue', *Commentary*, 112 (Dec. 2001), pp. 31–7.

Levinas, Emmanuel, *Totality and Infinity* (Pittsburgh, Pa.: Duquesne University Press, 1969).

Difficult Freedom: Essays on Judaism (Baltimore, Md.: Johns Hopkins University Press, 1990).

Otherwise than Being or Beyond Essence (Dordrecht: Kluwer Academic Publishers, 1991).

Lewis, Bernard, *The Crisis of Islam: Holy War and Unholy Terror* (London: Phoenix, 2004).

Lindbeck, George, *The Nature of Doctrine: Religion and Theology in a Postliberal Age* (Philadelphia, Pa.: Westminster, 1984).

Lipner, Julius, *Hindus* (London: Routledge, 1994).

Lipner, Julius, and George Gispert Sauch (eds.), *The Writings of Brahmabandhab Upadhyaya, Including a Résumé of his Life and Thought* (Bangalore: United Theological College, 1992).

Lloyd Jones, Gareth, *Hard Sayings: Difficult New Testament Texts for Jewish–Christian Relations* (London: CCJ Publications, 1993).

Lochhead, David, *The Dialogical Imperative* (London: SCM, 1988).

Loughlin, Gerard, 'Prefacing Pluralism: John Hick and the Mastery of Religion', *Modern Theology*, 7.1 (1990), pp. 29–55.

Louth, Andrew, *St John Damascene: Tradition and Originality in Byzantine Theology* (Oxford University Press, 2002).

McAuliffe, Jane Dammen, 'The Quranic Context of Muslim Biblical Scholarship', *Islam and Christian–Muslim Relations*, 7 (1996), pp. 141–58.

'Is There a Connection between the Bible and the Quran?', *Theological Digest*, 49 (2002), pp. 303–17.

MacCulloch, Diarmuid, *A History of Christianity* (London: Penguin, 2009).

McDade, John, 'Catholicism and Judaism since Vatican II', *New Blackfriars*, 88 (July 2007), pp. 367–84.

McGrane, Bernard, *Beyond Anthropology: Society and the Other* (New York: Columbia University Press, 1989).

McIntosh, Mark A., *Mystical Theology: The Integrity of Spirituality and Theology* (Oxford: Blackwell, 1998).

McLoughlin, Sean, 'Religion and Diaspora', in John Hinnells (ed.), *The Routledge Companion to the Study of Religion*, 2nd edn. (London: Routledge, 2010).

Macy, Joanna, *World as Lover, World as Self* (London: Rider, 1993).

Madra, Amandeep Singh, and Parmjit Singh (eds.), *'Sicques, Tigers or Thieves': Eye-Witness Accounts of the Sikhs (1606–1809)* (New York and Basingstoke: Palgrave Macmillan, 2004).

Main, John, *Christian Meditation: The Gethsemani Talks* (New York, Continuum: 1998).

Malka, Salomon, *Emmanuel Levinas: His Life and Legacy* (Pittsburgh, Pa.: Duquesne University Press, 2002).

Marshall, David, *God, Muhammad and the Unbelievers* (London: Curzon, 1999).

Marty, Martin, and R. Scott Appleby (eds.), *The Fundamentalism Project*, 5 vols. (University of Chicago Press, 1993–2004).

Mathewes, Charles T., 'Pluralism, Otherness and the Augustinian Tradition', *Modern Theology*, 14.1 (1998).

A Theology of Public Life (Cambridge University Press, 2007).

Maududi, S. A. A., *Towards Understanding the Quran* (Leicester: Islamic Foundation, 1988).

Melloni, Javier, *The Exercises of St Ignatius Loyola in the Western Tradition* (Leominster: Gracewing, 2000).

Mullett, Michael A., *Martin Luther* (London: Routledge, 2004).

Neusner, Jacob, *Jews and Christians: The Myth of a Common Tradition* (London: SCM, 1991).

Telling Tales (Louisville, Ky.: Westminster John Knox Press, 1993).

The Four Stages of Rabbinic Judaism (London: Routledge, 1999).

O'Collins, Gerald, 'Jacques Dupuis's Contributions to Interreligious Dialogue', *Theological Studies*, 64 (2003).

Salvation for All: God's Other Peoples (Oxford University Press, 2008).

Oberoi, Harjot, *The Construction of Religious Boundaries: Culture, Identity and Diversity in the Sikh Tradition* (Delhi: Oxford University Press, 1994).

Ochs, Peter, 'An Introduction to Postcritical Scriptural Interpretation', in Peter Ochs (ed.), *The Return to Scripture in Judaism and Christianity* (Mahwah, NJ: Paulist, 1993).

Pierce, Pragmatism and the Logic of Scripture (Cambridge University Press, 1998).

'Response: Reflections on Binarism', *Modern Theology*, 24.3 (July 2008), pp. 487–97.

Panikkar, Raimundo, *The Trinity and the Religious Experience of Man* (New York and London: Orbis/Darton, Longman and Todd, 1973).

The Intra-Religious Dialogue (New York: Paulist, 1978).

'The Dialogical Dialogue', in Frank Whaling (ed.), *The World's Religious Traditions* (Edinburgh: T & T Clark, 1984), pp. 201–21.

The Silence of God: The Answer of the Buddha (New York, Orbis, 1989).

The Cosmotheandric Experience: Emerging Religious Consciousness (New York: Orbis, 1993).

Patwant Singh, *The Sikhs* (London: John Murray, 1999).

Pecknold, C. C., *Transforming Postliberal Theology: George Lindbeck, Pragmatism and Scripture* (London: T & T Clark, 2005).

Pieris, Aloysius, *An Asian Theology of Liberation* (Edinburgh: T & T Clark, 1988).
Love Meets Wisdom (New York: Orbis, 1988).
'Does Christ Have a Place in Asia? A Panoramic View', *Concilium*, 2 (1993), pp. 33–47.
Prophetic Humour: Doing Inter-religious Studies in the Reverential Mode (Colombo: EISD, 2005).

Pope, Stephen J., and Charles Hefling (eds.), *Sic et Non: Encountering Dominus Iesus* (New York: Orbis, 2002).

Putnam, Hilary, *Cambridge Companion to Levinas* (Cambridge University Press: 2002).
Jewish Philosophy as a Guide to Life (Bloomington: Indiana University Press, 2008).

Queen, Christopher S. (ed.), *Engaged Buddhism in the West* (Boston, Mass.: Wisdom, 2000).

Queen, Christopher S., and Sallie B. King (eds.), *Engaged Buddhism: Buddhist Liberation Movements in Asia* (New York: State University of New York Press, 1996).

Queen, Christopher [S.], Charles Prebish, and Damien Keown (eds.), *Action Dharma: New Studies in Engaged Buddhism* (London: Routledge-Curzon, 2003).

Race, Alan, *Christians and Religious Pluralism: Patterns in the Christian Theology of Religions* (London: SCM, 1983).
Interfaith Encounter: The Twin Tracks of Theology and Dialogue (London: SCM, 2001).

Radcliffe, Timothy, 'The Sacramentality of the Word', in Keith Pecklers (ed.), *Liturgy in a Postmodern World* (London: Continuum, 2003).

Rahner, Karl, *Theological Investigations* (London: Darton, Longman and Todd, 1965–79).
Foundations of Christian Faith (London: Darton, Longman and Todd, 1978).

Rahula, Walpola, *What the Buddha Taught* (London: Gordon Frazer, 1967).
Zen and the Taming of the Bull: Towards the Definition of Buddhist Thought (London: Gordon Fraser, 1978).

Rajkumar, Peniel, *Dalit Theology and Dalit Liberation* (Farnham: Ashgate, 2010).

Ramadan, Tariq, *Western Muslims and the Future of Islam* (Oxford University Press, 2004).

Reps, Paul, *Zen Flesh, Zen Bones* (Harmondsworth: Penguin, 1972).

Richard, Yann, *Shi'ite Islam* (Oxford: Blackwell, 1995).

Ricoeur, Paul, *Time and Narrative*, vol. i (University of Chicago Press, 1984).
Oneself as Another (University of Chicago Press, 1992).

Rose, Gillian, *The Broken Middle* (Oxford: Blackwell, 1992).

Rosenzweig, Franz, *The Star of Redemption*, trans. William W. Hallo (Notre Dame, Ind.: University of Notre Dame Press, 1985).

The New Thinking, ed. and trans. Alan Udoff, and Barbara E. Galli (New York: Syracuse University Press, 1999).

Understanding the Sick and the Healthy: A View of World, Man and God, trans. Nahum Glatzer (New York, 1953), second introduction by Hilary Putnam (Cambridge, Mass.: Harvard University Press, 1999).

Saayman, Willem, and Klippies Kritzinger (eds.), *Mission in Bold Humility* (New York: Orbis, 1996).

Sacks, Jonathan, *Faith in the Future* (London: Darton, Longman and Todd, 1995).

The Dignity of Difference: How to Avoid the Clash of Civilizations, 2nd edn. (London: Continuum, 2003).

The Home We Build Together: Recreating Society (London: Continuum, 2007).

Saha, Santosh C. (ed), *Religious Fundamentalism in the Contemporary World* (Lanham, Md.: Lexington, 2004).

Saldanha, Chrys, *Divine Pedagogy: A Patristic View of Non-Christian Religions* (Rome: Libreria Ateneo Salesiano, 1984).

Samy, Ama, *Zen: Waking to your Original Face* (Thiruvanmiyur, Chennai: Cre-A, 2005).

Sanders, E. P., *Paul and Palestinian Judaism: A Comparison of Patterns of Religion* (Minneapolis, Minn.: Fortress, 1977).

Schall, James V., *The Regensburg Lecture* (South Bend, Ind., St Augustine's Press, 2007).

Scharf, Rafael F., *Poland, What Do I Have To Do With Thee ... Essays Without Prejudice* (Cracow: Fundacja Judaica, 1999).

Schineller, Peter, *A Handbook of Inculturation* (New York: Paulist, 1990).

Schreiter, Robert, 'Inculturation of Faith or Identification with Culture', *Concilium*, 2 (1994), pp. 15–24.

Schwab, Raymond, *The Oriental Renaissance* (New York: Columbia University Press, 1984).

Schwager, Raymund, *Must There be Scapegoats? Violence and Redemption in the Bible* (Leominster: Gracewing, 2000).

Schweig, G. M., *Dance of Divine Love: The Rasa Lila of Krishna from the Bhagavata Purana, India's Classic Sacred Love Story* (Princeton, NJ: Princeton University Press, 2005).

Selengut, Charles, *Sacred Fury: Understanding Religious Violence* (Walnut Creek, Calif.: AltaMira Press, 2003).

Shanks, Andrew, *Against Innocence: Gillian Rose's Reception and Gift of Faith* (London: SCM, 2008).

Sheldrake, Philip, *Spirituality and History: Questions of Interpretation and Method* (London: SPCK, 1991).

Spirituality and Theology: Christian Living and the Doctrine of God (London: Darton, Longman and Todd, 1998).

Spaces for the Sacred: Place, Memory and Identity (Baltimore, Md.: Johns Hopkins University Press, 2001).

(ed.), *The New SCM Dictionary of Christian Spirituality* (London: SCM, 2005).

A Brief History of Spirituality (Oxford: Blackwell, 2007).

Shomali, Mohammad Ali, *Discovering Shi'i Islam* (Qum: Jami'at al-Zahra, 2003).

Shi'i Islam: Origins, Faith and Practices (London: ICAS, 2003).

Singh, Gopal, *The Man Who Never Died* (Honesdale, Pa.: Himalayan International Institute of Yoga Science and Philosophy, 1990).

Singh, Pashaura, 'Sikh Identity in the Light of History', in Pashaura Singh, and N. Gerald Barrier (eds.), *Sikhism and History* (Delhi: Oxford University Press, 2004).

Smith, Jonathan Z., *Imagining Religion: From Babylon to Jonestown* (University of Chicago Press, 1982).

'Religion, Religions, Religious', in Mark Taylor (ed.), *Critical Terms in Religious Studies* (University of Chicago Press, 1998).

Smith, Wilfred Cantwell, 'A Human View of Truth', in John Hick (ed.), *Truth and Dialogue: The Relationship between World Religions* (London: Sheldon, 1974).

Religious Diversity, ed. W. G. Oxtoby (New York: Harper and Row, 1976).

The Meaning and End of Religion (London: SPCK, 1978).

Towards a World Theology: Faith and the Comparative History of Religion (London: Macmillan, 1981).

Faith and Belief: The Difference between Them, new edn. (Oxford: Oneworld, 1998).

Sottocornola, Franco, 'The Tea Ceremony and the Mass', *Japan Mission Journal*, 44.1 (1990), pp. 11–27.

'Seimeizan 1987–1992: Five Years of Interreligious Experience', *Japan Mission Journal*, 47.2 (1993), pp. 119–29.

'Zazen and Adoration of the Eucharist', *Japanese Mission Bulletin*, 49.1 (1995), pp. 44–56.

Southern, Richard, *St Anselm: A Portrait in a Landscape* (Cambridge University Press, 1999).

Strenski, Ivan (ed.), *Thinking about Religion: A Reader* (Oxford: Blackwell, 2006).

Sullivan, Francis A., *Salvation Outside the Church: Tracing the History of the Catholic Response* (London: Chapman, 1992).

Swearer, Donald K., *Me and Mine: Selected Essays of Bhikkhu Buddhadasa* (Delhi: Śri Satguru Publications, 1991).

Tanner, Kathryn, *Theories of Culture: A New Agenda for Theology* (Minneapolis, Minn.: Fortress Press, 1997).

Taylor, Charles, *Modern Social Imaginaries* (Durham, NC and London: Duke University Press, 2004).

A Secular Age (Cambridge, Mass.: Harvard University Press, 2007).

Thera, Nyanaponika, *The Heart of Buddhist Meditation* (London: Rider, 1962).

Thich Nhat Hanh, *Living Buddha, Living Christ* (London: Rider, 1995).

Essential Writings, ed. Robert Ellsberg (Darton, Longman and Todd, 2008).

Thomas, Edward J., *The Life of the Buddha as Legend and History* (London: Routledge, 1996 [1927]).

Todorov, Tzvetan, *Hope and Memory: Reflections on the Twentieth Century* (London: Atlantic, 2003).

Totten, Samuel, William S. Parsons, and Israel W. Charny (eds.), *Century of Genocide: Eyewitness Accounts and Critical Views* (New York and London: Garland, 1997).

Tracy, David, *The Analogical Imagination: Christian Theology and the Culture of Pluralism* (New York: Crossroad, 1981).

'Comparative Theology', in *The Encyclopaedia of Religion*, vol. xiv (New York: Macmillan, 1986).

Dialogue with the Other: The Interreligious Dialogue (Louvain and Grand Rapids, Mich.: Peeters/Eerdmans, 1990).

Tylor, Edward, *Primitive Culture* (London: John Murray, 1871).

Upham, E., *The History and Doctrine of Buddhism* (London: R. Ackermann, 1829).

van Beeck, F. J., *Loving the Torah More than God? Towards a Catholic Appreciation of Judaism* (Chicago, Ill.: Loyola University Press, 1989).

Vandana Mataji, *Christian Ashrams: A Movement with a Future?* (Delhi: ISPCK, 1993).

'Living with Hindus': Hindu–Christian Dialogues, My Experiences and Reflections (Delhi: ISPCK, 1999).

Veliath, Dominic (ed.), *Towards an Indian Christian Spirituality in a Pluralistic Context* (Bangalore: Dharmaram, 1993).

Volf, Miroslav, Ghazi bin Muhammad, and Melissa Yarrington (eds.), *A Common Word: Muslims and Christians on Loving God and Neighbor* (Grand Rapids, Mich.: Eerdmans, 2010).

Vorgrimler, Herbert, *Commentary on the Documents of Vatican II*, vol. iii (London: Burns & Oates, 1979).

Waldenfels, Hans, 'Buddhism and Christianity in Dialogue: Notes on the Intellectual Presuppositions', *Communio*, 15 (1988), pp. 411–22.

Ward, Keith, 'Truth and the Diversity of Religions', *Religious Studies*, 26 (1990), pp. 1–18.

The Case for Religion (Oxford: Oneworld, 2004).

Wasserstein, B., *Divided Jerusalem: The Struggle for the Holy City* (London: Profile Books, 2001).

Weber, J. G. (ed.), *In Quest of the Absolute: The Life, and Works of Jules Monchanin* (Kalamazoo, Mich.: Cistercian Publications, 1977).

Webster, John, *The Dalit Christians: A History* (Delhi: ISPCK, 1992).

Webster, John, Kathryn Tanner and Iain Torrance (eds.), *The Oxford Handbook of Systematic Theology* (Oxford University Press, 2007).

Weil, Simone, *Waiting for God* (New York: HarperCollins, 2001).

Weinberg, Leonard, and Ami Pedahzur (eds.), *Religious Fundamentalism and Political Extremism* (London: Frank Cass, 2004).

Weitz, Eric D., *A Century of Genocide: Utopias of Race and Nation* (Princeton, NJ: Princeton University Press, 2003).

Weller, Paul, *A Mirror for our Times: 'The Rushdie Affair' and the Future of Multiculturalism* (London: Continuum, 2009).

Wellman, James K. (ed.), *Belief and Bloodshed: Religion and Violence across Time and Tradition* (Lanham, Md.: Rowan & Littlefield, 2007).

Williams, Paul, *Mahayana Buddhism: The Doctrinal Foundations* (London: Routledge, 1989).

Williams, Raymond, *The Long Revolution* (Harmondsworth: Penguin, 1965).

Keywords: A Vocabulary of Culture and Society (Oxford University Press, 1976).

Williams, Rowan, 'Postmodern Theology and the Judgement of the World', in Frederic B. Burnham (ed.), *Postmodern Theology: Christian Faith in a Pluralist World* (San Francisco, Calif.: Harper and Row, 1989), pp. 92–112.

On Christian Theology (Oxford: Blackwell, 2000).

Lost Icons (Edinburgh: T & T Clark, 2002).

Wolfson, Harry Austryn, *The Philosophy of Kalam* (Cambridge, Mass.: Harvard University Press, 1976).

Woodhead, Linda, and Paul Heelas, *The Spiritual Revolution: Why Religion is Giving Way to Spirituality* (Oxford: Blackwell, 2005).

Wright, N. T., *Jesus and the Victory of God* (London: SPCK, 1999).

Yazbeck Haddad, Yvonne, and Jane I. Smith, 'The Quest for "A Common Word": Initial Christian Responses to a Muslim Initiative', *Islam and Christian–Muslim Relations*, 20.4 (2009), pp. 369–88.

Ye'or, Bat, *Eurabia: The Euro-Arab Axis* (Madison, NJ: Fairleigh Dickinson University Press, 2005)

Zaehner, R. C., *Bhagavad Gita* (Vatican City and Oxford: Libreria Editrice Vaticana/Oxford University Press, 1966).

Index

Index